WE, THE PEOPLE OF INDIA

T.M. KRISHNA

context

WE, THE PEOPLE OF INDIA

DECODING A NATION'S SYMBOLS

cntxt

Published by Context, an imprint of Westland Books, a division of Nasadiya Technologies Private Limited, in 2026

No. 269/2B, First Floor, 'Irai Arul', Vimalraj Street, Nethaji Nagar, Alapakkam Main Road, Maduravoyal, Chennai 600095

Westland, the Westland logo, Context and the Context logo are the trademarks of Nasadiya Technologies Private Limited, or its affiliates.

ISBN: 9789371973069

10 9 8 7 6 5 4 3 2

Typeset by Jojy Philip

Printed at Thomson Press India Private Limited

To Gopalkrishna Gandhi,
who reminds me of the beauty
in the smallest of things

Contents

Introduction

For years now, month by twelve-month, I have watched with mounting anxiety as the ground I stood on as a citizen of India began shifting, cracking, crumbling. As always, I turned to music, books and history for comfort and answers. As I frantically cast around, I found myself with more questions than ever, but also with a kind of clarity, and a renewed belief in the idea of a nation that we, the people of India, willed into existence.

The most fundamental question confronting me was this: can we envision a society that has the capacity to breathe a more humane way of being into our lives? In other words, to inspire us towards overcoming our narrowness of spirit. Is it possible to seek a society of love, where choices are based on empathy and concern?

The pessimist in me tends to believe that the natural condition of individuals is to control, regulate and oppress in order to further themselves—and so a compassionate society appears to be an unattainable fantasy. But history challenges this gloomy point of view, with evidence of social, philosophical, religious and political movements that have proliferated down the ages. These movements have questioned the status quo and the hierarchies of power. On many occasions, they originated from those who were at the receiving end of oppression. But across the world, over and over, people have attempted to discard the old, suffocating order even when they were acting against their own individual interests. In the face of this evidence, I have to admit that there is indeed something upstanding in all of us, something that needs cultivating.

And yet, as humans, we seek group affinities to reaffirm our own existence. This process is not unidirectional; we receive and offer. The potency of what travels in each direction is determined by the heterogeneity of the people who reside in it. Since diversity is inevitable within a large circle of people, every aspect of difference becomes a sphere of influence. We are then affiliates of these subsets and interact as representatives of one lot or another. From within this maze, identities and placements emerge, and negotiations are initiated. What, how, when and who receives or shares resources, material or intangible, is determined by inter–intra battles for supremacy.

Do we choose to be members of all these groups, or is membership preordained? There can be no doubt that we are born into associations of sex, caste, language, colour, race, etc. But what of free will? The philosophical question of whether or not choice is born of free will is going to plague this discussion, and we might as well address that entanglement. There are those who insist that choice is entirely determined by pre-fixed contexts over which we have no control. If nothing is in our hands, and we are mere instruments, we can happily lay all blame at the feet of karma. A thief can say that the poverty they were born into made them take to robbery. Or a colossally rich person can claim a right to push ahead, no matter the impact of their actions on others. These are not equal claims, and yet, unforgivable though such a comparison might be, it could be argued that both speak a partial truth.

There is free will in every one of us, but we must be wary of accepting the claim of absolute free will, just as we should dismiss the idea of a 'fate' that dictates all our actions. Every individual's socio-cultural conditions, temporal realities, and access to education, health and livelihood determine how strongly free will and fate—or instilled conditioning—operate in our lives.

Only the extraordinary buck this norm. The nature of the subset we belong to undeniably affects our choice-making ability. If we belong to a subset that clings to its past and confines us to its sphere of influence, there is a very high probability that free will is constricted.

What we should really be thinking about is the nature of our actions, rather than their source. Whether they germinate from free will or conventions, do our actions disregard, hurt or destroy natural life, for instance? What we are, and are becoming, as a people matters much more than whether our thoughts come from individual intellection or a borrowing. We need a social environment that allows for the fulfilment of every individual potential, not just a lucky few. And a society where differences meet and exchanges are encouraged, where mutual respect is spontaneous.

Jurist, philosopher and chairperson of the Drafting Committee of the Constitution of India Dr B.R. Ambedkar spoke of Buddhist sanghas with great admiration: 'A study of the Buddhist Bhikshu Sanghas discloses that not only were there Parliaments—for the Sanghas were nothing but Parliaments—but the Sanghas knew and observed all the rules of parliamentary procedure known to modern times ....'[1] Similarly, there is some evidence of cooperative living during the Chola reign in South India. The history of this region contains attempts by political and religious establishments to nurture such a society—brief flares that never did manage to truly bring down the towers of privilege. They are examples of partial, early experiments with people's participation in governance. But these prototypes were not overarching systemic shifts. Real power was wielded by a few—a sobering thought that must inform our celebration of such instances.

Still, philosophers realised the potential in those glimpses of freedom. They saw the possibility of life through a burden-free, non-oppressive lens. And realised the imperative to transform this emotional learning into a tangible way of organising society. This inner seeking inspired human beings to keep trying to create a higher order of politics. Even if imperfect, it needed to be an enabler of goodness in every individual. We called this formulation 'democracy'.

This imperfect democracy of ours is as precious as it is new, as fragile as it is vital. But how do we understand something so intangible? I sought to look for it in what was tangible, beginning my search with the visible symbols of the Indian republic. I have been studying them to understand where we came from, trying to wrap my mind around these unnerving times and hoping to find a way to move forward.

1

The National Flag

A Symbol of Freedom

I remember the day the colour television came home. Though it had been introduced in India in 1982, we were a little late in acquiring this new technology. It was 1985, and our house buzzed with excitement as all of us crowded around the square carton. Those were the days when a technician came home, unboxed the television, set it up, checked the antenna, and taught us how to use the circular knobs on the control panel. We could vary contrast, brightness, volume and colour levels. There was an option to change channels, I think, but all we had then was one channel: Doordarshan.

In about half an hour, it had been set up, and we finally saw the world on TV, as we did in real life, in colour. No longer was everything in shades of grey, black and white. The trees were green, and the flowers pink, blue, magenta, yellow and every shade in between.

Colour is such a powerful force in our lives. The world is dynamic because we see it in so many shades. The intermingling of colours, the contrasts and highlights create a visual symphony that is the background of our daily lives. The patterns on a snake's skin, the sharp blue of the kingfisher, the white froth on the rapids in gushing rivers, the leaves in autumn, and the Aurora Borealis

... they enthral, move and excite because they are coloured. Those pictures of our blue planet from space tug at our heart.

The interplay between cognition and emotions is complex, and over the millennia, we have come to associate colours with emotions. These may vary from culture to culture, but it is possible to see some universal patterns. Red is often associated with anger, fear, protest, revolution, agitation and auspiciousness; yellow with positivity, happiness, warmth, sickness and cowardice. Colours can thus trigger a corresponding emotional response, be it of welcome or rejection.

Yet, colour is a creation of the human optical apparatus and does not exist in the real world. Anyone who has studied physics in high school knows that when light hits a surface, certain wavelengths of the electromagnetic spectrum are absorbed and some are not. Our brain interprets this dispersion as colour, just as the brains of other animals interpret it in a range of different colours, depending on the number of colour-specific receptors in their eyes. What truly exists is light, the object and energy.

Indeed, our own visual range is fairly narrow. But imagine a world where our eyes and brains are not engaged in this continuous interpretation. If colour were not an active trigger for our emotions, symbols in specific colour combinations might mean little. Would the Nazi symbol have had the impact it did without the bright red surrounding the black swastika placed within a white circle? It's hard to say.

I am beginning this chapter on 15 August, India's Independence Day, when everything from clothes to garlands, and even food, is painted in three specific colours. Social media is flooded with videos of songs, dances and poetry readings, the visuals tinged with saffron, white and green in that specific order. For most Indians, this combination evokes a sense of patriotism, a nationalistic spirit. Even those of us who know very little about the freedom struggle respond emotionally. These colours give us a place in the world, an identity. Especially when we gaze upon them on the national flag of India.

Through the early part of the twentieth century, flags that represented different imaginations of this land were touted as ideal representations of India. It was only when we inched closer to achieving political independence that the flag we now hold close to our hearts came into being. On 22 July 1947, Jawaharlal Nehru moved the resolution regarding the Indian flag in the Constituent Assembly. Sarojini Naidu—who was the last to speak—responded by describing the anguish she felt when there was no Indian flag to look up to.

> I was asked to speak at a peace celebration in New York soon after the peace had been signed. Forty-four Nations and their Flags fluttering in the great hall in which the Assembly met. I looked at the Flags of all the Nations and when I spoke I cried that though I did not see in that great Assembly of Free Nations the Flag of Free India, it would become the most historic Flag of the world in the not distant future. It was also a moment of anguish for me when a few months later forty-two Nations sent their women to an International Conference in Berlin. There they were planning to have, one morning, a Flag parade of the Nations. India had no official flag. But at my suggestion some of the women Indian delegates tore strips from their saris sitting up till the small hours of the morning to make the Tri-colour flag, so that our country should not be humiliated for the lack of a National Banner. [1]

If no country had a flag, Sarojini Naidu would not have felt this way. But the quest for a national identity is not an Indian creation, nor a recent one. Indians had long been burdened by the presence of the British flag. We fought to establish our own identity—the multicoloured fluttering fabric an assertion of it. As Nehru said in his address to the Constituent Assembly, '... this

Flag that I have the honour to present to you is not I hope and trust, a Flag of Empire, a Flag of Imperialism, a Flag of domination over anybody, but a Flag of freedom not only for ourselves, but a symbol of freedom to all people who may see it.'[2]

Evident in his words is a recognition of the danger underlying this nascent sense of nationhood. In our love for the flag, does there lie a streak of competitiveness, a show of power? Our love for, and pleasure in, the symbol of our nation could so easily slide towards jingoism.

Nehru presented the flag as a symbol of hope and freedom for anyone who beholds it, exquisitely dismantling the insider–outsider nation-building rhetoric and elegantly smudging national boundaries, even citizenship. This is even more startling given the context: undivided India was being partitioned.

C. Rajagopalachari had expressed a similar thought back in 1923, at a time when the flag bore a different design. In an article in *Young India*, he wrote, 'The Flags of other nations are yet emblems of war and aggression. Ours is from the inception an emblem of peace. Our flag is not at war with any other standard. It bears the message of peace to everyone on earth.'[3]

In a similar vein of inquiry and reflection, we too must ask, what is the meaning of the Indian flag? In all flags, the choice of colours, the segmentation in the design, are meant to convey a particular meaning—meanings endowed on the flag by those endowed with the power to choose. With constant reiteration, over a few generations, the composite form reflexively invokes the desired response in citizens.

It is a fact that most Indians see the three colours on our flag as representing the three major religions practised in the country: saffron (Hinduism), white (Christianity and others) and green (Islam). This perception may not be off the mark, even though Nehru made it a point to say, 'Some people, having misunderstood its significance, have thought of it in communal terms and believe that some part of it represents this community or that. But I may say that when this Flag was devised there was no communal significance attached to it.'[4]

Many members speaking after him in the Constituent Assembly described the flag as a bearer of religious symbolism. H.V. Kamath is known to have said, 'The *Chakra* symbolises the *Dharma Chakra* or the Wheel of the Law, the Wheel of *Samsara* which revolves on these eternal verities of *Shantam, Shivam, Sundaram*.' Syed Mohammad Saadulla evoked religion too: 'But it has more than a sentimental or symbolical value to us Muslims because green was the colour of the Flag of the Muslims from the time of the great Prophet of Arabia thirteen centuries ago.'

Until the late 1920s, all the designs prepared for a national flag were conceived and interpreted in communal terms. Religion was the most dominant and identifiable socio-cultural marker; when the British sought to divide us, as also when we fought them, religion was the fulcrum. This original tethering with religion continues to plague our understanding of the 'self'. We do not know what it means to be Indian without reference to religion or how to conceive of the two identities as belonging to separate spheres.

In the words of Pingali Venkayya of Andhra Jatheeya Kalasala, in Musilipatnam, who prepared the prototype of what became the Indian national flag: '[T]o us people who walk according to religion, who eat according to religion, who think according to religion, there can be no such thing as a political flag separate from a religious flag.'[5]

Since 1907, this employee of the Andhra Jatheeya Kalasala had been obsessed with creating a flag that represented all Indians. Finally, in 1916, he published a booklet titled *A National Flag of India*, which contained thirty designs. Out of these, twenty-eight were his own creations. Nor was this Venkayya's first publication.

In the author's note in the booklet, he mentioned a previous book, his biography of Dr Sun Yat-sen, a leading figure in the Chinese Revolution of 1911.

Andhra Jatheeya Kalasala had been founded in 1910 by Kopalle Hanumatha Rao Panthulu. According to the website of the Andhra Jatheeya Vidya Parishad, Venkayya worked as a staff member at the Kalasala, also known as National College, which was set up with the objective of guiding young people to join the cause of independence and helping national development. Venkayya was thus working in an environment that encouraged national fervour, drawing inspiration from the Swadeshi Movement of the early 1900s.

Based on visual commonality, Venkayya grouped his flag designs into nine lots and provided detailed descriptions for each suggested design. He had his colleague, the artist E. Venkatasastry, illustrate the designs in colour along with a few of the latter's students. Venkayya was not a powerful man with political connections or ambitions, but he felt deeply about the need for a unifying symbol that would allow Indians to move towards self-rule. The flag was not merely a visual fancy, he wrote. 'If at all there is any simple remedy for the disunion in this country, it is a common national flag.'[6] In his opinion, the religions of India had to be the foundation of its flag—it was only a question of whether the eight most practised religions needed to be represented or only the major four. He conceded that there were many more minor religions that he was unable to accommodate. According to him, the eight religious communities that mattered the most were the Hindus, Muslims, Christians, Parsis, Buddhists, Jains, Sikhs and Jews. Each religion was assigned a colour, though there were some variations in the allocations between designs. Venkayya said he was open to changing these based on suggestions from people of the faith. The four major religions (Hinduism, Islam, Christianity and Zoroastrianism in his opinion) were also assigned symbols. In some of his designs, the space that each religion occupied on the flag correlated with the social significance of the religion.

Venkayya followed the accepted political discourse of his time. Seeking dominion status within the ambit of the British empire, India saw itself as independent like Australia and Canada were, not as the United States of America was. This meant that every flag Venkayya designed had the Union Jack on the left top corner.

Besides religion, he considered one other determinant: the provinces. In his division of Indian provinces, Venkayya foretold the future. Provinces, he believed, could be demarcated only on a linguistic basis. Inspired by Lord Hardinge's dispatch on linguistic provinces and B. Pattabhi Sitaramayya's linguistic delimitation scheme, he zeroed in on the nineteen most important languages. He ignored English, Sanskrit, Arabic and Persian on the grounds that too few spoke them. Urdu did not make the cut either, because it was spoken by a population spread out across the country, making it impossible to draw out a single province. Nineteen linguistic provinces were represented by nineteen stars placed under the Union Jack. This part of the design was obviously inspired by the American flag and remained a constant in all his designs.

Venkayya's designs were complex and contained far too many elements. The rectangular flag area was divided horizontally or into square blocks. In one set of designs, there was an inner annular ring painted in different colours representing different religions. His choices for the central motif were equally quixotic. Mount Kailash and the goddesses Kali, Saraswati and Lakshmi were options, and so were mythological characters such as Bheeshma and Abhimanyu. The peacock, elephant, plantain tree and cow, too, showed up. An occupational symbol, the plough, representing the Indian farmer, found its way into one design. Apart from these illustrated designs, he offered in his book seventy-odd options for the central image of the national flag and flags for festivities.

Venkayya had his favourites, which he ranked in order of preference. The first place went to design B4. This flag was horizontally divided into eight bands, each representing one religious community. The surface area assigned to the coloured bands was proportionate to the importance of the community. In this arrangement, the colour–symbol–religion association, top to bottom, was as follows:

Hindus: yellow canton with a shankhu, trishul and chakram
Muslims: red canton with a crescent and star
Buddhists: orange canton
Christians: indigo canton with a cross
Sikhs: green canton
Jains: white canton
Parsis: rose canton with the rising sun
Jews: blue canton

In the centre was a lotus. And as on all his flags, in the top left corner was the Union Jack, with nineteen stars just below it. There was an error in the number of stars in all the designs: twenty-one stars (three rows of seven stars) and not nineteen, which Venkayya noted was a mistake.

In 1921, Gandhi said of these efforts: 'I have always admired the persistent zeal with which Mr Venkayya has prosecuted the cause of a national flag at every session of the Congress for the past four years.'[7] In reality, Venkayya had made his presence felt even earlier, at the December 1916 Congress session in Lucknow.

At some Congress sessions, flags were placed on top of the session tents. For example, a picture of the 1914 Madras venue reveals two flags. One is most likely the Union Jack. The other, interestingly, looks like a tricolour. Unfortunately, it's a black-and-white photo, and all I can say with some confidence is that the top band is a dark colour and the bottom light; the central band could have been yellow, white or some pastel shade. There is no mention of the flag in the session report. But at that stage, there was certainly no emphasis on establishing any one flag as a national symbol. The 1916 Congress session report has very little to say about the images used inside or outside the pandal. A photograph used in the report shows a large tent with streamers and flags. The flag on top of the central flagpole seems to be the Union Jack. There are other, smaller, fluttering flags that are unrecognisable. The introduction to the report informs us that 'Loyalty to the British Crown and Devotion to the Motherland found prominent mention in numerous mottos decorating various parts of the hall.'

Among these numerous mottos was a Venkayya creation. On 10 January 1917, *New India*, a newspaper published by Annie Besant, carried an article titled 'A National Flag for India: A Timely Suggestion'. The piece opened with this long sentence:

> For the first time in the history of the Congress, two flags designed as the National emblems of this country were seen floating over the dais at the last Congress. Perhaps they were not observed by a vast majority of the delegates or visitors; but those who are conversant with the latest literature on the subject must have known that the designs were those of Mr P. Venkayya, one of the workers at the Andhra Jathseya Kalasala at Masulipatnam ...

The article describes Venkayya's designs and quotes from his book, and concludes by saying that Venkayya hoped his book would give 'impetus to the movement for a National Flag'.

Venkayya was not making a case for his own designs to be adopted. He wanted people to read his book and send him suggestions. Unfortunately, very few had the drive or the interest, as is evident from an appeal that Venkayya put out in August 1917, which was also published in *New India*. Before describing the plans of the Indian National Flag Mission, of which he was the organiser, Venkayya described his participation in the 1916 Congress session in detail. He had taken with him 900 copies of his book. Of these, 400 were given to the press so that they might review and publicise his work. The remaining 500 were given to leading citizens, including members of the All-India Congress Committee and the Congress's Subjects Committee. He also gave copies of the book 'to such of the members of the All-India Muslim League whose names could be easily ascertained by us'.

Venkayya's comment gives us a glimpse into the mind of the average Congress supporter. His knowledge of Muslim League leaders was minimal, and one has to assume that supporters of the Muslim League, likewise, knew little about the Congress. In December that year, the Muslim League also held its session in Lucknow. This was the momentous session at which the Congress and the Muslim League signed an agreement, which came to be known as the Lucknow Pact, regarding communal representation in legislatures, among other things.

Venkayya took to Lucknow eight designs painted on cloth. Gokaran Nath Misra, secretary of the Reception Committee, chose one that had the figure of 'Mother India' set amidst the colours of the rainbow. Each colour represented an important religion practised in India, with the Union Jack in the top left corner. In Venkayya's words,

> ... this flag had the unique honour of being present on the platform when the Home Rule Resolution was adopted by the Congress for the first time in the history of British India.

The flag Misra chose for display was not in the initial set that Venkayya had published. He had, since then, been desperately canvassing public support for his plans. He planned to print flags on art paper, either the design with Mother India or the one with the lotus in the centre, so that families could hang them at the entrance to their homes. He also wanted to make small cloth flags for use in processions, and buttonhole badges and handkerchiefs. He was on a mission to make the flag a cultural and intellectual phenomenon. He did not, however, have the financial wherewithal to do all this. Through *New India*, he appealed for people to donate Rs 8,000. But there was not enough interest, and I could find no evidence that he was able to gather the necessary funds.

Venkayya had wanted to continue publishing material on the subject, reiterate the need for a National Flag Day, and encourage organisations like the Congress to use only flags that represented Indian culture and were made out of Indian cloth. Even before Gandhi and others began insisting on khadi fabric for the flag, Venkayya declared that the flag should not be made of 'videshi' cloth.[8]

Gandhi was not impressed with Venkayya's creations. It is possible that initially he did not consider the flag an urgent need. But when the non-cooperation movement was launched in 1920, everything changed. Gandhi's mind veered towards a flag that could unite all Indians. As he himself said in 1939, 'It was designed when non-co-operation was at its height.'[9]

Gandhi travelled in Punjab between November 1920 and March 1921. He visited Rohtak, Lahore (multiple times), Gujranwala, Rawalpindi, Amritsar, Lyallpur, Multan, Bugana, Nankana Sahib, Sialkot, Jullundur, Hoshiarpur, Ludhiana and Ambala. It must have been on this journey that the educationist Lala Hansraj suggested that the spinning wheel, or charkha, be used as an image on the swaraj (self-rule) flag. The charkha, after all, was the soul of the movement.

Hansraj might just have tapped into something that was already in Gandhi's subconscious mind. He was excited, and wrote:

> A wise friend has suggested that the picture on our swaraj flag must be that of the spinning-wheel. This idea has appealed to me as very beautiful. We use all manner of flags. A gentleman

> from Andhra Pradesh has suggested many designs for a flag. But I find no other idea as attractive as that of having a spinning wheel on the flag of swaraj. I commend this idea to the leaders who will be in charge of the forthcoming Congress session.

Soon after his return from Punjab, Gandhi headed to Bezwada for the All-India Congress Committee meeting to be held on 31 March and 1 April. On the second day, he asked Venkayya to prepare a flag with the charkha as its central symbol. The background colours suggested by Gandhi were red (for Hindus) and green (for Muslims). Venkayya prepared the design in three hours, but too late to be presented at the meeting. A couple of weeks later, on 13 April, Gandhi wrote in *Young India*:

> On maturer consideration, I saw that the background should represent the other religions also. Hindu-Muslim unity is not an exclusive term; it is an inclusive term, symbolic of the unity of all faiths domiciled in India. If Hindus and Muslims can tolerate each other, they are together bound to tolerate all other faiths. The unity is not a menace to the other faiths represented in India or to the world. So I suggest that the background should be white and green and red. The white portion is intended to represent all other faiths. The weakest numerically occupy the first place, the Islamic colour comes next, the Hindu colour red comes last, the idea being that the strongest should act as a shield to the weakest. The white colour moreover represents purity and peace. Our national flag must mean that or nothing. And to represent the equality of the least of us with the best, an equal part is assigned to all the three colours in the design.

While Venkayya is referred to as the designer of the flag, going by Gandhi's accounts—our only source of information—it seems likely that he executed a design that Gandhi had come up with. Venkayya almost certainly did not draw the flag himself. He'd had an artist draw the designs for his own book too.

Gandhi himself explicitly claimed credit for the design in February 1931. 'The present design was suggested by me,' he said. Again, in April that year: 'The flag is my own personal creation.'[10] Sixteen years later, on the eve of India's independence, when the national flag was being finalised, he once again reiterated that he had come up with the original design.

Venkayya's perseverance needs to be admired, and his influence on Gandhi in the matter of the flag cannot be underestimated. But the credit for being the designer of the Indian flag must indeed go to Gandhi. Consider the aesthetics: all of Venkayya's designs were cluttered and had far too many elements. None of them possessed the clarity or simplicity of the final design.

Although Gandhi finalised the design of the flag in 1921, it was not officially approved via a resolution in the Congress. Instead, it became the default flag of the Congress, although for many it was also the national flag. A report of the 1921 Indian National Congress session at Ahmedabad has a photograph of Gandhi standing below the flag as people walk past in an orderly fashion, and the caption reads: 'Volunteers saluting the National Flag'. This fluttering flag is, in fact, a set of four repeated images printed on one large piece of cloth. The charkha motif is placed in the middle of the tricolour bands. Other pictures of volunteers also feature this tricolour flag in the background.

The description of the venue reads thus:

> The Congress Pandal was erected in a spacious enclosure bearing the appearance of a castle. The area of the enclosure was about 15 acres, while the area covered by the Pandal proper was about 8000 sq yards. The main entrance to the enclosure, named Lokmanya Darwaja was a facsimile of the famous historical Three Gates of Ahmedabad and was a special feature of attraction. At the top of the main gate was flying the national tricolour flag. Below the flag was placed a huge Charkha, decorating the central arch of the gate. The

entrance to the Pandal proper, named the Swaraj Dwara, was about 85 yards from the Lokmanya Darwaja.

Compare this with the description of the dais at the twenty-third session in Madras in 1908:

> The interior of the pavilion was draped entirely with white giving added lightness to the well-proportioned building. The dais, running the whole breadth on the northern side from east to west, was draped with red and immediately in front of the President's table was the Union Jack bearing an inscription 'Truth, Light, Love' and 'Vande Mataram' and an outline of India.

It must be noted that Vande Mataram, in this context, was an expression of Indian autonomy within the British framework. At this time, the viceroy's flag—the Union Jack with the star of India at the centre and the crown slightly above it—was often treated as the flag of India. The Union Jack itself was, of course, supreme.

Flags are no small matter. The fabric and design must convey the gravitas of an entire political apparatus. The Union Jack had for centuries fluttered over lands far away from Britain, establishing the nation's superiority and evoking obedience, faith and fear among those who lived under its command. Even after its greatest defeat, finding an appropriate resting place for that symbol of power would become a subject of paramount importance.

In the British Library there exists a file titled 'Flag of Last Viceroy of India—Disposal'.[11] In 1948, as Lord Mountbatten prepared to leave India, he sent the British government and the navy into a tizzy. Mountbatten was the only naval officer to become viceroy, and he wanted the flag of the 'Last Viceroy of India' to find its post-retirement home in St Ann's Church located at His Majesty's Naval Base in Portsmouth. However, the commander-in-chief of the base 'firmly rejected' the offer because the church was only adorned with naval war flags that commemorated naval war actions. Windsor was offered as an option. The Union Jack that once flew over the Residency in Lucknow had been moved to Windsor castle at the behest of the king.

British government officials wondered if the matter should be informally referred to the king through his private secretary. It was a delicate situation: Mountbatten had written directly to the commander-in-chief and would now wonder how the king had got to know about his request. File notings seem to suggest that the matter might indeed have reached the king's ear, and the flag finally found its place on the wall of Ramsey Abbey. Nehru and Vijayalakshmi Pandit visited the abbey in October 1948 and viewed this symbolic remnant of the Raj.

Between 1900 and 1920, references to the British flag at Congress sessions were respectful, with routine expressions of loyalty to His Majesty's Government. The British flag stood for the birth right of Indians to be 'free' under it. Delegates spoke of the bravery of the Indian troops who fought under the British flag. In the 1900 session held at Lahore, Viceroy Lord George Hamilton, the Secretary of State for India, was quoted by S. Gurcharan Singh from Lahore as saying:

> The dash and determination of our Indian troops has once more demonstrated to the world, the fighting power which the loyalty and courage of the great dependency can contribute.[12]

Singh went on to elaborate this point: 'These services have been rendered not only in India, but also all over the world wherever the British flag waves. And we are justly proud of it. Our men can and are willing to serve wherever their employers want them to serve.'

The only time the flag took a beating as a symbol of freedom was when Congressmen spoke for the rights of Indians in South Africa. When the 'Great War' began, it was still relatively untainted. But when questions began to be raised about Indians in India not being treated as equal citizens, the flag also became a metaphor to express that angst. At the 1915 Congress session, among the captions on the arches and flags were these slogans: 'Long live King and Queen', 'Victory to the Allies', 'Victory to the cause of Righteousness', 'Hail Motherland', 'Britain's cause is India's cause', 'Rally round the Congress Flag, Children of Hind', 'India aspires to have her right place in the Empire', 'India has responded right loyally and expects England to respond right royally'.[13]

At the conference, D.E. Wacha, while appreciating the British government for some of its actions, also had this to say: 'Of course, there yet remains the recognition of the principle that all subjects of His Majesty the King Emperor are entitled to equal rights and privileges of British Citizenship in every nook and corner of the Empire where waves the British flag. [applause]'[14]

Another Congressman, Jahangir B. Petit, asked the question directly: 'I should like to know what citizenship should mean to India, if we are going to be treated in the manner we have been treated outside, even under the British flag and under the aegis of the British Crown.'[15]

Today, we tend to gloss over the complex discussions on what freedom and swaraj entailed, and how these words incrementally gathered the meanings now ascribed to them. Freedom has always meant different things to different people and from one generation of freedom fighters to the next. For a long time, it meant equality, representation and respect. The fight was against discrimination, corruption, oppression and slavery, with an emphasis on the right to self-govern—not the immediate exit of the British.

In his book *Hind Swaraj*, Gandhi provides a nuanced interpretation of home rule. Home rule was never merely about kicking the British out of the subcontinent. Gandhi was far more interested in the response to a follow-up question: What kind of swaraj did we envisage? The removal of the British was immaterial if we were not going to change, for true freedom was freedom from all forms of tyranny—external, internal and within each individual. To him, equating independence with liberation from an 'external power' and that too by using any means possible, was a vulgarisation of the idea of swaraj.[16]

> EDITOR: Supposing we get self-government similar to what the Canadians and the South Africans have, will it be good enough?
>
> READER: That question also is useless. We may get it when we have arms and ammunition even as they have. But, when we have the same powers, we shall hoist our own flag. As is Japan, so must India be. We must own our navy, our army, and we must have our own splendour, and then will India's voice ring through the world.
>
> EDITOR: You have well drawn the picture. In effect it means this: that we want English rule without the Englishman. You want the tiger's nature, but not the tiger; that is to say, you would make India English, and, when it becomes English, it will be called not Hindustan but Englistan. This is not the Swaraj that I want.

In the free India of Gandhi's imagination, British presence or absence was inconsequential because he hoped for an awakening in everyone, including the British. If those in power could be made to understand the unethical nature of their presence through non-violent means, they would leave of their own volition. Everyone needed to understand what lay behind the Indian condition, which according to him was only a reflection of the larger human condition. From the realisation of this universality, he believed, would emerge freedom—freedom in the truest sense.

> READER: It is impossible that Englishmen should ever become Indianised.
>
> EDITOR: To say that is equivalent to saying that the English have no humanity in them. And it is really beside the point whether they become so or not. If we keep our own house in order, only those who are fit to live in it will remain, others will leave of their own accord. Such things occur within the experience of all of us.
>
> READER: But it has not occurred in history.
>
> EDITOR: To believe that what has not occurred in history will not occur at all is to argue disbelief in the dignity of man ...[17]

Gandhi wrote *Hind Swaraj* in 1909 on a ship bound for South Africa from London. The previous few years had been tumultuous for India and the Indian National Congress. The partitioning of Bengal had resulted in a groundswell that became the Swadeshi Movement of 1903–08. This was, without doubt, a crucial time in our history. It could be said that Indian independence was largely born from this coming together of political activists, the general public, especially the youth, and artists. The movement called for the boycott of foreign goods and the making and buying of local-made products, and created a massive churn all over the country. It was what led someone like V.O. Chidambaram Pillai to launch a shipping company in Tuticorin in the Madras Presidency.

At this time, while Congressmen such as Bal Gangadhar Tilak and Aurobindo Ghosh—referred to as extremists by their baiters—demanded a confrontational approach, the other group, labelled moderates, including leading Congressmen such as Gopalkrishna Gokhale and Rash Behari Ghosh, adopted a more reconciliatory position. It took years of negotiations between these groups, incremental changes in political positions and expressions in the Congress resolutions and even violent clashes for 'purna swaraj', or complete independence, to become a point of reckoning within the Congress. The Rowlatt Act of 1919 and the massacre at Jallianwala Bagh further tilted the scales in favour of severing all links with the British government. The resultant Non-Cooperation Movement also changed the complexion of the struggle.

Gandhi wished to accommodate both sets of views. In 1920, at the Nagpur Congress, he moved a resolution on Article 1 of the Congress constitution that read:

> The object of the Indian National Congress is the attainment of Swarajya by the people of India by all legitimate and peaceful means.

He further clarified:

> If the British Connection is for the advancement of India we do not want to destroy it. But if it is inconsistent with our national self-respect, then it is our bounden duty to destroy it. [Hear, hear] There is room in this Resolution for both, those who believe that by retaining British connection we can purify ourselves and purify the British people, and those who have no such belief. As for instance, take the extreme case of Mr. Andrews. He says all hope for India is gone for keeping British Connection. He says there must be complete severance, complete independence. [Hear, hear] There is room enough in this creed for a man like Mr. Andrews also.

This debate on swaraj lasted a whole decade. There were repeated demands for a change in the Congress creed with small alterations to the text, such as poet and political activist Hazrat Mohani's 1921 proposition: the 'attainment of swaraj or complete independence free from all foreign control, without any foreign connection by the people of India through legitimate and peaceful means'. It was appropriate that the suggestion came from Mohani, the person who coined the phrase 'Inquilab Zindabad'. Gandhi opposed the resolution. Each time the idea of complete independence was brought up, the resolution was rejected, until British missteps changed the tide of opinion. During this intervening period, the charkha and the flag emerged as unifying ideas and captured the public imagination.

Despite Gandhi's open-ended interpretation of swaraj, he never considered the possibility of the Union Jack being included on the Indian flag. It was meant to unify the people of this land, and there could be no room for the Crown on its fabric.

We must place Gandhi's notion of swaraj within this clear creative impulse. He sought an Indianness that everyone could celebrate and participate in. The flag provided him with an imagery that could temper religious differences. And in the charkha he recognised an actionable, symbolic social unifier. Despite all its contradictions and inequalities, to him, India came alive through simple acts of self-sufficient living and its people's spiritual quests. His logic was simple: if the British respected our identity, they would not demand the inclusion of the Union Jack on the national flag. They would feel secure being amongst us and participating in our public and political life. By embracing this way of life, they too would become free from all burdens. The question of whether India remained in the dominion or not would be moot, because the flag and the charkha would have become as much theirs as ours.

Much is known about the Salt Satyagraha of 1930, but little has been written about the Flag Satyagraha of 1923. This is probably because it remained limited to two towns in the Central Provinces: Jubbulpore and Nagpur.

The struggle was triggered by the district magistrate's act of vetoing the municipal commissioner's decision to hoist the Indian flag on the town hall at Jubbulpore, as part of a welcome event for visiting members of the Congress Working Committee (CWC). The satyagraha began on 10 March, and C. Rajagopalachari addressed angry protesters on 11 and 12 March. The following month, on Jallianwala Day (13 April), conflict arose in Nagpur. This further galvanised the Congress and fuelled more energy into the satyagraha. In the minutes of the CWC, we find repeated appreciation of the bravery, non-violence and sacrifice of the satyagrahis. In July, Sardar Vallabhbhai Patel was sent to Nagpur to guide and control the satyagraha.

Rajaji's book, *India's Flag,*[18] was published in 1923 when the satyagraha was still on. It contains articles written by him and Gandhi for *Young India*, the transcript of a speech he delivered in Nagpur and some other material. Rajaji believed that the satyagraha was a very important moment in the fight for independence. Why else were the British taking this struggle so seriously, he asked. Police officers waited for satyagrahis to come up to the 'civil-lines frontier line' all day under the beating sun to arrest groups carrying the 'tricoloured khaddar'. Occasionally, even individuals who walked all alone with a flag were arrested.

The British, Rajaji said, understood the power and the message of a unifying flag, and knew that, if allowed to grow, this could snowball into a national movement. It was an act of civil disobedience, another platform for Indians to demonstrate that they would not obey laws or orders that were unjust. According to Rajaji, what really rattled the government was the combination of colours on the flag. The coming together of red (Hindus), white (Christians, Jews) and green (Muslims) represented 'great danger to the British Empire'. Rajaji also hinted that some people questioned the 'correctness' of calling it the 'National Flag'. And then went on to explain,

> The government recognises the flag and fights it. The flag is a symbol for battle and when the enemy recognises it, it becomes the flag ...

> You do not find on our flag, a tiger, a lion or unicorn, but only a charkha. It represents industry, and goodwill, and our new weapon against brute-force. The government would not have minded if we had put the sign of a Gun, as they have bigger Guns.

An intriguing explanation. Apart from internal consensus, a symbol also finds sanction from the 'enemy' that is threatened by its symbolism. The use of the term 'enemy' might have been a Freudian slip, but it does reveal that, even in a non-violent political act, there is still an enemy, an opponent.

Rajaji, Gandhi and others positioned the flag as a representation of collective consciousness and religious cooperation, but it was also undoubtedly a display of collective strength. Even in non-violent movements, power is always in play. When non-violence becomes a political tool, it becomes an intimidating force.

The intimidation experienced by the oppressor is a consequence of their own actions. When we choose to court arrest or withstand physical torture, display resilience or sacrifice, the oppressor, perhaps initially amused, becomes irritated, tired and then afraid. The fear comes from the ineffectiveness of their aggression. They want us to retaliate so they may be further aggrieved. Fear of non-violence may seem paradoxical, but it is a reality.

We were all witness to such a moment in 2020–21. Farmers from Punjab and Haryana set up camp on the National Highway near New Delhi and peacefully protested the implementation of three new farm laws by the Union government. Farmers in western Utter Pradesh lent their support. Essentially, they were resisting laws that would hand over power to private operators, and in the long run, lead to the disintegration of all support from the government. Hundreds of lives were lost and a great deal of suffering was endured before the agriculturalists got the Government of India to repeal the laws on 29 November 2021.[19]

It was a triumph, though the government's retreat was partly impelled by the electoral power the farmers wielded. With Uttar Pradesh and Punjab elections nearing, the government finally gave in.

Compare this with the anti-CAA (Citizenship Amendment Act) and anti-NRC (National Register of Citizens) protests that took place across the country from 2019. Students were attacked within university campuses by the police and mobs, North-East Delhi witnessed communal riots, and yet there was no groundswell of support for these movements. If anything, the BJP and its affiliates were able to use them to further polarise society. The pro-CAA/NRC stance of many in the majority community and the lack of concern among many others directly impacted the effectiveness of the anti-CAA satyagraha. A swelling anti-Muslim sentiment overrode everything else. It was proof that non-violence wins only if it tilts the scales of power, and that depends on the political power of those who take to the streets. During the independence movement, there was a common enemy: the outsider. This helped galvanise people of all hues despite their differences.

For non-violence to prevail in its truest sense, it needs to be internalised in our social life. Homes, schools, social interactions, economic models and political structures will have to be reformed. Gandhi often articulated the need for personal evolution. Yet, when his satyagraha became a mass political programme, it became trapped in a thoughtless demonstration that succeeded in achieving its immediate goal, but ceased to be imbued with the spirit of thoughtful non-violence. The Anna Hazare–led movement against corruption is another case in point. It seemed like a resurgence of Gandhian resistance, but in reality the movement was quietly encouraging ugly sectarian divisions.[20] Once it ended, the anti-corruption plank was ditched, but the hatred it had cultivated remained. It is only when the resistors undergo an internal metamorphosis that satyagraha can embody non-violence. Mere absence of physical violence is not non-violence.

Right through the 1920s, although Gandhi was clear that no religious insignia should find a place on the flag, he continued to correlate the colours with religions. There were others who had their own colour preferences. In 1924, Gandhi received a letter for publication in *Young India*. Signed by Dwijendranath Tagore among others, it suggested that geru/gairika/gerva (ochre) represented Hindus and not the colour red. Ochre, the writers said, was associated with sanyasis, tyaga and ahimsa. They recalled Rabindranath Tagore's poetic references to the colour, its presence on Shivaji's flag and its acceptance among many 'Hindu sects', brahminical, Buddhist and Sikh. According to them, ochre was representative of the Indian darwesh, pir and yogi, while red had a limited relevance for Hindus and 'does not strike the Hindu note of Ahimsa'.[21] They also made a distinction between ochre and saffron. Saffron or red, though used by some Hindu sects, was unacceptable because it was the 'colour of war' and did not represent ahimsa for Hindus. Additionally, since red could also be associated with Christians, the three colours on the flag could be red, ochre and green. If that did not work, then possibly ochre (for Hindus), white (for other faiths and cultures) and green (for Islam).

As these direct connections were being drawn between colours and religions, Sikhs began to express unhappiness over the fact that they were not represented on the Indian flag. They appealed to the Congress party and Gandhi to consider a separate colour (black) for their community. Gandhi was of the opinion that there were no differences between the Sikh and Hindu communities. Muslims were being represented because, in his words, Hindus and Muslims 'have remained apart for so long and that their mutual distrust has been an effectual bar against the realisation of national aspirations'. If every community began adopting colours, a colour would be needed for Parsis, Jews and others too. This was exactly what Venkkaya had done in his earlier designs.

From 1921, images of the flag or mentions of its significance began to show up more often in Congress session reports. Flag-hoisting also became a regular ritual at Congress meetings and other nationalistic gatherings across India. This resulted in inconsistencies when it came to reproducing the design of the flag. At times, the material was not khadi, and the charkha would be missing. When such instances were brought to Gandhi's notice, he responded by reiterating the significance of each element on the flag. He was most troubled when the charkha was absent or the cloth was not khadi. These two elements were at the core of his nation-building exercise, and any disregard towards them hurt him deeply. At one point, in 1934, he said: 'If Congress men do not believe in the message of the wheel, we must remove it from the National Flag and khaddar from the constitution.'[22]

Gandhi's vision of a unified and free India demanded not just an intellectual concordance, it had to be reflected in people's life choices too. Only when there was such an un-demarcated internalisation of community could harmonious coexistence take root. This resulted in Gandhi's keenness to standardise the flag, its colour, shape and size. He also believed in centralising flag production. To him, this form of conformity was not homogenisation, it was a sign of respect and national pride.

A flag is not only a visual representation, a piece of cloth with colours and designs. It is a moving body of art. When the wind blows, it flutters and swings. When the breeze dies, it gently settles on itself and rests. The flag's dance depends on its dimensions and the nature of the cloth and weave. Any change in these qualities and the flag changes, not merely in appearance, but also in what it represents. In 1947, soon after the Indian national flag was approved by the Constituent Assembly, Rajendra Prasad wrote to Nehru stating that only hand-spun and hand-woven cloth (khadi), whether cotton, silk or wool, must be used for the making of the flag.

This was not included in the Constituent Assembly's resolution. To Prasad's surprise, the Constituent Assembly placed an order for 3,000 flags from a textile mill. He immediately reversed the order. He told Nehru bluntly, 'Apart from the fact that use of any other cloth will touch Bapu to the quick, and will alienate him still further from us, I think we should not discard Khadi in an indirect manner, and if we wish to discard it we should do it openly and directly after taking a deliberate decision to that effect.'

Many years earlier, in his presidential address at the 1934 Congress Session, Prasad had articulated his affinity to khadi and spinning thus: 'The spinning wheel and khadi are not only the living link between the classes and the masses. They are symbols of 'the country's determination to resist all forms of exploitation by non-violent means. They represent an era of purification of politics and private life.'

Nehru responded to Prasad on the very same day, agreeing that all flags intended for government use would be made of khadi. On the floor of the Constituent Assembly, on 31 July 1947, to a notice of a resolution on the khadi issue put forward by Rajkumari Amrit Kaur, Prasad reiterated that nothing but khadi would be used.

Prasad's passionate letter and statements demonstrate how deeply imbued khadi was with the spirit of resistance and self-reliance. Handmade and hand-woven cloth is uneven; it is soft but also rough, some threads untied, others knotted, the hand-spun threads mildly spotted and the interweave complex. In some ways, the material represented who we were: a set of diverse and plural groups searching for ways to coexist. The cloth was both a reminder of our unequal, divided reality and the dream of a better tomorrow.

In the early 1950s, the Indian State vigorously pursued the bureaucratic standardisation of the national flag. In 1951, for the first time, the Government of India established the flag standard. The symbol of swaraj was given textural specificity. Exact measurements, ratios regarding the length and breadth of each colour band, every spoke of the chakra in the centre, exact colour tones and brightness, yarn details, stitching methods, even measurements and the choice of wood for the toggles were prescribed. Standards were prepared for the khadi cotton, silk and wool that could be used. Like with every government standard, innumerable tweaks were made subsequently. But only one organisation had the permission to manufacture the flag: the Karnataka Khadi Gramodyog Samyukta Sangh in Bengeri, Hubballi in Dharwad district.

Yet, in 2022, as India approached its seventy-fifth year of Independence, the Government of India decided that it would permit flags made of polyester to facilitate availability at scale. The government wanted a flag in every house; a campaign it called Har Ghar Tiranga. The flag code was accordingly altered—a change that was widely criticised as diluting the principles on which we got our freedom and founded the nation.[23] Cutting the flag's umbilical link with khadi also severed our memory of all those who spun, wove, marched and sacrificed for the idea of India. It especially undermined the common person, the weaver, and handed over to the powerful and privileged that small place in our aesthetic architecture that ordinary Indians could until then call their own. Nehru used a beautiful phrase to describe khadi: 'the livery of our freedom'.

The sudden acceptance of polyester flags is in many ways representative of the India we have become: synthetic and plastic. Is it surprising then that so much of the public discourse is fake today? That we provide only unfeeling responses to the horrors that abound? Oppression and violence are not just perpetrated, they are encouraged and justified. India's citizens watch from the sidelines, unfazed. Those from the margins who pour out into the streets, hoarse from crying for justice, are called unpatriotic. Majoritarianism is today seen as fair, as is revenge against real and imagined historic wrongs. Polyester, in many ways, represents these qualities: slippery and glittery.

The establishment argued that polyester was cheap and accessible to all, that this move democratised the flag and empowered the poor to celebrate their country. A decision that took away from the poor their livelihood and handed it over to corporations and importers was heralded as democratic. If the government wanted to make the flag accessible to all, they could have given permission for the making of khadi flags to a larger number of units much earlier. It could also have subsidised the higher cost of the flag. Instead, it deprived the poor and forced upon everyone a damaged symbol. The aggression with which the flag was commercialised and higher sales demanded from various departments pushed it further away from the spirit of the Constitution of India.[24] In polyesterising the flag, we sold our soul to the homogenising juggernaut.

This fabricated spirit of uniformity spilled over to the internet when the prime minister of India told citizens, 'I have changed the DP [to the Indian flag] on my social media pages and urge you all to do the same.' It is ironic that present-day India, which noisily rejects the West, is mimicking the worst of American nationalism: the vulgar display, planting and waving of the national flag.

But there is another layer to this argument, an uncomfortable one. And that is the changing nature of ideas and yearnings. Today, the privileged see synthetic cloth as cheap, exploitative and alienating. Synthetic sarees and nighties are objects of scorn. But not so long ago, they were considered fashionable. If anything, khadi was unappealing, rough and unfashionable, even a sign of backwardness. A person wearing khadi clothes, with a khadi bag hanging from their shoulders, was thought of as trapped in the past, an irrational contrarian. Then came the privatisation of handloom and handmade clothing, with companies working with weavers and block printers to make clothing that suited the aesthetic palette of the privileged, their modern, urban needs and economic stature. All this made handloom expensive, beyond the reach of the common person. By this time, khadi had lost its moral, aesthetic and political stature. The original government-owned Khadi Gramudyog shops became unattractive. The fabric of the common person in India was now synthetic, cheap, aspirational and durable.

Ironically, in 1929, Gandhi had said of mass-producing swaraj flags:

> The cheapest and the most expeditious method is for the All-India Spinners' Association to have these flags prepared and kept for sale on behalf of the Congress at the different stores. As it would be impossible for any individual committee to compete with the All-India Spinners' Association in point of cheapness the flags should find a ready sale all over India ...

Much like Bollywood blockblusters that attract audiences all over, the glittery synthetic flag is now a relatable, yet inexpensive emblem.

By 1927, Indians were calling for complete and untethered independence, and Gandhi's accommodative posturing was no longer resonant. At the Madras session of the Indian National Congress, we witnessed an assertion by the next-generation leader, Jawaharlal Nehru: Swaraj had to mean complete independence.

Rising to the sound of cheering, he moved the Independence Resolution: 'It is my high privilege to place before you the resolution on Independence. [Cheers] The resolution reads thus: The Congress declares the goal of the Indian people to be complete national independence.'[25]

Though it was passed, the resolution itself may not have been fully understood by the Congressmen. At the time, the notion of complete independence was not a matter of urgency within the Congress, though it might have been the feeling among the general public. Nehru's popularity was on the rise, and everyone, including the British government, was taking note. Gandhi wasn't present at the session, and later criticised the resolution. His objections were not to do with the principle of complete independence but, as he had articulated in *Hind Swaraj*, the inner nature of swaraj.

He said to a journalist, '[M]y disapproval of the Independence Resolution is based upon grounds that are not common to those who generally condemn the Independence Resolution.'

On 5 January 1928, in *Young India*, he called the resolution 'hastily conceived and thoughtlessly passed'. Then again, on 12 January, in an article titled 'Independence vs Swaraj', he elucidated, 'What independence do we want? ... It will be determined not by my definitions but by our acts, voluntary and involuntary ... If we are wise, we will take care of the present and the future will take care of itself.'

He once again made the point that swaraj is not the same as independence, which to him was only an external demand. But he did not dismiss the need for freedom from the British. 'Personally, I crave not for "independence", which I do not understand, but I long for freedom from the English yoke ... My ambition is much higher than independence. Through the deliverance of India, I seek to deliver the so-called weaker races of the earth from the crushing heels of western exploitation in which England is the greatest partner.'

Nehru was not the least bit impressed by Gandhi's blunt criticism and penned a powerful and emotional rebuttal to his mentor.

You have described the Independence Resolution as 'hastily conceived and thoughtlessly passed'. I have already pointed out to you how the country has discussed and considered this question for years past, and how I have personally thought over it, discussed it, spoken about it in meetings, written about it and generally been full of it for the last five years or more. It seems to me that under the circumstances no stretch of language can justify the use of the words 'hastily conceived'. As for 'thoughtlessly passed', I wonder if you know that the resolution was discussed in the Subjects Committee for about three hours and more than a dozen speeches for and against were made. Ultimately as you know it was passed almost unanimously both in the Committee and the open Congress. Were all the people in the Committee and the Congress who voted for it 'thoughtless'? Is this not rather a large assumption? And why should it not be said with greater truth that the small minority opposed to the resolution were mistaken?

You mention that last year the resolution was rejected by the Committee. I do not know what inference you draw from this but to me it seems obvious that this can only mean that the Committee and the Congress have been eager to pass it in the past as in the present but refrained from doing so out of regard for you. I hope you will agree with me that it is not healthy politics for any organization to subordinate its own definite opinion on a public issue out of personal regard only. [...]

You know how intensely I have admired you and believed in you as a leader who can lead this country to victory and freedom. I have done so in spite of the fact that I hardly agreed with anything that some of your previous publications—Indian Home Rule, etc.,—contained. I felt and feel that you were and are infinitely greater than your little books.

The following year, at the Calcutta session, though the old guard still managed to pull its weight, another leader from the younger generation made it clear that it was time to move ahead.

Subhas Chandra Bose said,

> We want our older leaders—we revere them, we love them, but at the same time we want them to keep abreast of the times. I have told them on behalf of the younger school that I and my esteemed friend Pundit Jawaharlal Nehru and others may be regarded as the Moderates among the Extremists and if our older leaders do not come to a compromise with even these Moderates, a breach between the old and the young will become inseparable. Thanks to this Youth Movement that a new self-consciousness has dawned upon the youths of India. They are no longer prepared to follow blindfolded any policy. They have realised that they are the heirs of the future, that it is for them to make India free. And with that self-consciousness they are preparing themselves for the arduous task that awaits them. I do hope that at this juncture the Congress will give a bold lead to the country.

Right through all these political re-positionings, the primary meaning drawn from the colours of the flag, that symbol of freedom, remained communal, even for its originator. It was only in 1929 that Gandhi began articulating an alternative vision. In early 1930, he said, 'The red colour in the flag signifies sacrifice, the white, purity and the green, hope. The three colours stand for one ideal, that of unity.' He was also glad to accept other explanations that were on similar lines. 'A correspondent some days ago sent me a cutting describing a new meaning a lady gave to the colours. So far as I recall her speech, red was suggestive of bravery, green of calmness and white of purity. I have no hesitation in accepting this meaning in the place of mine.'

He also had this to say about his original interpretation: 'With the growing consciousness of oneness, Congressmen have begun to dislike the communal meaning that as inventor of the design I gave to the colours on the flag.'

This was an optimistic Gandhi who was happy to alter his explanation because he believed that there had been a change of heart among the people, especially Hindus and Muslims.

While these movements towards abstraction were ongoing, the flag with white, red and green horizontal bands, on which was superimposed a large charkha in blue, was hoisted as a declaration of Purna Swaraj by Jawaharlal Nehru on 31 December 1929 in Lahore. At the stroke of midnight, as the year turned, the resolution was passed. Later, in 1939, in his correspondence with Muhammad Ali Jinnah, Nehru pointed to 1929 as the year when the flag was adopted by the Congress. I could not find a record of a formal resolution on the adoption of the flag, but the Congress report of the 1929 session described the beauty of that night:

> The National Flag under which the declaration of independence was made on the memorable night of December 31st, was a structure deserving special mention. The flag was perched 115 ft. high from the ground. The flag post consisted of pipes with 6 ft. diameter at ground level gradually tapering to 4 ft at the upper end; by a mechanical device a man could reach the pinnacle in one minute and come down again. He had only to sit in the wooden box and the pully block system did the rest. On the top the flag was fitted with tricolour electric light 15 in number, each of 200 candle power, besides one lamp of each colour of 2,000 candle power. The post was also of the tricolour scheme. It was a glorious sight at night.

On New Year's Eve, it appears, Nehru danced around the flagpole![26]

Appropriately, the Purna Swaraj flag was hoisted in Lahore. This was the city in which twenty-three-year-old Siris Chandra Bose had made a flag in 1883 to function as a national standard. That flag was paraded through the streets of Lahore to the singing of nationalist songs in English and Hindustani, probably written by Siris Bose. An image of his flag can be seen on the title page of the book of songs published by the Indian National Society that Bose was instrumental in founding. The society was meant to work for Hindu–Muslim unity and the social, moral and spiritual upliftment of society at large. The flag is a swallowtail with a sun-face as the image at the centre. We can only speculate that the sun must have been yellow or orange in colour.

Meanwhile, the symbolism of the flag hoisted by the Congress continued to be disputed. The Sikh community was unhappy at not being represented on it. In December 1929, representatives met Gandhi demanding either the inclusion of a Sikh colour or an entirely non-communal flag. Finally, in April 1931, in order to find a way out of this impasse, the Congress constituted a Flag Committee. The committee included Congress heavyweights such as Sardar Vallabhbhai Patel, Abul Kalam Azad and Jawaharlal Nehru. The convenor was Bhogaraju Pattabhi Sitaramayya. Before they began their deliberations, a questionnaire was sent to the various Provincial Congress Committees and circulated amongst the public through the press. The Flag Committee members wanted to know if the feelings of any particular group or community needed to be taken on board, and they wanted specific suggestions to make the flag more popular; they also welcomed criticism of the present flag.

The Flag Committee met on 8 and 9 July 1931 to review the responses received from many Provincial Congress Committees, the Central Sikh League and the public. Other than the members of the committee, Sardar Sardul Singh from the Central Sikh League was also present at the meetings. Abul Kalam Azad, a member of the committee, did not attend the meeting on the second day. The committee's main concern was the communalisation of the flag. It was torn between de-communalising the present flag through an explanatory reinterpretation and coming up with an entirely new one. By this time, Indians had a decade-long emotional attachment to the flag, turning it into an important symbol of nationalism and freedom. This made giving it up a very difficult decision. Finally, with 'great reluctance', the committee decided that a new flag was the only way forward. Its members rationalised that the religious symbolism of the flag was so deeply entrenched in the psyche of people that a clean break was necessary. Further, they pointed to how similar the present flag sans the charkha was to the Bulgarian and Persian flags.

They proposed instead a 'distinctive, artistic, rectangular and non-communal flag'. The chosen colour was kesari (saffron), explained as a colour with historical significance for India. The device on the flag had to be the charkha (in blue), the symbol of the nationalist movement. The charkha was to be placed on the top left quarter, with its wheel towards the flag staff.

The report of the Flag Committee was submitted in early August 1931. The CWC wasted no time in refusing to accept the new idea. After thanking the Flag Committee for its work, and accepting its central point that the flag needed to be non-communal, the CWC reverted to the old tricolour design, albeit with some changes:

> The flag is to be three coloured, horizontally arranged, as before, but the colours shall be saffron, white and green in the order stated here from top to bottom, with the spinning wheel in dark blue in the centre of the white stripe; it being understood that the colours have no communal significance, but that saffron shall represent courage and sacrifice, white peace and truth, and green shall represent faith and chivalry, and the spinning wheel the hope of the masses.

The All-India Congress Committee during its meetings on 6–8 August also asked Congress organisations to celebrate 30 August 1931 as National Flag Day.

Although there were objections from others, I will venture to speculate that Gandhi may have influenced this rollback. A kesari-coloured flag would have been instinctively perceived as

Hindu (although it is a Sikh colour too). It is truly astounding that the Flag Committee chose a colour that was in no way universally representative. If anything, it would have only furthered inter-religious tensions, especially between Muslims and Hindus. This is not something India could have risked at a time when the freedom struggle was turning a corner. It is inexplicable why a committee that consisted of secularists like Nehru did not consider this. Nehru, in fact, was very interested in the aesthetics of the flag, and initially wanted to retain the red-and-green scheme. He was also clear that there should be no community-colour association. That he finally signed off on a kesari flag, knowing full well how society would receive it, is unexplainable.

Gandhi was very happy with the final CWC flag resolution. He regarded the change from red to saffron as an aesthetic choice and was immensely pleased that the 'the hope of the masses'—the charkha—had been retained. This flag, he said, 'has been authoritatively robbed of any communal meaning, and has a definite meaning assigned to each colour'. Here he was wrong. Reverting to the three-colour scheme, albeit with a substitution, only confirmed the colour–religion association. No amount of explaining could dislodge that impression.

The flag now became a factor in all kinds of skirmishes. Some princely states felt it diminished their state flag. There were also times when it was paraded at religious functions. All the while, Gandhi continued to insist that the national flag must be a harmoniser and should not be weaponised. By now, the acceptance of the flag seemed complete—at least until 1937, when the All-India Muslim League led by Mohammad Ali Jinnah launched a frontal attack on the symbols that the Congress propagated as 'national'. Along with the ritualised singing of *Vande Mataram* and a Congress-proposed Hindi/Hindustani language policy, the flag became an anti-Congress rallying point for the Muslim League.

It is nearly impossible, and unfruitful, to try and fix the blame for this battle on any one organisation. Letters, public statements and scholarship indicate that both the Congress and the Muslim League played a part in it. The conflict was a reflection of their divergent political aims, but it was also, without a doubt, muscle-flexing. In the eyes of the Muslim League, the tricolour flag represented Congress domination and arrogance. Jinnah insisted that it was the Congress flag and not the national flag;[27] there was no need for any member of the Muslim League to respect or salute it.

Insinuating that the flag was representative of the Hindu majority, Jinnah asked Muslims to rally around the Muslim League flag. It was a battle for political territory. The results of the 1937 provincial elections had shown the Congress that it had lesser traction among Muslims. In order to rectify this shortfall, it initiated a Muslim mass contact programme, which was a direct challenge to the Muslim League. The flag became a symbolic battleground. In an agenda note Jinnah prepared on 1 February 1938 for a proposed meeting with Nehru (which did not fructify), one sub-head read, 'National Flag must go.'[28]

In mid-1937, Gandhi made a draft note which was 'subject to alternations and additions', to be circulated within the Congress. It addressed many of Jinnah's criticisms and enunciated the Congress's position on the Hindu–Muslim question. The last point he made was regarding the flag. Gandhi suggested that the flag be used only in Congress gatherings, and not be hoisted on public buildings, municipal buildings, state offices, schools or, for that matter, anyplace where there was opposition to it. This draft was in private circulation among Congress members for over one and a half years. According to Rajendra Prasad, opposition to the flag was growing due to the 'thoughtless and inopportune action of our [Congress] workers and sympathisers at certain places.'[29] There were also accusations that, after the Congress came to power in the United Provinces, Bihar, Central Provinces and Berar, their ministers ordered the hoisting of the Congress flag on public buildings, schools and other places, and went to smaller towns and hoisted the flag, making a spectacle of it. In December 1939, at Allahabad University, Muslim students took objection to the Congress flag and declared that the only flag on top of the building should be the university flag. They demanded that, if the Congress flag was hoisted, the Muslim League flag should flutter alongside. From the sidelines, the British watched these disputes gleefully. Viceroy Linlithgow was happy that such contestations were emerging between the Congress and the Muslim League. In a letter to the Secretary of State, he had this to say: 'Nothing, I need not say, could be more satisfactory from our point of view than that this problem, presenting as it does an awkward feature from our side, should be resolved by the interplay of party jealousies ...'[30]

Right through this phase, Nehru stoutly defended the tricolour flag in his correspondence with Jinnah and others.[31] In his mind, the tricolour was the national flag. It represented the hopes, courage and sacrifice of all Indians—Hindus, Muslims, Sikhs and everyone else. The flag had a presence in remote villages, and mattered to Indians living in Asia and Europe, to worlds beyond the Congress circle. This most beautiful flag had been chosen after much deliberation and inter-community consultation. For seventeen years, across generations, the flag had been a part of the national movement.

Nehru noted that, unlike the tricolour, the Muslim League flag was communal. In his letters, he consistently spoke of the 'National Flag' and the 'Flag of the League' (even as he occasionally made the point that a national flag needed to be created!).

But he also mildly conceded that the number of Muslims in the Congress had diminished: 'In those days Muslims were present in large numbers in the Congress and the flag was frequently used by the Khilafat Committee.'[32]

At the same time, in mid-1937, during his public war of words with Jinnah, Nehru had this to say to the *Bombay Chronicle*:

> During the last seventeen years there has been no period when the Muslim membership of the Congress has not been counted by thousands and tens of thousands. We do not keep separate communal records of members; for us a Muslim or a Hindu member stands on the same footing. But if Mr. Jinnah desires to compare the Congress Muslim membership with the membership of the Muslim League, I can have the necessary statistics gathered together. I imagine he will find that the number of Muslim members of the Congress is enormously greater than the total membership of the Muslim League.

Nehru could not fathom how any religion-specific flag could represent a diverse country. In late 1937 he said, 'The Hindu Mahasabha and the Sikh League and Christian associations will put up their flags in public places with equal justification. That surely is not the way to promote unity and consolidation and nationalism or to advance to the freedom of India.'[33]

Indeed, the Hindu Mahasabha did make its own claims. In his presidential address at the All-India Hindu Mahasabha session in December 1938, Sarvarkar urged Hindus to form a 'United Nation Front under an unalloyed Hindu National Flag'. And then added, 'Whether this attitude on the part of the Hindu Mahasabha is called by the tyrants or the pseudo-Nationalist Congressites as anti-national or communal or parochial or otherwise—we care a fig for the name.' In his presidential address the following year, Savarkar went a step further and suggested a design for this 'pan-Hindu flag'.[34]

> The 'Kundalini Kripanankita' Gerua Flag shall be the Flag of the Hindu Nation with its OM, the Swastik and the Sword. It appeals to sentiments cherished by our race ever since the Vedic days. Those who like to realise the inner spirit and

know the 'raison d'etre' of its design and the symbols would do well to read the special tract I have written styled 'the Pan-Hindu Dhwaj'.

Others were welcome to have their own flags and those would be respected as long at this flag was respected. 'But Hindudom as a whole will be represented by the Pan-Hindu Flag alone,' he declared. In Savarkar's mind, Hindudom was India and hence, equal reciprocity with the minorities was a charade.

With so much religious baggage, it is hardly surprising that the tricolour never lost its communal associations. Even today, three-quarters of a century later, most people believe that the saffron stands for Hindus, the white for Christians and other minorities, and the green for Muslims.

Perhaps a deeper meditation on each of these colours will help us arrive at another kind of understanding. And since green is so tightly bound to the Muslim identity, let's begin with an examination of this colour.

According to the Pew Research Centre, sixty-four of the world's 195 countries have religious symbols on their flags.[35] Out of the fifty-five Muslim-majority countries[36], twenty-three have declared Islam as their state religion. Among these twenty-three countries, fifteen have flags with an element of green, though not all of them interpret the colour in a religious context.

It is a curious fact that green may not have been the colour of the early Islamic flags. Islamic scholar A. Faizur Rahman tells me that the Sunni caliphates used black flags, and the green flags probably emerged from the tenth-century Shia Fatimid Caliphate. Hence, Saiyid Muhammad Saadulla's comment in the Constituent Assembly that green has sentimental or symbolic relevance to Muslims, as it was the colour of the flag from the time of the great Prophet of Arabia, may not be entirely accurate.

The question is, does green have a special significance in Islam?

Green represents jannah, paradise. 'Jannah' means garden, a metaphor for abundance, tranquillity and happiness. Paradise is imagined as a garden of peace—a powerfully attractive idea in the desert terrain that the people of West Asia inhabited.

In the Constituent Assembly, S. Radhakrishnan, an advaitin, said of the green in the tricolour, 'The green is there—our relation to the soil, our relation to the plant life here on which all other life depends. We must build our Paradise here on this green earth.' Saiyid Muhammad Saadulla, while discussing the colour white on the flag, described such a land in picturesque detail: 'When the crystal-clear white raindrops and the water from the snow-capped mountains and rivers comes down we get our arid areas converted into smiling green fields the crops of which sustain us and conduce to the growth of the people.'

But green symbolises more than the natural world. Faizur Rahman says, 'The Quran goes on to state that those who have been good enough in life to win accommodation in the Garden would be seen "reclining on green cushions (*rafrafin khuzrin*) and beautiful carpets" (55:76), and wearing "green garments of fine silk (*siyaabu sundusin khuzrun*) and heavy brocade" (76:21).'

Both the Quran and the Hadiths describe incidents from Prophet Mohammad's life in which nature has a central place. The relationship between human beings and nature is not transactional but symbiotic in this worldview. The Quran speaks of the natural balance and the importance of equilibrium, as well as the need to conserve, share with all and not squander all that nature provides. Stories from the life of the Prophet as described in the Hadiths are even more specific. The Prophet chastises his companion Sa'd for using excessive water for his ceremonial ablutions.

'What is this excessiveness (israaf)?'

Sa'd responds, 'Can there be any excessiveness in ablution?'

He insists, 'Yes, even if you are on the bank of a flowing river.'[37]

A repeated theme in the Hadiths is the need to cease the unjust, unnecessary felling of trees and the killing of animals or birds. Hell is the punishment for those who slay without reason, while those who serve animals will be rewarded. The planting of a tree or sowing of a seed is an act of goodness not only because it creates life, but even more so because it contributes to nature's life cycles, providing food for animals, birds and human beings. Imam Bukhari, in his collection of Hadiths titled *al-Adab al-Mufrad*, quotes Prophet Muhammad as saying, 'If the Final Hour comes while you have a shoot of a plant in your hands and it is possible to plant it before the Hour [the Day of Judgement] comes, you should plant it.'[38] This dharma of conservation, protection, nurturing continued after Prophet Muhammad's time. Abu Bakr, the first Caliph of Islam, advised Yazid, who was to leave on a military expedition: 'Do not kill women or children or an aged, infirm person. Do not cut down fruit-bearing trees. Do not destroy an inhabited place. Do not slaughter sheep or camels except for food. Do not burn bees and do not scatter them. Do not steal from the booty, and do not be cowardly.'[39]

The Hadiths and the Quran display an acceptance of the needs of human beings and their dependence on nature for survival; at the same time, they instruct the faithful to curtail greed and exploitation since it is known that these faults come naturally to humans.

The scriptures have an influence on our relationship with the world at a personal level. Democratic constitutions, on the other hand, beckon citizens to a life of positive thought and action as a cohesive collective. Our rights are not grants of authority, they are gateways to social evolution. Some of these are stated directly, while others are inferred, interpreted and affirmed.

Article 21 reads:

Protection of life and personal liberty

> No person shall be deprived of his life or personal liberty except according to procedure established by law.

The Supreme Court of India has in judgement after judgement expanded the scope of this right. The court reads into Article 21 the right of Indian citizens to a viable life on this planet, the right to live in a pollution-free environment. Contained in this guarantee is the hope that we will protect the living species and non-living elements of our world.

Constitutions are written by human beings for human beings; they are anthropocentric. The rights they guarantee relate to inter-human, social relationships. The demand for a pollution-free environment, clean water, protection of forests, mangroves, marshlands and swamps are all connected to our quality of life, and above all, the creation of a liveable future for our children.

While everything is by inference and judicial interpretation and expansion as far as Article 21 is concerned, our laundry list of duties is not so ambiguous. Article 51-A (g) says we have a duty

> to protect and improve the natural environment including forests, lakes, rivers and wild life, and to have compassion for living creatures;

The burden on the citizen is explicit, but the state has wiggle room, with a mention of its responsibility to the natural world restricted to the directive principles (Article 48A).

The Indian constitution was authored at a time when conversations about the environment were largely utilitarian. In contrast, the South African Bill of Rights legislated in 1996 responded to a world that was far more aware of the perils of neglecting the environment. It directly empowered the citizen to promote conservation and prevent ecological degradation. Everyone has the right, it said,

> (a) to an environment that is not harmful to their health or wellbeing; and

(b) to have the environment protected, for the benefit of present and future generations, through reasonable legislative and other measures that—
   (i) prevent pollution and ecological degradation;
   (ii) promote conservation; and
   (iii) secure ecologically sustainable development and use of natural resources while promoting justifiable economic and social development.[40]

Writing laws from the seat of evolutionary superiority limits human comprehension of natural life. We want to save the earth for our grandchildren, not because birds, animals, insects and plants have a natural and equal right over this blue planet. What if we were to enshrine the right to life of all of these beings? Humans are one among millions of interconnected species on this planet, and natural resources are the common heritage of all life on the planet. The meaning of the right to life changes the moment we perceive ourselves in this way.

The crossover from self-realisation to constitutional rights is a complex one. Until we are able to detach our own immediate needs and future from the larger question of right to life, it will be impossible to make just decisions. We will remain trapped in the development vs sustainability quandary—the only choice being between immediate degradation and postponed degradation.

In the late 1940s, industrialisation was synonymous with development, progress and well-being. India was an extremely impoverished country, and the urgent goal before its leaders was to feed and economically uplift the poor. The world was mechanising, new things were being created every day, and buildings and factories were seen as the route to progress. Whether we chose to be a socialist country or capitalist, progress was equated with industrialisation.

At one point, Nehru wrote to Gandhi saying,

> You have criticized strongly the many obvious defects of industrialism and hardly paid any attention to its merits.

> Everybody knows these defects and the utopias and social theories are meant to remove them. It is the opinion of most thinkers in the West that these defects are not due to industrialism as such but to the capitalist system which is based on exploitation of others. I believe you have stated that in your opinion there is no necessary conflict between capital and labour. I think that under the capitalist system this conflict is unavoidable.

Nehru was concerned with the control of production and profit, believing that human development was a natural corollary. The glitter of factories, roads and buildings, and their contrast with the country's abject poverty, made it impossible not to walk the industrialisation route. The only person who took that risk was Gandhi.

He spoke about the dangers of imitating the West and of corporatisation; he wrote about the need to view the condition of workers holistically; and above all, he stressed the importance of differentiating between need, want and materialism. Gandhi's ideas regarding the primacy of the local and the natural—the result of deep contemplation—were far ahead of his time. Though socialism mirrored a lot of what he said, his mind was not trapped in that model. He envisaged a democratic, rights-based sharing. But the problem with Gandhi's discourse was its ascetic extremism: abstinence and rejection. He demanded from everyone a non-materialistic, personally detached way of living. This order of asceticism infringed upon the dreams of people.

Gandhi had experienced what material development had to offer before giving it all up. But all sacrifice is not equal. How does one preach to a poor farmer that material gain is unnecessary, that all it will bring is unhappiness? This is an especially important question in a country where education and healthcare, the gateway to material development, are determined by caste and gender. The problem with Gandhi's model for society was its inability to deal with this unevenness in a composite manner.

Hence his suggestions, far-sighted though they were, became regressive in tone and substance. Khadi, swaraj and village-level economic self-reliance were acceptable philosophies to resist British might, but it was not the preferred lifestyle choice of a poor nation. The people of this country yearned for material security.

Desire and aspiration cannot be dismissed as either evil or unnecessary. Pleasure, whether physical, aesthetic or material, needs to be negotiated within the ethics of materialism. How then does the constitution provide an ethical direction to material desires? For this, we need to begin with the acceptance that destruction is an inherent part of any human action. There is nothing that is purely, universally constructive. Someone or something is always being exploited, destroyed or manipulated. When we enter a conversation on desire (i.e., 'development') and the natural world, conflict is unavoidable. But it is necessary to be able to make choices that are not purely anthropocentric—which, of course, is easier said than done. In the contradiction between self-centred desires and justice for all life lies an imperfect and non-dogmatic channel. We need to find our way to it.

This was not a philosophical question that the constitution-makers considered in their day. But it is one that India, its citizens as well as its political and judicial structures must contend with today.

As we move towards the white on the flag, I am conflicted by the associations it evokes. There are not many uncomfortable images that white brings to my mind. Every other colour represents a wide range of human characteristics, but white is flat, uncoloured, even untrue, I would say. Nothing can be so faultless. White is so good that it can cover any stain; all that's needed is whitewashing. Politicians wear white to hide the grime beneath.

In India, white is also the colour that widows were forced to wear. But even then, white signified purity; the colour was not sullied. All forms of colour and physical beauty were stripped away to render the woman 'pure'—without desires, asexual and undesirable. A marginalisation represented by the puritanical nature of white.

In the normal course of things, though, white captures within its brightness all things we consider good or positive. It is possible that this is the product of an Occidental interpretation, nevertheless it is our reality.

White is one of the most prominent colours in biblical imagery, especially in texts that evoke purity, divine presence and eschatological hope. In much of Western Christianity, it serves as the liturgical colour for Christmas and Easter, symbolising joy, light and resurrection. Members of the Constituent Assembly while describing the white on the flag spoke of purity, truth, peace, tranquillity, simplicity, the dispeller of darkness, innocence, honesty, wisdom, birth, goodness and virginity. Ideas that they drew from Christianity.

As my friend, a senior minister, explained to me, in Ecclesiastes 9:8, white garments point to readiness before God. In Revelation 7:9, 13–14, robes are made white through the blood of the lamb, a paradox of suffering transformed into healing. The angel at the tomb wears white (Mark 16:5), signifying divine presence; and in Revelation 19:14, the armies of heaven ride out clothed in white, representing final justice. Yet, the Bible also warns against superficial purity: prophets condemned leaders who 'whitewashed' crumbling walls (Ezekiel 13:10–15) and Jesus compared hypocritical leaders to 'whitewashed tombs' (Matthew 23:27)—clean on the outside but corrupt within. In sum, biblical whiteness carries both the radiance of holiness and the danger of false purity.

To understand white, however, we need to comprehend the stigma that surrounds black. Exceptions aside, black has come to denote everything that white is not. Antonyms to every quality associated with white are acceptable representations of black. Racist notions about dark people come from this binary of good and bad that the two colours conjure up. Just as white has been assigned monochromatic emotional possibilities, so has black. Even day and night are viewed with warmth and suspicion respectively.

In an attempt to invert presumptions about darkness, the renowned Tamil writer Perumal Murugan wrote two songs: on the night and about the owl. The night, in his words, becomes a point of origin, the land of dreams, the cradle of romance, a balm for suffering, the state from which awareness is born. The owl becomes the voice of the night, the interpreter of its beauty, from whose words we can draw many a meaning.[41]

Here are a few excerpts from these songs.

Darkness
For the pining heart, it is the panacea
Cup your hands and consume it for solace

Darkness calls, Darkness embraces
Darkness helps flourish, Darkness helps mould
Darkness helps punish, Darkness helps distil
Darkness is grace, and darkness do I savour

Owl
It is the sound of darkness
That hoot of the owl
Tune in and heed to it
For it conveys many a meaning

Listen to it with an open mind
Hear the peals of a child's glee
See the darkness dissolve away
And a grace fills your heart

On the other hand, a piece by Jacqui James, a retired Unitarian Universalist religious educator, paints a powerful picture of the bleakness that black is burdened with.

> Blackmail, blacklist, black mark. Black Monday, black mood, black-hearted. Black plague, black mass, black market.
>
> Good guys wear white, bad guys wear black. We fear black cats, and the Dark Continent. But it's okay to tell a white lie, lily-white hands are coveted, it's great to be pure as the driven snow. Angels and brides wear white. Devil's food cake is chocolate; angel's food cake is white!
>
> We shape language and we are shaped by it. In our culture, white is esteemed. It is heavenly, sunlike, clean, pure, immaculate, innocent, and beautiful. At the same time, black is evil, wicked, gloomy, depressing, angry, sullen. Ascribing negative and positive values to black and white enhances the institutionalization of this culture's racism.[42]

India has a multi-million-dollar skin-whitening industry. Mothers and grandmothers grade their own children on the basis of skin colour. 'White as milk' is used as a compliment. I am often told by conservatives that our worship of Krishna, the dark lord, is proof that we are not racist. If that were how real life operated, we would not be a land that kills the girl child—we worship the goddess, don't we?

As a musician, I have travelled across the globe. When touring the US, I often stay at the homes of upper-caste Hindus, and I've noticed that my hosts seldom have friends who are African-American. Their neighbourhood is almost always privileged white, with the competitive Chinese looming large.

If I am to accept white as a symbol of purity and propriety, I would rather interpret it as a reminder to us, the citizens, to keep the people in public life in check. Every time we look at the flag, we must tell ourselves that not only should we remain incorruptible, we should make our representatives at every level answerable.

The Right to Information (RTI) Act was a watershed moment in India. This campaign for transparency began at the village level, finally ending in a path-breaking legislation that has changed the relationship between the citizen and the State. The provision has teeth, which gives it power—the fulcrum of which is the ease with which it can be accessed. It has allowed the poor to demand information regarding the functioning of government schemes and welfare programmes, forcing the State to open its books to citizen scrutiny, giving people the opportunity to challenge authority with proof and make the government accountable at every level of its functioning.

I have heard people in the administrative services call the RTI a nuisance that does not allow them to take bold decisions and move the country forward. If we had a culture of both justification and transparency, the Act would have been unnecessary. As things stand, unnecessary applications are a small price to pay for making sure work is not just done, but done in the right manner. RTI is the whiteness in our flag that shines a light on injustice.

And yet, it is under attack today. The Union government intends to use the Digital Personal Data Protection Act, 2023 to undermine the RTI. The RTI had balanced the need for privacy and information beautifully. As per its original provisions, the government had to only release personal information that was relevant to public activities or public interest. All other personal information was protected. Now, through an amendment, access to all personal information has become taboo. This means that the public cannot ask for the names of officials and contractors who have sanctioned and built faulty public infrastructure. We cannot find out the names of wilful loan defaulters. The marginalised, who are often forced to pay bribes to get their ration card or pension, cannot find out which official is sitting on their files. The RTI had placed the citizen on par with members of Parliament and legislative assemblies. No citizen could be denied information that could not be denied to MPs and MLAs. This is no longer the case. Furthermore, the 2023 Act infringes on the free functioning of journalists and gives sweeping powers to the Union government. The government, which is only a custodian of public information, is now behaving like it is the owner. The 2023 Act disempowers citizens while simultaneously allowing the State to violate their rights and privacy.

In a democracy, the citizen is deemed sovereign. The people articulate their will through methods of election and selection. When India's sovereignty came into question in the Constituent Assembly debates, M. Ananthasayanam Ayyangar said unambiguously, '"We, the people of India, having solemnly resolved to constitute, etc." We are the persons who have met to give a Constitution for ourselves. Unless we are sovereign, we cannot give a Constitution for ourselves.' But our right to ask questions and make rightful change does not begin and end with suffrage. The burden of sovereignty requires that we remain active citizens, pushing for a greater stake in governance and decision-making.

The white in the national flag is a reminder that all is not white in public life. White is the colour we see when a surface reflects light back instead of absorbing it, a reminder that nothing can remain hidden in a democracy. We cannot blindly celebrate the success of the RTI without remembering the hundreds of RTI activists who were killed, assaulted, harassed or threatened.[43]

In the eyes of many Indian Hindus, the colours green and white are tinged with fear and suspicion. Disdain towards these colours has been instilled from childhood. I remember hearing the term 'Muslim green' used to describe what my family saw as a garish green. The army green, on the other hand, signified bravery. A certain white is also unacceptable: the white of a priest's robe. The loyalty of those who follow the white man's religion has always been suspect.

Things were not very different in 1947. Prominent educator and Bengali Christian leader H.C. Mookherjee said in the Constituent Assembly:

> From one point of view we have been misunderstood. It has been held that because we profess Christianity—essentially an Asiatic religion—and because we have certain contacts with foreign missions, therefore the Indian Christian community has what is known as Christian mentality. It is not so and I stand here to say that it is an incorrect idea. It is a misconception and I want it to be clearly understood that today I on behalf of my community, am pledging our allegiance once more to the Flag.[44]

The responsibility to change the narrative lies with the Hindus, the majority community in India that wields the power to set the narrative.

When I was growing up, the colour saffron simply meant auspiciousness. At religious events, the colour palette ranged from yellow to red. Traditional colour combinations for Kanchipuram silk sarees included yellow, orange, magenta, red and green. White jasmine flowers and green mango leaves contrasted with the orange, yellow and red flowers that dominated all celebrations. The colours bring back memories of laughter, gossip, sweets and afternoon siestas. Milk turned yellowish orange with just a pinch of saffron and turmeric. Add black pepper to that milk, I was told, for it was the cure for colds and coughs. Being a singer and hoping for a richer vocal tone, I consumed it.

When my mother took me to a Hanuman temple in the suburb of Mylapore in Chennai, the kunkuma was not red and powdery; it was a distinct, sticky, orange application. This should not be surprising because 'kunkuma' denotes the saffron flower. The word 'kesara' means the 'filament of a flower'. 'Kunkuma kesara' thus means the 'filament of the kunkuma flower', which is saffron-coloured. Over time, both kunkuma and kesara became synonyms for saffron itself. Nehru called the saffron colour on the flag 'kesari', the Hindi word for it. In mythology, Hanuman's father's name is Kesari. And so, the colour of the kunkuma in the temple dedicated to Kesari's son Hanuman came to be saffron (kesara/kesari).

Hanuman is the lord of strength and intellect, and the protector of the weak. Whenever I was afraid of sleeping alone, my mother would ask me to close my eyes and recite a shloka in praise of Hanuman. But now, Hanuman frightens me. A sticker image of an aggressive Hanuman in orange or yellow stares at me ferociously from the rear end of cars or from the small, transparent plastic shades that protect the gauge on a motorbike.

It is the same colour that shows up on the sketch of the constructed Rama temple in Ayodhya used by some as their Facebook profile picture, not as a prayer but as an in-your-face assertion of supremacy. Those who attack dalits, Muslims and Christians in the name of Hinduism flaunt saffron headbands. Today, saffron signifies ferocity and thuggishness. It is no longer the colour of renunciation or selflessness; it is the colour of aggression and revenge. Saving Hinduism from turning into a bitter, heartless, chauvinistic faith will require the reclaiming of the colour saffron.

We now equate saffron with Hinduism and hence, the flag as representative of Hindus. Yet, at the time of finalising the flag, Govind Malaviya, elected from the United Provinces, had felt the need to explain its significance as a rebuttal to Hindus who thought it did not represent them.

> The green portion in the flag may be taken to represent our Muslim friends, the white one the Christians and other communities and the saffron the Sikhs ... They represent the Hindus as well ... Some people have complained in the press

> that there should be predominance of Hindu colours in the flag and that the present flag should be changed. They ask if, along with other communities, have the Hindus not shed their blood and sacrificed their kin for this flag? How can we forget the call of those Hindu martyrs through whose sufferings and sacrifices, these disgruntled (Hindus) have had the chance to see the dawn of independence?
>
> With due respect, I would like to tell even the most orthodox Hindus that this flag amply represents the Hindu sentiments. This flag is the true expression of the sentiments of the Hindus and Hinduism ... The red colour at the top represents fire and the sun. The white represents the moon. Now according to the Hindu mythology, the first thing that the Creator (Brahma) did was to create the sun and the moon. The Hindus, the Aryans have since their very beginning been worshiping the Sun, Fire and the Moon. The Sun and the Moon are worshipful deities. This flag represents these very gods—the fire the sun and the moon. The green colour at the bottom, as I have said, should be taken by our Muslim friends to represent them. But at the same time, this colour in a way represents the Hindus as well. You know of all the nine planets Budha is supposed to be the most important. This green colour represents the Budha ... What better flag can the Hindus adopt for themselves, than the present one which represents the Fire, the Sun, the Moon and Budha? ... Therefore, far from opposing it, Hindus should adore it and should be prepared to sacrifice their all to protect its honour.[45]

Radhakrishnan called the saffron on our flag 'bhagwa'—an interesting name for the colour. According to Sanskritist Naresh Keerthi, the word 'bhagwa' can be traced to the word 'bhagavan' (god) which is 'bhagavo' in Pali. Buddha was probably the first person to be addressed as 'bhagavo'. Later, it becomes a generic social honorific associated with renunciates who joined a monastery or took to a life of spiritual seeking. There is a very old tradition in Buddhism of monks wearing saffron or red robes. In a later transformation of meaning, Keerthi explains, the colour worn by the bhagavo must have become bhagwa, saffron. The robe communicated the ideal of giving up all levers of control and power.

There is a beautiful verse in the *Gaha Sattasai* believed to have been compiled by the Satavahana King Hala (early first century CE) that describes the bright orange flame of the palash flower lying on the ground, which further establishes the connection between the colour ochre and Buddhist robes.

> The palash flowers resembling
> parrots' beaks,
> strewn on the forest floor;
> are like a congregation of monks,
> paying homage to the Buddha.[46]

The next time you see this flower, place it on the ground and look at it. It does look like a Buddhist monk bent forward on the floor, face down in prayer.

Another text, *Harivamsha*, probably from the Gupta period and attributed to sage Vyasa, has this to say about the kali yuga: '... and shudras who follow the Buddha of the Shakyas will practice their religion dressed in ochre robes, with shaved heads, white teeth, and uncowed eyes'.[47]

The era is described as apocalyptic, everything is topsy-turvy, the traditional social order (varna) is collapsing, members of the different varnas are not behaving or working within their prescribed domains and people's behaviour in general is uncouth and violent. This degradation is not just social, the natural world is also deteriorating. The text, a sort of sequel to the Mahabharata, seems to suggest that the social normative and environment crumble together—an indicator of the ochre age.[48]

Radhakrishnan had this to say: 'The red, the orange, the Bhagwa colour represents the spirit of renunciation. It is said:

Sarve tyage rajadharmesu drsta.' He was quoting from the Shanti Parvan of the Mahabharata. The verse reads:

> Every benevolence is seen in
> every hardship is prescribed for
> every discipline is enjoined for
> and all people are encompassed by just governance.[49]

Radhakrishnan was speaking of renunciation in political and public life and the detachment that needs to be inculcated in those who wish to serve. This was rajadharma. Saffron was a message, he said, that the 'World belongs not to the wealthy, not to the prosperous but to the meek and the humble, the dedicated and the detached.'

Selflessness does not begin at the moment of action. It happens before the act, when we remove ourselves, see it for what it is, with a mind free of prejudice. Saffron robes are not just about renunciation. Like the rising sun, sacrifice and detachment should give rise to wisdom. There is work involved; it is not spontaneous. Renunciates wear the colour saffron to remind themselves of tyaga and jnana, renunciation and self-realisation.

On the day the flag was introduced, Nehru and Radhakrishnan were making every effort to erase social divides using this new flag as a metaphor. Yet, members of minority communities felt compelled to pledge their allegiance to the flag as representatives of their specific community. This demonstrated the power imbalance that existed between the majority and minority communities then. I am not sure much has changed in the past seventy-five years.

Ever since Independence, we have referred to our flag as the tiranga, or tricolour. But our flag is not a tiranga. It is a chaturanga: four colours. At the very heart of the flag is a striking navy blue, the colour of the wheel. The chakra finds mention always, but rarely its colour.

Before the chakra, it was the charkha that had been the central ornament on the flag. The charkha was used much larger, its outline extending over the three original colours (white, green and red) of the flag. A version of this flag was adopted as the national flag by Subhas Chandra Bose in 1941, in Berlin. In his interpretation, the springing tiger—reminiscent of the Mysore warrior king Tipu Sultan—replaced the charkha in the centre. Later, in South East Asia, Gandhi's charkha came back to take centre stage on the flag of the Indian National Army (INA). One of the pages of the original Indian constitution has a painting of Netaji saluting the flag as the army moves ahead. The emblem in the middle is not recognisable on the fluttering flag.

The Non-Cooperation Movement of 1920 had catapulted the charkha and the act of spinning thread into a symbol of nationalism. In Gandhi's construal, the charkha was not just a benign tool for change, but a device of active resistance. He endowed the charkha with metaphorical meanings that ranged from the physical to the esoteric. He said that national programmes, such as improved sanitation, the settlement of village disputes, anti-malarial campaigns and the conservation and breeding of cattle, could be built around the charkha. Thus seen, the charkha embodied the personal and the collective.

In 1920, at a special session in Kolkata, the Congress decided to embark on what it called 'progressive, non-violent non-cooperation'. It was agreed that foreign goods would be boycotted. And to further push this agenda, it was decided:

> And in as much as Non-cooperation has been and conceived as a measure of discipline and self-sacrifice without which no nation can make real progress, and in as much as an opportunity should be given in the very first stage of Non-cooperation to every man, woman and child, for such

> discipline and self-sacrifice, this Congress advises adoption of Swadeshi in piece-goods on a vast scale, and in as much as the existing mills of India with indigenous capital and control do not manufacture sufficient yarn and sufficient cloth for the requirements of the nation, and are not likely to do so for a long time to come, this Congress advises immediate stimulation of further manufacture on a large scale by means of reviving hand-spinning in every home and hand-weaving on the part of the millions of weavers who have abandoned their ancient and honourable calling for want of encouragement.[50]

In this resolution, there was a double emphasis: on self-sacrifice and discipline. Though foreign goods were to be boycotted, the specific target was piece-goods, or textiles. A boycott would not help unless there was a viable indigenous option. In came the mass production of hand-woven cloth. This was both an act of resilience and a reminder of self-worth, made plausible by that instrument of action, the charkha.

Most of the country celebrated this move; those who objected did so for political reasons. Only one man stood on the other side of the chasm on philosophical grounds—for Rabindranath Tagore, the charkha was a specific target of critique, articulated in a series of exchanges with Gandhi. Readers became witness to a complex and thoughtful exchange between two wonderful minds that went on for about five years.[51] Tagore raised many issues that need deeper engagement and appear particularly relevant today. His criticism was not based on the immediate needs of politics. He was concerned about the impact of this path on future generations. While Gandhi was addressing the present, Tagore was looking into the future, and hence reconciliation was near impossible.

There were a few points on which the two men agreed. Both of them unequivocally stated that love is swaraj and truth, and this love needs to be found within, not outside, each person.

But when venturing to describe the nature of the internal and external, they parted ways. For Gandhi, good, bad, right, wrong were all near-perfectly differentiated, a definiteness that guided his personal and public actions. So certain was he that he believed everyone else would benefit from following the path he had charted for himself. This belief did not stem from narcissism or an inability to listen. Quite the opposite. It came from his life experience, religious and spiritual reflections, and interactions with society at large. It was this clarity that provided him with the immense strength needed to fight and lead from the front. And yet, although he was constantly learning throughout his life, Gandhi did not allow his foundational value system to be altered. He was unable to live ambiguously, in the grey. His compassion came from being convinced of the 'right', not from being doubtful of it. Tagore, on the other hand, was an artist, and like all artists, thrived in the in-betweens, the uncertainties and vulnerabilities that come from not knowing.

In the Non-cooperation Movement, all Tagore heard was shouting, a 'congregated menace of negations shouts'. In that negation, he perceived a negation of life, the material and real. He said he was 'frightened of an abstraction which is ready to ignore living reality'. It was a form of violence against the living. He sought harmony between the physical and the spiritual. He did not believe that the kind of austerity Gandhi was trying to instil in every individual would lead to understanding and love. Tagore was not interested in love among Indians alone, he sought universal love.

It is difficult to disagree with Tagore in principle, but he definitely did not account for the role of power in this equation. Gandhi explicitly dealt with this inequality; a fair relationship with the West was only possible on an equal footing, not when Indians were being oppressed. A borderless, limitless sharing, which Tagore called 'one grand harmony of all human races', was not possible without dignity. Hence, regaining the power to say 'no' to evil was the first step towards freedom within. Negation was necessary then, and in all arenas—cultural, social, educational and political. The charkha embodied all these challenges to power. If employed effectively, it could invert the power equation and force the powerful into a position of weakness—though it is unlikely that Gandhi employed the word 'weakness'. Therefore, within Gandhi's spiritual strategy lay a tactical attack.

Yet, Gandhi's acute comprehension of the workings of power did not extend to a reckoning of his own power over others. Tagore saw through this. People blindly followed Gandhi's diktat to spin and adopt khadi, without any intellectual participation in the action. Gandhi's own unbending ethical engagement combined with his status as a sort of saint-teacher who used the semantics of the spiritual tradition in politics made it very difficult for those on his side of the political arena to reject his recommendations. In Tagore's words, 'And therefore I am afraid of a blind faith on a very large scale in the charkha, in the country, which is so liable to succumb to the lure of short cuts when pointed out by a personality about whose moral earnestness they can have no doubt.'

But Gandhi was convinced of his vision for the country, and the people, in turn, became convinced that the charkha was part of a spiritually energised political action. Unfortunately, spinning became much like the ritual of praying: a mechanical act that suppressed all mental faculties. The words 'self-sacrifice' and 'discipline' in the Congress resolution are right out of Gandhi's vocabulary, but Tagore saw it as a homogenising process. In other words, to reject external tyranny, internal oppression was being unleashed, and the charkha was its instrument. Gandhi even suggested that membership in the Congress could be limited 'to those who gave a certain amount of self-spun yarn ...'

Tagore titled one of the later essays in his parleys with Gandhi as 'The Cult of the Charkha'. He suggested that Gandhi was mechanising people, especially the young, stripping individuals of their mind and free will. In some ways, he was industrialising minds in exactly the way he himself would not want. Tagore used the phrase 'mechanical mortar pounded homogeneity' to describe such a state. He was even more scathing when he said,

> If in any country we find no symptom of such rebellion, if we find its people submissively or contentedly prone on the dust, in dumb terror of some master's bludgeon, or blind acceptance of some *guru's* injunction, then indeed should we know that for such a country, *in extremis*, it is high time to mourn.

But the larger cause had taken over Gandhi's mind, and perhaps individual awakening was pushed to the back burner. He argued that the act of spinning was meditative, a silent and powerful revival. This might be true for some, and would certainly have been true for him. But was it universally true?

In this context, we must also consider difficult questions about the repetitive nature of certain kinds of work. Today, the substitution of people with machines is spoken of as a form of liberation for those who are forced to do menial, repetitive jobs. Emancipation from such work could indeed open up creative possibilities for individuals and thus for society. But there is a catch. The mechanisation of jobs on the factory floor must necessarily be preceded by access to education, especially for the marginalised, and a society that guarantees equality and equity. Without this, mechanisation only means the taking away of a scarce source of livelihood from the worker for the gain of those who hold power.

Tagore was an artist. For him, freedom meant the flow, intermingling and exploration of whatever life had to offer. This openness engendered love and empathy. Any limitation put on it would cause suffocation. This is what the spinning of the charkha was doing. It did not allow each person to learn and respond to the crisis of unfreedom in their own manner. Instead, they resorted to mindless acts such as the burning of foreign clothes—an act Tagore found insensitive because it ignored those individuals who had no clothes to wear.

> Secondly, I feel that the clothes to be burnt are not mine, but belong to those who most sorely need them. If those who are going naked should have given us the mandate to burn, it would, at least, have been a case of self-immolation and the crime of incendiarism would not lie at our door. But how can we expiate the sin of the forcible destruction of clothes which might have gone to women whose nakedness is actually keeping them prisoners unable to stir out of the privacy of their homes?

Gandhi countered:

> I must refuse to insult the naked by giving them clothes they do not need, instead of giving them work which they sorely need. I will not commit the sin of becoming their patron, but on learning that I had assisted in impoverishing them, I would give them a privileged position and give them neither crumbs nor cast off clothing but the best of my food and clothes and associate myself with them in work.

'In burning my foreign clothes I burn my shame,' he said. And yet, how could Gandhi or anyone else take a moral stance on behalf of someone else? Placing the burden of a certain moral choice on the shoulders of someone who has nothing is also a form of violence. Does such a person become impoverished by accepting foreign cloth? Is it not their right to possess clothing, no matter what its origin?

It is hard to ignore the fact that neither individual involved in this lofty discussion had experienced such forced deprivation. It is, all the same, one of the great debates at the moral heart of this country.

Restoration of the human spirit, to Tagore, meant the undaunted flow of ideas in every direction, not the compulsive execution of a predetermined act of making or destruction. Protest had meaning when each person found their own language to break free. Leaders needed to provide the environment for such 'creative courage' to emerge.

It could be said that Gandhi did exactly that. The spinning of the charkha unified people, bringing Indians to a level playing field, even if it was only for a limited period. Irrespective of caste, gender and class, everyone spun in unison. Unison was not a sign of sameness; it was a rejection of differences. Which is why Gandhi called it noble. It also gave the privileged an understanding of labour, which Gandhi hoped would help give human labour the rightful place it deserved in society. Most Indians were labourers of some sort, after all. His objection to machines replacing handlooms was as much about the dignity of labour as it was about mass production and the destruction of livelihood in the name of modernisation. The charkha sought to give back honour to every individual by giving them work, food and clothes. Tagore understood this, but he said,

> Where Mahatma Gandhi has declared war against the tyranny of the machine which is oppressing the whole world, we are all enrolled under his banner. But we must refuse to accept as our ally the illusion-haunted magic-ridden slave mentality that is at the root of all the poverty and insult under which our country groans. Here is the enemy itself on whose defeat alone swaraj within and without can come to us.

The Tagore–Gandhi debate also raised questions about the role of art in society, in personal evolution, and how we imagine freedom. For Gandhi, art, especially music, had a spiritual place in the nationalist imagination. Every song he chose had a role to play in his grand socio-religious-political reformation movement—it wasn't mere aesthetic luxury. Gandhi referred to the role of a creative person at least twice in his exchanges with Tagore. In the first instance he said,

> I do indeed ask the poet and the sage to spin the wheel as a sacrament. When there is war, the poet lays down the lyre, the lawyer his law reports, the schoolboy his books. The poet will sing the true note after the war is over, the lawyer will have occasion to go to his law books when people have time to fight among themselves. When a house is on fire, all the inmates go out, and each one takes up a bucket to quench the fire. When all about me are dying for want of food, the only occupation permissible to me is to feed the hungry.

What does a poet, or indeed a singer, do during war and civil strife, I ask myself. Even during turmoil, we need songs of courage, words of encouragement, and poetry describing a post-war future. Without that, there would be no hope. Poets must not lay down their lyre; they should allow it to respond with power and kindness. Bards have always travelled with kings on conquests, not to pick up the sword but to call upon the intangibles of nature to bless them with victory.

I don't know how I feel about this near supernatural power of words, but I believe in my heart that art has kept society emotionally alive. Unlike a burning house which has only one solution, the fire of social and political turmoil needs to be addressed in both, the physical and emotional domains. Songs douse the fire as much as direct political action. While the impact of a political action is limited to a time and space, the poem lives on, playing its part each time a fire erupts. 'Hum dekhenge', I sang at protest meets, many decades after Faiz passed on.

Gandhi made one other sharp comment: 'I have found it impossible to soothe suffering patients with a song from Kabir. The hungry millions ask for one poem—invigorating food.'

Is that a flattening of the needs of the hungry? Do the poor not sing to their babies even when there is no food at home? Art exists because it is an essential part of life, not because it provides livelihood. This recognition of the role of art in society has always been missing from Indian society. If art had little value among the poor and the oppressed, we would not have had innumerable genres of poetry, painting, music and dance. People make art to share their real and imagined worlds. There is an audience that receives it, but the art itself is not made for them. Art objects are not carbon copies of life, they excavate the emotional contours behind the physical façade. A poet creates a poem that invents reality; a dancer's deer is independent of the deer in the forest and a painted tree is a different self. These objects carry in them the feelings they evoke in the artist. When the real is suffused with imagination, art happens. This potential exists in every human being, irrespective of the social context.

Tagore claimed that the urgent push for swaraj had created an illusion of coming together. The Hindu–Muslim unity on display was not real. We know that after more than seventy-five years as an independent nation, there is still an enormous gap between our constitutional dreams and our lived reality. We have to concede that there has been a cultural failure. Tagore wanted us to work towards that change by evolving cultural rather than political networks between communities. Through osmosis of word, sound, movement and design, he believed a free society would materialise, even if it took time.

There has been progress, no doubt, but a large section of Indian society still lives within a feudal set-up. Laws and constitutional guarantees haven't managed to change minds that remain holed up in a distant past. The idea of Hindu–Muslim unity has proven to be largely an artificial construct. We are socially separated and economically transactional. Saying that we are a land of many religions is a half-truth; we are a land of many competing religions, although the frenzy of seeking political independence from the British led us to believe that we had moved forward as a unit.

> Human nature has its elasticity; and in the name of urgency, it can be forced towards a particular direction far beyond

> its normal and wholesome limits. But the rebound is sure to follow, and the consequent disillusionment will leave behind it a desert track of demoralisation.

Despite this prophetic warning from Tagore in 1925, the violence of Partition and the assassination of Gandhi, India brushed everything under the carpet and prayed that subsequent generations would not carry forward the anger. Today it appears that, with each generation, the memory of unattended hate has been aggravated. Tagore's vision of swaraj was of a cultural environment, where learning was freely shared, where the Indian identity was not wedded to nationalist euphoria and where unfettered creativity was the norm. But this is not the vision we chased. Today, we are a country that is free but made up of individuals who are not. We are free of the external villain, but have failed to exorcise the demons within. Even Gandhi's charkha has been unable to keep us together.

The charkha on the flag morphed into the chakra for multiple reasons. One of them was a visual complication that Nehru laid out in the Constituent Assembly.

> Normally speaking, the symbol on one side of the Flag should be exactly the same as on the other side. Otherwise, there is a difficulty which goes against the rules. Now, the Charkha, as it appeared previously on this Flag, had the wheel on one side and the spindle on the other. If you see the other side of the Flag, the spindle comes the other way and the wheel comes this way; if it does not do so, it is not proportionate, because the wheel must be towards the pole, not towards the end of the Flag. There was this practical difficulty.[52]

This was a point made by S.D. Kalelkar in his note on the flag, which was considered by the ad hoc committee headed by Rajendra

Prasad, chairman of the Constituent Assembly. The committee members included Abul Kalam Azad, C. Rajagopalachari, Sarojini Naidu, K.M. Panikkar, K.M. Munshi, B.R. Ambedkar, Frank Anthony, B. Pattabhi Sitaramayya, Pandit Hiralal Shastri, Satyanarayan Sinha, Sardar Ujjal Singh and S.N. Gupta.

Kalelkar also felt that any image on the flag must be such that even a common person could draw it on their own. Over-decorativeness would make that impossible. He suggested that a simple chakra worked visually, and represented a wide range of people, principles, occupations, having been the 'substratum of all civilisations'. He included 'revolution' in his interpretation—especially refreshing now, when revolution is considered anti-national. In fact, Kalelkar believed that the original red that was changed to saffron in 1931 was a better choice because red is distinct, unlike saffron, which can be interpreted in so many shades. He also defended red on philosophical grounds: 'A symbol of revolution, red need not necessarily indicate a bloody revolution; it may very well stand for the non-violent revolution that we have witnessed in India.'

Kalelkar used the word 'wheel' in his note, while Nehru used 'chakra' in the Constituent Assembly. It would be fair then to assume with some certainty that they were aware that the wheel on the abacus of the Sarnath pillar was a chakra and not the dharmachakra. In fact, Kalelkar only infers that the wheel might include the idea of the dharmachakra. Ananya Vajpeyi, in her book *Righteous Republic*,[53] informs us that there is no documentation of discussions on this subject between archaeologists, historians and the Constituent Assembly. But she has hinted that advice may have been received.

The minutes of the 10 July meeting of the ad hoc committee included the following statement (emphasis mine):

> (5) The emblem on the flag should be an *exact reproduction of the wheel on the capitol of Asoka's Sarnath pillar superimposed in the* middle of the central band and (white) of the flag.[54]

In the minutes of the 18 July meeting, it is further stated (emphasis mine): 'The design of the Wheel shall be that of the *Wheel (Chakra) which appears on the abacus of the Sarnath Lion Capitol of Asoka*.'[55]

This may be interpreted as some expert informing members of the committee after the 10 July meeting that there was, at present, no wheel on the capital. Hence, in the minutes of the 18 July meeting, there was a specific reference to the wheel as that which appeared on the abacus.

Gandhi was not entirely pleased. In his jottings we can sense disappointment and reluctance. His mind was also filled with arguments made by others for and against the replacement of the charkha with the chakra. Aesthetically he found the charkha to be more elegant. He said, 'Even if they cast it away, I will still have it in my hand and in my heart.' He felt that the charkha was a symbol of non-violence, which was the soul of India's past. The acceptance of the new flag did not make the old redundant.

> Even after the king is dead, the kingdom remains and old coins are not discarded for the new ones. When the new coins are issued old coins do not suffer any depreciation of value. Therefore, so long as there is even one old flag in stock at the Gandhi Ashram the two flags will have the same value.

Gandhi accepted the Indian flag only as an 'improved design' that was 'innocent', 'a concession to art', not as a philosophical shift from the past. If it did not represent the charkha, he would not salute it. Beneath this apprehensive acceptance lay Gandhi's emotional bond with the representative significance that he had constructed around the charkha: 'Whether the Asoka Chakra and the spinning-wheel are the same thing will ultimately depend on the behaviour of the people.'

Gandhi did find some solace in the fact that some saw in the chakra the compassionate king Ashoka who 'represented all faiths'; his symbol 'represents [the] eternally revolving divine law of ahimsa'. For Gandhi, all this circled back to the charkha: 'Seeing the charkha in his chakra adds to the glory of the charkha.' In his eyes, it remained a spinning wheel.

It would, however, have been simply wrong to retain the charkha on the national flag. With Independence, the Indian National Congress became a political party, on par with other parties, even if they were smaller. India had to move ahead and become a part of the world of nations. The replacement of the charkha with the chakra endowed the flag with an echo of the past while establishing the distinctiveness of the present standard. There is, of course, a counter argument that Gandhi's charkha was a contemporary signifier of the common person. Replacing it with a conceptual symbol that was constructed by a monarch thousands of years ago distanced the state from its people.

It is possible that members of the Constituent Assembly were addressing Gandhi's discomfort while explaining various aspects of the new design.[56] For Nehru, the presence of Ashoka on the flag was justification enough. Others spoke of the wheel as a symbol of peace, prosperity, progress and spiritual values. The wheel has also been interpreted by scholars as unity in diversity, a symbol of federalism.

Unsurprisingly, there were religious interpretations too. The chakra was seen as Krishna's sudarshana chakra. Correlations were also made with the Upanishads and the Buddha. In a castigation of religious bigots, Seth Govind Das, elected to the Assembly from Central Provinces and Berar, said, 'Those who have been maddened by Communalism today, should not take this flag to be a communal flag. You see that it has the Asoka chakra in the middle.' The chakra was the peacemaker, the symbol that unified religions and brought them together under one voice of dharma. I am tempted to speculate that the sudden emergence of a Buddhist symbol on the flag suggests the influence of Ambedkar. But there is no information to back such a suggestion. Nehru's own fascination for Ashoka may have been the primary motivator.

But why was the colour of the chakra blue? I could find no discussions that explain this choice of colour, although it appears to be a continuation of the blue of the charkha on the Congress flag.

There is another story that has emerged from Laila Tyabji, the daughter of Badruddin Tyabji, an Indian civil servant, and Surayya Tyabji. She claimed that her parents were instrumental in placing the image of the chakra from the abacus of the Sarnath pillar in the centre of the Indian flag. She also dismisses the claim made by the then ambassador of the Republic of China to India, Chia-Luen Lo, that he had suggested the use of Ashoka's wheel as a motif for the flag, at a dinner party that took place on 26 July 1947—a few days after the flag had been presented by Nehru in the Constituent Assembly. It is just possible, though, that the ambassador got the date of the dinner party wrong.

Surayya Tyabji was one of the members of the Flag Presentation Committee on the night of 14 August 1947 and supervised the making of the first official Indian flag. Laila Tyabji writes: 'Originally, my mother had painted a black chakra, but Gandhiji objected so it became navy blue.'[57]

Even if we were to accept this contention, it still does not explain why the original blue charkha became a black chakra. In the minutes of the ad hoc committee meeting, there is no mention of a change of colour for the chakra; only the image was debated. Perhaps we can conclude that there was no great thought put into the choice of blue. It may have been a purely aesthetic decision. But we are at liberty to interpret it, and I am going to do just that.

In India, the colour blue has an age-old association[58] with the struggles of the marginalised. In early 1859, peasants in Bengal, who had been exploited by white planters for decades, took a cue from a magistrate's notice that made the sowing of indigo non-obligatory, and for the first time refused to cultivate the plant. Though many historians have termed the protests that ensued as non-violent, some others say that besides non-cooperation—passive resistance and boycotting of Indians who served British planters—peasants attacked factories and defended themselves against armed goons sent by the planters. The Bengali bourgeoisie were careful not to antagonise the British government. This fence-sitting by the intellectuals may have been one of the reasons why this 'blue movement', which sustained for over a year, remained local and anti-planter, and did not develop into a larger anti-colonial campaign. Nearly sixty years after this episode, the indigo blue came back into focus. But this time, it was as the launch pad for an entirely new method of anti-colonial activism. One that played a pivotal role in freeing us from the colonial yoke in 1947.

Gandhi's first experiment with satyagraha, or civil disobedience, in India was in Champaran, Bihar, in 1917. Champaran was full of indigo plantations. The tenants of the plantation were bound by law to plant indigo on a portion of their land. 'This system was known as the tinkathia system, as three kathas out of twenty kathas (which make one acre) had to be planted with Indigo,' Gandhi noted. The tenants lived in oppressive conditions, and landlords used force and extortion to make sure they remained subjugated. Even when the price of indigo began falling, they had no choice but to grow the crop.

Gandhi first went to Champaran on the invitation of Rajkumar Shukla, an agriculturalist. Very soon, he realised the gravity of the situation. He studied the problem, listened to the voices of the tenants, and mobilised public participation for a peaceful agitation. His overtures to the office-bearers of the planters' association were rudely rebuffed; he was an outsider.

Still, Gandhi's investigations were having an impact and made the government uneasy. He was issued a notice to leave Champaran, but he stayed on. Then the administration issued him a summons. The night before Gandhi was to appear in court, crowds gathered around the house where he was staying. The following day, the court was overflowing. In his characteristic style, Gandhi said,

> In my humble opinion it is a question of difference of opinion between the Local Administration and myself. I have entered the country with motives of rendering humanitarian and national service. I have done so in response to a pressing invitation to come and help the ryots, who urge they are not being fairly treated by the indigo planters ... As a law-abiding citizen my first instinct would be, as it was, to obey the order served upon me. But I could not do so without doing violence to my sense of duty to those for whom I have come. I feel that I could just now serve them only by remaining in their midst ... I venture to make this statement not in any way in extenuation of the penalty to be awarded against me, but to show that I have disregarded the order served upon me not for want of respect for lawful authority, but in obedience to the higher law of our being, the voice of conscience.[59]

Soon enough, the case was withdrawn. Gandhi continued his inquiry and recorded thousands of statements by tenants and held multiple public meetings. The result was the abolishment of the tinkathia system. The satyagraha began as a response to violence in the name of blue. Momentarily, blue also became the colour of ahimsa, satyagraha and righteousness.

But the dark blue of indigo soon faded from memory. It needed Ambedkar to bring it back into the public imagination. Ambedkar statues, seen in innumerable street corners across the length and breadth of the country, have him attired in a blue suit, holding the constitution in one hand and urging us to move forward. There are many theories about how the association between blue and dalit movements came about. Was it Ambedkar's favourite colour? Ambedkar's suit was a social statement and the choice of blue possibly just his preference. Some associate blue with the expanse of his vision and the non-discriminatory nature of the sky itself. Blue is also considered the colour of equality, representative of the working class. Buddhist and folklore associations with the colour blue have also been pointed out.

We know that Ambedkar gave blue a political presence by choosing it as the colour of the flag of the All India Scheduled Castes Federation that he founded in 1942. Part XI of the amended constitution of the Federation, published in 1955, states: 'The flag of the Federation shall consist of stars against a blue cloth cut in triangle.' The Republican Party of India, founded by Ambedkar in 1956, also had a blue flag.

Could there have been another reason for the choice of blue?

In his *Riddles of Hinduism: An Exposition to Enlighten the Masses*,[60] Ambedkar reviewed what the Puranas had to say on the origin of the varna system. He quoted from John Muir's translations of some sections of the Mahabharata and the vulgate version of *Harivamsha*.

From the Mahabharata: 'The colour (varna) of the Brahmans was white; that of the Kshatriyas red; that of the Vaishyas yellow, and that of the Sudras black.'

From *Harivamsha*: 'The Brahmans, beautiful (or, dear to Soma), were formed from an imperishable (akshara), the Kshattriyas from a perishable (kshara), element, the Vaisyas from alteration, the Sudras from a modification of smoke ... Hence in the world men have become divided into castes, being of four descriptions, Brahmans, Kshattriyas, Vaisyas and Sudras ...'

That the colours blue and black are used as interchangeable shades was not important in these correlations. The scholar Nick Allen demonstrates that equivalences between certain colours and people's social functions, nature and even appearance are found in many cultures.[61] These cultural associations also reveal that people at the lowest rung of society are invariably allocated dark colours, very often blue or black. Allen calls black a 'non-colour' which is connected with the semiotics of inferiority and otherness.

Although Ambedkar wrote this particular essay in the 1950s, he had been seriously engaging with the Hindu scriptures for a long time. This makes me wonder if his choice of blue was influenced by the association of this colour with shudras.

Be that as it may, the blue has come to stay. Dalit protests across the country are flooded with blue flags. Political parties that represent dalit communities have at least a spatter of blue on their emblems and flags. Homes are coloured blue; activists, musicians and movie makers use blue to signify battles against oppressors. The spirit of the blue has also changed with every generation of dalit voices. It used to be about gentle appeals, then a strong collective demand. Today it is a forceful assertion of identity and rights, a powerful pushback that informs the oppressing majority that their time is up.

The blue chakra is at the literal heart of the Indian flag, holding within itself the strength of the dalit community and the spirit of civil disobedience. It is a reflection of our right to assemble peaceably and without arms. An assertion that we will assemble to protect our rights and ally with all those society forgets to notice. It is also a reminder of our unkept promises.

Interestingly, Ambedkar doesn't seem to have been present in the Constituent Assembly on 22 July 1947, when the resolution to accept the flag was moved by Nehru. With the partition of Bengal, Ambedkar had ceased to be a member of the Constituent Assembly. In late June, an anxious Rajendra Prasad wrote to the prime minister of Bombay, asking him to elect Ambedkar so that he could attend the next session commencing on 14 July. Ambedkar was re-elected in July and signed in his credentials on the first day of the session. He came in on 21 July too, but is conspicuously absent on the next day. Perhaps he did not care very much for symbols and signs; it was minds and actions that needed to change. The blue wheel of dharma moves only when those on the periphery are placed at the hub of social, cultural, economic and political activity. Or maybe his reasons were purely mundane, for he only attended the Constituent Assembly sessions on 14, 21 and 29 in the month of July.

While speaking of the non-sectarian nature of the flag, Nehru had also said, 'We thought of a Flag which ... in its combination and in its separate parts would somehow represent the spirit of the nation, the tradition of the nation, that mixed spirit and tradition which has grown up through thousands of years in India.'

For Nehru, colours—separately and in their coming together—needed to represent the spirit of India. To contain the religiousness that saffron, white and green brought forth, we needed a shared treasured value. That was secularism.

Secularism is a word that sounds obscure and unrelatable because of its non-representational nature. Secularism is not a physical body, a place one can go to, a rule that can be followed or a destination that we can see in front of our eyes. It is a sensibility that we hope to inculcate through social mores and directions. Consequently, it is easy to malign. The dictionary defines secularism as the separation of the State and religious bodies. A word that has roots in European history, and the need to keep an all-powerful church out of matters of governance. But the meaning of the word has grown beyond that definition. In France, it can be traced to the 1905 law regarding the separation of Church and State. Article 1 of the French constitution (1958) states: 'France shall be an indivisible, secular, democratic and social Republic. It shall ensure the equality of all citizens before the law, without distinction of origin, race or religion. It shall respect all beliefs.'

Neutrality of the State means non-interference in religious life. Yet, over the past three decades, France has passed laws that prohibit or restrict the expression of religious identity in public schools; even private enterprises are empowered to restrict such expressions. This, too, is a definition of secularism.

India's secularism is of an entirely different register. Religion is not institutionalised in quite the same way here. The philosophical problem with the sort of uncompromising separation between religion and State is that it does not account for the natural seepages between the private and the public. For long, France was predominantly single-religion and ethnically homogeneous. But its socio-religious composition has been changing, and its traditional interpretation of secularism has manifested as insensitivity and discrimination. The State is unable to respond to the specificity of issues that its minority citizens, say Muslims, face. And so the much-touted neutrality of French secularism is turning into a majoritarian order.[62]

Religions are amorphous and porous, and bundles of contradictions. They can be welcoming and uplifting, and also oppressive. Indian culture is a product of the intermingling of various faiths as well as agnostic and atheistic traditions. It has offered to the world as much as it has received from it. As Nehru put it:

> It is folly for any nation or race to think that it can only give to and not receive from the rest of the world. Once a nation or a race begins to think like that, it becomes rigid, it becomes ungrowing; it grows backwards and decays ... India's greatest periods are those when she stretched her hands to others in far off countries, sent her emissaries and ambassadors, her trade agents and merchants to these countries and received ambassadors and emissaries from abroad.[63]

Nehru conceived of the Indian identity as borderless and hoped that even the creation of Indian nationhood would not stifle that quality. Our secularism is cultural and religious internationalism. This spirit flourishes only when faiths rub shoulders with each other; when we see, recognise and learn from each other's spiritual paths. In the Indian version of secularism, religion is to be seen in our attire, symbols and headgear, not hidden away as private practice. In 1947, we were becoming a country and wanted a culture of secularism that allowed everyone to ask questions of, and about, faith. This is our secularism: the freedom of conscience and conduct. The freedom to believe, not to believe, or remain indifferent.

A critical aspect of our secularism is its recognition that all religions do not enjoy equal social power. This reality is taken cognisance of in Article 30 of the Fundamental Rights:

> Right of minorities to establish and administer educational institutions
>
> (1) All minorities, whether based on religion or language, shall have the right to establish and administer educational institutions of their choice
>
> (1A) In making any law providing for the compulsory acquisition of any property of an educational institution established and administered by a minority, referred to in clause (1), the State shall ensure that the amount fixed by or determined under such law for the acquisition of such property is such as would not restrict or abrogate the right guaranteed under that clause
>
> (2) The State shall not, in granting aid to educational institutions, discriminate against any educational institution on the ground that it is under the management of a minority, whether based on religion or language

This special consideration is not limited to religion; it includes linguistic minorities. The empowerment of the weaker sections of society was a central principle for India's constitution-makers. In Article 29, there is a direct reference to cultural minorities.

But god has always been a touchy subject. Even as the constitution was being conceived and finalised in 1948–49, there were requests from some members of the Constituent Assembly that god and the seeking of the Almighty's blessings must find mention in it. One humorous response to this came from Sardar Bhopinder Singh Mann, a Sikh representative in the Constituent Assembly.

> Tomorrow, you are going to associate his name somewhere in the Preamble. I am doubtful whether God will at all like this. It may be a clever piece of Constitution for you; but still He may not like this Constitution. He may not like to be associated with this Constitution. He may be a communist God or He may have strong socialist inclinations. I would ask the Members and Dr. Ambedkar, 'suppose without ascertaining His wishes you incorporate His name, what would happen to the Constitution if tomorrow He in His wisdom would withdraw His consent and would refuse to be associated with this Constitution at all?' Then, I would request you, before you incorporate His name in various ways and associate Him with your Constitution, to ascertain His wishes. In case Dr. Ambedkar had no access to God, then I request you Sir, to use your good offices to ascertain His wishes and let the House know that He is a willing party to this affair. After all oath taking means two parties, the person who swears and the Person by whom you swear. Indeed, it is a point of Order with me and I submit whether at all we can incorporate or use the name of a person who is not a Member of this House and without His consent in the Constitution. It is really of great constitutional importance. Tomorrow, the whole labour will be lost if He withdraws his consent and refuses to be associated with your Constitution.

Jokes apart, this was a serious discussion. Govind Malaviya asked Ambedkar to consider a 'reference to the Supreme Power which guides the destinies of the whole world'. Finally, H.V. Kamath's proposal to include the phrase 'In the name of God' to begin the Preamble was put to the vote, and the Ayes lost forty-one to sixty-eight. According to B. Shiva Rao, who compiled all the documents relating to India's constitution-making process into the iconic six-volume series *The Framing of the Indian Constitution*, some members felt that invoking god would not be consistent with the freedom of faith which the Preamble promised and the Fundamental Rights guaranteed.[64]

A theist might surmise that the constitution-makers disregarded the sentiments of millions of believers. But the same Constituent Assembly did not include the word 'secular' in the Preamble. In the non-inclusion of both these words lies our constitutional understanding of faith and secularism. India was imagined as a secular country that would be respectful and celebratory of faith. Its democratic ethos was meant to exist in the intersection of equality and religious freedom. The agnostics and atheists are not excluded either, because freedom of consciousness includes the freedom to reject.

During the Emergency of 1975, along with a number of other amendments, the word 'secular' was included in the Preamble. It is an inclusion that diminished its meaning and our catholic understanding of the expression. The forced inclusion has also emboldened those occupying high political offices to falsely claim that secularism was not originally part of our constitutional spirit.[65]

The flag took its place as India's primary symbol of identity just as the date ticked over to 15 August 1947. The presentation of the flag was India's first act after the president of the Constituent Assembly announced that the viceroy was to be intimated that

(1) the Constituent Assembly of India had assumed power for the governance of India, and

(2) the Constituent Assembly of India had endorsed the recommendation that Lord Mountbatten be Governor-General of India from 15 August 1947.

The flag was presented immediately after this, by Constituent Assembly member Hansa Mehta 'on behalf of the women of India'. She was standing in for her colleague Sarojini Naidu and had with her a list of seventy-four women from different communities who wished to be associated with the presentation.

Hansa Mehta said proudly,

> It is in the fitness of things that this first flag that will fly over this august House should be a gift from the women of India. [Cheers] We have donned the saffron colour, we have fought, suffered and sacrificed in the cause of our country's freedom. We have today attained our goal. In presenting this symbol of our freedom, we once more offer our services to the nation. We pledge ourselves to work for a great India, for building up a nation that will be a nation among nations. We pledge ourselves for working for a greater cause, to maintain the freedom that we have attained.

It was only appropriate that the flag was presented by women. After all, three of the early ideas for an Indian flag came from women. The most dramatic unveiling of all was by Bhikaji Rustom Cama at the International Socialist Congress held in Stuttgart in August 1907. The story is now part of India's political folklore.

Madame Cama, as she was known, was attending the Congress along with S.R. Rana, a Paris-based businessman who supported Indian revolutionaries. The invitation had come through Henry Mayers Hyndman, a well-known British Marxist and anti-imperialist.

Cama was born in 1861 in Bombay into a wealthy Parsi family. In the early twentieth century, she moved to Britain—a migration that was necessitated by illness after a volunteering stint during the plague in 1897. During her initial years in Britain, Cama was drawn to the Indian National Congress's moderate form of politics and even campaigned for Dadabhai Naoroji in 1906 when he stood for election for a liberal seat in the constituency of Lambeth North in London. But as political divisions within the Congress became more obvious, she moved towards the confrontational camp and was associated with Britain-based Shyamji Krishnavarma, who was already well known in rebellious anti-British circles. In 1905, he had started a publication called *The Indian Sociologist*, which was banned by the Government of India. One of the communications in the Home Department files of the Government of India in 1907 speaks about the difficulty of stopping the spread of the publication, which was gaining popularity because it was sent out in closed envelopes, like letters.

Krishnavarma provided scholarships for Indian students, one of whom was V.D. Savarkar. He bought a house in London that came to be known as 'India House' and hosted these young students, aiming to cultivate a nationalistic mindset in them. He also established the India Home Rule Society. Krishnavarma moved from London to Paris in 1907, but Cama shuttled between the cities until 1909, when she too moved to Paris.

In August 1907, Cama and Rana were not official delegates at the Stuttgart Conference. Yet, due to Hyndman's influence, she was allowed to address the gathering. Among the many dramatic descriptions of her presentation in Stuttgart that are in circulation, here is one from a biography published by the Publications Division of the Ministry of Information and Broadcasting, Government of India.

> She has been the cynosure of all eyes, as she stood, proud, tall and erect, dressed in a longsleeved blouse and the traditional Parsee sari. She spoke with bitterness, she spoke with vehemence, she was out for vengeance, she was not going to mince matters. India spoke through her, an India enslaved, impoverished, and humiliated. At the end of her speech she proudly unfurled the tricolour which she had kept concealed

and to the thunderous cheers of the delegates, demanded justice for India.[66]

This sounds like a highly memorable moment, but there is no mention of it in the *International Socialist Review* of September 1907. In his recollections of the conference, Lenin mentions in passing that there were some delegates from 'Asia' (Japan, and some from India). There is no specific mention of Cama's speech, though he makes a political observation about the British bourgeoisie exploiting millions in India. This fact was, in any case, known around the world. In fact, in 1904, the International Socialist Congress that met in Amsterdam had adopted a resolution condemning the British capitalist colonial system and the exploitation of Indians, and demanded Indian 'self-government under British Supremacy'. Dadabhai Naoroji was a delegate at that conference and spoke in great detail about the financial drain, the lack of equal rights, the barbarism and predatory politics the British were indulging in. He asked for the support of the Congress and wanted an end to the slavery and ignominy that Indians were being subjected to.

Prior to the 1907 conference, a resolution was prepared by Indians living in Paris. The prime movers were Shyamji Krishnavarma and his cohorts. The text, printed in the August issue of *The Indian Sociologist*, states:

> That the continuance of British rule in India is positively disastrous and extremely injurious to the best interests of Indians, and lovers of freedom all over the world ought to cooperate in freeing from slavery one-fifth of the whole human race, in habiting that oppressed country, since the perfect social state demands that no people should be subject to any despotic or tyrannical form of Government.[67]

This was forwarded through the Social Democratic Federation of London to the office of the International Socialist Congress. It was hoped that the resolution would be passed in

Stuttgart, but that did not happen. According to a report in the *Manchester Gaurdian*, the resolution was not discussed.[68] It is, however, believed that there was moral support for the resolution from the delegates, except for Ramsay MacDonald of the Labour Party (Britain). This is understandable because, at that very conference, Ramsay was campaigning for a shift in the socialist view of British colonialism since, he argued, many of its colonies were self-governed.

The specifics of what transpired in Stuttgart are further confused by Rana's recollections published in January 1950 in *The Modern Review*. At the time of its publication, Rana was about eighty years old. In the piece titled 'Hyndman and India', he recalled that Hyndman had insisted that the resolution be summitted to the Congress. Cama, he said, proposed the resolution in her speech, and just before concluding, she unfurled the Indian flag. And then he added, 'the whole audience stood up to salute the flag'.

The image evokes a vision of Cama, much like a magician, suddenly materialising a magnificent, large flag out of thin air. In reality, it was a small flag that she probably held folded in her hands and then held aloft for the audience. The flag that Cama presented was a tricolour, and it is said to be the same one on display at the Lokmanya Tilak Museum in Kesari Wada, Pune. The top band is green (faded in its present state), the central golden-saffron and the bottom strip red. On the green are embroidered eight lotuses. They most likely represented the eight Indian provinces. On the golden-saffron band, 'Vande Mataram' is inscribed in Devanagari. On the red portion are the sun and the crescent. The sun may have represented Parsis or Hindus, while the crescent is clearly indicative of Muslims. All the embroidered elements are silver coloured. It is most likely that the colours were also directly associated with specific religions. Green for Muslims, golden-saffron for Sikhs and red for Hindus. The unusual aspect of the flag is the crescent. In the

Islamic crescent moon, the concave side usually faces right or upwards. On this flag, it faces left towards the sun. We do not know if this was deliberate, and if so, its implication.

The flag that Cama unveiled is said to have found its way back to India with the socialist Indulal Yajnik. He, in turn, handed it to G.V. Ketkar, a grandson of Lokmanya Tilak. In 1937, Savarkar unveiled it on Indian soil. The Lokmanya Tilak Museum, where it is housed, is also the office of the Marathi newspaper *Kesari*, which was founded by Tilak and launched in 1881. The launch announcement included a Sanskrit stanza in which the leader of an elephant herd is asked to leave the forest as the lion (kesari), the king of the jungle, tears into rocks thinking they are elephants.

Cama's association with Savarkar, the secretive return of the flag to India and its second unveiling have all given the Stuttgart event a mythical status, especially in certain nationalist circles. But these might not be the only reasons why it is remembered. Cama's political work continued in Paris, and she continued to exhibit the flag on other occasions. She created networks with Russian, Irish and Egyptian anti-colonialists and launched a publication named *Bande Mataram*, which was printed in Geneva. Its very first issue caught the attention of Gandhi, but not for the right reasons: 'It contains open incitement to violence, as if that would make India free this very moment. Even if India could be free that way, what would it do with that freedom.'

Gandhi, who was then in South Africa, was angry that Gokhale had been attacked in a piece that referred to him and his colleagues as 'mean and cowardly'. This was not the way to serve one's motherland, he said. He called the author 'puerile'.

I do not know if this criticism reached Cama's ears. Even if it did, she may not have cared. She was already having an impact within the European leftist revolutionary circles of the early twentieth century. The famed Russian author Maxim Gorky, for instance, invited her to write a piece on the role of Indian women in India's freedom struggle.

There is another story about the Stuttgart event that further highlights its importance within certain quarters. Hemchandra Das Kanungo, an associate of the Bengali revolutionary (and later saint) Aurobindo Ghosh, was in Paris in 1907. (Learning bomb-making among other things!) He had lunched at Cama's home several times and she knew him as an art student. According to him, Cama, though a Parsi, introduced herself as Hindu, and her speech in Stuttgart was powerful. However, his recollection[69] of the flag's colours contains some errors, which is perhaps telling in itself. What mattered then was the visual statement being made and the optics of the event, not the meanings embedded in the flag.

> At the time of delivering the speech she had in her hand a tricolour flag designed for the future independent India. It had three colours, red, saffron and blue one after the other. The red was at the top, and against it were eight half-blossomed white lotuses; in the middle, against the saffron was written 'Bande Mataram'; at the bottom against the blue was an image of the sun on one side, a crescent moon and stars on the other.[70]

He also said that the sight of a

> pardanashin saree-clad Hindu lady, standing on the stage of the world conference and delivering a speech, was an unimaginable sight for Europe. As a result many photographs of her (and) the flag appeared in newspapers as well as translations of her speech, causing quite a commotion.[71]

The reference to 'pardanashin', or veiled woman, points to the European impression of Indian women as coy, suppressed and voiceless. In Hemchandra's view, Cama broke these stereotypes. Even within the Indian community, the idea of a woman standing up to imperial power in their territory would have been enormously significant.

Neither the flag nor Cama's speech found much mention in the European press, so the excitement was probably generated by, and among, the Indian revolutionaries in Europe. Hemchandra Das was not in Stuttgart himself, but picked up the stories that were circulating within the Indian community in Paris. The factual accuracy of his account does not matter as much as the impression we gather from it about the impact of the event.

The report of the conference published by Buchhandlung Vorwärts, Berlin, gives us details of Cama's speech on 22 August 1907.[72] From the audience response noted in the report, we can surmise that she did make an impact. The afternoon session opened with Paul Singer, the chairman of the Congress. Cama was next. She spoke about the economic hardships faced by Indians living under the oppressive capitalist British government, the poverty, the high mortality rates and epidemics that ravaged the country. India, she said, gave Britain £35 million every year and got nothing in return.

> I am standing here before the court of human justice. What is socialism if it is not justice? If there is justice, why do millions of despondent Indians have to languish? [Resounding applause] One fifth of the world's population is concentrated in India. India is an English crown colony—a subjugated country under despotic rule. An unbearable tyranny reigns supreme over there. I beseech the congress to oppose this diabolical tyranny. [Applause][73]

She asked delegates to read the documents collected by Comrade Hyndman and complained that they were all being ignored. She wanted to present the Indian problem in economic terms to her largely socialist audience. Suffering and injustice is born out of capitalist and imperial greed, she said. 'The Indian question is also an economic issue.'[74] From the applause captured in brackets in the Vorwärts report, it is clear that, in that moment, Cama impressed.

Just before concluding, she strategically mentioned the Russian struggle and greeted 'Russian Freedom Fighters', and that worked too, going by the 'thunderous applause'. S.R. Rana was partially right: Cama did mention the proposed resolution. Though she did not read it out, her speech was an elucidation of the resolution, and she did request the Congress to adopt it.

In conclusion, she said: 'Indians demand their human rights, their autonomy. We want our right to self-determination; we demand justice and right to self-rule. [Resounding applause and clapping]'[75]

At least a few delegates remembered Cama's flag too. In 1920, the Marxist Karl Kautsky apparently told Bhupendranath Datta, the Bengali revolutionary and editor of *Yugantar*, 'I remember an Indian lady waving a flag.'

From within Cama's circle there emerged a report. The *Indian Sociologist* published by Shyamji Krishnavarma printed the 'main portion' of what it called an 'impressive speech' in its September 1907 issue.[76] This report needs to be taken with a pinch of salt. But it is important because many Indian revolutionaries would have read it at the time.

The article was titled 'India at the International Socialist Congress', with a subhead that said it all: 'The Indian National Flag Unfurled'. In the opening paragraph, the author claimed that the proposed resolution had been unanimously adopted. The excerpt from Cama's speech more or less matches the details in the German report. But there are some differences of note. The *Indian Sociologist* said that Cama had reiterated more than once the financial loss to the Indian exchequer. She framed the India problem as a class conflict, with the wealthy becoming wealthier at the expense of the poor who died. She demanded that socialists bring the India issue to the table and issue resolutions of support at every Congress. They ought not to wait for Indian representation at the Congress. 'How can they start representation in that land where liberty does not exist?'

she asked. The socialists had to stand in support of the 'suffering millions of Hindusthan'. While acknowledging the sufferings of the Russians and the Polish, she said that it was still nothing compared to what Indians were going through. Interestingly, this report did not contain the greetings that Cama offered Russian freedom fighters.

Cama was aware of the heated discussions regarding colonies in socialist circles. At the Congress, it was resolved that socialism and colonialism could not coexist—a resolution that was voted on after Cama's speech. This was also why her speech was well received. She is supposed to have said, 'You are discussing colonies all the time, what about dependencies? First of all, let me ask you, should there be such a word as dependency in Socialism?' She referred more than once to the pamphlet that Hyndman had written for the Congress, titled 'The ruin of India by British Rule'. The pamphlet was banned in India. Beyond these generic statements and appeals, she also spoke specifically of two freedom fighters, Lala Lajpat Rai and Sardar Ajit Singh, who had been sent to Burma in May 1907: 'Two of our most enlightened friends have been deported, without trail, kept in captivity in some fort in Burmah for the last three months, simply for speaking and writing the truth about tyranny and injustice in the land, and even for discussing the economic question of India.'

According to the *Indian Sociologist*, Cama's final act of unfolding the flag was backed by some potent and prophetic statements.

> I unfold this little Indian National Flag before you friends, and I ask you in the name of the Indian Nation to fight for Justice ... so I wave this Indian National Flag before you once again, and before concluding let me tell you that I have every hope of seeing the Republic of India established during my lifetime.

While the Indian National Congress in India was still working with the 'dominion' model, Cama apparently spoke in front of a European audience, which included British delegates, about her ambition for the future of India as an independent republic.

Was the resolution adopted or not? Soon after Cama unfurled the flag, Paul Singer addressed the gathering. He explained why the resolution could not be considered. It had not been submitted to the International Bureau and, more importantly, the 1904 resolution already spoke of British tyranny in India. In other words, the new resolution did not add anything new to what had already been resolved. Yet, the Indian statement was added to the resolutions on women suffrage, militarism, immigration, trade unions and colonialism that were passed in the Congress. Interestingly, though the *Indian Sociologist* version of Cama's speech ends with the dream of an Indian republic, the suggested resolution itself said nothing of the sort. Singer did say that the spirit of this resolution (1907) was endorsed both by the Bureau and the Congress. I suspect that this 'in spirit' endorsement and the publication of the statement along with the resolutions was interpreted as an official endorsement by Rana and Shyamji Krishnavarma.

Bhupendranath Datta's spy novel–like narration of the resurrection of Cama's flag in Berlin makes for interesting reading.[77] Datta travelled through many countries, in disguise, and reached Berlin in 1915. There, at the home of a member of the revolutionary Berlin Committee, he saw a flag. But it was not the flag Cama had launched in Stuttgart. This version was a tricolour, no lotuses, crescent or sun. He asked Berlin Committee member Virendranath Chattopadhyay about the variance and was informed that those symbols were Cama's doing and had since been removed. The tricolour may never have been seen in public in Berlin, but according to information received by Berlin Committee members, it was probably used by the Indian Volunteers Army. Datta writes that this army came into being when deserters from the British Army in Mesopotamia and Indian revolutionaries from Berlin joined hands. If we are to believe his account, a sample of this flag too found its way back to India. We do not know whether this is true, and if the flag does still exist or who has possession of it.

It is not possible to discuss the Cama flag without mentioning its close resemblance to another pre-independence Indian flag. If Cama's presentation was dramatic, the unfurling in Calcutta was grand. The occasion was the first anniversary of Boycott Day, 7 August 1906. The previous year, a boycott resolution had been adopted at the Town Hall in Calcutta as a response to the partition of Bengal initiated by Viceroy Lord Curzon and announced on 19 July 1905. It called for the boycott of foreign goods, which meant that the manufacture and consumption of India-made goods would be encouraged. According to Surendranath Banerjea, a leading moderate political figure, Congressman and editor of the *Bengalee* newspaper, the boycott was to some extent inspired by the Chinese boycott of American goods in 1905. *The Statesman*, though unsure whether such a boycott would be successful, mentioned the Chinese parallel and the need for the government to not ignore it as 'froth and insincerity'.[78]

The seeds of swadeshi had been planted well before 7 August. It was clear that industrialisation was a powerful force, but the benefits of it were accruing elsewhere. The weak state of India's industry was also evident. Therefore, the boycott was a political and economic gamble that intended to push the government to reverse its decision to partition Bengal. In Banerjea's words, it was 'a temporary measure adopted for a particular objective'.

Public resentment against His Majesty's Government had been brewing for some time. The antecedents of many of the arguments Gandhi would make more than a decade later—

swadeshi, charkha, resisting industrialisation—can be found in the discussions that evolved during this time. Significantly, these protests drew the younger generation into politics, the reverberations of which could be felt across the country. Some chose non-violent activism, while others took to the revolutionary path.

In November 1905, soon after dividing Bengal, Curzon left India from Bombay. The *Mahratta* reported that he was rightly not given an honourable send-off by the intellectuals of the city. India was glad to see the back of him, a great load had been lifted. In his farewell speech, Curzon claimed that the partition would be a boon to Bengalis, and future generations would thank him. The *Mahratta*'s response to this was, yes, it was a gift not only for Bengal but the whole of India, because it had given rise to the Swadeshi Movement. The *Karachi Chronicle* claimed that in Sind, while the younger generation were supporting the Swadeshi Movement, the older generation too joined in because of their hatred towards the expensive and 'foppish' dresses worn by the young.

The student-powered Anti-Circular Society came into being on 4 November 1905. It was a response to various repressive measures enacted by the British government, but one order led directly to its formation: the Carlyle Circular of 10 October 1905 addressed to magistrates and collectors. The circular stated that the government would withdraw grants and scholarships and disaffiliate any institution that did not prevent students from participating in politics. It also said that heads and teachers of educational institutions might be required to act as 'special constables' in order to keep the peace. In the following months, the government acted on these threats, banning students, dismissing headmasters and asking for the disaffiliation of schools. Students retaliated by boycotting educational institutions. Many of these students were from upper-caste communities that placed a great premium on education. This meant that independent, privately funded institutions had to be set up, and a lot of energy and money was invested in making that happen, not only in Bengal but also across the country.

The launch of the Anti-Circular Society was a powerful affair, with 3,000 students in attendance at College Square. Its principal founders were Sachindra Prasad Bose, a college student, and Ramakanta Roy, a Japan-returned engineer. The society's backbone was Krishnakumar Mitra, a well-known Brahmo leader. It established schools, provided support for the setting up of swadeshi mills and assisted in the supply, distribution and sale of swadeshi cloth. Interestingly, music was one of its areas of work—it collected and disseminated swadeshi songs. Society members raised funds for various causes, assisted in smothering communal clashes, and were often on the front lines against the police force.

There was also an uncompromising commitment to the idea of Hindu–Muslim unity. In many circles, the Swadeshi Movement had turned into Hindu assertion, but the Anti-Circular Society maintained its secular heart. It refused to participate in the Shivaji Festival of 1906, where Bal Gangadhar Tilak was in attendance, on the grounds that it was Hindu-dominated. It was this society which designed the national flag that was introduced on 7 August 1906.

A report in the *Bengalee* newspaper, published the next day, gives us a blow-by-blow account of the celebrations.[79] The festivities began early in the morning at College Square, where hundreds of people gathered. From there began a grand procession led by Krishnakumar Mitra. They proceeded down streets, lanes and by-lanes singing national songs. People were wearing garlands around their neck, some wore a white or gerua pagdi. Members of the Natya Samaj played clarinets, cornets, drums and other instruments, adding to the general atmosphere of joyousness. Grand gerua flags flew high.

Later in the afternoon, scenes from Boycott Day, the first anniversary of which was being marked, were re-enacted. Young men and students from leading technical, medical and arts colleges, cultural organisations, Brahmo institutions, hostels and schools poured into College Square. There was not enough space to accommodate everyone. The crowd spilled over into the streets around the square. Flags with slogans such as 'Bande Mataram', 'Boycott Celebrations' and 'Long Live Surendranath' could be seen all around. The *Bengalee* described it as a 'huge mass of humanity shouting Bande Mataram'. Those gathered were carrying flags with red, green and gerua- or yellow-coloured bands. Surendranath Banerjea was the leading political figure at the celebrations, and members of the Anti-Circular Society were seen wearing paper garlands and holding flags.

We then encounter what the newspaper report unambiguously called the 'national flag' consisting of the colours red, green and yellow. The motto 'Bande Mataram' was placed in the centre, eight half-blossomed lotuses on the top, and the sun and moon at the bottom. The report doesn't explicitly mention the order of the coloured bands. If I follow the order in which the symbols were described in the report, then the central band would have been red, with green on top and yellow at the bottom. If the colours were mentioned in the top-down sequence, then it would be red on top, green in the centre and yellow below. In either case, the order of the colours made it different from the flag Cama would present in Stuttgart the following year.

The significance of the half-blossomed lotuses is for us to try and decipher. Perhaps they indicated the potential in the people of India which could not reach fruition because of the oppressive British government. Though Bengal was divided in 1905, the imperial gazetteer published in 1908 still listed Bengal as a province, with a footnote: 'In 1905, Assam with a large portion of Bengal was constituted a new Lieutenant-Governorship under the style of "East Bengal and Assam".' The eight half-blossomed lotuses were possibly an act of defiance against the partition of Bengal.

The *Bengalee* says there was a sun and a moon in the bottom band, and I infer that the moon was a crescent, since the flag symbolised Hindu–Muslim unity.

The flag was carried by Babu Jetindra Kumar, a young Bengali from Allahabad, on horseback. The procession moved slowly as Surendranath followed on foot. People continued to gather, and at one point, the procession was about a mile long. With such a huge gathering, one would assume there was heavy police bandobast. But as per the report, the police were conspicuous by their absence. The *Bengalee* exclaimed, 'The scene from a housetop was perhaps one of the grandest ever seen in Calcutta.' As music continued to be played on the ground, women from Hindu households blew conches from their housetops. The exact route taken by the procession to Parsi Bagan has since been mapped out. According to my friends from Kolkata, who spent an hour trying to work it out, the total distance travelled by the procession was about seven kilometres.

The *Bengalee* estimated that there were roughly 50,000 people assembled in the park and spilling out from it. The atmosphere was lively. Crackers were burst and women cheered from the balconies and windows of nearby buildings. Over twenty-five leading political figures were present. Hindus, Muslims, Christians and Jains, as well as people of various nationalities came together. In his book, *A Nation in Making*, published in 1925, Surendranath noted that a number of English friends were sympathetic, and advised and provided moral support. Although much time had passed since then, he refused to reveal their names. Maybe some of those friends were present on that Monday.

The official meeting commenced with Narendra Nath Sen delivering a long prayer in English. Not a poem or a song, but a scripted speech requesting divine benediction for all, including the British, the Indian leaders and youth volunteers. He asked the 'Benignant King and Master of all creation' for blessings so that they may work for goodness and the welfare of their countrymen and sought forgiveness for any disharmonious actions of theirs. He thanked the lord for the strong national sentiment and patriotism that was present and gave credit to the almighty for the spirit of self-help and the development of Indian industries. Sen was upset that certain sections of society felt estranged. And with the 'somewhat strained relations between our rulers and ourselves, which at the present time saddens our hearts'. He wanted an environment where everyone could speak and act freely, living in unity and concord; he wanted the lord to fill the hearts of the rulers with love for Indians and their lawful aspirations. For Indian leaders, he sought self-control, earnestness and just action. He prayed that the supreme being would instil in the youth the 'highest moral principles' and help them avoid excesses and evils. And he hoped that the partition would be withdrawn and peace restored.

Next, the politician Bhupendranath Bose was called upon for the presentation of the flag. He first recalled the 'monster meeting' of the previous year. Noticing the presence of a large number of women in the audience, he said that the Swadeshi Movement was successful because of their involvement. It was in their honour that the new cotton mill was named 'Banga Luxmi Cotton Mill'. He said the hoisting of the flag must be a sign of unity among India's communities. He believed Banerjea was the ideal person to unfurl the flag—a proposal seconded by A.H. Gaunavi on behalf of the Muslim community. Despite the bonding over the past year, because of the rise of religious nationalism, there were suspicions on both sides of the religious divide. The flag was viewed as a way to bring Hindus and Muslims together under one symbol—a coalition that was much needed in the fight against the Empire.

Finally, an overwhelmed Banerjea asked the thousands present to salute the flag and swear to give their life for the 'fatherland'.

The flag, he said, was its emblem, a sign of unity among Hindus, Muslims, Christians, Jains and Parsis. If 7 August 1905 had given them new life, 7 August 1906 would give them 'an outward token and emblem of unity and devotion'. And then he 'unfolded the flag amidst loud and prolonged cheers'.

Considering the scale of the celebrations and the fanfare with which it was conducted, the event must have left a deep impression on the minds of the people present there that day. The flag was not only on the stage, but also in the hands of thousands, much like the paper flags we carry today. The celebrations of the day did more than mark the anniversary of Boycott Day; it was equally an attempt at moving forward.

In his book *Bharater Dwitiya Swadhinata Sangram*,[80] Bhupendranath Datta pieces together information collected from a few sources and his own recollections to reconstruct events that took place behind the scenes. The idea of creating a flag had come from a friend of Sachindra Prasad Bose, who took it to his guru Surendranath Banerjea. The senior leader approved of the idea. Bose, Sudhir Chandra Bandhopadhyaya and other comrades then came up with the tricolour flag.

Datta writes that the flag had three colours, green, yellow and red, presumably in that order from top to bottom. But this is not the order deduced from the *Bengalee* report of 8 August 1906. Funnily enough, Datta's order tallies with the colour sequence of the Cama flag. Though they presented the flag as the coming together of Hindus, Muslims and Sikhs, Bhupendranath Datta suggests that it was, in fact, inspired by the spirit of the French tricolour. Datta claims that it was he who, in the pages of *Yugantar*, had lauded the flag as representing equality, fraternity and liberty (samya, maitri, svadhinata). His account puts the number of lotuses at seven, not eight. He also asserts that the flag was preserved at the home of Krishnakumar Mitra.[81]

Datta mentions that there were those who mocked the flag ceremony. He also claims that the Calcutta flag was hoisted once again at the Congress session of December 1906. This event was referred to by R.K. Sidhwa on 22 July 1947 when the national flag was adopted by the Constituent Assembly. He got the year wrong and was promptly corrected by Rajendra Prasad. Sidhwa claimed that Dadabhai Naoroji (the president of the conference) while raising the flag had said, 'I present this Flag. Under this Flag we should fight our battles.' But there is no mention of a flag being hoisted in the Congress session report; only renditions of *Vande Mataram* and other national songs find place in it.

Considering the fact that many of those involved in the August event were Congressmen, it is possible that a flag-hoisting event did take place. It is also distinctly possible that the 7 August flag continued to be part of Congress session decorations for some more years.

Why did this symbol not capture the imagination of the Bengalis in the same way that the slogan of Bande Mataram or the Bharat Mata depiction did? The answer lies in the question itself. Though the secularists attempted to find a foothold in cultural imagery, religious symbols were what really took hold, deep-seated as they were. The line between a nationalist spirit and religious parochialism is a fine one, and almost invisible. It is not hard to float from one to the other, and before we even register the move, Indianness would have been myopically reconstructed. This happened within the Swadeshi Movement too. The Anti-Circular Society members who were responsible for designing the flag were conscious of these currents. They did not reject religion. If anything, they chose to use it on the flag to bridge these gaps. It was a cultural statement, possibly targeted at the younger generation of freedom fighters. A new, shared symbol of inclusivity. Through this grand presentation, they may have hoped to destabilise an ingrained religious conservativism. Unfortunately, the flag was no match for the goddess.

At any rate, it seems most likely that Cama's version of the flag was influenced by the 7 August flag. But what was the connection between the two? Scholars have suggested that the revolutionary Hemchandra Das Kanungo might have been the link. However, Kanungo's autobiography makes no mention of the Calcutta flag and only mentions that he had heard of Cama's flag. Confusingly, in *Bharater Dwitiya Swadhinata Sangram*, Bhupendranath Datta refers to a letter from Kanungo in which he states that, though he had never claimed it in his autobiography, he was the inventor of this national flag. He also states that he was opposed to having the words 'Bande Mataram' in the middle. Considering the power of that phrase among the nationalists, especially revolutionaries, this contradiction is surprising in itself. Kanungo also slides in a subtle critique of Savarkar, who was being published in the Bombay papers. Apparently, Sarvakar had been asserting that the moon was not a symbol of Muslims and was taking credit for the flag design.

Could Kanungo have seen the unfurling of the Calcutta flag and been a carrier of the design? It appears unlikely, because he left Calcutta in July 1906 and travelled to Colombo via Cuttack, Madras, Coimbatore and Tuticorin in the hope of meeting more revolutionaries. He probably sailed from Colombo to Marseilles on 13 August. Although, one supposes he could have been around when the flag was in its preparatory stages.

Bhupendranath Datta suggests that Cama unfurled the flag on other occasions too, when delivering speeches. And that she would say, 'This is the flag for which Khudiram and Prafulla Chaki died.' These were two young Bengali revolutionaries who had attempted to assassinate a magistrate. Datta's version, if it is to be believed, only confirms the Cama flag's Bengal connection.

Datta proposed two sociological explanations for the link. Either it was a case of 'parallelism in history', wherein two sets of people separated by time and place come up with a near identical idea. A theory that, he reflected, was now considered ahistorical. The more likely explanation lay in the theory of 'diffusion of culture'. Somehow, knowingly or unknowingly, the 7 August flag had influenced Cama and the Paris revolutionaries. Either a copy of the Calcutta flag or a description of its design reached Paris through someone, or an imprinted memory was carried across the seas.

During that period, Calcutta was the epicentre of nationalist activity, and continued to be an ideational hotspot for flag designs. In 1909, Margaret Noble, who by that time had become Sister Nivedita, devised another flag for India. Born in 1867, Noble met Swami Vivekananda in Britain when she was twenty-eight. Her entry into spiritual work was not very different from the kind of stories we hear today. She was seeking religious centring and purpose, and when she heard Vivekananda, something clicked. She was willing to redraft her entire life.

On his part, Vivekananda recognised her strengths, her background in education, her passion and dedication. He felt that India lacked such women, and we should 'borrow them from other nations'. At the same time, he wanted Margaret to understand what she was getting into. Indian society would not be easy to deal with. She would encounter narrowmindedness, casteism and distress and, as a foreigner, she would face antagonism. Besides, she would have none of the material comforts that she was used to.

Margaret was undeterred. She moved to India in 1898. A few months later, Vivekananda initiated her into brahmacharya, the vow of celibacy, and christened her Nivedita. She began a small school, but soon found herself travelling with Vivekananda, in India and abroad. After Vivekananda's passing in 1902, she went back to the idea of setting up a school and established both, a high school and one for women. But she did not tie herself to either institution. She toured extensively in India and other countries, speaking and writing about a wide range of subjects. Besides a number of lectures on Vivekananda and his teachings, her writing covered the entire gamut of private and public life: faith, rituals, gods, goddesses, temples, mythology, Islam,

Christianity, morals and Upanishadic thought. She shared her thoughts on caste, women, education, civic issues, modernity and health.

Nivedita also responded to the politics of her time, the spirit of nationalism, interactions between Western thought and Indian knowledge, freedom, the Swadeshi Movement and the Bengal famine. As was the case with many in Bengal, the partition of 1905 drew her directly into political activism; she was convinced that India needed to be liberated from the British. She also had a keen interest in aesthetics, specifically visual art. She wrote a series of appreciations on art and artists, many from the Santiniketan school, but also French, German and Italian painters. The intersection of art, visual imagery and nationalism fascinated her. She was drawn to interpreting meaning and messaging in art.

In 1909, Nivedita went a step further, combining her aesthetic, spiritual and political imagination. She published an article in *The Modern Review* describing her flag for India and its philosophical underpinnings.[82] The Swadeshi Movement of 1904–08 had triggered a deluge of visual and aural images of India. Symbols, colours and phrases were being recovered from the past, newly constructed or reinvented, giving shape to various impressions of India's emotional and psychological landscape. Nivedita's flag was one such expression.

The 1909 article, as it turned out, had an impact on Pingali Venkayya. But he was unaware of the identity of the author. In the introduction to his book he wrote,

> [S]ubsequently, when I was one day discussing the subject with a friend of mine who is a teacher at the National College at Masulipatnam, he drew my attention to an article published on the same subject in The Modern Review for November 1909 in which a certain writer R S suggested 'Vajra' (the famous weapon of Indra) as a suitable emblem for the National Flag of India.

Venkayya reproduced the article in his publication, but stated that the vajra or thunderbolt would have been appropriate only if the entire population of India was Hindu.

Sister Nivedita did not see the symbol as purely Hindu. The thunderbolt, she said, had resonances in Christian, Greek, Roman and Buddhist cultures. She even wondered if it had given birth to the trishul. The Indian vajra, she believed, was far superior to the 'crude realism' of the Roman thunderbolt. She felt a symbol must come from deep within the heart, with links to history and mythology. The myth that the vajra was made from the bones of Rishi Dadhichi, a sage who was willing to give up his body for the making of this powerful weapon, only emphasised its suitability, epitomising sacrifice for the cause of humanity. A symbol also needed to have 'phonetic power'. For Nivedita, the vajra ticked all these boxes. Her flag had two crossed vajras, its power multiplied, representing the aspirations of every Indian and demanding sacrifice from all, not just a few sanyasis.

Venkayya published a coloured drawing of Nivedita's flag. It was red in colour with an annular ring around the crossed vajra in the centre. Within the ring on the top curve was written 'Vande Mataram' and on the lower curve 'yato dharmas tato jayah' (where there is dharma, there is victory).

The Ramakrishna Sarada Mission publication of 1955, *Sister Nivedita's Lectures and Writings*, contains another image of the vajra. This is a single, vertically positioned vajra, with the words 'Bande Mataram' written across it in Bengali. It was embroidered by her pupils and displayed at an exhibition organised alongside the 1906 Congress session. The publication doesn't specify the colour, but I imagine it would have been red or saffron.

Despite Nivedita's arguments for it, the vajra is not a compelling symbol. Besides the obvious visual complications, the vajra was not widely known. It did not tap into any religious or cultural memory, nor did it have any particular emotional charge. So, doubling the number of vajras would have had no effect either. Even if one's construction of nationalism is narrow and steeped in, say, Hinduism, the chosen symbol needs to be accessible. The vajra was a contrivance—an inelegant attempt to create a mythological universal out of a religious symbol. Though religion was also at the heart of the Calcutta flag and Cama's Stuttgart flag, despite the political divergence between the two groups, there was an attempt to use imagery that most Indians could relate to. This was not true of Nivedita's vajra; it was also an othering of non-Hindu Indians. In short, most unsuitable on a national flag.

For nearly a decade after this, no noticeable progress took place on the flag front. Then, in 1916, when Venkayya was working hard in Machilipatnam writing his flag booklet, another woman created a flag standard. Annie Besant, unlike Venkayya, was far from unknown. A noted figure in social and philosophical circles, she was also by this time a prominent political personality and an influential member of the Congress. She had bought the newspaper the *Madras Standard* (first published in 1841) in 1914 and renamed it *New India*. She used this publication and her weekly newspaper, *Common Weal* (1914), to disseminate information, provide commentary and actively participate in the struggle to achieve political self-governance and socio-cultural transformation. These were relatively small publications, but they became active platforms for debate and discussion.

By 1915, Annie Besant was convinced that a Home Rule League was an urgent necessity, an umbrella platform to bring together all major organisations that subscribed to self-government. The league could force them all to act in concert. On 16 December 1915, nine days before a meeting in Mumbai, scheduled for the eve of the Indian National Congress's thirtieth gathering in the very same city, Besant published the essay 'A Personal Explanation' in

New India. She said that initially she had conceived of the league as a sort of 'light cavalry regiment' that would serve the Congress. But her friends in Madras advised against it. Instead, she had an 'influential Congressman' bring together representatives of the Hindu and Muslim communities, and 'leaders of the two great representative bodies looked on the idea with favour'. Besant was speaking of the Indian National Congress and the All-India Muslim League. The political position and form of the organisation was to be left to their judgement. Besant positioned herself as a foreigner who would be glad to help in any manner they saw fit. She hoped to be accepted as A.O. Hume had been, helping Indians with his knowledge of 'British ways and political methods'. If her proposal was not agreeable, she would continue working towards this end in an individual capacity.

The timing couldn't have been better. Differences within the Congress were slowly but surely being ironed out. Besant, who saw herself as neither a moderate nor an extremist, wanted politics to become more action-oriented. The work of the league as she saw it would be exactly that: educating people and continuing civil activism. Significantly, the Muslim League and the Congress were both holding their respective annual conferences in Bombay. Rapprochement was on the cards. Representatives of the Muslim League were invited for the first time to attend the Congress session, with a special seating area allocated to them. Besant knew this was the best time to propose such a coming together. She had sent out personal invitations to all those who mattered in Indian politics. The 'Grand Old Man of India' Dadabhai Naoroji wrote back saying that he was not in good health and hence, she should not appoint him to any office. Signed by over a hundred political figures from British India's eight provinces, including the big stars of Indian politics, the official invitation for the meeting read:

> We, the undersigned have the honour to invite you, as a member of All-India Congress Committee or All-India Muslim League Council to be present at a conference to

> decide on the establishment of a league for the education of the people of India and Great Britain on the necessity of Self-government in India for the good of both nations and for the safety of the Empire, and of such Self-Government forming a part of Reconstruction of the Empire after the war. The conference will, if it approves the idea, choose the name of the League, formulate its basis, draw up its rules, and elect its All-India officers.

But things did not go as Besant had expected them to. Chaired by Surendranath Banerjea, the meeting had about 250 attendees. When she proposed a simple resolution calling for the formation of the Home Rule League, questions were raised about the capacity in which each person was attending the meeting. Were they there as individuals or as representatives of their respective bodies? In Besant's version of the events, published under the heading 'From the Congress Camp—The Home Rule Conference—The Majority for the League', she noted that a few among the attendees had tried sabotaging the meeting using technicalities. But the others effectively doused their attempts by giving them a hearing. Besant made a special mention of the Muslims: 'the Musalmans are splendidly firm'. A lot of Hindus were also ready to go along. In any case, she said, 'We shall know by the 29th what the Congress has done, and on that evening, so far as prophesy is permissible, we shall form the league ... This is the vital point for India's future—a working body, containing both, labouring for the motherland.'

In the Congress session soon after, a detailed resolution was passed regarding self-government, built on Article 1 of the Congress creed and the resolution of 1914. It asked the All-India Congress Committee to frame a reform scheme and confer with the committee appointed by the All-India Muslim League for the same. The Congress did not stop with resolutions. It showed shades of the activism Besant had proposed—one could even say it tried taking the wind out of Besant's sails. As she noted in *New India*:

> Another good point is that the All-India Congress Committee is to formulate a programme of continuous work, educative and propogandist, to be carried on during the year. So, we shall have, if the order of the Congress be carried out, a steady agitation carried on throughout the year 1916—exactly the proposal made by me for the Home Rule League taken by the All-India Congress Committee!

Given the Congress's own plans, Besant knew that her league might not get the go-ahead—an opportunity to create a common platform for Hindus and Muslims would be 'destroyed', she felt. But she would keep her promise of going ahead only if the Indian leadership approved.

On 29 December, a meeting was held to discuss the Home Rule League. *New India* titled its news report on the meeting 'A Most Heated Discussion'. According to the report, many Muslims were in favour of such a formation. Yet, a vote led to the decision that they would wait for the report from the Congress and the Muslim League. Besant decided to wait and watch.

As G.S. Arundale, Besant's theosophist colleague, said when the Home Rule League was finally inaugurated in September 1916:

> You are all aware that, at first, our league was only brought into existence for the purpose of giving some definite direction to the Xth resolution of the National Congress held in 1914 in Madras. In the hope, however, that the 1916 Congress Committees would take up the question definitely and energetically, as a consequence of the passing by Congress of Resolution XIX, the league was temporarily suspended when about to be organised.

Besant did not remain a silent bystander. From early 1916, she cranked up the heat. There was a flurry of home rule literature—

pamphlets in the thousands, a series of articles, regular columns in *New India* and *Common Weal*—and public lectures. During this period, the Madras, Bengal and Bombay Provincial Congress prepared schemes for self-governance. These reached the All-India Congress Committee, which after considering all the suggestions, drew up its proposal and, in typical bureaucratic fashion, sent it back to the Provincial Councils to elicit their views. Nothing was moving at the pace Besant was looking for. At a talk in Palghat in May 1916, 'She followed the advice of the leaders, and suspended the formation of the league. But suspension with her did not mean giving up.'[83]

Besant believed she had made a mistake by thinking of the league top-down. Now she was working on the ground, trying to get as many people as possible to buy into the idea, so that, as soon as the league started, she would have a ready army of volunteers. An army from which she intended to send a large number of delegates to the 1916 Congress session in Lucknow. She hoped that the home rule resolution would be passed at the next session by both the Congress and the Muslim League. The army she was building was to be a pressure group. She knew that the Congress was the primary political force in the country and she would need their active participation.

On 4 April 1916, *New India* published a small news item from the *Maharatta* titled 'Poona Home Rule League by Western Indian Nationalists'. The report referred to a conference of the nationalists of Bombay, Central Provinces and Berar held in December 1915. This was just a few days before Besant's first home rule meeting and the Indian National Congress session in Bombay. That conference by 'Western Nationalists' was spearheaded by Bal Gangadhar Tilak, among others. At the conference, a committee was formed to consider the setting up of a Home Rule League, its constitution, and the modalities of collaborating with similar organisations in the country. The report said that, based on consultations, a pioneer organisation would be launched to work in Bombay, Central Provinces and Berar at the outset. A letter was sent to Besant sharing the resolution that was passed and detailing the nationalists' plans for the creation of a home rule body. She was requested to share copies of the proceedings and the resolution that might emerge from the home rule meeting she had called for. Considering this overture, it is indeed odd that *New India* published two articles on 23 and 25 December 1915 with the headers 'A Rival Home Rule Conference' and 'Rival Home Rule League'. Rival to whom?

Unlike Besant, Tilak was not going to wait until August for the Congress to make up its mind. Having just returned to politics after serving a six-year prison sentence, he was trying to find his way back into the Congress, but there was resistance from some 'moderates' within the group despite Tilak's mellower stance and acceptance of self-governance within the British empire.

At Belgaum, on 28 April 1916, Tilak, along with Joseph Batista, G.S. Khaparde and others, formally launched the Home Rule League. *New India* published a two-line wire report that said the Provincial Home Rule Committee had met in Belgaum and announced the launch. The league's membership application form articulated its intentions: to attain home rule within the British empire through constitutional means and to educate the general public regarding the same so that they may help fulfil this aspiration. *New India* did not dedicate more space to this news though, unlike other publications, it was an agenda-driven newspaper and Besant's call for home rule was on top of its list.

In May, Besant travelled to Poona, where Tilak chaired her lecture. In his introduction, he said, 'Mrs Besant is lecturing for the first time on a non-theological lecture.'

When Besant realised that the Congress would do nothing, she launched her own Home Rule League and set up chapters in towns such as Benares, Bombay, Kanpur, Calicut and Allahabad. This was followed by the inaugural meeting of the league in Madras on 3 September 1916.

According to C.P. Ramaswamy Iyer, a founding member of Besant's Home Rule League, it was 'a daughter association of the Congress'. They were not going to work in opposition to the Congress but focus their energies on the specific demand for home rule, which was also one of the Congress's objectives. Iyer proposed that the league must apply for recognition within the Congress constitution. Besant's league also stressed that it would work with other home rule leagues, with a specific mention of Tilak's league—a declaration that was received with a huge ovation. Proposed by league member Jamnadas Dwarkadas and seconded by Besant, it was considered 'a pleasure and privilege to co-operate with the work of the Poona League'. The arrangement between the two leagues was simple. Tilak would mainly operate in Maharashtra, while Besant covered the rest of India. There were places of overlap in the Bombay Presidency and Central Provinces. During this period, *New India* covered Tilak's speeches and activities.

Despite the expressions of mutual respect and shared public meetings, it is difficult to gauge how closely the two organisations engaged with each other. Besant is supposed to have said that the leagues were separate because there were those in each camp that did not like either Besant or Tilak. The leagues did come together for political ends, such as when Jinnah spoke on behalf of both organisations in January 1918, and among other things, requested E.S. Montagu to implement the Congress–Muslim League scheme.

Interestingly, while emphasising the collective power of the two leagues, Jinnah used different names for each league. The Tilak-founded one was called the Indian Home Rule League and Besant's was the Home Rule for India League. Jinnah was definitely a member of the latter, but I am unable to ascertain whether he was also an official member of Tilak's league.

It appears that the differentiation in nomenclature was not often used. At the 1916 Congress session, Jamnadas Dwarkadas spoke of home rule leagues in the plural, and the two leagues were identified with Tilak and Besant respectively. It is my reading that, while the two leagues worked on a common cause and under a territorial arrangement, they did not often actively collaborate and retained a degree of distinctness. Besant's was the larger organisation, and there may have been some underlying tension. There was also some noise about Besant not being Indian. A piece in *New India* mentioned that an Indian (Tilak) had started a league, and it was active and engaged in wonderful work. This was followed by a lengthy paragraph proving Besant's Indian credentials.

This is the background against which we must discuss the home rule flag. Let me first describe Tilak's flag, which consisted of horizontal strips of alternating red and green bands, the Union Jack on the canton and the Great Bear constellation with its seven stars occupying a large portion of the central, lower section of the flag. The flag also had a crescent and a star in the right-hand top section representing the Islamic community. Tilak was an upper-caste Hindu nationalist and the initiator of religious-fever-driven celebrations such as the Ganapati and Shivaji festivals. Today, Hindu extremists have dragged Tilak into the cesspool of religious extremism, which is different from Hindu conservatism. As problematic as Tilak's position on various social issues was, we need a contextual understanding that comes from observing his political trajectory.

At the 1916 Congress session, when the Lucknow Pact was agreed on, Tilak said:

> It has been said, Gentlemen, by some, that, we Hindus have yielded too much to our Mahomedan brethren. I am sure I represent the sense of the Hindu community all over India, when I say that we could not have yielded too much. I would not care if the rights of Self-Government are granted to the Mahomedan community only. [Hear Hear] I would not

care if they are granted to Rajputs; I would not care if they are granted to the lowest classes of the Hindu population, provided the British Government consider them more fit than the educated classes of India for exercising those rights; I would not care if these rights are granted to any section of the Indian community. Then the fight will be between them and other sections of the community and not as at present a triangular fight.

And then he went on to say,

[N]othing can be gained by passing resolutions on this platform by the simple union of the two races, Hindus and Mahomedans, and the two parties, Moderates and Nationalists. The union is intended to create a certain power and energy among us and unless that power and energy are exercised to the utmost you cannot succeed, so great are the obstacles in your way.

As the main architect of the Lucknow Pact, Tilak was attempting to win over the conservatives and build bridges with others for the realisation of their combined objective: home rule.

On the home rule flag attributed to Tilak, the Hindu community was represented by an uncommon symbol: the Great Bear constellation. In Vedic tradition, the Great Bear is known as the Saptarishi Mandala, representing the seven rishis who are believed to be guides to humanity. Born from Brahma's mind, these rishis are endowed with knowledge of the ultimate truth of existence and are tasked with keeping an eye on all of creation. Despite this, the Saptarishi Mandala was an unexpected choice as a Hindu symbol. Like Nivedita's vajra, it is not an integral part of a Hindu's religious or cultural recollective registry.

An online search for the home rule flag brings up different versions of the flag I just described. It is also assumed that this flag was common to both the leagues. But I propose that the two leagues did not use the same flag. There is no mention of a specific flag design in Besant's home rule files until December 1917. All the information that I have gathered is through news reports in *New India* and *Common Weal*. The crescent, star and Saptarishi constellation are conspicuous by their absence in all mentions of Besant's home rule flag. It is only described as consisting of two colours: red and green. These two colours kept recurring at the league's celebrations. A library set up by the league is said to have had a green notice board with red letters. The *New India* editor provides a detailed explanation for the colours in 1917: 'Red is sacred to Hindus, especially in struggles for liberty, and green is sacred to Muslims. And the unity of both is thus significant of the times we live in.' This unity, the editor says, was in the service of the mother (India) for achieving freedom. In his opinion, there was nothing in the flag that could perturb the bureaucracy. Those who were trying to import other meanings were either ignorant or mischievous. Perhaps this editorial note was a result of some criticism that had been levelled against the design of the flag. Further, the Home Rule membership card informed each member that they would be given a silver pendant with a red-and-green ribbon.

When Besant arrived in Madras in 1920, national home rule flags 'in flaming red and green' were on display. I came across two black-and-white photographs in which the flag makes an appearance. One is a group photograph taken in Lahore in 1917, on the occasion of the first anniversary of the Home Rule League. The picture shows many volunteers, standing and seated cross-legged, with a picture of Besant placed at the centre on a table. On a banner behind the group are small painted flags interspersing the slogans 'Home Rule', 'Swaraj' and 'Self-Government'. Behind and to the side are a few large (out of focus) flags. But all the flags are undoubtedly twin-coloured. From these images and the literature, one can deduce that this home rule flag had two broad vertical stripes of red and green, with no other symbol on them. In contrast, a picture of the Indian Home Rule delegation that called on the viceroy in November 1917 has Tilak's red-and-green striped flag—again, a deduction I make based on the literature—with the Union Jack, crescent, star and Saptarishi Mandala.

It is interesting that Besant did not use any theosophical or Hindu spiritual insignia on her flag. She separated her philosophical and spiritual inclinations from her political activism. In fact, *New India* carried very few theosophy-related articles.

Besant's home rule flag became a flashpoint in June 1917. On 16 June, Besant, Arundale and B.P. Wadia, all office-bearers in the Home Rule League, were served an order dated 7 June. They were not allowed to enter Madras city, it said, and were required to remain within a few specified districts of the Madras Presidency. They were also prohibited from attending any meetings, delivering lectures or publishing their views.

Besant left for Ooty on 21 June and the three of them stayed there for a few days before travelling to Coimbatore. The governor of Madras, Lord Pentland, who had publicly criticised the Indian Home Rule movement, had met Besant on 16 June, a courteous but cold meeting that achieved nothing. In fact, he suggested to Besant that she stop all political activity and go to Britain and stay there until the end of the War.

There was a national outcry against the order. Gandhi, who opposed Besant's methods, spoke in her support at public meetings and wrote to the viceroy's office asking the government to accept its folly and withdraw the order. Despite warnings issued by the Government of Bengal, Tagore publicly chastised the British and expressed his dismay.

Besant and her colleagues arrived in Coimbatore on 24 August and were hosted by N.S. Ramaswami Iyengar in his rented property. On the afternoon of 25 August, the home rule flag was hoisted. Red-and-green lights (the home rule colours) were strung up after midnight and lit again the following day. On 27 August, the day the magistrate passed his order, the police arrived and demanded that the flag be brought down; they finally did so themselves. Photographs show three constables removing the anchoring and dismantling the flag as another constable looks on. The district magistrate issued an order on that morning forbidding Besant, Arundale and Wadia from flying the home rule flag. He claimed he had personal knowledge that relations were strained between brahmins and non-brahmins in Coimbatore Town and riots would break out if the home rule flag was allowed to be raised.

This was the first time that caste was being brought up in the context of an Indian flag. While it is clear that the magistrate was inventing an excuse, it does bring to light the prevailing perception that the Home Rule League was brahmin-dominated.

Interestingly, even today, religious hatred rarely works as a political strategy in Tamil Nadu. The same parties that use religious divisions for political gain all over India change course when it comes to this state—here, caste is the central fissure.

There is a backstory to all this. On 19 and 20 August, Coimbatore hosted two political conferences. One was the Home Rule District Conference and the other was a Non-Brahmin Conference. After the first day of the Home Rule District Conference, the district magistrate said that 'there was some objection to the Home Rule Flag alone flying and it was advisable to put up the Union Jack also.' His issue with the flag was obviously the exclusion of the Union Jack, but he used the underlying caste fissures to show just cause for his obstructive actions.

Both conferences discussed home rule among other things, and it is clear that there were some differences between them. Apparently, the non-brahmins had a separate conference because they wanted to press the point of communal representation, but they had no disagreement on the issue of home rule or the protests against the internment of Besant and her colleagues. One witness claimed that on the issue of home rule, the resolution of the Non-Brahmin Conference went farther than that of the Home Rule

District Conference. Witnesses, brahmin and non-brahmin, who appeared before the magistrate in defence of Besant, repeatedly emphasised the fact that there were no clashes between the two groups, before, during or after the conferences.[84] In fact, there were non-brahmins who had participated in both. The Home Rule League itself had a majority of non-brahmins. The league's flag flew high inside and outside the pandal of the conference and no one objected, they claimed. Other than flags, merchandise such as badges and pendants were also used to propagate the movement. The flag could only instil 'noble sentiments' and not violence of any kind, witnesses emphatically asserted.

Even in these witness statements, the home rule flag is described as having only two colours, green and red, representing Muslims and Hindus. One witness speaks of how, after the first day of the conference, a nervous magistrate advised him to also have the Union Jack flying since an objection had been raised about the home rule flag flying alone.

Meanwhile, *New India* published statements and articles by non-brahmins in support of the Home Rule League and its flag, and highlighted reports of solidarity meetings held by non-brahmins in various towns. According to one witness, there were differences between the league and the conference, but these were intellectual and would not have led to any kind of violence. Another made it a point to say that a 'few men with criminal inclinations' were the cause for a separate Non-Brahmin Conference.

The perception that the Home Rule League was brahmin-dominated ties very closely to the brahminical character of the Theosophical Society. *New India* published criticism from non-brahmins about articles and opinion pieces related to caste. One member of the public—named Radhakrishnan, who identified himself as Tamil—wrote a letter accusing Besant of being 'carried away by pro-brahmanical sympathies'. He accused the paper of providing space and 'passive support' for the varnashrama movement. Another person who signed off as 'A NON BRAHMIN' wrote in asking specifically what status the league's conception of home rule assigned to non-brahmins. Most of the brahmin and non-brahmin partnerships in this period were between brahmins and socially privileged brahminical non-brahmins. It is unlikely that those beyond this circle were convinced by Besant's explanations.

After the flag case, the only mention of the home rule flag that I found in Besant's papers was of a resolution at a conference of the All-India Home Rule held in Calcutta on 31 December 1917. It was decided that 'the present flag be retained, with the addition of the Union Jack in the corner'. This was a tactical move. Having the Union Jack on the flag would make it impossible for the government to bring it down. The fact that it had not been part of the design thus far substantiates my point that the flags of the two leagues were entirely different. It was also resolved at the conference that 'the family of the Tagores should be approached with the request to design a National Flag for India'. I am unable to find any information on whether the Tagores were indeed approached, and if so, whether they sent any design options. In the following years, with many changes on the political front, and with Gandhi emerging as the fulcrum of the freedom movement, the significance of the league diminished and it eventually merged with the Congress. The home rule flag became irrelevant.

Through all these variations that emerged from different groups, the term 'national flag' was not applied to any one flag. Each of them was intended to challenge the Crown and the subordination it represented, lending to their bearers a sense of control. When *New India* published articles about Venkayya's flags, Besant's home rule flag already existed. There were several 'national' flags, and they were representative of the social aspirations of the time. They coexisted, with the shared principles of religious unity and self-governance under the British Crown. Each association had distinct, though divergent views on the mechanics of how this could be achieved, but they did not disagree on the goal. The word 'national' in the phrase national flag was not defined by geography or political boundaries. It was a synonym for collective self-respect, resistance and dignity.

If one thinks about it, even after Independence, other flags have emerged, contesting with each other for relevance. When travelling in the hills of Karnataka some years ago, I noticed the brightly coloured yellow-and-red flags hoisted on poles along the road. Initially, I thought these represented a local political party, but soon realised that was not the case. Auto drivers too flew the yellow-and-red. Utensils, plastic tubs, mugs and buckets in stores were painted in these colours. This was the Kannada flag, I discovered—not the state flag, but one born out of the need for Kannada self-assertion in the midst of what was perceived as Tamil cultural dominance. In the 1960s, the Dravida Munnetra Kazhagam (DMK) had a significant influence on the political imagination of the Bangalore region. It is said that DMK flags could be seen flying across the city. Kannada activists then wanted a visual assertion of their linguistic identity. After much discussion among different groups, this finally took the form of the yellow-and-red flag.

Every flag has its own power, and political and cultural specificity. It is one among the many symbols that emerge when an antagonist of some sort is perceived to be threatening a community's sphere of influence. The Kannada flag did that job, and though it is not the official state flag, it has become a de facto representation of the Kannada people. In 2018, the state government approved a flag design that bore the same yellow and red colours with the addition of the state emblem in the centre. There has been no further movement on this front, but the battle between identities is perpetual. Recently, a young man graduating from a university in the United Kingdom unfurled the yellow-and-red flag representing Karnataka. Soon enough, there were questions raised about the kind of identity Indians should project when they are abroad. The present Karnataka chief minister (then in the opposition) came out in support of the young man.

Even within a broader national identity, the flag and the constitution of a particular region can serve as an acknowledgement of its special status within that nation by virtue of its history. It was on this basis that, under Article 370, Jammu and Kashmir had its own constitution and flag.

> **Flag of the State.** The Flag of the State shall be rectangular in shape and red in colour with three equidistant white vertical strips of equal width next to the staff and a white plough in the middle with handle facing the strips.

With the abrogation of Article 370 in August 2019, both of these were taken away from the people of the region. On top of government buildings, where both the state flag and the national flag used to be seen, now only the Indian flag flutters. The state, in any case, no longer exists—bifurcated and designated as federally administered Union Territories.

A state flag may also mark the recognition of a region's particular culture. Among the key demands of those calling for a larger Naga state are a separate flag and constitution, symbols of the Nagas' assertion of cultural and historical uniqueness. The flag, they say, is a symbol of their people, their sacrifices, pride and courage. As far as Chief Th. Muivah of NSCN (I-M) is concerned, 'The Nagas were never under the Indians either by the conquest of their forces or consent of ourselves.' And so the community's ask for its own symbols is not exceptional.

Flags are unusual artefacts. On the one hand, they can be unifying; a coming together of different people, free people. At the same time, they can be used to establish control and identity. When flags are in contestation with each other, we know that there is a tug of war between freedom and control.

Think of the freedom fighters who saw the Indian flag raised for the first time in 1947. As the flag was unfurled, they would have experienced relief and joy, a feeling of strength and victory, and the possibility of freedom. Yet, while a spirit of festivity took over the entire country, one man stood on the other side of the chasm: the anti-caste warrior, social reformer and political ideologue, Periyar. Beyond his anti-Congress stance, his erroneous understandings of the then developing constitution and the bluster-filled rhetoric, the anxieties he expressed are worth paying attention to, especially in contemporary India.

Periyar said that all we were witnessing was a transfer of power from the British to North Indian banias and Aryan brahmins; it was not true independence. The South and the North were very different economically and socially, he said, and he was concerned that the country would be dominated by the North. In today's parlance, the region he is referring to would be the 'Hindi heartland'. He was worried that this would lead to the centralisation of power, religious persecution and inequality. Hence, he demanded a separate state (nation) for Dravidians.

> The main reasons we are asking for a separate state is to counter the economic pillage of the North Indians and to remove the Aryan idea of communal suppression ... Like the states of Nizam, Travancore and Mysore, the 4.75 crore Dravidian population of the Madras state too want an independent state to preserve their culture and their economy.[85]

Twenty-five years after Independence, in 1972, Periyar reminded people of his comment about Independence Day in 1947:[86] 'Even when the declaration of Independence was announced, I had declared it as a dark day and a day against our country and humanity.' He then went on to offer a critique of the past twenty-five years. A quarter of a century had only brought 'slavery, idiocy, immorality, and dishonesty'. He spoke of the rampant corruption in the political system, the silencing of those who raised their voice, the casteism and religious superstition. He also pointed to how principled public action was being manipulated: 'There is rowdyism under the guise of striking work. Dishonesty goes under the label of Ahimsa. Obstinacy is called Satyagraha.'

The lack of education and illiteracy, especially among women, worried him. He went on to ask: 'Are we independent or do we just have different masters now?'

Clearly a man ahead of his time, Periyar also referred to sedition being a punishable offence: 'Is there any country that has a law that states, "If anyone in this state, raises his voice for total independence, he would be considered a criminal with punishment of imprisonment up to seven years?"'

Every freedom that Article 19 guarantees is limited by 'reasonable restrictions'. When we gave ourselves the constitution in 1950, 'the right to freedom of speech and expression' was not limited by 'reasonable restrictions'. This might have been an oversight, and was corrected in the first amendment with retrospective effect.

In its original form Article 19 (2) read as:

> (2) Nothing in sub-clause (a) of clause (1) shall affect the operation of any existing law in so far as it relates to, or prevents the State from making any law relating to, libel, slander, defamation, contempt of court or any matter which offends against decency or morality or which undermines the security of, or tends to overthrow, the State.

This was changed by the First Amendment (1951) to:

> (2) Nothing in sub-clause (a) of clause (1) shall affect the operation of any existing law, or prevent the State from

> making any law, in so far as such law imposes reasonable restrictions on the exercise of the right conferred by the said sub-clause in the interests of the security of the State, *friendly relations with foreign States, public order*, decency or morality, or in relation to contempt of court, defamation *or incitement to an offence.* [italics mine]

Madras High Court lawyer and eminent legal commentator Suhrith Parthasarathy makes the point that if reasonable restrictions had not been added 'in the interest of public order', the courts would have had to define free speech itself. This could have had dangerous consequences.

The other side to this amendment is that it opened the door to the adding of more categories to sub-clause (a) of clause (2).

The restrictions on freedom of expression and speech were further deepened in 1963.

> (2) Nothing in sub-clause (a) of clause (1) shall affect the operation of any existing law, or prevent the State from making any law, in so far as such law imposes reasonable restrictions on the exercise of the right conferred by the said sub-clause *in the interests of the sovereignty and integrity of India*, the security of the State, *friendly relations with foreign States, public order*, decency or morality, or in relation to contempt of court, defamation or *incitement to an offence.*

The italics are mine, and point to the conditions that have been added via the amendments to this sub-clause. Has anything been removed? Yes, 'libel' and 'slander'. But these are, in any case, covered under defamation.

When the first amendment was proposed in Parliament, Nehru cited the violence of the recent past in Delhi and Punjab to justify it:

> These amendments that we have placed before you are an attempt to balance between that stability of approach and at

> the same time that flexibility, an attempt to balance between the idealism and the realism, between the conditions in the country as we see them today and the possible dangers that may confront us, and at the same time to keep the whole, entire spirit of the Constitution, the spirit which ensures us freedom, freedom of the Press and various other freedoms.

But every government finds reasons to put a lid on the voice of the people. As the Opposition then argued, phrases like 'public order' allow the State to easily clamp down on public dissent.

The fact remains that, despite the words in the constitution and the original intent, the interpretation of what is 'reasonable' lies in the hands of the court. History informs us that the courts have swung both ways. In a recent judgement, however, the Supreme Court made some forceful assertions: The reasonable restrictions provided for in Article 19(2) must remain reasonable and not fanciful and oppressive. Article 19(2) cannot be allowed to overshadow the substantive rights under Article 19(1), including the right to freedom of speech and expression ...[87]

The Supreme Court stressed that the courts must play a proactive role in protecting these rights.

> The Courts are duty-bound to uphold and enforce fundamental rights guaranteed under the Constitution of India ... Courts, particularly the constitutional Courts, must be at the forefront to zealously protect the fundamental rights of the citizens ... As a matter of fact, the Courts must remain ever vigilant to thwart any attempt to undermine the Constitution and the constitutional values, including the freedom of speech and expression.

Crucially, it was scathing about the police force's failure to safeguard these rights.

> This case shows that even after 75 years of the existence of our Constitution, the law enforcement machinery of the

> State is either ignorant about this important fundamental right or does not care for this fundamental right ...
>
> By this time, the police officers ought to have been sensitized about their duty of abiding by the Constitution and respecting the ideals of the Constitution. If the police officers are not aware of these obligations, the State must ensure that they are educated and sensitized by starting massive training programs.

The highest court of our land is having to ask the State to begin sensitisation programmes for the police after seventy-five years of freedom.

There are enough examples of abuse of power by the police which have sometimes even led to the loss of lives. In 2018, in my own state of Tamil Nadu, the Thoothukudi police fired on protesters who opposed the Sterlite Copper company. Thirteen lives were lost that day. This callous attitude emanates from the State's weaponising of the phrase 'reasonable restriction' for the sake of 'public order'. Governments across India regularly reject applications for protest meetings at the very last moment, making it impossible to get any relief from the court. To some, these 'reasonable' restrictions may sound harmless, even fair, on paper, but in real life they are grim and ominous.

A further restriction on our freedoms is imposed with regard to our national symbols. This need to protect them from any symbolic act of resistance has its roots in an episode in Tamil Nadu in the year 1957, leading to the passing of the Prevention of Insults to National Honour Act.

Periyar had often initiated and participated in acts that symbolically targeted upper-caste Hindus, such as the public breaking of Ganapathy idols. (Do note that he demanded that those who wanted to break the idols must use their own money to buy one, not damage what others possessed.) Periyar had also announced plans to burn pictures of Rama and Gandhi, break idols of Gandhi and burn the national flag. Not all of these plans were actually acted upon. Nevertheless, in early November 1957, when his birthday was being celebrated on a grand scale in Thanjavur, Periyar announced that he would hold an event where the Constitution of India would be burnt. This was to make the point that the constitution sheltered the caste system. The date was also set: 26 November 1957. This announcement rattled the Congress government led by K. Kamaraj, a leader Periyar had great regard for and had even publicly supported for a few years.

The government of Tamil Nadu hurriedly brought in an Act that disallowed citizens to wilfully desecrate, burn or insult a picture or portrait of Mahatma Gandhi; wilfully damage or destroy a statue or bust of Mahatma Gandhi; wilfully burn, desecrate or insult the national flag; and wilfully burn, desecrate or insult the Constitution of India. The punishment for these actions was imprisonment for up to three years, a fine, or both.

Many readers may feel this was entirely justified, that we need to treasure and respect our national symbols. But one could argue that these symbols also represent the State. One way to express anger against the State, which is a non-physical entity, is to target its symbols: the constitution, flag and anthem, for instance. On 11 December 1957, DMK leader C. Annadurai, who was then in the Opposition, beautifully explained the intention behind Periyar's actions in the legislative assembly:

> When Periyar says he will burn Gandhi's picture or the constitution, it is not because he hates them. He wants the government to fix the deficiencies he is pointing to. It is in order to get their attention that he is calling for burning these symbols. We need to understand that he does not hate them. Have these people (government) understood the reasons for his anger and taken any action to address his concerns? It is eight [ten] years since we got independence but what have you done to annihilate caste, is the question Periyar is asking through this action ... The most deep-seated feeling in society is religious affinity and that has been passed on

> for generations. When Periyar broke and burnt symbols of religion, like the pillaiyar [Ganapathy] statue and the picture of Rama, what did you say? You claimed Rama and Pillaiyar become greater by these acts. That logic seems to have disappeared now! ... The police minister said that they consider the constitution as being as sacred as the Vedam [vedas]. I have no objections if they consider it Vedam and keep it in their puja room. I will not stop them. But if people, especially the marginalised point at mistakes, errors in it that need to be corrected, does that become a crime?[88]

The burning was a symbolic act that sought to highlight the dichotomy between what we promised ourselves in the constitution and the reality of citizens' lived experience. In principle, it was not very different from Gandhi's own words on the day the Constituent Assembly approved the Indian flag after replacing the charkha with the chakra: 'What I do know is that even if the charkha was shown on the flag but was not in people's hearts, both the flag and the charkha would be fit only to be burnt.'

The Union government's legislation in 1971—the Prevention of Insults to National Honour Act—was built on the 1957 Tamil Nadu Act.

> **Insults to Indian National Flag and Constitution of India.** Whoever in any public place or in any other place within public view burns, mutilates, defaces, defiles, disfigures, destroys, tramples upon or [otherwise shows disrespect to or brings] into contempt (whether by words, either spoken or written, or by acts) the Indian National Flag or the Constitution of India or any part thereof, shall be punished with imprisonment for a term which may extend to three years, or with fine, or with both.

The Act then goes into the details of what would be considered disrespectful of the flag.

(a) a gross affront or indignity offered to the Indian National Flag; or

(b) dipping the Indian National Flag in salute to any person or thing; or

(c) flying the Indian National Flag at half-mast except on occasions on which the Indian National Flag is flown at half-mast on public buildings in accordance with the instructions issued by the Government; or

(d) using the Indian National Flag as a drapery in any form whatsoever except in State funerals or armed forces or other para-military forces funerals; or

(e) using the Indian National Flag—

  (i) as a portion of costume, uniform or accessory of any description which is worn below the waist of any person; or

  (ii) by embroidering or printing it on cushions, handkerchiefs, napkins, undergarments or any dress material; or

(f) putting any kind of inscription upon the Indian National Flag; or

(g) using the Indian National Flag as a receptacle for receiving, delivering or carrying anything except flower petals before the Indian National Flag is unfurled as part of celebrations on special occasions including the Republic Day or the Independence day; or

(h) using the Indian National Flag as covering for a [statue] or a monument or a speaker's desk or a speaker's platform; or

(i) allowing the Indian National Flag to touch the ground or the floor or trail in water intentionally; or

(j) draping the Indian National Flag over the hood, top and sides or back or on a vehicle, train, boat or an aircraft or any other similar object; or

(k) using the Indian National Flag as a covering for a building; or

(l) intentionally displaying the Indian National Flag with the 'saffron' down.

Restrictions such as these, and later the Flag Code of 2002, were not new, nor unique to India.

In May 1948, in a note prepared in consultation with the governors of the various provinces, Nehru had set down rules and instructions for where, when and how the flag could be displayed. The consensus was that use of the flag should not be unrestricted. Nehru was careful to mention that these regulations were not meant to 'punish anyone for not falling in line'. But experience informs us that advice alone does not stop the State from acting like a bully.

In 1950, the Uttar Pradesh government issued a flag code regarding ceremonial and flag salutations to be adopted at educational institutions. The Government of India wanted the code to be adopted across the country so that a 'uniform tradition' could be developed.

It was not until 2004, in *Union of India v. Naveen Jindal,*[89] that an Indian citizen's fundamental right to fly the national flag was recognised. But even in that judgement, the Supreme Court was worried about unrestricted use. This obsession with national pride overflows from every branch of government: 'The extreme proposition of law taken in the American decisions that burning of the Flag is an expression of anger cannot be accepted in India as it would amount to disrespect of the National Flag.'

Having said this, the court guardedly granted Indians the right to fly the national flag, while repeatedly emphasising that, although the Flag Code was not a statute, it had to be followed so that dignity and respect for the flag could be maintained. The court said, 'The right is not [an] unfettered, unsubscribed, unrestricted and unchanneled one.' It was subject to the Emblems and Names (Prevention of Improper Use) Act, 1950 and the Prevention of Insults to National Honour Act, 1971.

From the very beginning, we have worried about disrespect being shown towards the flag. The number of frivolous cases filed in courts across the country against institutions and individuals based on the 1971 Act and the Flag Code is illustrative of our mindset. The accusations have included not lowering the flag in the evening,[90] accusing a publisher of insulting the flag by having reproduced a picture of a grocery bag that had the flag printed on it[91] and another person for hoisting the flag on the terrace of a school building while teachers and students stood or sat on the ground.[92] There was even a demand that the court must issue a writ in the nature of a mandamus directing officials to hoist the flag in anganwadis.[93] Most of these cases were thrown out by the courts. But, in many of the judgements, the courts felt it necessary to mention the need to protect national honour and the respectability of a symbol. This, in a country where citizens struggle to be noticed by the courts, even when it is for a habeas corpus petition.

Ironic, isn't it, that an abstract symbol of freedom is actualised and protected while those who hope to derive their rights and freedoms from its symbolism are repeatedly trampled upon.

2

The Lion Capital

An Emblem for Justice

Names have a way of lingering on in memory. Some names act like mnemonic tools, reminding us of certain qualities, attributes and registers. The characteristics associated with a near-mythical person who held a certain name override any linguistic meaning the name itself may have.

Ashoka is one such name.

Our understanding of the life of Ashoka (c. 304 BCE–232 BCE) can be encapsulated thus: a tyrannical Mauryan king oversaw a genocide in Kalinga and then metamorphosed into an ahimsa-adhering Buddhist monarch. Some may also know that he inscribed his vision for a compassionate society in messages (edicts) addressed to his subjects. Ashoka, whose name means 'one without sorrow', continued to be recalled in various narratives until about the sixteenth century. Several centuries after he passed, travellers were being told of his greatness and tales were written about his rule. Rulers who came after him commissioned pillars with capitals like he did. However, over time, any meaningful memory of Ashoka became shrouded in mystery. And by the sixteenth century, he disappeared from public imagination, his name confined to Buddhist circles.

Layers of history and culture got imprinted over Ashoka's legacy, and his writings were lost to the world. In some locations, subsequent kings had their declarations written around Ashoka's edicts. Perhaps his cylindrical pillars were considered to be of little value. Ashoka's architectural feats were also buried. But Buddhist monasteries knew of him, and since his story was important for religious reasons, it stayed alive within the community.

The resurrection of Ashoka began in 1837, when James Prinsep of the Asiatic Society cracked the Mauryan Brahmi script, which meant the edicts could be read again. The voice of the emperor came to life, opening the doors to a long-lost period.

In many of the edicts Ashoka addressed himself as 'Devanampiya' (Beloved to the gods) or Devanampiya Piyadasi (Beloved to the gods and of amiable appearance). He did not mention his father's name or ancestry. Initially, Prinsep believed Devanampiya was King Tissa of Sri Lanka since he used the same prefix. But this theory did not make sense because the person who called himself Devanampiya in these inscriptions also said he was the King of Magadha and a resident of Pataliputra. This, along with the fact that the Pali text *Dipavamsa* also attached the prefix Piyadasi to Ashoka's name, forced Prinsep to change his mind. He concluded correctly that the mind behind these edicts was King Ashoka, the son of Bindusara. Identifying the names of contemporary Egyptian and Greek kings in the edicts further strengthened his argument. The discovery of the Maski edict by a British gold-mining engineer in 1915 put all doubts to rest. For the first time, archaeologists and philologists discovered the name Ashoka etched in stone: (A proclamation) of Devanampiyasa Ashoka. This unlocked not only the memory of the king but also allowed us to look into his mind.

The early twentieth century was a time when Indian nationalism was finding new directions. The end goal of the freedom struggle was constantly changing. Concepts and vocabularies were evolving. What freedom meant was being framed with greater clarity. As Ashoka was being revived, Mohandas Karamchand Gandhi returned from South Africa, having already shown the world that non-violence was indeed an active form of resistance. Very soon, he captured the imagination of the Indian public.

As India turned from asking for dominion status to demanding self-rule, modernists began looking back at India's civilisational history for a leader to remember. Someone who would suit a new democratic vision. In Ashoka they found the perfect icon. Who could better represent hope than a reformed tyrant? Here was a bloodthirsty overlord who had metamorphosed into a personification of kindness. A useful allegory for a country moving from colonial oppression to compassionate self-rule. Ashoka's post-Kalinga persona was held up for emulation, his pre-Kalinga image serving as a warning.

India needed to discover self-realisation and forgiveness to move ahead with positivity. And never more so than after Partition. Healing was required not only for the wounds of the colonial past, but even more urgently between the scarred Muslim and Hindu communities. Jawaharlal Nehru, more than anyone else, saw in Ashoka's reformed avatar an enlightened form of governance, an approximation of a democrat and an internationalist with a socialist temper.

The memory of Ashoka was carefully chosen from the pantheon of monarchs who had ruled large tracts of India. But the choice was not a connivance, as some have tried to say, nor a whitewashing of other histories. An active recognition of the dangerous breaches in our society necessitated Ashoka's resurrection. It was hoped that the Ashokan spirit would serve as a balm. So, when the decision-makers of the new nation began looking for visual symbols to represent India that is Bharat, it was Ashoka's imagination that they turned to.

Quite aside from his utility for modern India, Ashoka was an unusual emperor. Rather than focusing on expanding his vast empire, he wrote a new text for governance. In fifty locations across the subcontinent, from Kandahar in Afghanistan to Dhauli in Odisha and Erragudi in Karnataka to Girnar in Gujarat, Ashoka's words were inscribed on rocks, pillars and inside caves. He began with short messages and went on to articulate lengthy sermons. The messages were mostly inscribed in the Brahmi script in various dialects of Prakrit, which was then the language of administration. Even if the script changed, as in the case of Shahbazgarhi and Mansehra (Pakistan), where it was Kharoshthi, the language remained Prakrit. Only in the north-west frontier of the kingdom, today's Afghanistan, was there a shift. This region had been a part of the Achaemenid empire, with Aramaic as the official language, and later the Greeks had ruled. The edicts here were bilingual, in Greek and Aramaic. It is likely that in places like today's Karnataka and Andhra Pradesh, where Prakrit was not spoken, there were people who were bilingual (dubhashi) and could translate the edicts for the common person. Imagine in your mind's eye regular gatherings before a set of edicts on a rock where a translator-orator proclaimed to the locals the king's intentions. Maybe there were dramatic interpretations of the edicts in the form of street plays. One thing is obvious from the sheer number of edicts that existed: Ashoka wanted to communicate directly with his people.

He repeated certain messages in multiple locations. He first experimented with publishing on rock or stone about ten years after being crowned as emperor, and then built upon the idea. The most definitive and detailed set of messages are referred to as the Major Rock edicts. They consist of fourteen messages that were issued over four years and published in multiple locations. Though the edicts were the same, changes in the dialect and interpretations by the local government heads or the inscriber resulted in variations. Much later in his reign, Ashoka created a new set of six pillar edicts that, once again, he had inscribed in multiple locations. Unlike the Major Rock edicts, these were consistent in style and content. The two later collections are recognised as the essence of what Ashoka wanted to communicate; his teachings, so to say. On occasion, he had other, smaller and specific messages inscribed.

Through these edicts, Ashoka informed citizens of his conversion to Buddhism and the change he underwent, and instructed them on moral values, the cultivation and sharing of dhamma, respect for various sections of society, and fraternity. He expressed concern for the environment, the need for animal protection and concord between various faiths. He had specific messages for those living at the edge of his kingdom—the borderers, so to speak. Ashoka directed his administrative officers to take care of his subjects, and informed his subjects that he was always accessible. At times, he sounds like a high priest giving orders to members of a Buddhist sangha. The tone of the message changed according to its content and the addressee. Nevertheless, it was always clear that it was the king speaking, his authority undiminished. Having chosen the Shakya way for himself, he was convinced that this was the only way forward for his kingdom and its people.

When politicians speak to citizens, it is often only to reaffirm their own status. There were shades of this in Ashoka too. He did emphasise that his reign was better. That it was a break from the past, that his was a land of equality. As he metaphorically put it: 'Those gods who during that time had been unmingled (with men) in Jambudvipa have now been made (by me) mingled (with them).'[1]

We don't know if this averment was indeed true. But often, his words were reflective. Unlike other monarchs, Ashoka was unafraid of being publicly vulnerable—something that is considered a sign of weakness for those in public life even today. He recognised the necessity for change, and made listening the basic tenet for welfare. This focus on listening is what draws me to him. From his description of how accessible he intends to be and the instructions he gives his officers, we gather that he was attempting to establish a radically different model of governance.

Ashoka said, 'Reporters have to report to me the affairs of the people at any time (and) anywhere, while I am eating, in the harem, in the inner apartment, at the cowpen, in the palanquin, (and) in the park.'[2]

He also wanted to visit his people, to hear directly from them: 'But this is considered by me (my) principal duty, visiting (the people) personally.'[3]

I've often said that musicality is in the listening, not the rendering. We can acquire all the skills needed to enable our voices to leap, glide and speed as and when we command, but that is not the essence of music. The quality of the music depends on how well we listen to our teacher, co-musicians, the aural-scape in the place of performance and, more than anything else, to ourselves. When musicians listen to every ripple, drop, swirl and delay in a song, almost as if it is present in front of them and not coming from them, the song becomes their own. At that point, the song is feeling itself. Ashoka was not just attempting to transform citizens; he wanted his administrators to alter the relationship between the government and the governed.

His officers who were in charge of sensitive regions were given specific orders:

> For you are occupied with thousands of men, with the object of gaining the affection of men.
>
> All men are my children.
>
> As on behalf of (my own) children I desire that they may be provided by me complete welfare and happiness in this world and in the other world, even so is my desire on behalf of all men ...
>
> Now you must also pay attention (to this), though you are in prosperous circumstances.
>
> It happens frequently that a single person undergoes imprisonment and suffers harsh treatment.

> In this case (an order) cancelling the imprisonment is (obtained) by him accidently, while many other people (continue to) suffer.[4]

At the same time, he made it clear who was the boss, and the boss had to be listened to.

> In this case you must strive to deal (with all of them) impartially.
>
> One fails to act (thus) on account of the following dispositions: envy, anger, cruelty, hurry, want of practice, laziness and fatigue.[5]

And his officers had to obey and please him.

> If one fails to observe (this), (there will be) neither attainment of heaven nor satisfaction of the king.
>
> How (could) my mind be pleased if one fulfils this duty badly.[6]

There were aspects of his life that Ashoka was reticent about. He never mentioned his ancestry or his likely bloody rise to power. He spoke of the past only to compare it with his own 'just' rule. Even during his time as king, there were moments when he was not entirely golden-hearted. Unlike the Buddha, he did not walk away from power and live the life of a renunciate. Ashoka was always the king. Though he is flagged as proof of consummate Buddhist leadership, his words are also criticised by some for being shallow in their understanding of the faith. I imagine that Ashoka would not have cared. He was not placing grand spiritual propositions before the public; he was fashioning a role for Buddhist ethics in the political and administrative domains. Also, perhaps, attempting to construct a new public order that he hoped would become a socio-political habit.

Scholars argue about whether Ashoka was already a Buddhist before the Kalinga massacre. This scrutiny does not interest me. But the possibility that his wife/partner Devi influenced his choice of Buddhism is intriguing.[7] Ashoka's grandfather Chandragupta Maurya had, after all, moved towards Jainism, yet Ashoka did not follow his lead. It was when he was sent by his father to Ujjayini as a viceroy that Ashoka met and fell in love with Devi. She was probably already a Buddhist, and may have swayed his mind in the direction of the faith. Unfortunately, she is rarely mentioned as an individual in her own right. We know more of her as the mother of Mahinda and Sanghamitta, her children who became ambassadors for Ashoka's vision.

What did Ashoka himself have to say about Kalinga?

> When king Devanampiya Priyadarsin had been anointed eight years, (the country of) the Kalingas was conquered by (him).
>
> One hundred and fifty thousand in number were the men who were deported thence, one hundred thousand in number were those who were slain there, and many times as many who died.
>
> After that, now that (the country of) the Kalingas has been taken, Devanampiya (is devoted) to a zealous study of morality.
>
> This is the repentance of Devanampiya on account of his conquest of (the country of) the Kalingas.
>
> For this is considered very painful and deplorable by Devanampiya that while one is conquering an unconquered (country), slaughter, death and deportation of people (are taking place) there.
>
> ... Therefore even the hundredth part of the thousandth part of all those people who were slain, who died, and who were deported at the time in Kalinga, (would) now be considered very deplorable by Devanampiya.[8]

This thirteenth edict (part of the set of fourteen edicts) is extraordinary. Here, Ashoka declares the extent of the violence he unleashed in Kalinga and then expresses deep remorse for what he has done. This is indeed a watershed moment in the history of politics. Rarely has a leader thought, let alone acted, in such a manner. The pessimist may interpret this as grandstanding, but the courage to say all this in public—or indeed, the wisdom to see the necessity of it—cannot be attributed only to his absolute power, invincibility and shrewdness. If that was the case, many monarchs, dictators and wildly popular leaders would have done the same. Our elected leaders have remained mute about ghastly pogroms they have watched over. Does an apology change anything, you may ask. True, it cannot undo the past, but when it comes from sincere contemplation, it has the potential to change the course of the future.

But even goodness is not a perpetual state. We have to constantly battle our own demons, compulsions, desires and ego just to remain decent. Ashoka was no different. The thirteenth edict does not end on the vulnerable note at which I just left it. The king goes on to make the point that he still wields the power to kill. To the forest dwellers he says,

> And even (the inhabitants) the forests which are (included) in the dominions of Devanampiya, even those he pacifies (and) converts.
>
> And they are told of the power (to punish them) which Devanampiya (possesses) in spite of (his) repentance in order that they may be ashamed (of their crimes) and may not be killed.
>
> For Devanampiya desires towards all beings abstention from hurting, self-control (and) impartiality in (case of) violence.[9]

Despite his resolve to propagate ahimsa, Ashoka sends out a veiled threat, the message that violence remains a part of his arsenal. Paraphrased, this amounts to saying: Just because I abstain from violence, don't think of me as weak; don't push me—if needed, force will be used. This reminds me of a composition of Tyagaraja's, where he describes Rama as a person adept at gentle persuasion, concession, dividing the enemy and, if needed, using force. Ashoka was not a mendicant; he was aware of and used statecraft, which included the possibility of unleashing the might of his army.

This fissure remains largely undiscussed, in large part because of the need to present Ashoka as a perfect ahimsavadi. It closes us to an understanding of this very real ethical conflict, and the opportunity to reflect upon this tension—one that many of us experience. We do not have the power of a monarch, but we do issue instructions from positions of power or rebuke those who are weaker. We, too, are capable of indulging in violent demonstrations of power. As our strength compounds, our threshold for what is permissible and what is not shifts, almost inevitably to the detriment of the powerless. If we were on Ashoka's throne, we would probably have struggled with similar choices. Hence, this dynamic movement between remorse and aggression within the space of a few lines needs to be discussed.

One thing that bothers admirers of Ashoka is the conspicuous absence of the thirteenth edict in the Dhauli and Jauguda regions of Kalinga (much of which lies in modern-day Odisha), the land of the genocide. The first inference we must draw is that its absence is not a mistake. Ashoka did not want it published in Kalinga. The question then is, why? Was he too proud to apologise directly to the people who suffered at his hands? Or was he avoiding this conversation in order to move forward? Ashoka himself provides an answer to this quandary. In both Dhauli and Jauguda, he had a couple of individual edicts inscribed. They make it abundantly clear that he was attempting to find a way forward, hoping that the people of Kalinga would forget the past and, in forgetting, forgive. In these edicts, he calls his subjects 'my own children', donning the role of a loving father. He doesn't want these 'borderers' to be afraid of him; he wants to build trust. In order to achieve this, he instructs his administrators and judicial officers to work tirelessly, take care of people's welfare, make sure justice is served and no unnecessarily harsh treatment is meted out. He promises to send kind-hearted officials every five years to check on them. This is a ruler who is trying to make things right, seeking to make amends for his past actions. He does not mention the genocide in as many words, but he definitely wants acceptance. The question of whether the people of Kalinga were convinced remains unanswered.

As are some other questions. Did Ashoka have conversations with his ministers and regional governors on the content of the edicts? Did they advise him not to open up old wounds in Kalinga?

Another indication that Ashoka was well aware of local sentiments and edited or omitted edicts accordingly is found in the last line of his fourteenth and final Major Rock edict. 'But some of this may have been written incompletely, either on account of the locality, or because (my) motive was not liked, or by the fault of the writer.'[10]

There is something similar about the way Ashoka and Gandhi recorded their thoughts, even if one recorded them on rocks and pillars and the other wrote on paper. It is possible Ashoka had many more messages etched on wooden pillars and boards, which were lost because of the perishability of the material. This was clearly someone who had a lot to say! What binds the two men, to my mind, is the unsettling coming together of honesty and power. Whether or not we agree with either of them, both spoke with integrity and questioned prevailing socio-political mechanisms. They also wielded power, each in his own way. There is no doubt that the respect, or lack of it, that honesty receives is determined by the extent of power wielded by the individual. And it is also true that such honestly can further empower the powerful. This is evident in the case of both Ashoka and Gandhi.

Their inner urge to do what they considered good is unquestionable. But the reason they could open themselves up to vulnerability is because they knew their strength. Is it really possible for everyone else to follow suit? How can a powerless person gather the courage to say what they feel? The repercussions could be terrible. Even with all his authority, Gandhi paid a price for his openness. This web that entangles power and honesty remains another complex philosophical conundrum.

Ashoka's most significant and dramatic political pivot was his decision to rely on persuasion rather than force as a medium for social change.

And he said as much:

> Now this progress of morality among men has been promoted (by me) only in two ways, by moral restrictions and by conversion.
>
> But among these (two), those moral restrictions are of little consequence; by conversion, however, (morality is promoted) more considerably ... (because it leads) to abstention from hurting living beings (and) to abstention from killing animals.[11]

For Jawaharlal Nehru, who was leading a new country embarking on democracy, this was the romantic past he wanted to mirror. It would not be wrong to surmise that Nehru was inspired by Ashoka. Some may even say he saw himself as a twentieth-century Ashoka. A caring, listening leader of a country that was in urgent need of moral leadership. Like Ashoka, Nehru too occupied a righteous high ground. But Ashoka couldn't have dreamt that a symbol of his would come back to life after two millennia. Nehru likely played an important role in making some of those symbolic choices. But Lo Chia-Luen, ambassador of the Republic of China to India, made an unusual claim while relating a conversation he had with K.M. Panikkar (who later became ambassador to China) in the presence of Nehru on 28 July 1947:

> Panikkar suddenly raised a question: 'What shall we do with the three lion heads on Asoka's pillar?' To this, I smiled and replied: 'With your erudition, you will surely find ways to use them, perhaps as the Indian emblem of state on the gates of government buildings or on official stationery, like the lion and unicorn on the British coat of arms?' 'That's exactly what was on my mind, too!' he said, and we both laughed heartily.

A few days earlier, on 23 July 1947, the *Hindustan Standard* had published a piece titled 'India's National Flag' with a subhead that read 'Ashoka's Historic Singha and Chakra as Union Seal and Symbol': 'It is understood that the Ad Hoc committee of the Constituent Assembly on the National Flag and Seal have drawn their inspiration from the famous Sanchi Pillar of the time of Asoka, the Great.'

The writer goes on to describe the pillar at Sanchi in detail. He had obviously got mixed up between the Ashoka pillars at Sanchi and Sarnath. The article also explains the centrality of the 'lotus' in Indian culture. It is obvious that the writer had been informed that it would be part of the symbol.

This long discussion on Ashoka is necessary—if we are to comprehend the significance of the Indian emblem, we must situate its first dwelling place. Unsurprisingly, we do not know the names of the designer and sculptor of the lion capital. An invisible architect and a set of skilled masons brought Ashoka's dream to life. We can gather with reasonable certainty that the mind behind the lion capital was indeed Ashoka. His edicts and pillars were not mere symbols of the State; they represented his radically new vision for society.

In the minutes of the meeting on 10 July 1947 of the ad hoc committee, which was constituted by the Constituent Assembly to look into the national flag, we find the following notes:

> The question of the designs of the State emblem and seal was then considered, and the following tentative decisions taken:
> (1) The emblem and the seal should be of the same design.
> (2) The design should be an exact reproduction of the whole of the Sarnath Asoka capitol till it joins the stem of the Pillar (sthambha).
> (3) The words 'Republic of India' should be superscribed round the emblem, and 'Seal of the Republic of India' round the seal.

In the next meeting a week later, on 18 July, it was decided that any decision on the State seal and emblem could wait: 'As regards the design of State seal and emblem, it was considered that a decision in this matter was not of immediate urgency, and should be postponed until more designs were prepared.'

Nehru was a special invitee to these meetings. The conversation between the Chinese ambassador and Panikkar on 28 July now makes sense. Panikkar's leading, rhetorical question about the 'three lion heads on Ashoka's pillar' probably came from the discussions of the ad hoc committee a few weeks earlier.

This committee constituted by the president of the Constituent Assembly asked prominent artists to send in designs for the emblem and many were received. After which the committee decided that a decision on the matter must be made by the government and not the Constituent Assembly. Consequently, these designs were considered by Nehru, but it is likely that he had already made up his mind.

Nehru was not alone in being convinced that democratic India needed to remind itself of the Ashokan era. The discovery of the edicts gave Ashoka an unparalleled moral force. There was nothing about him or the old Buddhist world that anyone could object to. Even staunch Hindu members of the Constituent Assembly, such as Govind Malaviya, considered Buddha an avatara of Vishnu. All this helped the liberal Nehru sidestep the danger of a forced choice from Hindu, Islamic and Christian symbols or creating a modern symbol that would lack historical significance. The latter would have been a hard sell. And in a polarised religious environment, the last thing the leaders would have wanted was another inflection point. Ashoka came to their rescue.

Though it was only from 26 January 1950 that the emblem officially replaced the Crown on government buildings, the design itself had been approved by the Government of India by 29 December 1947, five months after the flag was finalised in the Constituent Assembly. The cabinet approved Nehru's proposal for the emblem on 11 December 1947. 'After a short discussion the cabinet approved of the Prime Minister's proposal with the direction that the seal should so far as possible conform to the original of the Sarnath Lion Capital of Asoka minus the lotus.'[12]

Following which, on 15 December 1947, *The Hindu* published a short report that read, 'Free India's Emblem will consist of the Sarnath Lion Capital of Ashoka as it exists at present.' A short description of the emblem was also provided. On 28 December, the Ministry of Home Affairs sent out a letter to all state governments. This was followed by a public announcement about the emblem.

On 30 December 1947, *The Hindu* declared,

> The Government of India have now approved a design for their State emblem and seal, says a Press communique. It has been decided that the State emblem and seal should consist of the Sarnath Lion capital of Asoka as it exists at present, looked at from the side which shows the lions standing on an abacus which has a Dharma Chakra in the centre, a bull on the right and a horse on the left, and the outlines of the

> Dharma Chakras on the extreme right and left. The bell-shaped lotus at the bottom of the capital has been omitted as the capital would become too long for effective use as a State emblem or seal. The reproduction of the capital should be enclosed in a plain double line (the inner line being thin and the outer thick) rectangular frame.

Despite this decision, the official reports of the Constituent Assembly of India Debates (Legislative) continued to use the emblem design that included the bell-shaped lotus on the cover page until the end of 1948. It is only in the report for the period 1–17 February 1949 that the bell-shaped lotus is missing.

Within weeks of the cabinet finalising the emblem design, anomalies began to appear in the public domain. This assertion, for instance, from the above quoted report dated 30 December, was erroneous.

> The reproduction of the capital should be enclosed in a plain double line (the inner line being thin and the outer thick) rectangular frame.

At the cabinet meeting on 7 January 1948, Nehru pointed to this mistake. No decision on an enclosure for the crest had been taken, he said. He also observed that a rectangular frame for an emblem which consisted of a circle (chakra) would be aesthetically inappropriate.[13]

A year later, Governor General C. Rajagopalachari flagged a square border problem. He noticed that, in government publications, the emblem was cased in a square frame. A letter was sent from his office to the prime minister's personal secretary and orders were promptly passed for its removal. But this question of whether or not to enclose the emblem lingered on for nearly a year.

In March 1949, the prime minister's secretariat wrote to the Ministry of Works, Mines and Power, under which the

Office of the Controller of Printing and Stationery functioned, complaining that there was too much variance between the crest printed on the stationaries of the governor general, ministers of the Central government, provincial governors and Indian missions abroad. There was a need for standardisation. From then on, the government took up the issue of formalising a consistent design with vigour. The final crest design which included the motto sans an enclosure was finalised in September 1949. On 21 September 1949, a letter was sent out with samples of the design to all provincial governments and chief commissioners. The Ministry of External Affairs was asked to do the needful with regard to the Indian embassies.

In 1949, the prime minister's secretariat pointed to an anomaly. The Ministry of Home Affairs had sent out the design of the emblem twice that year. First in late May, when the motto was finalised, and then again in September. The September release was supposed to be the final iteration. According to the prime minister's secretariat, in neither version did the lion capital look like the standard that was originally approved by the cabinet in December 1947.

In its response, the Ministry of Home Affairs claimed that the 1947 design was done in a 'great hurry' and was not a correct depiction of the Sarnath lion capital. The present design was a more accurate representation. The ministry explained that this newer design also made reproduction and resizing much easier, and argued that going back to the old design would be a 'retrograde step'.

The Ministry of Home Affairs was right. The design that the cabinet had approved was visually shabby and would have been difficult to replicate, especially in smaller sizes. Unlike the Sarnath capital in which the lion's legs are smooth, the lion on the approved emblem had hair on it, and its mane was drawn with many more strokes. The new design avoided these mistakes and was indeed a closer adaptation of the Sarnath capital. The background of the abacus was lighter, the wheel cleaner, and the bull and horse sharper. But the back and forth between the prime minister's secretariat and Home Affairs on which design to use for which print size continued. In December 1949, the principal secretary to the prime minister noted that the prime minister has approved the 'original' design for larger sizes and the design used by the legation in Berne for smaller sizes! Finally, the two offices came to a compromise. It was decided that, for bigger size reproductions, the government would go with the old design approved in December 1947, including the motto, and for smaller sizes it would use the design released by the Ministry of Home Affairs in September 1949.

It is evident that the prime minister was involved in these design-related discussions. Though the crest design did not have a border, in the form of a seal, an enclosure was included. The prime minister asked for samples of the seal with a circle and oval enclosure to be sent for his perusal and personally approved the oval seal design in December 1949. By May 1950, all decisions regarding seals, rubber stamps, stationery and colour of ink had been finalised.

Beyond the specifics of the design, it is refreshing to see how the political and bureaucratic class took keen interest in the design and wanted to get it just right.

The British kept track of these symbolic changes in their erstwhile territory. In January 1948, *The Illustrated London News* published an image of the new emblem with a description.[14] The Office of the High Commissioner for the United Kingdom followed happenings in the Constituent Assembly (Legislative) and sent the Commonwealth Relations Office in London transcripts of the discussion in February 1949 'on the substitution of the Crown Emblem by the Emblem of the Indian Dominion by the High Courts ....'[15]

The British government seemed more interested, though, in the symbolic changes adopted by our new neighbour, Pakistan.

There are exchanges between the High Commissioner for Pakistan and British officials on whether a dominion could have a crest that was distinct from the coat of arms of the United Kingdom. They wondered if the Garter King of Arms needed to be consulted in this matter. It was then suggested that this was best avoided, and that no special constitutional measures were needed to give an emblem formal recognition. The adoption of a floral emblem through a statute passed by the local legislature of the Province of Ontario was given as an example. The use of the crest, a letter said, had to be left to 'local custom and sentiment'.

In October 1949, the Government of India sent a letter to all provincial governments asking them to replace the Crown and other pre-Independence symbols with the new Indian emblem. Included in that message was the additional advice that this should be done 'gradually and unobtrusively without any undue publicity'. One can conclude that the government did not want this change to become a flashpoint or be used for any kind of chest-beating or point-scoring in such turbulent times. But this process of replacement took a while.

As India neared its twenty-fifth Independence Jayanti, the Government of India wrote again to state governments and union territories asking them to ensure that all the old symbols were replaced.

Curiously, the Constituent Assembly discussed nearly every aspect of India's future in great detail, but the emblem hardly got a mention. There seem to have been only two occasions when it was spoken of, and both occurred after it had been chosen. On 15 November 1948, Shibban Lal Saxena moved an amendment to include a description of the emblem in the constitution.

> Mr. Vice-President, Sir, the amendment moved by Mr. Tyagi is a very important amendment. I have myself given notice of a similar amendment (No. 189) which runs as follows:

'That the following new Part be inserted after Part I and the subsequent Parts and articles be renumbered accordingly: -

Part I-A

General Principles ...

13. The Arms of Bharat consist of the Three Lions above the pedestal and the Dharmachakra, as are depicted on the top of the Asoka pillar at Sarnath.'[16]

The other mention, on 26 May 1949 by B.H. Zaidi, is interesting. He had this to say:

> So far as I know, there has been no occasion in the history of India when the Hindus have persecuted a minority. They have turned themselves from a minority into a majority on one occasion. When Buddhism was reigning supreme in this country, when the Hindus were in a minority, they gradually saw to it that from a minority they converted themselves into a majority. But as against the Buddhists there were the Jains who were a minority. There were the Syrian Christians, the Parsis, and many others. Indeed, India has given asylum and protection to a number of minorities, and the only example I can think of, the only unhappy episode in the history of India was the fate which Buddhism met in the land of its own birth, but it can hardly be called persecution of a minority. The present generation, I suppose is atoning for that, and we are now going back to Buddhist symbols and in our flag, in our national emblems we are giving a place of honour to something from which we ran away, something which we did not sufficiently honour at that time.

Zaidi interprets the adoption of Buddhist symbols as an expiation for that 'unhappy episode'.

The Sarnath Pillar, on which the lion capital sits, marks the place where the Buddha gave his first sermon—the deer park in Isipatana, later known as Sarnath. The capital was fashioned from buff sandstone procured from Chunar in the Mirzapur district of

Uttar Pradesh. The stone is greyish-cream in colour with dark brown and black spots. The capital glows! A shine that is the product of a labour-intensive polishing technique. The Chinese traveller, documenter and monk Xuanzang, who visited Sarnath in the early seventh century, wrote about the pillar's dazzling brightness and jade-like softness. But he does not mention the capital. Did he not see it? It is curious that he did not document its majestic presence.

The capital has four lions, sculpted back-to-back and facing the four cardinal directions. They are seated on a circular abacus. The abacus's annular is carved with a horse, bull, elephant and lion. These animals are interspersed with four smaller chakras with twenty-four spokes. Each chakra is carved directly below a lion. When the Sarnath Pillar was found, it was broken and the lion capital was dismembered from it. The heads of two of the four lions were detached (these were refixed later, but are still damaged). Fragments of a large dharmachakra that used to sit on top of the four majestic lions were also discovered. There is much to say about the sheer beauty of its sculpting. The lions' manes are intricately carved, and look like they are swaying in the breeze. Similarly, the pleated layers of skin hanging from the bull's neck are beautifully achieved.

What we have adapted as our emblem is a partial image of the lion capital. The dharmachakra with thirty-two spokes that once stood on top of the lions was excluded. The amendment that Professor Saksena moved in late 1948 in the Constituent Assembly asking for the emblem to include the 'Dharmachakra, as are depicted on the top of the Ashoka pillar at Sarnath' was obviously also a demand for the inclusion of a reconstructed design of the dharmachakra on top of the lions. Nearly a decade later, in 1956, Member of Parliament Dr Radha Kumud Mookerji wrote a few articles about this issue. He forwarded them to President Rajendra Prasad, asking him to look into the matter. Prasad took it up very seriously, had his office investigate the process by which the emblem was selected and even received inputs from the director general of the Archeological Survey of India (ASI). He also brought all this to the notice of the prime minister. But Nehru made it clear that 'whatever justification there might be in Dr Mookerji's remarks', the emblem was too well established across the globe for any alterations to be made it. While the president's secretariat gathered facts, the General Purposes Committee of the Lok Sabha also heard Mookerji out.

Since none of this had any impact on the prime minister, Mookerji sent a co-signed letter directly to Nehru a year later. The complainants wrote that the chosen design was flawed because it had edited out the dharmachakra with thirty-two spokes that once stood upon the shoulders of the lions and 'distorted the significance originally sought to be conveyed'.[17] Nehru, of course, did not budge.

There are those who believe that the smaller chakras on the abacus are miniature dharmachakras, while others disagree.

In 1951, R.R. Diwakar, the Minister of Information and Broadcasting, published an article about the emblem in which he quoted Kannada poet and scholar Govind Pai as having said to him, 'How can the Dharmachakra be under the feet of the Lions? It must be on their heads'.[18]

The constraints of two-dimensionality required that the emblem consist of three lions. Among the smaller animals on the face of the abacus, it was decided to expose the bull and the horse with a chakra in between, in the centre.

Without getting caught up in these debates, we can definitely conclude that dharma lay at the heart of this choice. The selectors were making a statement about the kind of country we were attempting to mould—not one that beat its chest in pride or boasted about its military might. The newly independent nation was giving the fallen lion capital its rightful place, and in doing so, reinstating the principle of virtuous governance—echoes of which can be found in the words of the Buddha. In one of his previous births, when he was born as a deer, the bodhisattva teaches the Kosala king the principles of just rule:[19]

> Great king, it is good for a king to rule a kingdom by forsaking the ways of wrongdoing, not offending against the ten kingly virtues and acting with just righteousness.
>
> Generosity, moral restraint, self-sacrifice, integrity, leniency, fervour, non-anger, non-ill-will, patience and non-enmity.
>
> These noble virtues I have ascribed to, thereby, arise joy and self-actualisation, without diminishing.

Symbolism, though, changes with time, place, people, culture and context. Since Independence, replicas of the Sarnath Pillar have been erected in various cities and Ashok Nagar is a common name for residential localities. The emblem has found a place on traffic islands, bridges and public parks, but as a symbol of State presence and power and not a representation of the ideas it embodied. I cannot imagine that anyone looks at the emblem in these places and thinks of dharma.

Wherever the entire pillar has been replicated, all four sides of it are visible. In the city of Chennai, there is an Ashoka Pillar at the centre of a busy four-road intersection. Not surprisingly, that suburb, established in 1964, was named Ashok Nagar. I am not certain that the pillar was specifically modelled on the Sarnath Pillar. But that doesn't matter. The bus conductor shouts out 'Ashok Pillar' every time the bus approaches this bustling junction. Commuters on bikes and cars hardly notice the pillar that stares at them when they circumambulate it, and no doubt fewer still know or care about its origin.

Ashoka has become so much a part of our public imagination that we don't notice his presence. At the Kozhikode airport, as I walked towards the aeroplane, I noticed a not-so-well-done large copper engraving depicting some king's coronation. How very odd, I thought. But when I looked more closely, just below the feet of the king, there lay a dharmachakra with thirty-two spokes.

Every time we dig into our wallets and purses for the right denomination of a bill or coin, this symbol of dharma makes an appearance, but we do not see it. And I doubt that acknowledging its presence, and its significance, would stop us from indulging in dubious transactions. The bills will continue to be used for illegal, unaccounted, unethical exchanges. Even on counterfeit currency bills, the lion capital remains intact. If we stood in the presence of the original Sarnath Pillar, we may be touched by its philosophical enormity. But now that the emblem has become just one more element in our everyday life, its meaning is eroded. It is just another design element.

The lion capital is also, of course, an art object. Meanings accrue to it and diminish. From the time it was conceived by Ashoka's inner circle of philosophical and aesthetic advisors to when the sculptor gave it form, there were probably many additions and subtractions to its inferred meanings. When it was placed at its location, the capital gained another kind of significance. As time passed, people saw what they wanted to see in it and interpreted its import as they deemed fit. Social norms, faiths, cultures are always in flux, and the pillar also became irrelevant, just another broken old column. The old meanings were lost in the sands of time. Centuries later, the same pillar was recovered, pasted back together, its long-lost sheen retrieved. Religious and political meanings from the past were revisited and given life anew. The lion capital became the coat of arms of the Indian nation state. It continues to fulfil that function, even though we rarely think about it.

Symbols are ideas that are abstracted from temporal objects and thus imbued with trans-temporal identities. Not every art object that is trapped within a specific event or period, or is associated with one person alone, may possess the suppleness needed to acquire a new symbolic meaning. Even so, after being confined for some length of time, a piece of art may suddenly transform into a symbol quite free of its original meaning. The passage of time could de-baggage it of its historical load.

When the Constituent Assembly met for the first time on Monday, 9 December 1946, at 11 a.m., at the seat of the Imperial Legislative Council, Indians were occupying that room for the first time on their own terms. I don't know if the royal coat of arms hung from any of the walls there, but a painting of His Majesty King George VI might have adorned some panel. Did the viceroy's standard find a place somewhere? The emblems of the dominions of the Empire had already been carved into the tall side walls of the central hall. The 209 members, including the temporary chairman, who presented their credentials on that day, were preparing to reimagine the chamber and everything it represented. On a day not so far in the future, that room would belong unequivocally to Indians.

The sight of a lion on official insignia would not have been new to the people of the subcontinent. They had seen it on the coat of arms of the East India Company as well as the royal coat of arms of the United Kingdom. For obvious reasons, the emblem of India needed to be the antithesis of what the British represented. India's choice for its state emblem had lions too, but the similarity ended right there. These lions were not aggressive creatures that threatened to kill and conquer. They sat in peace, regally watching over their land. In Pali scriptural teachings, the lion is a symbol of compassionate power, meditative majesty, benevolent grace and dignified leadership.

In July 2022, an unusual debate erupted over the installation of an enormous bronze replica of the Ashokan lions at the site of our new Parliament. The critique was that this replica was wantonly aggressive and overtly muscular, the antithesis of what the Indian State intended in its founding days. Those who defended this manifestation believed that the original lions themselves were neither benign nor toothless, that the Sarnath lions possess fangs, but we chose to overlook what they signify. The defenders of the new design questioned the eulogisation of Ashoka as a pacifist. Some also said that the real Indian lions (meaning Hindu representations) were always fierce, ready to defend good, and hence, if anything, this modern adaptation was truer to 'our' civilisational history. The more direct defence was that this brawny look represented India under Narendra Modi.

It is necessary to put these assertions to the test of reason. The problem is not with the lions showing their fangs or muscles or sharp claws. The impression an artwork creates is not the result of a summing up of its attributes. What needs to be considered is its sensibility, the quality it exudes. The emotional landscape and the social and philosophical continuum within which it was created and within which it now exists. This futuristic flow is charted by the artist and the conversations that resulted in the artist's response at the time of its creation. Viewed in such a manner, and in the light of what we know about Ashoka's philosophical trajectory, it becomes obvious that the Ashokan lions are not there to attack anybody. They have presence, farsightedness, composure and command, but they do not threaten.

The contradictions between Ashoka the emperor and Ashoka the Buddhist do not diminish his empathetic inclinations and policies. There seems to be an urge to trivialise non-violence by claiming that the celebration of such public action during the independence struggle—satyagraha, for instance—and imbuing our national symbols with its message marginalises revolutionaries and revolutionary action.

This line of thought should not surprise us in an era where the 'killer instinct' is a mantra. Till some years ago, Indian sportspersons were accused of not possessing this much-needed quality. They were too nice, would roll over easily, did not know how to win and did not give it back to their opponents—or so the talk went. But today, commentators describe the new Indian cricket team as illustrative of the 'new, confident India'; in other words, players with the killer instinct. In these casual observations, meanings are bundled together: soft, timid, weak, diffident are placed together with decent, dignified, compassionate and concerned. On the other side, we conflate anger, aggression, vulgarity and intimidation with strength, confidence, determination and self-assurance. This muddled understanding fosters a belief that, to win, you have to be threatening.

Though we adopted national symbols and a constitution that paved a path away from this competitive social order, our social infrastructure galloped along the killer instinct trajectory, valourising the powerful and the dictatorial. As India's economic power grew, this only became more blatant. The new lion capital is the Indian State's symbolic course correction—bringing it in line with a chosen social direction rather than allowing it to remain as a symbol of what we should be seeking.

Ashoka was probably one of the first proponents of a welfare state. But his idea of welfare extended beyond the economic and social needs of his people. The propagation of dharma as he understood it—and the desire to convince his subjects to follow such a trajectory in life—was at the very heart of his welfarism. He created an entire class of administrators called the dharma mahamatras just for this purpose. Their work included ensuring that moral practices were adhered to, and that the social requirements of all his subjects were fulfilled. One could say this was how Ashoka imagined a land of dharma.

'Land of dharma' has a good ring to it, a nobler sort of nationhood. For most Indians, the very word 'dharma' signals an end to all arguments. All you need to say is 'this is dharma' or 'this is the dharmic way of life' or 'this is dharma shastra', and your proposal is instantly sanctified. The word is imbued with the headiness of antiquity, and parables from the lives of 'enlightened' saints and mythical figures have drilled the idea into our psyche.

The most immediate understanding of dharma is righteousness or justice, although the import of these words in a person's lived experience is not very clear. Each one of us holds a certain interpretation of these concepts that is unique to us. There may be broad parameters we agree on, but the divergances are considerable. There is no one dharma that is universal. We cannot even be sure if violence can be universally categorised as adharmic. What about the power of the individual or entity indulging in the violence? Is there a difference between the violence inflicted upon citizens by a person fighting for his basic rights and the State using violence (sometimes in the form of its laws) to suppress citizens for reasons it finds justifiable? In an even more complicated comparison, is there a difference between the violence unleashed by an errant individual and the State?

Where is the dharma in all this?

Dharma is a near untranslatable Sanskrit word. Its etymology can be traced to the aphorism 'dhriyate anena iti dharmah': that which is the substratum (or that which preserves, sustains), that is dharma. The philosophical question is, what is it that sustains humankind? Not varna or jati, or a foundational social order, but a realisation of reality. Dharma has an exterior and an interior. The meaning written on the shell of the word consists of customs, a code. The kernel is reflective, a conscience. Religious, social and political orders adhere to the outer meaning to establish control in the name of decorum. Philosophers stress the primacy of inner meaning in order to free themselves and others from the control of these very orders. It is impossible to go into every understanding of dharma. In this chapter, I attempt to take a path that can be best described as inspired by the Buddhist way.

Dharma, in its larger sense, directs our attention to something very subtle—phenomena, nature, the way things are. We need to be careful with this meaning. Used thus, dharma does not refer to accepting reality as it is. It speaks of the true phenomena that we are unable to see, an underlying quality to life that we are unable to grasp. This is not a mystical idea, but an empirical observation we are all familiar with. Our place of birth, gender, caste, race, colour, sexuality and such-like factors filter and process all the information we receive. So, all that we know is tailored by socio-cultural determinants that impact our moments of anger, happiness, regret, jealousy—the entire range of human responses. The question that arises is: what are we actually seeing? When we assess the nature of something, are we comprehending its attributes or reconfirming our own character? Understanding the nature of dharma relieves us of these intermediaries. If our social facets were absent, our relationship with everything around us would be radically different. Dharma is uncoloured reality. To be able to observe in such a manner requires us to discard all that we think we know and are, so that we may free ourselves and awaken our conscience. This is a living practice.

It is also a mode of thinking we can carry over to our observation of the natural world. The birds, trees, animals, insects, water, the sun, clouds and rain live and behave as per their nature. But we may not perceive their true nature. Knowing the natural world does not come to us instinctively. I am reminded of the Oscar Wilde quote, 'life imitates art far more than art imitates life'. What, how and when we notice something is not dependent on its existence, but in our ability to pay attention to it. Imagine being introduced in a piece of art to a common garden bird we don't much heed. The next time the bird flies into your line of sight, you would look at it very differently. To my understanding, dharma is the ability to recognise this reality of awakening.

Our relationship with nature needs critical observation too. What is nature, separate from our need for sustenance? Is it possible to have with it a relationship that is non-transactional?

At this juncture, let me introduce you to a Tamil word, 'poromboku', or the commons—the grazing lands, rivers, mountains, lakes, marshlands, backwaters, mangroves, all of which existed long before we entered the scene. Human beings, birds, animals, fish and all living things have a right to the poromboku. Nomadic tribes, fisherfolk and other such communities have lived on the poromboku, knowing full well that they are one of many creatures who share the space and what it has to offer.

The State is the caretaker of the poromboku. But the poromboku is also seen by mainstream society as being of no value for one simple reason: it does not generate revenue. It is not owned by anyone and is hence non-taxable, and so 'it is going waste'. An extractive society is unable to fathom why any part of the earth should not be directly beneficial to it. The birds, trees, grass, animals, fish and people who survive on the land-of-no-value are thus as useless and valueless as the poromboku.

The caretaker, the government, exploits the poromboku as it chooses, asserting that this is done for the benefit of the citizens, so they may have better employment and a higher standard of living. But, as we have repeatedly seen, these promises are rarely kept. Instead, polluting factories, uncontrolled mining and deforestation lead to the annihilation of flora, fauna, water bodies and the air. People lose their cultural identities, ways of living, livelihood and health, and gain little to nothing in return.

The only true beneficiaries of this destruction live far away in the safety of their urban homes.

The word 'poromboku' is now used as an abuse—an unworthy person, a good-for-nothing. This negative connotation is what opens up the poromboku for exploitation.

It is this very utilitarian view that informs our social models too, constructed as they are for convenience, utility, control and power. The title of dharma is bestowed upon every discriminatory social practice to sanctify it. Thus, people with caste privilege pontificate on how only 'certain' people can do certain things; that this is the natural order of life. The word 'dharma' is used in so many contexts, not all of which even adhere to the basic tenets of decency or justice.

A corrective to this corroded idea of dharma is urgently needed. The abolishment of untouchability as included in our Fundamental Rights was one such extraordinary intervention. Untouchability was once justified on the basis of varnashrama, which was considered a dharmic model. We, the people of India boldly tackled this falsity.

> **Abolition of Untouchability:** Article 17 abolishes 'untouchability' and forbids its practice in any form. The enforcement of any disability arising out of untouchability shall be an offence punishable in accordance with law.

Article 15 had already addressed discrimination on the grounds of religion, race, caste, sex or place of birth. Yet, the makers of the constitution of India felt the need for a separate and specific article addressing untouchability. This article is not a right in the traditional sense, but the criminalisation of an inhuman practice. Untouchability was so widely prevalent that this Land of Dharma had to explicitly put an end to it. Calling out 'false dharmas' and acting to correct the wrong is itself a dharmic act.

Have we moved far away from our first understanding of dharma? We now seem to be discussing the nuts and bolts of life. But dharma is not a fanciful, impractical idea; it is something derived from lived reality. In order to realise dharma in its most subtle form, we need to practice it in everyday life, not through organisational structures such as religion. Dharma can only be based on universal empathy, love, equality, compassion and non-violence, and above all, the courage to act, to not remain passive observers. And for it to flourish, an entire architecture of dharma is needed—constitutional guarantees, effective justice systems and socio-political structures born of its spirit.

For all of Ashoka's efforts, we cannot be sure if his subjects changed the way they lived or society at large became more compassionate. After all, despite his good intentions, the political practice of his empire remained unfree, hierarchical and violent.

Article 15 of the constitution guarantees Indian citizens a right to live free of discrimination. It is a right, but also a hope. We are hoping that this course correction will lead us to co-exist and cooperate as citizens without the blinkers of prejudice.

Our constitution was supposed to be a pathway to dharma. Unfortunately, it is people who write constitutions and, hence, there are always rough edges. At the very least, there tends to be a gap between design and execution. Despite Article 15, Article 17 and the seventy-five years that have passed since the constitution was first adopted, India still witnesses 'honour' killings, rapes, mass killings of dalits and Muslims and denial of access to dalits to public spaces like wedding halls, temples, pathways and cremation grounds. Dalits are still offered separate glasses to drink from, and casteist slurs are commonplace. Caste-belonging remains strong.

Mahatma Gandhi rightly understood untouchability to be the worst manifestation of the evil human beings are capable of. He believed that the Hindu house would be cleansed only once this abomination emanating from within the faith was discarded and the upper castes atoned for their sins. There was a time when he did not subscribe to the view that varnashrama, the caste edifice that enabled such a practice, was necessarily ugly. But his views changed with time. From defending the practice in its entirety, he slowly moved to looking at the possibility of a re-envisioned, non-hierarchical varna system. He saw a dharmic possibility in the system and reasoned that it was the mutilated form of it that was adharmic. Gandhi's attempt at reconceptualising varnashrama was born from an ingrained belief that, at some point, it had to have been a social ideal. It is clear from some of his comments that Gandhi knew deep down this ideal never existed, yet he held on to his dream of a non-hierarchical, occupation-based, equal and respectful social structure. An unreal hope!

Scholars such as Akeel Bilgrami and Anil Nauriya have argued that Gandhi's attempt to excavate and revise an indigenous social order came from his deep-seated resistance to the market economy and the monetisation of people and their skills. In other words, he was fighting against the divorcing of society and culture from the economy. There is also the argument that there was practicality and social strategy in the way Gandhi approached the issues of untouchability and caste—attacking untouchability first before he moved on to caste.[20] This idea was to establish partners from within caste Hindus and take the community along as he incrementally dismantled their ugly practices without destabilising their cultural anchor. He also appeared to believe that, with untouchability gone, the ugly form of caste would dissipate. There can be no doubt that the change in Gandhi's attitude towards varnashrama was influenced by Ambedkar. There are suggestions that his final position on caste was in consonance with Ambedkar's, but I am not entirely convinced.

Even in the oft-quoted piece written in November 1935, Gandhi clings to the mirage: 'I believe in the varnashrama of the vedas ...' Or: 'Varnashrama of the shastras is today non-existent in practice.' And, 'The present caste system is the antithesis of varnashrama. The sooner public opinion abolishes it the better.'[21]

In most discussions on the subject of Gandhi and caste, Gandhi the individual, his internal struggles, emotional baggage and anxieties are ignored. Caste is, unfortunately, the most intimate social bind in Indian society. Within its ambit exists every imaginable social and cultural experience. The 'caste collective', even if it is not recognised as such, is the only reference point for community. For a person with caste privilege, its effects are incredibly significant—they never experience discrimination. All the joy experienced while growing up comes from social relationships constructed within caste. This is true of even an anti-caste savarna. Unsurprisingly, there is a sense of cultural belonging associated with this caste-limited past. I am suggesting that Gandhi was emotionally trapped in this web. It is quite possible that his yearning to find social justice within a varna construction was a product, at least in part, of wanting to hold on to his own personal socio-religious experience. It could have been born of a fear that the removal of varnashrama would lead to the erasure of cultural and religious bonds.

The fact that Gandhi was deeply affected by the grotesqueness of caste and that he took on the orthodoxy at great personal risk cannot be questioned. Neither can the fact that, both in his personal and political life, Gandhi constantly challenged caste boundaries. And yet, he sought a solution that would emerge from within that very tangle. It is privilege that allows a person to straddle radicalism and protectionism at the same time. I am not accusing Gandhi of duplicity. It is just that privilege allows such incongruities to co-exist with ease. I do not know what

Gandhi had in his mind when he moved between these two diametrically opposite positions. The way I see it, what's at play is tension between two different types of discomfort. On the one hand, Gandhi was courageously putting himself in a state of discomfort by challenging caste oppression. At the same time, he was agonising over the possibility that his cultural-religious paradigm would collapse if varnashrama were to vanish. Gandhi was struggling and grappling with this breach. So, instead of committing to one of the two positions in totality, he repeatedly readjusted his balance without really rocking the varnashrama boat—something his own privilege allowed him to do. This is not a choice that an activist from an oppressed community would have. Beyond the analytical reasons provided by scholars for Gandhi's ambivalence lie emotional tugs and the blind spots of upper-caste activism.

The very idea that varnashrama could ever have been a non-discriminative cultural arrangement is irrational. Even in a society that is not driven by money and is non-transactional, power would have manifested in innumerable other ways. Who evaluated a person's abilities? What was the process of evaluation? How were people allocated various vocations? Our everyday prejudices, unconscious biases, the need to control and oppress in various contexts, not only caste, make it obvious that varna could have never been fair. It was, in fact, adharmic in its very conception.

The other common assertion in support of the 'ideal' varna system is that it was not based on birth. This too is false. Right from the Buddha's time, there are many narrations that inform us that varna, even in its proto form, was not practised on the basis of birth or ability. The Buddha, for instance, explains to a brahmin what it means to be brahmin or an outcast; that it is not by birth, but based on the thoughts and deeds of an individual. We also find the Buddha challenging the notion of hereditary caste purity. The earliest record of this seems to appear in the

Vinaya Pitaka of the Pali canon, where some Sakyan princes, who were the Buddha's cousins, ask the Buddha to ordain Upali, their barber, before them—an act that is seen as a way of curtailing their own class and caste pride. The Buddha is said to have approved of this enthusiastically. The Buddhist text *Vajrasuchi*, written sometime in the middle of the first millennium, is also a critical discourse on varnashrama.

The story of Buddha's disciples Ananda and Prakriti is another example: Ananda refuses to acknowledge Prakriti's outcaste status as a chandalini.

The exchange between Adi Shankara and the chandala, who opened his eyes to the illogic of considering another human impure, is also conveniently forgotten, but it too reinforces the realities of his time.

It doesn't matter whether these incidents actually occurred or not—they are still a record of how, right from its early days, varna worked on the premise of birth. The working of the varna system varied depending on the local culture and, with time, developed into the complex labyrinth of jatis. The accounts of Chinese travellers confirm that an individual's social status was shaped by associations of caste, occupation and purity. The Manusmriti was not some obscure text that had no real-life relevance. It built on the foundations that had already been laid down in practice, with birth being the pivot for the function and social status an individual was assigned. It is shocking then, that a statue of Manu stands within the grounds of the Rajasthan High Court in Jaipur. That its removal requires a battle speaks volumes for how deeply entrenched the tenets of the Manusmriti are, even if it has hardly been read!

Savarnas need to understand the limitations in Gandhi's conception of social equality to avoid the pitfalls that lie ahead. This is the place from which I critique Gandhi—not to make him out to be the 'devil in khaddar' and not to announce my hyper-liberal credentials. And I refuse to fall into the Gandhi vs Ambedkar trap. I discuss their exchanges only to understand the problems in Gandhi's interpretations and not to bring one of them down. One thing is for certain: neither Gandhi nor Ambedkar held back on their opinions just because their cohorts disliked them.

The man who wrote about his experiments with truth was unable to see the truth that was staring at him. Once he saw himself as a dharmic Hindu messiah, it became imperative that he protect Hinduism. To be fair to him, the faith he was trying to protect was not the one the casteist conservatives were holding on to. He felt the need to be a representative for everyone within the fold, especially the voiceless. This was coupled with a need to save Hinduism from moral decay. I believe that Gandhi would have welcomed this critical evaluation of his ideas, and it is distinctly possible that, had he been born in our time, he would have thought and acted differently.

Referring to a statement made at one specific moment in time does not help us understand a person's mind. Words can be used in the heat of the moment, in defence of a point of view or in order to put down an opponent. But Gandhi's observations on untouchability and varnashrama, even conceding that he was on a learning curve, had some recurring themes. He did not accept that he was an outsider in the untouchability dialogue. His role was to be an ally, especially when there were many voices of force and intellect from the affected communities. But Gandhi centred himself, and in turn the Congress, as the true representatives of the untouchables. Even after accepting the political necessities of such a positioning, it is obvious that this was personal, and there was irritation in his words at the suggestion that he could not occupy such a place. He spoke of his willingness to personally atone for the sins of the caste Hindu community. This personalisation, keeping with the Hindu tradition of prayaschitta, turned the entire focus of the conversation on the sacrifice, which he also expected other orthodox Hindus to make. What should have been a fight for rights became a push for reform that came from repentance. This, in turn, disempowered those from the community who spoke up.

Gandhi refused to even consider Ambedkar as the voice of all untouchables or, for that matter, allow him to take that seat and be by his side. He spoke of Ambedkar as a regional player, while he who had travelled the length and breadth of the country, and had lived with the dalits, knew what needed to be done for all untouchables.[22] Gandhi often acknowledged Ambedkar's intellect, but would keep reiterating that Ambedkar was a bitter man. He said that Ambedkar had every right to 'even spit upon me, as every untouchable has'[23] or 'if he really hits us with shoes we must bear even that'.[24] Gandhi may have thought that he was publicly owning up to the wrongs of his community, but what this actually did was diminish the gravitas of Ambedkar's voice. By saying that Ambedkar had every right to be angry, and at times hinting that this anger was limiting his ability to think clearly, Gandhi was insisting that he knew best what was good for the dalits.

Ambedkar was sharp, brutal and, at times, unkind in his criticism of Gandhi. Beyond the obvious ideological differences, this probably came from being forced to incessantly argue and defend his legitimacy in the caste, reservation and untouchability dialogue. The fact that Ambedkar took all this in his stride and forged a way forward demonstrates his personal grit, resolve and commitment to social reform, and above all else, his belief that people are capable of changing.

It should not be difficult for us to empathise with someone who knew what it meant to be an untouchable, and had built philosophical, political and social arguments for change, yet had to repeatedly prove himself and even compromise. Gandhi, on the other hand, without any lived experience, was accepted as the realised soul who knew it all.

Gandhi spoke about how he had become a harijan by choice and hoped that caste Hindus would become bhangis by choice: 'I myself have become a Harijan by choice ... A Harijan by birth may repudiate his varna, but how can I who has become Harijan by choice.'[25]

And, 'If the caste Hindus would become Bhangis of their own free will, the distinction between Harijans and caste Hindus would automatically disappear.'[26]

I am reminded of something Bezwada Wilson, the social activist and founder of Safai Karmachari Andolan, said. I paraphrase: A person with caste privilege choosing to clean toilets is very different from a dalit being forced to do so because of his caste. As he rightly suggests, the former has a choice. Gandhi shed his modern clothes, wore a simple piece of cloth, cleaned toilets and learnt about the lives of the oppressed. This was a critically important personal learning; it allowed him to challenge the savarna elite, and it made him stronger, his message more universal. Ambedkar, a man of flaming intellect and incredible moral and philosophical clarity, was not acknowledged as a universal thinker. To my mind, there was only one reason for this fencing in of his relevance: caste.

It is well known that Ambedkar's *Annihilation of Caste* was originally a prepared speech to be delivered at the annual Jat-Pat-Todak Mandal conference in Lahore in 1936. The event was cancelled because the organisation wanted certain portions of the speech deleted. In a letter dated 22 April 1936, Har Bhagwan of the Mandal says that Ambedkar's declaration that he had 'decided to walk out of the fold of the Hindus' and that this was his 'last address as a Hindu' would not have been an acceptable statement at their forum:

> You have also unnecessarily attacked the morality and reasonableness of the Vedas and other religious books of the Hindus, and have at length dwelt upon the technical side of

> Hindu religion, which has absolutely no connection with the problem at issue, so much so that some of the passages have become irrelevant and off the point. We would have been very pleased if you had confined your address to that portion given to me, or if an addition was necessary, it would have been limited to what you had written on Brahminism etc. The last portion which deals with the complete annihilation of Hindu religion and doubts the morality of the sacred books of the Hindus as well as a hint about your intention to leave the Hindu fold does not seem to me to be relevant.[27]

This portion of the letter is an example of the intellectual bind progressive Hindus were caught in, one that persists even today, and not just among savarna Hindus. Ambedkar's emotional intensity lights up *Annihilation of Caste*. He was thematic, historical, religious, scriptural, political and logical, building his arguments with great acuity and detailing, unrelenting in his takedown of the Hindu social architecture. But it was not the debate that he was interested in. He wanted the world around him, everyone, to change. Despite his own lived experience, he believed change among Hindus was possible. But he does begin by saying:

> As a rule, I do not like to take any part in a movement which is carried on by the Caste Hindus. Their attitude towards social reform is so different from mine that I have found it difficult to pull on with them. Indeed, I find their company quite uncongenial to me on account of our differences of opinion.[28]

As a public intellectual, however, he was in conversation with everyone, including the 'caste Hindu', albeit on his own terms.

Unfortunately, Ambedkar has been siloed into the caste bracket. Savarnas either ignore him or use him as a crutch to target some other minority. Progressive savarnas attempt to appropriate his words. On the other side, many dalit progressives close the doors that he kept wide open. Their suspicion of savarnas is entirely justified. And yet, if we are unwilling to cross that dividing line and engage with each other with courage and respect, there is nowhere to go. So many across caste lines are afraid to speak or listen because they fear being 'cancelled'. Ambedkar's voice has not had the free rein it needs to fundamentally transform Indian society.

Progressive Hindus, meanwhile, continue to believe that the problem within Hinduism is largely a case of misinterpretation or misrepresentation. Discarding certain scriptures, or critically assessing them, remains outside the realm of the permissible. This is exactly what we see in the response from Jat-Pat-Todak Mandal. They were under pressure from powerful Hindu groups, but that was not the only problem. The fact that Ambedkar was pointing to scriptural immorality was unpalatable. Eight decades and many caste debates later, nothing has changed.

There is more to the Jat-Pat-Todak Mandal–Ambedkar story. The publication of the undelivered speech resulted in an exchange of intellectual volleys between Ambedkar and Gandhi. But there was an interpolator in their debate: the Jat-Pat-Todak Mandal. In an interesting letter, they responded to Gandhi. After providing their side of the story, Sant Ramji from the Mandal challenged some of Gandhi's arguments:

> Moreover I want to bring to your notice that your philosophical difference between caste and varna is too subtle to be grasped by people in general, because for all practical purposes in the Hindu society caste and varna are one and the same thing, for the function of both of them is one and the same, i.e., to restrict intercaste marriages and inter-dining. Your theory of varnavyavastha is impracticable in this age and there is no hope of its revival in the near future. But Hindus are slaves of caste and do not want to destroy it. So when you advocate your ideal or imaginary varnavyavastha they find justification for clinging to caste. Thus you are doing a great

> disservice to social reform by advocating your imaginary utility of division of varnas, for it creates hindrance in our way. To try to remove untouchability without striking at the root of varnavyavastha is simply to treat the outward symptoms of a disease or to draw a line on the surface of water. As in the heart of their hearts dwijas do not want to give social equality to the so-called touchable and untouchable Shudras, so they refuse to break caste, and give liberal donations for the removal of untouchability, simply to evade the issue. To seek the help of the Shastras for the removal of untouchability and caste is simply to wash mud with mud.[29]

Gandhi was deeply bothered by this. He responded by saying that there seemed to be no difference between the position of the Mandal and Ambedkar. When we read this 'mud with mud' phrase in conjunction with Har Bhagwan's letter to Ambedkar, where he expressed displeasure about what he called unnecessary attacks on 'the morality and reasonableness of the Vedas and other religious books of the Hindus', it is clear that a line is being drawn between shastras that can be, or need to be, discarded and those that are sacrosanct. This way of thinking is probably true of many progressive savarnas.

In his letter to Gandhi, Sant Ramji says, 'In spite of all this, I cannot help praising his address which is, as far as I know, the most learned thesis on the subject and worth translating into every vernacular of India.'[30]

So, do we just discard Hinduism in toto? Ambedkar's absolute rejection did not mean there was no hope—a point that is often ignored. He made a bold proposition:[31]

> [Y]ou must give a new doctrinal basis to your Religion—a basis that will be in consonance with Liberty, Equality and Fraternity, in short, with Democracy. I am no authority on the subject. But I am told that for such religious principles as will be in consonance with Liberty, Equality and Fraternity it may

> not be necessary for you to borrow from foreign sources and that you could draw for such principles on the Upanishads. Whether you could do so without a complete remoulding, a considerable scraping and chipping off the ore they contain, is more than I can say. This means a complete change in the fundamental notions of life. It means a complete change in the values of life.
>
> It means a complete change in outlook and in attitude towards men and things. It means conversion; but if you do not like the word, I will say, it means new life. But a new life cannot enter a body that is dead. New life can enter only in a new body.
>
> The old body must die before a new body can come into existence and a new life can enter into it. To put it simply, the old must cease to be operative before the new can begin to enliven and to pulsate. This is what I meant when I said you must discard the authority of the Shastras and destroy the religion of the Shastras.

Nothing, whether oral wisdom or written holy text, that translates to social abuse of any form—physical, emotional, psychological, economic or cultural—is acceptable. It is only from this position of uncompromising truthfulness that Hindus can hope to find a non-discriminatory belief system. This is the truth-seeking that I speak of in discussions on dharma. What remains of Hinduism if they venture down this path is for Hindus to find out.

It is in this context that an examination of Sree Narayana Guru's philosophy becomes vital. Narayana Guru unequivocally rejected caste, fashioning a Hinduism without any ifs and buts. This was a remarkable achievement. He wrote poems that named Hindu gods and goddesses, but he also evolved a new blueprint for ritualism, bringing social justice politics into the faith's emotional conscience. His spiritualism did not seek a convenient escape. Instead, he wrestled with the reality of religion as it was practised.

On the face of it, Gandhi and Narayana Guru seem to be converging, but they do not. Narayana Guru's socio-spiritual-religious movement emerged from a very different social experience and this showed in his approach. His idea of 'One People, One Religion, One God' was not a placating universalism that covered up inherently complex problems pervading the faith system, neither was it a simplistic placebo. Instead, Narayana Guru sought to reconfigure faith in society. He demanded from every individual spiritual nakedness. It was the kind of enquiry no faith system truly wants.

I would argue that if nothing remains after an honest enquiry, then it didn't deserve to exist in the first place. Progressive Hindus are terrified that they may become faithless, with nothing to hold on to. The natural reflex is to somehow restructure the past, find an angle for its relevance and hold on to an older vocabulary. But the presence of the older vocabulary could in itself be violent to others. Gandhi's fear that the rejection of the varnashrama system in its entirety would lead to the disintegration of the Hindu faith has a deep resonance for many today.

Gandhi and Narayana Guru met once, on 12 March 1925, when the Vaikom Satyagraha was on. Also present at the meeting were C. Rajagopalachari, Periyar, Ramdas Gandhi, Mahadev Desai and a few others. The dialogue was moderated by a lawyer, N. Kumaran.

Gandhi felt that Narayana Guru's 'One People, One Religion, One God' conceptualisation was unfeasible because differences are inherent to existence, and he used the trope of diversity in nature to make his point. He, instead, called for tolerance between faiths. A few days after meeting Narayana Guru, Gandhi had this to say at a public meeting in Aluva:

> Your motto is, 'One community, one religion, one God' ... I feel that the attainment of what is implied by this motto is also beyond our powers. I can understand the principle

> of one God. In spite of our worshipping Him in a million different ways, our adoration finds its way to Him. However, I feel that so long as the human race continues, differences of creeds and religions will indeed exist, since there are many minds and not one. If we look at Nature, we shall find that it is full of diversities and it is through them that the one God becomes many. To expect that at any stage in the history of the human race the world will have a single religion and a single creed is, I think, as good as wishing that the laws of Nature should become topsy turvy ... I feel that human society cannot do without the four-fold divisions of varna and ashrama. Hence, diverse religions and diverse creeds seem to be inevitable. Tolerance should be our aim. If all of us hold uniform views, where then is the scope for this generous virtue of tolerance?[32]

Narayana Guru's vision was far from an unimaginative homogeneous singularity, but for Gandhi to accept his proposition would have meant accepting that varnasharama had no legitimacy. A month later, in a response to a correspondent's criticism, Gandhi said,

> Swami Narayan Guru does not need to be called a Brahmin in order to enable him to be, what he [is] reported to be, a Sanskrit scholar. He who performs the duty of a Brahmin will easily become one in the next incarnation. But a translation from one varna to another in the present incarnation must result in a great deal of fraud. The natural consequence must be the obliteration [of] varna. I have seen no reason to justify its destruction ...[33]

Gandhi's and Narayana Guru's biographers refer to the latter's observation to Gandhi that untouchability would probably not end in their lifetimes, and that Gandhi would need to be reborn to see that happen. But there is an interesting exchange just before this comment.

> Gandhi: Does Swamiji have any suggestions to improve the conditions of marginalised classes besides the anti-untouchability campaign?
>
> Guru: They must acquire knowledge and education and wealth. I wouldn't rush to insist on inter-caste marriage and inter-dining. But they need equality of opportunity to get ahead in life.
>
> Gandhi: Doesn't Swamiji think Hindu religion is enough to help people attain moksha?
>
> Guru: Paths to moksha are offered by other religions as well. For spiritual salvation, Hindu religion is sufficient. People also crave for materialistic freedom.
>
> Gandhi: That will happen.
>
> Guru: Considering its rigidity, for that to happen in its perfection, Gandhiji may have to re-incarnate himself once again.[34]

The brilliance of Narayana Guru lies in his ability to place material needs alongside spiritual growth, not allowing them to compete with one another. He knew only too well that material gain would not happen on its own; it had to be demanded as a right. For an ascetic to speak of wealth as a tool for social equality is unusual. It was, in fact, a profoundly radical proposition. From Narayana Guru's point of view, only when some degree of this equalisation of material circumstances was achieved would inter-caste marriage and inter-dining hold meaning.

In 1934, long after the passing of Narayana Guru, Gandhi said,

> The assumption of superiority of one class over another is a poison slowly killing us. When Narayana Guru Swami enunciated his formula of one caste, one religion and one God, he had, in my opinion, no other meaning in his mind. He said, 'I will not tolerate this assumption of superiority on

> the part of anybody.' I do not recall in my many discussions with him that he had anything to say against the beneficent interpretation of varnadharma that I have given.[35]

Though Narayana Guru did not express disapproval of the varnashrama structure directly, his enunciation of equality was clearly an indication of it. He made this abundantly clear in an interaction with a devotee.

> Devotee: Varna is not caste. Gandhiji says that there is no connection between caste and varna.
>
> Guru: Gandhi may say so based on good deeds. But there is nothing permanent in good deeds. It is always changing. So how can we determine our varna?
>
> Devotee: The conservatives have gained some strength due to Gandhi's views.
>
> Guru: Why might Gandhi say that? Maybe it wasn't well thought out. What good is there in thinking that there is one, except harm? What a tragedy! This belief has not yet disappeared?
>
> [...]
>
> There is no virtue in caste. It hinders the freedom of people. It destroys intelligence. Without freedom and intelligence, how can a profession be good? Our carpenters, blacksmiths, etc., don't know anything. Those who do the same thing throughout in life and do not know anything else in the world will not be able to do any job well. Not everyone has the opportunity to engage in work as per their talents. When that happens, it becomes a matter of doing the work of the caste you were born into. Even if you have no ability or aptitude, you have to do it. When that happens, there is no way to improve the job ... Everyone should have the freedom to choose their own job and study.
>
> [...]

> Devotee: They say that if such a freedom is given, competition will increase. Therefore, the world will have more sorrow than happiness.
>
> Guru: This may be the argument of those who created caste. Those who get all the benefits of caste will say so. It may be necessary for their own benefit that others suffer. Do humans live for the sake of caste and the world? Or is it all for man? If man is destroyed, what good is there in the world? Caste destroys man. Therefore, it is not necessary. Caste does not exist. It is foolish to think that it exists.[36]

Gandhi seems to have ignored this, even though it was obvious in the 'One People, One Religion, One God' framing. Gandhi also reiterated his disagreement with Narayana Guru's 'One God' motto. He said, '[I]n practice, no two persons I have known have had the same and identical conception of God', and the best we could hope for was 'unity in diversity'.[37]

In an article titled 'Dharma and Caste in the Mahabharata', Rudrangshu Mukherjee studies the less-spoken-of 'lower caste' characters in the epic and makes an interesting point:

> The Mahabharata affirms the dominant ideology of Brahminical religion but that affirmation is not unqualified. Through the episodes discussed above it opens up the argumentative space in which the dominant ideology can be contested, even subverted ... By suggesting that the pursuit of dharma could be free from the shackles of the orthodoxy of the caste system, the epic is formulating a response to the message of the Buddha and thereby fulfilling its own post-Ashoka aspirations. It is suggesting, sotto voce, that the pursuit of a moral code by the half-caste, the son of a sudra, and a nishada is possible within the Brahminical religion which has space within it for difference and dissent and even for subverting orthodoxy. The pursuit of dharma and living a life of dhamma as promulgated by the Buddha could co-exist

and even be complementary. Nothing in dharma—a subtle art—is frozen: its pursuit and its wisdom are open-ended.[38]

Two thousand years later, Narayana Guru's subversive creation of a space for those oppressed by Hinduism within the religion's own framework manifested as a creative contemporary actuation of the above argument, albeit not within the brahmanical ambit. He did not demand the demolition of the Hindu faith. Beginning as an advaitin, he found his own path to remoulding Hinduism. He stands apart among seers as someone who shifted the theological, philosophical and social aspects of the faith.

When the untouchability clause was proposed in the Constituent Assembly, it was adopted amidst shouts of 'Mahatma Gandhi ki jai'. Gandhi had support across communities. It was not Ambedkar—a dalit who fought everyone, including Gandhi, for the rights of the untouchables, and the chairman of the Drafting Committee—who was lauded for this achievement, it was Gandhi the sanyasin. Ambedkar had to continually battle this mindset as he strove for social justice. Caste deprives people of personal and collective self-worth, and thus the relative value of contributions to the cause. Even in Ambedkar's own community, many chose Gandhi over him.[39]

Ambedkar himself did not prioritise any faith system. To him, faith did not matter, people did. According to him, the only way to transition to an equal society was by creating structures that secured the vulnerable and questioned the violence of caste. If religion came in the way, it would have to be removed. Since it helps to posit Ambedkar as a harsh rationalist opposite the spiritual Gandhi, even anti-caste voices deny Ambedkar his spiritualism. His reimagination of Buddhism was not merely a strategic socio-political act, it was an emotional endeavour. His spiritual internalisation of equality, of the possibility of sighting that unseen dharma, drove him to demolish every social superstructure that masqueraded as dharmic practice. I cannot help but believe that his resilience and unrelenting efforts towards bringing people together could only have come from a spiritual awakening.

We cannot ignore the fact that in the very same Constituent Assembly, H.J. Khandekar said:

> If we Sudras, today's Harijans, were to name our children according to our wishes we were not allowed to name them like Jawaharlal, Brahmadatta and so on but we could use only Manu. Now today, Sir, we are enacting a law of Independent India under the genius of Dr. Ambedkar, the President of the Drafting Committee. If I may do so, Sir, I call this Constitution the Mahar law because Dr. Ambedkar is a Mahar and now when we inaugurate this constitution on the 26th of January 1950 we shall have the law of Manu replaced by the law of Mahar and I hope that unlike the law of Manu under which there was never a property in the country the Mahar law will make India virtually a paradise.[40]

And then he went on to say:

> Now, Sir, we have embodied an article No. 17 in this Constitution to remove untouchability and I am sure that untouchability will be removed, but I have seen Act for removing untouchability in the Provinces, the Temple Entry Act and the Removal of Disabilities Act passed by the different Provinces in this country. What is the effect of these laws? Not an inch of untouchability has been removed by these laws and, therefore, if this law of removing untouchability remains in the book of Constitution itself, I do not think that untouchability will be removed. If at all the ghost of untouchability or the stigma of untouchability from India should go, the minds of these crores and crores of Hindu folks should be changed and unless their hearts are changed, I do not hope, Sir, that untouchability will be removed.

The dharmachakra symbolises the experience of 'reality' and all the steps that need to be taken for that to happen. I have used the Sanskrit expression 'dharma', but in Pali and Buddhism, it is 'dhamma', and the wheel of justice is the 'dhammachakka'. This second part of the compound word, 'chakka', the wheel of dhamma, needs to be able to move.

The Sarnath Pillar is unlike any other Ashokan pillar; it is grand and exquisitely carved. The other Ashokan pillar with a bell-shaped capital on which four lions are mounted is the Sanchi Pillar. But a dharmachakra did not sit on the four lions. The great archaeologist John Marshall was of the opinion that the Sanchi capital was not of the same level of workmanship as the Sarnath capital. Even in Sanchi, it is the Sarnath capital that is remembered. The pillars around the great Sanchi stupa have various interpretations of the dharmachakra. The Sarnath Pillar, marking as it does the location of the Buddha's first sermon, is the site of the Dhammachakkappavattana Sutta (the discourse that set in motion the wheel of dhamma). Sarnath is the place from where the message of the Buddha began its voyage around the world.

In his sermon, Buddha first articulated the four noble truths and the eight-fold path. The sermon was addressed to five of his old comrades: Kondanna, Assaji, Bhaddiya, Vappa and Mahanama. After the Buddha explained his middle path, it is said that the various realms reverberated with his message and divine beings rejoiced at the arrival of a new way. The wheel of dhamma had been set in motion. We do not know the immediate impact of the Buddha's words on these mystical beings. But in the real world, as Buddha ended his discourse, a moved Kondanna attained enlightenment.

> Then the Buddha expressed this heartfelt sentiment: 'Koṇḍañña has really understood! Koṇḍañña has really understood!'

And that's how Venerable Koṇḍañña came to be known as 'Koṇḍañña Who Understood'.[41]

Perhaps it was for Kondanna one of those moments of utter clarity we experience while listening to music or reading a poem. The difference being that his realisation was permanent, not a passing ray of light. Even before this moment arrived, we had been told that Kondanna was moving closer to understanding. 'And while this discourse was being spoken, the stainless, immaculate vision of the Dhamma arose in Venerable Koṇḍañña: "Everything that has a beginning has an end."'[42]

Though the wheel of dhamma was set in motion by the Buddha's first sermon, some interpreters say that it truly began rolling only when Kondanna realised the import of those words. This idea touched me. Knowledge by itself is useless. It needs to be shared among people. But even that will not do. It must touch their hearts and enter their minds. Condescension is not sharing, and what we hoard is valueless. The Buddha's words became real only because he gave with generosity and Kondanna received with abandon.

In music, gathi and nadai refer to the gait of a musical movement or composition. These expressions not only describe the way musical or textual syllables are spread across time signatures, but also define the nature of the music or poetry. The emotional import is also contained within these forms. Across all gathis there is a constant, and that is the feeling of consistent forward movement. There cannot be stutters, arbitrary gaps or an abrupt stop. There needs to be free and unfettered flow that establishes steady and cyclical momentum—if not, the entire structure will collapse. When the wheel of dhamma was set in motion by the Buddha, it moved generously across all lands in a gathi that invited everyone into its fold, and moved and transformed people. But when we gave ourselves a constitution, we did not let our constitutional dhamma spread far and wide and enter every home.

Within the chambers of the Constituent Assembly, we declared to the world our chosen path. But for the vast majority of us, the words written on those pages have remained abstractions. The constitution has remained the exclusive domain of those who haunt ominous red-coloured court buildings: the specialists, lawyers and judges. The higher up the justice system we go, the more intimidating and obscure its language becomes.

There was a time when the performing arts and the court shared space. Lawyers and judges would agree that court proceedings are a form of performance. A real-life theatrical enactment. Though art and law occupy diametrically opposite domains—one dances to the tunes of feeling, while the other marches to the rhythms of statutes—they do share one word: kutcheri. Evolving from the Hindi expression 'kachehri', in Karnatik music parlance, the word 'kutcheri' refers to a live music performance. Devotional and cinema musicians, too, use the word to indicate a performance. However, the word itself refers to a court or public office. In Tamil, lawyers use the same expression to mean arguments in the court house, 'court kutcheri'. The overlap of meaning occurred because music recitals and issues of law played out in the same darbar. The Marathas ruled Tanjore for about 125 years from 1676, and it is probably during this period that kutcheri became a common expression for musical performances and legal cases. Of course, the king's court hosted many a musical battle too. This intersection is so interesting. The maharaja's court was not egalitarian, yet it was open to settling all kinds of disputes. It was also the stage where music was produced, dancers held sway and dramatists conjured up new stories. Hopefully, this convergence helped legal minds develop an aesthetic sensibility.

Great artists and writers don't need a physically shared space to bring about an intersection of justice and art. Mirza Ghalib found himself in the court room too often for his own good. This is reflected in the generous use of legal terms in his poetry. In Urdu, even life imprisonment (daim ul-habs) sounds amorous. Maybe there is something we can learn from these intersections. Fluidity frees knowledge from its spatial entrapments, and when one comes in touch with another, a new language is born.

The members of the Constituent Assembly may have been erudite and well-meaning individuals, but they did not deliberate upon how to ensure that the ethos of the constitution percolated to India's citizens. Later parliamentarians fared no better. The gulf between citizens and the courts, Parliament and legislative assemblies is as wide as the Pacific Ocean. It is despite governmental inaction that some citizens have educated themselves.

When I discussed this matter with former diplomat and scholar Gopalkrishna Gandhi, he did not entirely agree with me. He believed that the situation was not as depressing as I thought it was. To illustrate his point of view, he recounted an incident from his time as governor of West Bengal. He was visiting a village of bidi workers in the district of Murshidabad. The men were out working. The women and children were making bidis in small, dank huts. The conditions were horrible. In one house, he met young Alwara (name changed). When Gandhi enquired whether she was attending school, Alwara replied in the affirmative. That day, she had to miss school because the governor was scheduled to visit, she said. Gandhi was curious about her school books, and asked her if she could show them to him. From a small box in that tiny hut, Alwara took out a book covered with brown paper. What was the book? To Gandhi's surprise, it was a children's edition of the Constitution of India, and that, too, in English. He gently asked her if she knew what was written on the first page. She promptly said yes, stood up and recited the Preamble in English. She knew it by heart. For Gandhi, this was a transformational moment. He prayed that someday Alwara would become the president of India. While acknowledging that this young girl was an exception, he also felt that the ignorance and disconnect we see around us is reversable.

I was not convinced. 'Isn't it so wrong that, after so many years of independence, Alwara is reading lines that express our promises to ourselves but is living in inhuman conditions?'

'But isn't it true that Alwara's mother was probably illiterate and wouldn't have even read the Preamble? This incident happened over fifteen years ago, and by now Alwara would have exercised her franchise and most likely knows her political rights,' Gandhi countered.

The lions on the capital are no ordinary ones, they are the Sakhya Simha, the Buddha himself. I hope he has watched over Alwara.

The simhas stand guard over the four cardinal directions, communicating the message of dhamma. Their roar reaches the four ends of the earth. While these majestic lions once represented a monarchy, in our adaptation, I would like to believe it represents the people's sovereignty and our own assurance of dhamma through a constitutional democracy. Some people associate the four simhas with equality, justice, liberty and fraternity. Others see in the three visible lions the legislature, the judiciary and the executive. These are easy and convenient connections.

But what of the fourth simha—the one we know exists but remains hidden? It is an unsolved puzzle. Does that lion have anything to say to us? Gopalkrishna Gandhi has offered the most eloquent interpretation of the unseen lion: the fourth lion is the constitutional morality that Ambedkar described. It is our antaratma, conscience. The conscience is invisible, but without it we are incomplete. Unfortunately, we tend to forget that there is a quartet of lions.

Our eyes are drawn to the lions on the pedestal. But what of the bull and the horse on the periphery of the abacus? Hidden from sight, much like the fourth lion, are the elephant and the lion which are on the same band as the bull and the horse. There are many commentaries on the significance of these animals. Perhaps Ashoka was merely continuing an older tradition of associating characteristics seen in the Buddha with these animals. Such as solitude (bull and elephant), courage and confidence (lion), quick to learn and mindfulness (horse), natural and rightful leadership and pre-eminence (bull).

The other, more complicated, explanation comes from Buddhist cosmology. Here is a gist. Indian architectural symbolism connects the temporal with the cosmic, and the Sarnath Pillar is no different. The pillar itself is like the axis of the cosmic world. At the centre of that world exists the Anatotta Lake in which the Buddha is said to have bathed. Its waters flow through four mouths guarded by these animals, one in each direction, and they become four major rivers. There are different versions to this central theme, but in all of them, the bull, horse, elephant and lion are the guardians of the four quarters. This is the ideal world in which the Buddha's dhamma resounds across the universe.

Is a rule by dhamma possible in the real world? Could it be that the king who installed dhamma inscriptions in all four directions achieved this too? In the Chakkavatti Sutta, the Buddha narrates the tale of King Dalhanemi, the wheel-turning monarch. His righteous rule was continued by seven generations of his descendants. The eighth-generation king decided to ignore his predecessors' dhamma. With that began the degeneration of society. Poverty, thievery, killing, lies, slander, immorality, greed, hate and disrespect reigned, and resulted in the reduction of the lifespan of the people and their near extinction. Only when those who remained decided to go back to the old ways of living, and rejected the negativity, could the resurgence begin. But for such a recovery to blossom, a wheel-turning monarch was needed. That was when King Sankha, who followed the principles of dhamma and whose dominion extended in all four directions, emerged.

I am tempted to conclude that Ashoka saw himself as this chakkavattin, the heir to King Dalhanemi and King Sankha. And that, more than a thousand years later, India hoped to usher in the rule of dhamma, giving democracy the place of the just Chakkvattin.

The elephant, bull, horse and lion on the Sarnath capital are seen in motion, pulling along the chariot of dhamma. The elephant we do not see on our emblem seems especially important to me. The symbol of the Constituent Assembly was an image of undivided India, with the face of the Indian tusker on it. But we have forgotten the elephant, the gentle giant who lives nearly across the entire length and breadth of India. The elephant precedes the lion in being part of our heraldry, but is now hidden, even on the emblem.

Within the umbrella of the lion capital exist many individual artistic symbols, one for each state. They are intended to provide every state in the Union with a distinctive identity. Some states have not bothered to invest in the creation of an emblem, instead adopting the lion capital as their motif. Except for seven states and three Union Territories, all other state emblems of India have incorporated the lion capital in their design. Among the states whose emblems are independent of the lion capital, the emblem of Bihar stands out. It is a simple sketch of the Bodhi tree. Prayer beads hang from one branch on each side of the trunk, and there is a svastika on either side of the tree. At the base of the tree is the name of the state, written in Urdu. There is something old-worldly and uncomplicated about this emblem. It is a beautiful coming together of faith and people. The Buddha attained enlightenment under the Bodhi tree in Bodh Gaya, Bihar. I see this emblem as an appeal for awakening in the land where the Buddha awakened. Dhamma, after all, is common to all.

The central image in Tamil Nadu's emblem is an ornate gopuram (temple tower) designed by the artist Krishna Rao on the basis of the west gopuram (temple tower) of the Madurai Meenakshi temple. The intricately sculpted and gigantic gopurams of Tamil Nadu are a delight to behold. Irrespective of who is worshiped beyond the temple gates, everyone who looks up at these towers marvels at their artistry and architectural brilliance. The gopuram is meant to represent the creativity and culture of the people of Tamil Nadu. As far as I know, even the atheist-rationalist Periyar raised no objections to this choice of emblem. Faith had little to do with it, wonderment was everything. The genius of the Tamil people was captured in that image. No one saw it as an unsecular act. Yet, a judge said to me in a private conversation that it felt unseemly that a temple tower should be part of the Madras High Court's emblem in a secular country.

The princely past lingers on too. States like Sikkim, Karnataka and Kerala retained the emblems of the erstwhile kingdoms of their region. They rejected the undemocratic nature of the past by including the lion capital in the design but opted for aesthetic continuity. Uttar Pradesh adopted the emblem designed for the united provinces of Agra and Oudh. Some state emblems include the cereals that are grown in the region. Trees, animals, even butterflies found place in others. States bordering the Himalayas chose to give us a glimpse of the snow-capped peaks that flank their northern extent. Mythical creatures appeared on the emblems of Manipur, Karnataka, Sikkim and Uttar Pradesh. Goa and Maharashtra's emblems foreground the lamp as a symbol of knowledge and glory.

Each newly created state has taken a different design route. Uttarakhand's emblem is drawn with sharp contemporary lines. A very modern depiction of the Himalayas, the Ganga, and the struggle for statehood. Chhattisgarh may be informing us about the electricity the state generates. On the other hand, the Telangana emblem is a coming together of two cultures: the Kakatiya-built arch, Kakatiya Kala Thoranam, and the Charminar. The designs are eclectic. Though the metaphorical meanings of most symbols hover around geographical and cultural beauty, abundance, learning and progress, each of these symbols is an assertion of the state's individuality.

India is a land inhabited by different people and cultures. It is an amalgam of manifold ways of thinking, linguistic imaginations, aesthetic sensibilities, aspirations, historical and social references, remembrances and perceptions of continuity. Every emblem is a statement of self-definition born out of these attachments. But this usually means that there is little or no thought for the people who surround the area that is being framed. Other states and their people become outsiders in this construction. Metaphorically speaking, how does Maharashtra's emblem speak to Karnataka's state symbol?

Unfortunately, these symbolic representations do not allow for porosity. The problem begins with the arbitrary manner in which the borders are drawn. Linguistic boundaries, like all separating mechanisms, are homogenising and create inflexibility. When we define and celebrate our specificity, we knowingly or unknowingly alienate others. Addressing this psychological separation, and in the process, holding the socially and politically powerful to account, requires the self-realisation of dhamma. State governments, when necessary, push back with the Union government, and may even come together to this end. But otherwise, the states function mostly in silos, even indulging in violence and othering. Our imagination of federalism is so trapped in the State vs Union archetype that we forget that being accepting, inclusive and cooperative is every state's responsibility towards every other state in the Indian Union. No form of assertion can be at the expense of another state. Being

Indian must mean that we push into the background all forms of parochialism. This, in the end, is what will keep us together when we are faced with a barrage of flattening nationalistic attacks from the Union government.

But what of the pillar that supports our national symbol of justice? Ashoka had an edict inscribed on it:

> Deva (nampriya) ...
> ... pata (liputa)
> ... the sangha (cannot) be divided by anyone
> But indeed the monk or nun who shall break up the sangha should be
> Caused to put on white robes and to reside in a non-residence.[43]

Ashoka's instructions to the Buddhist sangha may have little to do with our discussion. But it is unusual for a monarch to interfere publicly in the internal affairs of a monastic order, to go so far as to issue a warning. The Theravada scriptures include the Buddha's teachings on monastic accountability. In them, the master lays out ways in which laypeople can question the sangha. If the people find any monks to be corrupt, greedy or spreading hatred, they can stop offering them alms, robes and donations. The public can withdraw support to a monastic order and apply pressure in order to initiate a formal enquiry. But all these actions, the Buddha says, need to come from a place of objective observation and dhamma.

In the Theravada tradition, there is also a reference to Ashoka's teacher, the elderly monk Moggalliputta Tissa, performing a major clean-up of the sangha and expelling no less than 64,000 unruly monks and nuns. The twelfth-century temple in Myinkaba Kubyauk-Gyi in Bagan (Myanmar) houses a fresco depicting Ashoka, seen as one among others asking Moggalliputta Tissa to tell the monks that they need to hold the Uposatha festival.

We do not know if Ashoka was responding to a power struggle within the order—ideological differences or, perhaps, monks wanting to take different paths—when he demanded such unity.

The need for unity and permanence operates at every level of statehood. The fear of breaking away is used as an excuse to keep people in check with strictures and violence. But can a land that uses fear to maintain its territorial integrity be a land of dhamma? Even those who fight for the country do so without knowing what they are protecting. What if the disputes come from a place of dhamma? Should we accept them as just? Will we embrace a redrawing of our identity if dhamma demands it? Around fifty years after Ashoka's demise, the empire splintered. Although, why do I use the word 'splintered'? Maybe people found happiness, safety and freedom in their new and smaller kingdoms.

3

Satyameva Jayate

An Old Truth for a New Motto

I first encountered the tiny declarations we call mottos on my school badge and notebooks. School mottos usually intend to capture the mission or spirit of the institution, in the hope of instilling it in the students who pass through its halls. These maxims could tell us quite a lot about the antecedents of the institution. Those born of religious parent bodies tend to use Sanskrit, Urdu or Latin quotes with some religious or philosophical connection. Of course, non-religious educational institutions might also use such quotes to establish antiquity, but secular schools usually lean towards an educational ideal or social theme, while corporatised schools love words such as 'excellence', 'strive' and 'success'. Across the board—whether colleges or universities, voluntary service organisations, religious or sports bodies—most institutions tend to adopt a motto.

As do nations. When a new country is born, be it a democracy, dictatorship or monarchy, a phrase is chosen to encapsulate its identity or the dream that those in power may have for its future. Some of these mottos leave an imprint on our mind for their simplicity, ambition or profundity, or even for the way the words sound. Botswana and Losetho have mottos that reflect their semi-arid conditions. Botswana's motto is 'Pula!', or 'Let

There Be Rain'. Losetho's includes the prerequisites for a country to flourish: 'Khotso, Pula, Nala', or 'Peace, Rain and Prosperity'. For Cubans, it is 'Patria o Muerte, Venceremos', or 'Homeland or Death, We Shall Overcome', with the emotional uprising of the recent past spilling over into the new nation's symbolism. The phrase is taken from a slogan pronounced by the nation's larger-than-life leader, Fidel Castro. Mottos, like everything else, are born of the spirit of those who are taking over the reins of the emerging country.

The mottos of nations tend to share some common themes: unity, god, liberty, justice, freedom, peace, progress and work. At least on paper, every country recognises the need to come together, have conversations, iron out differences and urgently work towards equality. It is another matter that these mottos may be representing nations torn by civil strife or discriminatory constitutions.

The South African motto is an example of how common phrases can be reinterpreted in an ancient language to reflect indigenous assertion and moral yearning. Apartheid ended in 1994, following which the first non-racial general elections were held in the country. Six years later, on South Africa's Freedom Day, President Thabo Mbeki introduced the coat of arms and motto to his people. After being subjected to violent colonial rule and racial discrimination for centuries, the nascent independent nation chose for itself a phrase that means 'Diverse People Unite'.

President Mbeki said, 'By inscribing these words on our Coat of Arms—!ke e: |xarra ||ke—we make a commitment to value life, to respect all languages and cultures and to oppose racism, sexism, chauvinism and genocide.'

The South African government chose |Xam, an extinct Khoisan language, to craft its motto. This decision not only avoided the controversies that may have emerged from choosing one living indigenous language over another, but by recalling the ancient people of the land and honouring their ancestry, it sought to unite the people of today.

In an interview, Mbeki spoke about an expression used by the Khoisan people which exemplified their civilisational spirit: 'A dream is not a dream until it is dreamt by the people as a whole.'

It is rare indeed for an English phrase to be reinterpreted and repurposed in a long-lost language as a national motto. This effort to find a |Xam voice for an English phrase allows for multiple readings when the expression is translated back into English from |Xam, each one suggesting a different sensibility:

Diverse people unite.
People who are different are coming together.
People of different origins are joining together.
People who differ in opinion are talking with one another.

The mottos of South Africa and Cuba couldn't have been more different, influenced, no doubt, by the nature of the revolution that brought them freedom. They are also an indication that mottos are not mere decorations. When things get difficult, they are at least a reminder to the hopeful that there is a way to claw back to socio-political decency.

In the light of this, is it not surprising that the word 'truth' rarely features in national mottos? Perhaps it is the debatable nature of truth itself, and whose truth is being embodied, that makes leaders wary. Yet, in participatory constitutional democracies, truth must necessarily be an underpinning sentiment. Without truth, there can be no equality, unity in diversity, progress, faith, freedom or justice. On the other hand, the pessimist might argue, why place upon ourselves the burden of truth when we have 'our' truth and convenient truths?

India was not the first country to use 'satyam eva jayate' as its motto. Two tiny kingdoms in Central India—Jambughoda in Gujarat and Baraundha in today's Madhya Pradesh—had also adopted this phrase from the Mundaka Upanishad. Nor is India the only country to centre this ideal. The Czech Republic, and

Czechoslovakia (1918–90) before it, used 'Pravda vítězí' ('Truth Prevails') as its national motto. For a brief period between 1990 and 1992, they went with the Latin version of the same phrase, which is as loaded with philosophical, political and theological underpinnings as India's motto.

The internet informs us that Madan Mohan Malaviya used the phrase 'satyam eva jayate' when he presided over the 1918 Congress session. I have been unable to find the exact phrase in his presidential address or elsewhere during that Congress session. What he did say was:

> In the long past, the memory of which is still cherished, our ancestors had waged the greatest war recorded in our history—Mahabharata—and sacrificed the entire manhood of the nation to establish 'Triumph of Righteousness'. And for thirty years we have been carrying on a Constitutional agitation to obtain some measure of power to administer our own affairs.

It is difficult to confirm if Malaviya said 'satyam eva jayate', which got translated as 'triumph of righteousness'. It is more likely that he used another phrase that resembles it closely: 'yato dharmas tato jayah'. This phrase appears many times in the Mahabharata, and literally means, 'where there is dharma there is victory'. This phrase found its place in our symbolic vocabulary when it was chosen as the motto of the Supreme Court of India. Whether or not satya is synonymous with dharma depends entirely on the context and on how we choose to understand the two words.

At the Congress sessions, 'truth' was frequently thrown about in arguments. In 1909, when he was president of the Lahore Congress session, Malaviya narrated a story about two sages who were at loggerheads: Vashishtha and Vishvamitra. The latter was a kshatriya king who became a sage. Vishvamitra unleashed violence on Vashishtha and killed his hundred children only because Vashishtha refused to recognise Vishvamitra as a brahmin even though the entire world had done so. Malaviya said, 'Vashishtha had realised the truth of the ancient teaching satyam puttra-shatad varam. He valued truth more than a hundred sons. (Hear, hear.) He would not save them by uttering what he did not believe to be true.'

The Sanskrit phrase 'satyam puttra-shatad varam' comes from the Mahabharata, where it is used in a different context. In the grand epic, a fiery and eloquent Shakuntala castigates Dushyanta for not acknowledging her and the child she is carrying in her womb. She says,

> [Building] a lake is better than a hundred wells,
> [doing] sacrifice is better than a hundred lakes,
> [having] a son (child?) is better than a hundred sacrifices
> [upholding] the truth is better than a hundred sons.[1]

In my research, I found only a couple of instances where the phrase 'satyam eva jayate', or something that closely resembles it, was employed. And on both occasions, the context was freedom of expression.

In 1903, while arguing against Lord Curzon's proposed amendments to the Official Secrets Bill that targeted the press, the president of the session, Lal Mohan Ghose, said, 'A great historian and eminent statesman of the last century tells us that "the press may have absolute freedom without danger; *truth alone is formidable; whatever is false is powerless*; and the greater the exaggeration the weaker its effect" [emphasis mine].'

At the 1924 conference, when Gandhi was the president, Annie Besant used the line 'Truth only conquers and not falsehood' while arguing for free speech. This being a translation of the Upanishadic expression 'satyam eva jayate nanrtam'.

In July 1934, Sardar Vallabhbhai Patel was released after spending over two and a half years in jail for a civil disobedience campaign in which he had also brought together the peasants of

Gujarat. On his release, he spoke about the continued suffering of the peasants in Gujarat and Karnataka. He said, 'But from the depths of my soul, comes on every occasion the voice: Truth alone will triumph in the end, but never the forces of untruth and darkness.' *The Hindu* published a report titled 'Truth Alone Will Triumph'.[2]

Patel, it appears, learnt Sanskrit while he was in prison. Gandhi wrote in a letter to his son Devdas, 'Vallabhbhai is studying Sanskrit like a diligent school boy.'[3]

The intriguing question about 'satyam eva jayate' becoming the Indian motto is: who suggested it in the first place? Because of S. Radhakrishnan's serious engagement with the Upanishads, some have speculated that he was the source. Others think Jawaharlal Nehru may have been the instigator. Patel had already used it in public. Did he make the suggestion? There must have been discussions among the country's leading minds, such as Radhakrishnan, Nehru, Patel, Chandrashekhar Azad and B.R. Ambedkar, all powerful voices within the Constituent Assembly. But no record of these exchanges exists. The correspondence between V.K. Krishna Menon and Nehru from this time suggests that various people were chiming in with their opinions.

In November 1948, Menon wrote to Nehru[4] with the recommendation that there should be a scroll below the emblem. He believed that adding a scroll would make the emblem design more 'complete' and 'symmetrical'. He also suggested that the words could be in Sanskrit instead of Latin, which most European countries used for their mottos. The words that he recommended were 'truth, service and honour', adding that 'non-violence' would be hypocritical. Did the 'truth' in his suggestion influence Nehru? In the same letter, Menon also made an unusual point: the addition of a scroll would make it the 'seal of India and not of Ashoka'. It is possible that, among the intelligentsia, there was a feeling that our national symbolism needed some degree of independence from Ashoka.

There can be no doubt that the selection of 'satyam eva jayate' was influenced by the idea of satyagraha—the undaunted, non-violent seeking of, and standing by, the truth. Satyagraha was the vehicle to freedom, the truth of our struggle.

So, to understand India's motto, we must examine what we know of the historical record and reconstruct the possibilities that led to the adoption of our motto.

When the chakra replaced the charkha, it was a recognition of the present, a signalling of the need to move forward. The past was not abandoned; its energies were repurposed. The charkha—a symbol of self-reliance, a method of rejection and protest—metamorphosed into the chakra, the wheel of socio-economic progress. In using the phrase 'satyam eva jayate', the founders might have been pointing to the unprecedented way in which we attained freedom.

India won its freedom through a prolonged conversation between peoples and powers. When Nehru attended the coronation of Queen Elizabeth II in 1953, he gave his first television interview to the BBC,[5] where he was asked, '... why there is so little resentment in India towards the British, in view of our past history. It seems to us India is a most wonderfully magnanimous country. Can you explain this remarkable phenomenon of forgiveness?' Nehru responded by attributing this in part to Indians' inability to hate for 'long or intensively' and in (big) part to Gandhi's contribution. Whether one agrees with Nehru's explanation or not is immaterial. The question came from a member of the oppressor class. He was surprised because, in the normal course of things, the ousting of a colonist is followed by visceral hatred and disassociation. Despite the horrors of two centuries of colonial rule and the violent sundering of Partition, it appeared that Indians had been able to retain some level of philosophical equanimity. Could it be said that, at some unconscious level, the fabric of Indian society had been touched by the method of our freedom struggle?

Or perhaps this is a nostalgic, romantic view. When the British finally departed, Indians were left to deal with the horrors of Partition, not to mention the destruction and poverty that colonial rule had wrought. Unimaginable violence marred the creation of India and Pakistan. Satyagraha failed us at that moment in our history. The entire platoon of Indian leaders, including Gandhi, could do little to stop the retributive violence that engulfed large sections of eastern and western India. People who had marched hand-in-hand to demand the ouster of the British were now cutting each other up. Were Indians then truly truth-seeking in their independence movement, or was it only a temporary coming together against a greater evil?

'Satyam eva jayate' might have been an acknowledgement of this uncomfortable reality. Beneath the high ground of protest against the oppressor, there was a lot simmering—the falsity of religion, tradition, ritual, caste, gendered living and class. Ambedkar, Nehru, Gandhi, Maulana Azad and the other architects of Indian democracy were aware of these distortions and struggled to reconcile their idea of India with the society that they observed. None of these thought leaders attempted to justify the present in the light of the past. They attempted to address the present through a reckoning of what the country lacked. Was their choice of motto then a warning against falling into the trap of self-congratulation and moral lethargy?

Or was 'satyam eva jayate' a prayer for the future? The dream of creating a society that would live by the truth. In the face of the overwhelming challenges that a newly independent India faced, the makers of our constitution exuded progressive idealism. This is evident in the symbols that they chose and in their discussions in the Constituent Assembly. They were urging Indians to become better people, truthful citizens. 'Satyam eva jayate' may also have been referencing our wonderful unifying document: the Constitution of India. It was a document that forced reflection—

not perfect, but carrying within it the capacity for discernment and creativity, and the liberation of the last person standing.

The motto could easily have reflected India's glorious past or its future needs. Instead, we chose a universal principle, evidence of the catholicity and imaginative expanse of our founders.

India was to become an unusual union of states. A more diverse set of people could not have come together, entrenched in their respective pasts, languages, religions, castes and cultures. If India could imbue its democracy with truth, perhaps it would actually work. Despite being a feudal and casteist society divided by religion, most people who took the lead after India won its independence found their way to this spirit of openness. India would not be a walled, insular, antiquated nation. It would be an osmotic region that allowed for the flow of people and ideas into, and from, its land. 'Satyam eva jayate' was an open invitation to the world to participate in this principled democratic enterprise.

Readers may rightly wonder whether my creative interpretations are running away with me. In a conversation, Mbeki said that the South African motto 'is something that every child must grow up saying'.[6] I do not know about people in his country, but it is true that many Indians don't know their nation's motto, or even that there is one.

The motto does not have the recall of the anthem or the flag. Also, it is written in tiny letters under the emblem, is in Sanskrit and is taken from a brahminical text—all factors that make its relatability for the common person that much more tenuous. Only Indians who make it to middle or high school learn of its existence, and even they are not likely to encounter it often again.

Politicians see the motto every day in the buildings they occupy, the vehicles they get around in, and on their letterheads. This does not seem to affect their conduct. Bribery is rampant, votes for money is a norm, bigotry casual and commodification celebrated. Some state police emblems include the motto too, and it is part of their livery. But this does not stop the force from participating in all kinds of violence. The brutal murder by the Tamil Nadu police of P. Jayaraj and J. Benicks[7] in 2020 is an example of the disconnect between the motto and the State's actions. As I am finalising this chapter, Ajith Kumar, a security guard, has died in police custody.[8] In 2023, a group of young boys shared on social media details of the torture they endured at the hands of a policeman.[9] Between 2016 and early 2022, an astounding 490 deaths of individuals were reported either in police or judicial custody in Tamil Nadu.[10] The underlying cause of these deaths and attacks is caste. The number of people from the Scheduled Caste community who are detained under preventive custody in Tamil Nadu is disproportionately high. In 2022, 38.5 per cent of such detenues were from Scheduled Caste communities.[11] It is they who suffer the most at the hands of policemen, who often belong to higher castes. Needless to say, policemen almost never get convicted for their crimes. Between 2017 and 2022, not a single policeman was convicted.[12]

Tamil Nadu often makes the point that it is ahead of all other states in many socio-economic indices, and certainly higher than the national average. What we are not told is that Tamil Nadu has failed abysmally in protecting its most vulnerable. Untouchability still persists in innumerable forms. This is a state where dalits are still stopped from entering temples[13] and from using common crematoriums or cemeteries,[14] and where caste and honour killings are not uncommon. Recently, a young dalit man, Kavin Selvaganesh, was killed for having fallen in love and wanting to marry a woman from a dominant caste.[15] According to the Madurai-based NGO, Evidence, since 2017 there have been sixty-five cases of honour killings.[16] Individuals from dominant and landowning castes groups such as the vanniyars, thevars and kongu vellala gounders are often reported to be the perpetrators of such caste-related offences. Children, too, are indoctrinated into caste hierarchies and taught to function from their caste location from very early on. Dominant caste children believe that they have a licence to attack dalit children. In 2023, a dalit boy and his sister were attacked by their classmates. The reason—his academic proficiency.[17]

But why speak of only Tamil Nadu when this is a national menace? There are official mottos and there are unofficial ones, which are politically embedded into our psyche. Tamil Nadu has projected itself as the land of social justice, and of late used the phrase 'Dravidian model' to symbolise its non-discriminative, inclusive, compassionate development standard. In reality, these slogans ring hollow. Ironically, the Tamil Nadu police wears 'Truth Alone Triumphs' on its sleeve (quite literally).

Can words effect change?

As a young boy, I remember being taken to the crematorium following the death of a relative. I overheard people discussing the pointlessness of life. Wealth, hate, jealousy, avariciousness, competition was all pointless, they said. After all, everyone ends up in the same place, leaving everything behind. When we left the crematorium, another relative said of these dreary ramblings, 'This is called smashana vairagyam'—the detached philosophical wisdom of the crematory ground that disappears soon afterwards. In short, words mean little.

Yet, words have sparked revolutions. The French revolution was built around the cry 'Liberté, Égalité, Fraternité'. Rachel Carson's book *Silent Spring* launched the modern environmental movement. Martin Luther King Jr's 'I Have a Dream' defined the American civil rights movement. We need to hold on to the possibility that words, much like music, theatre and movement, are capable of influence. If not, what is the role of literature or poetry? But, for words to have a serious impact, the individual must be receptive. There needs to be a willingness to embrace a truth that causes discomfort. Usually, such serious engagement occurs in small circles. But even hidebound mainstreamers may find themselves transformed by a word, phrase, poem, essay or book. 'Satyam eva jayate' holds on to that idealism. This was the semantic risk that the constitution-makers were willing to take at the dawn of Indian democracy.

It could be argued that we should have selected a phrase that directly spoke to our reality. Something more immediately felt and material than 'satyam eva jayate'. The motto could have been a reminder of real-life challenges instead of a fantasy. But not everything is driven by pragmatism alone. We have to draw ourselves towards the light, even if it seems distant and unattainable. Because humans are fallible, we will only function in degrees of truth. But being reminded by the written word that truth is our destination, and that truth alone triumphs at the end, can be powerfully motivating. Maybe, over time, we will discard many of our charades and inch closer to this Utopian state, or so we can hope.

I have speculated about the possible intentions and ideas behind the selection of 'satyam eva jayate' in such detail because there is no evidence from that time to give us an inkling of why this phrase was adopted or who was instrumental in making it happen. We know even less about the how, that is, the process of its adoption. The motto is not mentioned even once in the Constituent Assembly or in any of the committee minutes.

To our RTI application regarding this matter, we received an unusual response from the Ministry of Home Affairs. Based on an October 1972 letter[18] from the 'Undersecretary, Ministry of Home Affairs' to all 'State Governments, Union Territories, Secretaries to Governors etc.', the reply stated that the motto was incorporated into the emblem in 1949. The letter also specified the exact position of the motto below the profile of the lion capital. There was no mention of any primary document that was the basis of this claim.

The Hindu reported on 26 January 1950, the day India became a republic, 'The Emblem of our Republic, which is a replica of the Lion Capital at Sarnath will from 26th January 1950 replace the Crown on the State buildings, structures, furniture and the like.'[19]

It went on to describe the emblem in which the motto is mentioned: 'The motto Satyameva Jayąte—Truth Alone Triumphs, in Devanagari script underneath the crest. The Motto is taken from the Mundaka Upanishad, an ancient scripture. It embodies a cardinal principle of Mahatma Gandhi.'

Six months earlier, on 31 May 1949, *The Hindu* had published a press note from the Ministry of Home Affairs announcing that 'Satyameva Jayati—Truth Alone Triumphs' would be the new state motto of India, and it would appear in Devanagari in a scroll under the crest in the seal. In 1947, when the emblem, consisting of a specific perspective of the Sarnath capital, was being finalised, the motto had not yet been decided upon. On 15 December 1947, while reporting on India's new emblem, *The Hindu* said that there would be an 'inscription of some letters' and that the language of inscription was under consideration.[20] A report on 30 December 1947 said that a suitable motto would be included in due course as soon as it was finalised.

On 26 February 1948, in the Constituent Assembly (Legislative), to a question from R.K. Sidhwa about the emblem, Minister of Home Affairs Sardar Vallabhbhai Patel clearly stated that the motto had not been finalised. But there must have been much back and forth during this period. Reports published in Britain about the emblem in early 1948 said that a motto would be decided and included. The cover page of the Constituent Assembly Debates (Legislative) reports for the six sessions that took place between 17 November 1947 and 24 December 1949 are revealing. From the first report of the November 1947 sitting until the last report of the September 1948 sitting, the cover page featured below the emblem the phrase 'Dharmachakra

Pravartanaya' written in Devanagari script in a bold font, with a hyphen between the words. It was designed in such a manner that the phrase was curved upwards, towards the emblem. The phrase itself is the Sanskrit translation of the Pali phrase 'Dhammachakkam Pavattetum' which means 'turning the wheel of dhamma'.

This phrase was obviously under consideration, and used for a period of time, even if unofficially. The choice would have been obvious—after all, the site of the Ashokan capital was where the Dhammachakkapavattana Sutta was delivered by the Buddha. This places in context Menon's comment that the seal needs to be Indian and not Ashokan. Though his letter suggests that no lettering beneath the emblem had been sanctioned, he might have been concerned that 'Dharmachakra Pravartanaya' would be finalised.

Fascinatingly, this phrase continued to be displayed above the Speaker's chair in the Lok Sabha of the old Indian Parliament until we moved to the new Parliament building. R.R. Diwakar noted in his 1951 essay titled 'Dharmachakra or the Wheel of Law': 'Everyone who had a look above the speaker's Chair in our Parliament Chamber on a working day, when the speaker is in his chair, must have noticed the words "dharmachakra-Pravartanaya" in Nagari script shining in electric light all the time.'[21]

It is unlikely that this was accidental. I suspect that someone believed that the person seated in the Speaker's chair and every parliamentarian within the chamber needed to be reminded of their duty towards the dharma of our constitution. How many members of Parliament noticed these words, understood their import or took them seriously is, of course, a different matter altogether.

Let's return to Menon's suggestions regarding the motto and its design. Nehru responded to him by saying that they were finding it difficult to describe India in Sanskrit or Hindi.[22] What were Nehru and his colleagues trying to capture in the words they were searching for? Why did they feel 'satyam eva jayate' represented India? Perhaps India needed a universal moral principle in those turbulent times, a universal ideal to aspire to. The freedom struggle was about truth, and the constitutional project was a search for truth. 'Satyam eva jayate' captured the spirit that the constitution-makers believed was embedded in the Indian ethos and at, the same time, in need of revival.

If I am allowed to speculate even further, it is possible that Gandhi's disappointment at the removal of the charkha from the flag weighed on the decision-makers. With Gandhi's assassination still casting a long shadow, Nehru, Radhakrishnan and others would have naturally gravitated towards words that were dear to him. 'Satyam eva jayate', they are likely to have felt, captured his ideal. I feel convinced that Gandhi's spirit guided the choice.

The Indian government began using both the motto and the emblem even before 26 January 1950. Its press release on 30 May 1949 concluded with: 'The State Emblem and Seal with the Motto will be adopted with immediate effect.' In July 1949, the high commissioner of the United Kingdom in India wrote to the Commonwealth Relations Office in the UK intimating them about the motto that India had adopted, enclosing newspaper clippings.

In the Constituent Assembly Debates (Legislative) report of the first session of 1949 (1–17 February), there are two noticeable changes. 'Dharmachakra Pravartanaya' has been replaced by 'Satyam Eva Jayate', and it is printed within a curved scroll placed just below the three lions. On 30 May 1949, the Ministry of Home Affairs sent out a letter to all provincial governments and chief commissioners with a copy of the press communique; an image of the finalised emblem and motto was attached. In that image, 'Satyam Eva Jayate' was enclosed in a scroll. The *Times of India* published this image in early June.

So Krishna Menon's scroll was included in that version of the emblem. But something changed afterwards. A letter from the prime minister's secretariat to the Ministry of Home Affairs reveals the possible reasoning.

The question of enclosing the emblem in a circle or oval is also linked up with the manner of attachment of the scroll with the lettering. [23]

The emblem-and-motto design of September 1949 was not enclosed. The motto was printed in a straight line below the emblem in Devanagari script. But when used as a seal, it was enclosed in an oval border. Perhaps it was the likelihood of the motto becoming illegible or smudged in smaller sizes that led to the dropping of the scroll. But the Constituent Assembly Debates (Legislative) reports of sessions held until April held on to the scroll.

The last session of the Constituent Assembly (Legislative) took place between 28 November and 24 December 1949. Oddly, this report did not print the emblem or the motto on its cover page.

A correspondence between the Ministry of Home Affairs and the Controller of Printing and Stationery dated 22 March 1949 states that the motto had not yet been finalised. We can, therefore, conclude that the motto was decided upon sometime between late March 1949 and mid-May 1949. By mid-May, there were indications that the government was going with 'satyam eva jayate'. This is evident from the letters that government functionaries received from private citizens about the impending choice.

Sanskrit purists groused, of course. There were complaints that the phrase 'satyam eva jayate' was grammatically wrong, and that the correct expression should be 'satyam eva jayati'. In fact, *The Hindu* on 31 May 1949 published the new motto as 'Satyameva Jayati'. It is likely that some Sanskrit expert in the newspaper's editorial team corrected the text provided by the government. The fact that the *Hindustan Times* published the press note on the very same day with 'SATYAM EVA JAYATE' supports my hypothesis.

The semantic challenge was strong, and came from scholars and institutions alike. A panicked government issued an 'express telegram' on 11 June 1949 to 'stop adoption of new motto for State Emblem and seal for India'.

The Government of India archives have an entire file on issues that cropped up after the public announcement of the motto. Most letters were directed to the prime minister directly, and it appears that a majority of the objections emanated from people living below the Vindhyas. Individuals from Eluru, Hyderabad, Narsapur, Coimbatore, Madurai, Mysore, Bangalore and Pune all wanted 'jayate' to be changed to 'jayati', not only because it was wrong, but also because such a mistake would bring 'disgrace' and affect the 'prestige and honour' of the country.

There were those who had other issues with the motto. One individual from Madras felt 'satyam vada dharmam chara' would be a better choice because the phrase embodied the essence of 'satyam eva jayate' and brought to the table the virtues of righteous thought, action and Gandhi's ahimsa. This would have a positive impact on the functioning of the judiciary and executive. There were complaints about the design and font. The seriousness with which so many citizens engaged with the subject is refreshing to note. It mattered, at least to some people, that we get it right in every way.

Besides the letters received by the Ministry of Home Affairs, it is evident that the debate on the motto was agitating India's intellectual circles too. Sri Prakasa, the governor of Assam and a friend of Nehru's, wrote to him in support of 'satyam eva jayate'. He explained the usage as 'poetic licence' and used quotes from Shakespeare, Kalidasa and Vyasa to make his point. His postscript is worth quoting:

> I am on tour. Rain falls in torrents. Still I feel I should get along. To my surprise, huge crowds gather everywhere and I feel like

> old days all the time. Assam is lovely with everlasting green everywhere and as I think of the old poems of Kalidasa about rain and cloud and Himalayan snows, I feel happy that our poor dear neglected Sanskrit has a chance of coming to its own again in its own land, and I feel so thankful to you for giving it the great fillip that you are doing.

Does this mean that the decision to choose 'satyam eva jayate' was Nehru's?

The government issued a clarification on 27 June 1949. This communique declared that, after consulting scholars, it had been concluded that there was no problem as far as grammar and classical Sanskrit were concerned. Since it was an ancient usage from the Mundaka Upanishad, strict grammatical rules from a later time could not apply, and that it was accepted practice to retain such expressions in their original form. It went on to say that they had scholars look into this issue and consult older manuscripts. There was also, the government said, 'collateral evidence' to show that 'jayate' was correct in Upanishadic form. We have to wonder which scholars were consulted, and whether Radhakrishnan was at the centre of issuing this clarification. In his letter, Prakasa had suggested that C. Rajagopalachari could help resolve this controversy: 'Rajaji, as a great student of the Upanishads should be able to put all doubts at rest.'

By the time Prakasa wrote in, Nehru had already done his due diligence. The prime minister received scholarly inputs from two individuals, Dr N.P. Chakravarti, the director general of the Archaeological Survey of India, and Governor-General C. Rajagopalachari. We don't know if Radhakrishnan was part of this consultatory process. He left for Moscow only in September 1949, when he took over as ambassador from Vijayalakshmi Pandit, and hence would have been in India when the controversy erupted. On 17 June, Nehru instructed the Ministry of Home Affairs to issue an explanatory press release.

Prakasa's father, Dr Bhagavan Das, who received the Bharat Ratna in 1955, chipped in with his authoritative input, albeit after Nehru had made his decision to stick to 'jayate'. He said that the form should not be altered as the phrase occurs in the Upanishads, which are part of the Vedas. And such a usage is permitted. Maybe he was the unnamed 'scholar' the government relied on.

It was an interesting beginning for a phrase that symbolised truth. There are probably Sanskritists even today who find this version of the truth—'satyam eva jayate'—unacceptable.

When Radhakrishnan published his translation of the Mundaka Upanishad, just below the verse that contains 'satyam eva jayate', he also noted that this phrase was the motto of India. And then provided the 'jayati' alternative.

Beyond the realm of official correctness, there were other issues surrounding the choice of motto. The government received letters from an ordinary citizen, a commercial organisation, a theistic order and a princely state—each of them claiming that they had been using this motto from before it was chosen as the Indian motto. They were seeking permission to continue the practice.

The government's answer to S.G. Chavan from Kolhapur whose family had been using 'satyam eva jayate' on their notepapers and envelopes was straightforward. No private citizen could use it, and hence the practice had to stop. The Bombay-based National Advertising Services Limited had been using 'satyam eva jayate nantrtam' since 1946 as part of their logo on their stationery and publicity material. In their letter they said 'they have prior claim', and hence the government should not disbar them from using the phrase. Since the phrase was not a replica of the motto, the government had no objections.

The ruler of Alirajpur (in Madhya Pradesh) was also using 'satyam eva jayate'. King Surendra Sinh wrote to the secretary of the Ministry of States saying they had been using this motto for over a hundred years, and it had been registered along with the crest during the British regime. They also felt that any change would hurt the feelings of their people. He stressed on the kingdom's antiquity and antecedents, founded as it was in 1437 by descendants of the house of Rathors from Kanoj. The government seems to have given in to the request because it believed that the crest of Alirajpur was unlikely to be confused with the national crest.

The final claimant was the Sadharan Brahmo Samaj. They, too, indicated their century-old association with the phrase. They claimed that it was 'Maharishi Devendra Nath Tagore, the brahmo leader and revered father of Rabindra Nath Tagore' who had insisted on including it as part of their creed. He had even published the shloka in 1848 as part of the book *Brahmo Dharma*, they said. The name of their founder, Raja Rammohan Roy, 'the father of the modern age', was also thrown in to add weight to their claim. Their letters also contained a subtle undertone, telling the government that even during British domination there was no interference in their theistic affairs and that they hoped a secular state would not intrude upon the freedom of expression and religious liberty of a religious order and of Indians at large. After having looked at how the phrase was used by the organisation, the government issued a no-objection letter.

St. Stephen's College in Delhi had 'Satyam Eva Vijayate Nanrtam' in Sanskrit and a translation in Hindi below it that read 'सत्य ही हमेशा विजयी होता है, असत्य कभी नहीं' (the truth always wins, never untruth) on the college assembly hall's balcony façade, facing the stage. It had probably been there from the time the building came up in 1941—almost a decade before India adopted its motto. Apparently, a Sanskrit teacher decided to correct the Upanishadic phrasing 'jayate' to 'vijayate'. It was removed a decade or so ago, and has not been put back.

Irrespective of how it came to be, this is a daunting motto. It is necessary, therefore, to investigate the phrase and critically evaluate its meaning.

Before we reflect on whether truth is always the victor, we must struggle with the multivarious understandings of truth. This word, like every other, exists in the temporal, inspires ideas, constructs histories and evokes emotions. It is not universally shared and manifests variously—as claim, reflection, power, defence, sorrow, oppression, victory, love and a range of other factors that run the gamut of human experience. Truth must, therefore, be investigated as something that meanders through society, handled by so many, if we are to differentiate it from its bête noire: falsehood.

Words move with and within people, cultures, geographies, politics, environments and time, evolving into complex beings that evoke diverse responses. A word is not a pictorial combination of lines, strikes, dots, slashes and curves. It comes alive through sound and listening. Vowels, consonants, phonemes combine vocables to produce a range of audible triggers. Body language and facial expressions also contribute to acquired meaning. The truth of any word meanders through these possibilities.

But what about truth itself?

This is the era of rancour, untruths, half-truths and post-truths. We argue that truth is merely a perspective, a point of view that is entirely dependent on our location. Truth as opinion, then? The reasons that drive us in our attempt to know something determine whether we will realise truth. When clouded by hatred, we only want to strengthen the revulsion. Every thought and action that arises from such manipulated seeking becomes a trigger for many more cycles of violence. We remain trapped in a maze of falsehoods.

During the second wave of the Covid-19 pandemic, pyres were burning twenty-four hours a day. The pictures of burning bodies left us aghast. This involuntary, visceral reaction makes it hard to explain what happened next. Instead of asking difficult questions of those in power, as a nation, we turned on those who took the pictures and accused them of insensitivity and being anti-Indian. The Indian government's Civil Registration System's data published in 2025 shows that the excess death (increase over expected numbers based on previous years, 2015–19) was 21 lakh, as opposed to the 3.32 lakh the government had claimed.[24] There can no longer be any doubt that there was a very substantial undercounting of Covid-related deaths. But people have moved on from this 'old news'. Power and immediacy determine our interest in the truth.

In another recent situation, the conscience of the nation appeared to have been shaken by the pictures of women being paraded naked on the streets of Manipur. Righteous anger flowed freely on social media. This lasted for a few days. Two years later, the violence in Manipur continues. Once again, Indians outside the affected area have all moved on. The personal investment needed to continue demanding the truth is too much. This is especially true if we have no social connection or interactions with the people participating in, or affected by, the turbulence. It permits us to discard humanity; the truth becomes irrelevant.

It shouldn't be surprising then, that the ongoing genocide of the people of Gaza gets such little attention. The daily updates and death counts have become the new normal. Further, the normalisation of Islamophobia in our current discourse makes what should have been an urgent national conversation even more marginal.

This demonisation of the Muslim has been cleverly crafted through false tellings in words and images across India. Consider the movies *The Kashmir Files* and *The Kerala Story*. No one can deny that the story of the Kashmiri pandits and of women who were inducted into ISIS must be told. But these movies have little truck with truth.[25] They were made to manipulate the mind to such an extent that the viewer leaves the theatre seeing the devil in every Muslim. The number of movies produced with this intention has only increased, each causing more ill feeling than the previous. The many meticulous fact-checking exercises annihilating their claims do little to mitigate the influence of these movies, the runaway success they enjoy or the official patronage they receive. *The Kerala Story* has also been feted with national awards.

What is the relationship of these filmmakers to truth? Or to the abstraction that art aspires to? Are they abstracting reality? One way to interpret abstraction is as a creative impression of the real. In real life, our own presence is foregrounded at every moment, but an abstracted experience removes us from the picture. Take fear, for instance. We may know when, why and what we fear, but we know little about the fear itself. It cannot be comprehended because of our personal investment in what causes it. Removing our individuality from the experience gives us an opportunity to get near that question—in other words, get closer to the truth of it. Art could be a window to such an opportunity. But a production that connives to exploit a real-world situation squanders that possibility. It fails in abstracting life, only stunting art and reducing it to a propaganda device.

Are fact and truth synonymous? Facts are not approximations, feelings or hearsay, or anecdotal. They are established through a transparent, rigorous process, and stand the test of logical scrutiny. If there isn't enough evidence to establish a fact, it must be presented in terms of probability. However, the establishment of a fact does not fix the truth. Every fact is a trigger, and truth grapples with these triggers, taking into account the various voices, contexts and human vagaries. Truth begins with the critical evaluation of everything that is presented as fact, peeling back every layer of human interaction with it. This evaluation cannot proceed along an organised path that proceeds to a planned destination. As philosopher J. Krishnamurti put it, 'Truth is a pathless land.'

Tyagaraja had this to say in one of his compositions:

chakkani raja maragmu lundaga
sandula duranele O manasa.

Why take the narrow by-lanes
when there is the royal high road.

Tyagaraja was referring to the moral and religious high road. I would rather interpret the raja-marga as the pathless land of truth.

An image of a woman, be it Bharat Mata, Annie Besant, Indira Gandhi, or a picture or drawing of an average Indian woman has so often been superimposed on the country's map that it is difficult for Indians to disassociate the two. Kashmir is her face, the southern states her legs and her saree sometimes drapes the east, extending downward to the northeastern states. The very name India brings to mind its territorial extent. But along the borders, there is nothing in the natural landscape that points to a division of land between nations. Only direction and mileage signs, the presence of the Border Security Force, international checkpoints, fences and warlike dramatics as performed in Wagah remind the viewer that they are abutting the edge of a nation. All astronauts see when they look down from high above the planet is a contiguous stretch of land, deserts, water bodies, mountains and various scales of habitation. A land mass that contains what our maps say are Asia and Europe.

In the map that a Pakistani child studies in school, Pakistan-administered Kashmir is placed within Pakistan's boundaries and not inside India. In it, Indian-administered Kashmir is called

'Indian Illegally Occupied Jammu and Kashmir'. For us, Jammu and Kashmir is that entire piece of land that completes the face of India. Any alteration to it is visually disturbing. The land becomes disfigured; the woman's face no longer fits elegantly on the map of Kashmir.

All countries are abstractions defined by the lines that demarcate them. By instilling that definition in the collective consciousness through political maps, the notion of country is solidified. We claim that the osmosis between diverse traditions and cultures is the glue that keeps us together. But, foundationally, it is this political map that gives us a sense of country. It is the same mechanism that gives us state-level identification. What then is the idea of love for one's country? A narrative is built on a series of historical incidents, politically assembled into a physical form and finally reiterated through a map, and we are then taught to love our country. What are we really loving? And is this constructed love the reason we see our neighbours as the other?

Pakistanis and Indians are taught different histories. Dislike and suspicion of the other is instilled in us generation after generation. Movies, sport and literature contribute actively across generations to ensure that we remain isolated from each other. There are periodic claims of cultural connectivity, but they are strategic and rarely run deep. When the intention is to keep our people separate, the muddy truths and complexities of a shared history will be ignored.

Caught in the vortex of the swirling currents generated by two nuclear powers is Kashmir. The people there have lived through decades of violence, with no end in sight. Even the mention of it is so sensitive that I find myself walking on eggshells. No doubt it is just the same for someone sitting on the other side of the border attempting to talk about it. Under so much self-scrutiny, no one, be it politicians, members of armed forces, bureaucrats or us, common citizens, can think with freedom or speak of

Kashmir with compassion. And yet, ironically, 'freedom' is the operative word for every player in the Kashmir imbroglio. India and Pakistan call each other occupiers, each accusing the other of crushing freedom. But if we want to ask truthful questions about Kashmir, we have to turn the focus away from political and military manoeuvrings to the people of the land.

Ashoka, our quintessential representative of political dharma, must be invoked once again. Though there does not seem to be a historical connection between Ashoka and this region, he finds a place in Kashmiri lore, an indication of his impact on the political histories of his time, and beyond. The seventh-century Chinese Buddhist monk Xuanzang attributes to Ashoka, who 'extended his power over the world, and was honoured even by the most distant people', the credit of constructing four stupas in Kashmir that contained the relics of the Tathagatha.[26] In the twelfth-century, Kalhana in his *Rajatarangini* not only lists Ashoka as one of the kings who ruled Kashmir, but also credits him with having built the city of Srinagari (close to Srinagar).[27] Kalhana says he 'freed himself of Sins and embraced the doctrine of Jina'. Further, that Ashoka was blessed with a son by lord Siva in order to remove mlecchas, or foreigners, from the country. Even a thousand years ago, this question of who belongs and who does not haunted the region.

Ashoka, the consummate monarch, recognised and struggled with the wedge between dharma and power. If he had been a modern-day democrat, would he have done things differently? A hypothetical question that has no answer. If we are to embrace the spirit of Ashoka, we will need to suspend many uncomfortable memories in relation to Pakistan. This is easier said than done. But there is no other way out of this mess—we have to plough our way through and find humanity. Humanity is not parochial, it does not distinguish between people, religions, citizens, non-citizens and refugees.

Kashmir has to cease being a legacy tussle between the two nations. Like Ashoka, India and Pakistan need to publicly acknowledge their failings. If they did so, the creative possibilities are immense. We could then listen to one another, keeping aside our enormous egos. Kashmiris need to be at the heart of this conversation between the two nations. Peace is a courageous act because, in seeking it, we fight our own inner demons. Peace does not just save lives in the present. It puts an end to inter-generational trauma and repeated cycles of violence.

In one of his edicts, Ashoka speaks of harmony as listening.

> harmony is the best,
> what is harmony?
> listening to reflections on Justice
> listening to another's reflections on Justice
> and listening to that willingly[28]

The people of India and Pakistan have to ask themselves: have we listened to the voices from Kashmir? Have we willingly listened to the voices from Kashmir?

All through my growing-up years, I heard the phrase 'Indian culture'. A belief in a cultural commonality that connects all Indians, holding the country together. Ancient civilisational history is trotted out as proof that India is not a modern idea but a continuum of sorts. Many leaders, including Gandhi and Nehru, periodically tapped into this notion in order to stress that the Indian people are inseparable. It was part of the nation-building exercise. The central element that broadly held this idea together was religion.

A religious Gandhi and agnostic Nehru, though very different in their approaches, imagined this culture to include Hinduism, Islam and Christianity, among other strands. They were not interested in the fallacious idea of who were 'original' or had 'first' claim on the land. This fluidity allowed them to carefully select features from different periods, places and texts, and bring them into a singular Indian narrative. The reason they needed to craft such a narrative is obvious. What lay before them was a deeply divided and damaged land. To bring people together, they needed a beautiful shared past. With a secular democracy as the goal, these leaders chose from the past ideals that they wished to instil in the citizens of India, and superimposed these on principles of modern democracy.

The problem with this kind of history-telling is that it can also be used to augment concepts such as 'Akhand Bharat'. Also, it allowed for problematic aspects, such as caste, to be cleansed. Those who believe in a Hindu Rashtra use this methodology too, choosing portions of the past that suit their narrative, and razing the contradictions of history to build a picture of a 'pure' era of Hinduism. Wherever this Hinduism had a footprint, those lands are Indian, they claim. In order to counter the argument that Buddhism and Jainism once dominated our territories, they subsume these faiths within the idea of 'Indic' religions and pit them against Abrahamic religions.

There is hardly anything that binds Hindus across the land—not language, daily rituals, understanding of the environment, gods, modes of social engagement or familial values. The Hindu faith is not the same across regions, or even among different castes in the same region; we are different Hindus. Proponents of Hinduism, particularly those who see themselves as liberal, circumvent this logical problem by calling it a 'way of living' that allows for plurality, if only within an unquestionable superstructure. Even atheists from the distant past who rejected the Vedic heritage are somehow coopted, and their opposition used to prove Hindu openness. The absence of one book or one god is described as intra-religious diversity. Yet, these liberals struggle to imagine a Hindu who rejects the Vedas or the Gita.

This is why we see a strong pushback when anyone criticises Hinduism's brahminical manifestations.

The most dire impact of all this jugglery is the sundering of Muslims and Christians from India's legacy. Hindutva commentators, in any case, demand that Muslims must publicly proclaim that they were originally Hindus. Although it is hard to deny the heavy presence of religion in the social life of Indians, our identity is crafted by much more. The local environment, seasons, vegetation, terrain, forms of livelihood, writings, songs, stories, everyday challenges, distances, the list is long and never ending.

The poet Kalidas said in his play *Malavikagnimitram*:

> पुराणमित्येव न साधु सर्वं
> न चापि काव्यं नवमित्यवद्यम्।
> सन्त: परीक्ष्यान्यतरद्भजन्ते
> मूढः परप्रत्ययनेयबुद्धिः॥

> All that is old does not glitter,
> nor does novelty make a play detestable.
> Gentlemen assay both, then pick one—
> the thoughts of dimwits go with the herd.[29]

It is from this philosophical standpoint that we must boldly call ourselves a modern democratic nation. This land and its people are old, but this country and its spirit are new, unburdened and free. I believe this was the ethos the framers of our constitution held close despite pushback from the old hawks. India is not Bharatavarsha or Jambudveepa. India that is Bharat was born on 15 August 1947 and its dreams inscribed in the constitution that was accepted on 26 January 1950. Only the rights and values we have given ourselves in that modern document can keep all those who are scattered over 36,87,263 square kilometres together.

When I was trekking in Uttarakhand a few years ago, I wondered whether there was any cultural interrelation between the people I spoke to in the villages and myself. There was very little common ground in terms of cultural affinities or shared histories. If I were to find a bond there, it lay in the present, not the past.

In the Mundaka Upanishad, death is seen as part of the never-ending cycle of karma; an interplay of birth, pleasure, possession, grief and loss. Here, death is one perishable aspect of material reality. It is not an end but a perceived momentary pause before another cycle takes over. The realisation of brahman—the truth, immutable and imperishable—leads to the transcending of the life–death cycle. This awakening is not necessarily something that happens after a physical death, it can happen during life too. As the Mundaka Upanishad states, 'One who knows this, my friend, hidden within the cave, cuts the knot of ignorance in this world.[30]

The Upanishadic world is not really interested in the how or why of dying because these reasons fall within the causative trap. All that lives will die. Yet, not all deaths are equal. Indeed, death could be commissioned, ordered, using the vocabulary of justice. We cannot let this pass as just a product of karma.

The phrase 'awarded the death sentence' is used with great regularity. It's an expression that has always made me uncomfortable. The word 'award' is derived from French, meaning 'to decide after due observation', and used both as noun and verb. As a noun, it refers to a prize or recognition. As a verb, it carries emotional neutrality and, when employed penologically, it has the distinct clang of finality to it: was awarded the death sentence.

This triggers a phonetic dissonance. My mind is unable to reconcile the image of the guillotine with the word 'award', the noun and verb forms getting tangled up. The lexical entanglement reminds me of the word 'loha', which Surdas says does double duty:

इक लोहा पूजा में राखत
इक घर बधिक पड़ो

One iron adorns the puja altar
Another the hunter's den[31]

From the kings of lore to modern democrats, those in power have always promulgated laws to prevent human deaths. Punishments are prescribed—impersonal institutional retribution that could vary from solitary confinement and life imprisonment to imprisonment for a certain period of time. They may also involve mental and physical torture, even though it is illegal in almost all parts of the modern world. Denying inmates food and social interaction, verbal abuse, intimidation and physical assaults are all par for the course in prison. Prison officials, too, are victims of the punishment culture and the oppressive environment. Army detention centres seem to be worse. The videos and reports of the treatment of Iraqi and Afghan prisoners by American soldiers are seared into public memory.

In India, there are over sixty offences for which the death sentence can be applied. Along with countries such as China, Iran, USA, Pakistan and North Korea, India retains the death sentence. Rwanda, a country that lost over five lakh people to genocide in the early 1990s, abolished the death sentence in 2007—a move that was seen as a way to facilitate the extradition of those accused of genocide who were living in other countries. Twenty-five African countries have abolished the death sentence, while some others are abolitionist in practice.[32]

Our neighbour, Sri Lanka, a country that endured three decades of armed conflict, when mass killings, attacks and assassinations were all commonplace, has the death penalty in its books. But not one person has been executed for nearly fifty years. In 2019, former Sri Lankan president Maithripala Sirisena tried to bring it back into practice by ordering the execution of four drug offenders. Hangmen were recruited after a gap of forty-three years. But the next president, Ranil Wickremesinghe, assured the Supreme Court of Sri Lanka that he would not sign warrants for their execution.

Taiwan moved in the other direction. Thirty-seven inmates on death row challenged the constitutionality of the death penalty. In 2024, the courts held that the death penalty was legal but also put in place more safeguards. The hope was that this would move Taiwan in the direction of abolishment. Unfortunately, that did not happen. In January 2025, Taiwan executed a person convicted of rape and murder. That was the country's first execution since 2020. According to Amnesty International, as on December 2024, 113 countries had abolished the death penalty for all crimes and 145 countries were abolitionist in law or practice.[33]

There is a lack of accurate data about how many people have been executed in independent India. As per Annexure XXXIV of the 35th Report of the Law Commission of India (1967), the total number of murder cases in which the sentence of death was executed from 1953 to 1963 was 1,410. As per the responses received from central prisons in India by Project 39A, National Law University, Delhi (now The Square Circle Clinic at NALSAR University of Law, Hyderabad), 134 people have been executed in India in the past five decades (1973–2023). However, certain prisons have provided information only for a limited period, refused to provide any information or did not have any records available. As of 2024, over 546 prisoners had been sentenced to death.

In the case of mercy petitions, our presidents have demonstr-ated varying inclinations over the decades. Gopalkrishna Gandhi records in his book *The Undying Light* that requests were made through him to the then president R. Venkatraman, including one from the Dalai Lama, to accept the mercy petition of Kehar Singh (convicted in the Indira Gandhi assassination case). But the president was unmoved.

And finally, after the dreadful deed was done on 6 January 1989, the president went on with his work. Gandhi notes, 'Kehar Singh was a file disposed of.'

K.R. Narayanan was probably not an abolitionist, but after scrutinising the death sentence files, he decided not to reject any mercy petition. A.P.J. Abdul Kalam was the only president who publicly stated his reservations regarding the death penalty, pointing to the fact that it was the poor who faced the brunt of it. He rejected just one mercy petition because he was convinced that the accused was directly responsible for the rape and death of a girl. In the other cases, there was, according to him, 'social and economic bias'. Kalam felt that in most cases, those who were being punished were the ones least involved with the crime. The next president, Pratibha Patil, most definitely leaned towards abolishment. She commuted thirty-five sentences.[34] Pranab Mukherjee, on the other hand, rejected thirty mercy petitions involving forty-two convicts. Ram Nath Kovind rejected six of the mercy petitions that reached his desk.[35]

Since Independence, there has been great progress in our laws and in the legal attitude towards the death sentence. Where once the norm was to award the death sentence for certain crimes, and judges needed to explain why they did not take that route, our system now requires judges to spell out reasons for awarding the death sentence. Though the death penalty is only applicable in the 'rarest of the rare' cases, its implementation is ripe with concerns. Guidelines have been put in place for the manner in which the death sentence can be imposed. The circumstances and mental health of the accused are to be taken into account. Additionally, in 2014, the Supreme Court took cognisance of the torture that inmates are subjected to in prison, including solitary confinement and having to wait years for presidents and governors to decide on mercy petitions. Such individuals, the Supreme Court said, cannot be executed. In 2022, the apex court even put down guidelines for the manner in which information about the prisoner is to be collected before the death sentence is pronounced.

Yet, the reality on the ground is that the death sentence continues to be awarded in trial courts, where citizens go to demand justice, and caste, class and religious discrimination are all-pervasive. According to the *Death Penalty India Report* published by Project 39A in May 2016,[36] which studied the death sentences imposed by trial courts between 2000 and 2015, 76 per cent belonged to the backward classes and religious minorities, 24.5 per cent to Scheduled Castes and Tribes, 61.6 per cent had not finished their secondary education and 74.1 per cent were economically vulnerable.

Evidence of how casual the process is can be seen in the fact that only 4.9 per cent of the death sentences imposed by trial and high courts between 2000 and 2015 were upheld through the appellate process by the high courts and the Supreme Court.

The powerless find it harder to navigate the court system, and between corrupt, inefficient or uncaring lawyers and judges apathetic to social disadvantages, they stand no chance. The few who are able to take their cases up to the Supreme Court are usually supported by legal collectives. Mental health professionals and social workers are not an integral arm of the justice mechanism. Until this integration is recognised as essential, there is a high probability that the disenfranchised will be sent to their death by law.

Over the past decade, the gamut of crimes for which the death penalty is applicable has expanded. After the Nirbhaya incident in 2012, rape that causes death or results in the victim having to live in a vegetative state was brought within the purview of the death penalty. Then, in 2018, the rape of children below the age of twelve was included too. The recommendation of the Law Commission in 2015 that the death penalty must be applicable only for terror offences has been ignored. The general public was jubilant about the execution of those involved in the 1993 Mumbai bombing, the 2001 Parliament attack, the 2008 Mumbai attacks and the 2012 Nirbhaya gang-rape case. It was unnerving to see citizens rejoicing over the killing of an individual. As Albert Camus suggests in his essay 'Reflections on the Guillotine', if executions are a deterrent, then people should be made to watch every execution and it must be broadcast on television.[37] If these are moments to be relished because justice is being served, we should take part in this accomplishment.

Public floggings in countries like Afghanistan and Saudi Arabia are the subject of opprobrium and disgust. Why? Is it only because these State-sanctioned punishments are happening in public for everyone to see? So, is it the public sharing and participation in the violence inflicted on an individual that is considered repulsive? We hide executions from the public because we know that such actions are inhuman, that this is not justice. This is the satiation of our savagery. Army combatants have reported that killing another person is shattering and that, with repeated participation, it strips them of empathy, pushing them into an emotionally dark place. This is why even the nature of the crime is not a good enough reason to sanction the death penalty. The Law Commission felt that terrorism was reason enough; some other countries believe drug smuggling is equally vile. Who is to be the arbiter of what that threshold should be?

When the death penalty exists, every other punishment is placed on a downward scale in relation to it. The wider the reach and scope of the death penalty, the harsher are the laws on the downward curve. The existence of the death sentence also has a psychological impact on how even brutal sentences such as life imprisonment are perceived. This allows governments to pass stringent laws for offences it wants to criminalise.

Every execution chips away at the nation's moral fibre. We watch from the sidelines as a death penalty case crawls up the judicial ladder. Finally, the Supreme Court pronounces a guilty verdict. A few years later, the president rejects the mercy petition.

Then, often for a very long time, the convicted person languishes in jail waiting for the dreaded day. Life in Indian prisons is itself torturous. The hierarchical, violence-entrenched environment takes away every shred of dignity, and the restrictions placed on access to family destroys the mental health of inmates. All of a sudden, one morning, we learn that the individual has been executed. As citizens, we have participated in the systemic destruction of a human life. Eventually, we move on. This numbness is the scariest consequence of legitimising the death penalty.

But how can I be accused of participating in that death when I am not involved in any part of the process that resulted in the execution? The truth is, when I seek to legitimise the death penalty, I have participated. When I brainwash my children into believing in this immorality, I participate. When I remain indifferent and silent, I participate.

The taking of a life is considered acceptable when it satisfies the current social standards. But these standards are changeable. Moral standards are easily lowered by tapping into fears and anger. The grounds for the death sentence may expand. An authoritarian state could lay traps for individuals that it fears, falsely accusing them of crimes they never committed. One of the intermediary stages in this social degeneration is the State equating legal justice and vigilantism. In India, we already see this in action. The killings of Muslims and dalits by mobs as well as attacks on citizens who do not subscribe to the Hindutva ideology have been taking place across the country.[38] The frequent intimidation of minorities in autos, buses, bazaars has become commonplace.[39] Those perpetrating these attacks claim to be protecting their country. They are standing in for a failed police force, judicial system and society. Indeed, state governments themselves play vigilante when they raze the homes or buildings of those they see as the 'other' without due legal process.[40]

In April 2023, a convicted gangster-cum-politician was shot dead outside a hospital in Uttar Pradesh while he was guarded by the police.[41] Political commentators saw nothing wrong with the incident—for many, a killing is a crime only if the victim is 'innocent'. This is the logic that the police have been using to legitimise encounter killings. It is a gang warfare understanding of justice.

A society that largely approves of the death penalty is also one where violence of various grades is justified. For all the complaints about the failure of our judicial system, the death sentence is perceived as a rare occasion when the courts get it right and complete their job. The logic being that the convict can no longer use loopholes in the law to subvert justice.

The disgust with which hardened criminals are viewed also needs introspection. Their entire life is reduced to their crime, everything else is wantonly erased. The voices of death row inmates are never heard. Their thoughts, aspirations, dreams are deemed irrelevant. Such single-minded demonisation empties them of any human qualities. But they, too, had friends and family, possibly watched the same films we did. We may share many traits and interests with them. It is these commonalities that we do not want to face up to. It scares us that they are people just like us. If life had not dealt us a good hand, a family, education, congenial circumstances and a supportive environment, we might have been one of them. Many of us may have momentarily stumbled but found our balance. The death penalty eliminates this sort of critical revaluation of our thoughts and actions.

As for the retributive demand for death that comes from family members or friends of the victims, it is emotionally understandable but beyond the scope of justice. Justice is an abstract weighing scale; it is civil society that needs to hold the hand of those who have lost someone to violent crime. Psychological support and care must be available to those in need of it. As long as retributive thinking prevails, the death penalty remains acceptable. Murder becomes justice.

The existence of a form of punishment that is entirely irreversible must trouble us. Even the Supreme Court has not been consistent or even-handed when it comes to the death sentence. In 2009, it admitted that fifteen persons had been wrongly sentenced to death.[42] Unfortunately, Ravji Rao and Surja Ram were executed before the Supreme Court declared that their cases had been wrongly decided. Who is to be held responsible for their killing? After the advent of DNA testing, it has been found the world over that many convictions were wrong, caused by flawed investigations, prejudiced officers or judicial processes, even the pressure of public opinion. Many people have lived for decades in prison, wrongly convicted, until they were proven right and finally released. These individuals can at least expect to experience life beyond the prison. But what of someone who was wrongly executed?

Every so often, there are discussions around more humane methods of execution—switching from hanging to the lethal injection, for instance. But the experience across the world has been that often, this process is botched up and the prisoner is put through horrifying agony. According to Professor Austin Sarat's book *Gruesome Spectacles: Botched Executions and America's Death Penalty*,[43] published in 2014, out of 1,054 executions by lethal injection in the USA, seventy-six were botched.

In conversations around the death penalty, one person is conspicuously absent: the executioner. Whether it is death by hanging or a needle, someone has to make it happen. Someone has to end a life as a few others watch. What happens to the mind and life of the executioner? Does the executioner find it hard to enjoy moments of ecstasy, happiness, love and romance, which most of us take for granted? This too must be investigated, for it is another kind of execution, one with a blameless victim. Just as the convict is dehumanised, so also is the executioner.

Even as our courts grapple with what constitutes the 'rarest of the rare', India must face up to the only two truths that matter in the context of justice: no authority is infallible, and a life once taken cannot be returned.

Kamban, the legendary Tamil poet and author of the Tamil Ramayana, described the kingdom of Kosala in terms of truth and lies. He wrote, '*Unmai illai poiurai illamayal*' (There is no truth, when people speak no lies).

The meaning of a word truly comes to life when the opposite exists. And in the case of truth and lies, I fancy that falsehood came first. Allowing my fancy to take flight, let me present to you a possibility. A set of cave dwellers looking for food find an abundance of deer in a specific location. Initially there was enough for everyone. But as the numbers of the prey dwindled, the mind of the early human began correlating need, availability and survival. Initially, group members fought with each other, even killed one another over food. Then they discovered a new and far more subtle method of winning. Some of them did not share information with the others about where food was available or a hunt would be successful. Lies were born.

Over millennia, as our needs and desires multiplied exponentially, we built lies upon lies. Some of these lies also manifest as destruction. In the way we aggressively and wilfully pollute the planet. In how narrow-minded territorial nationalism has darkened our hearts. And how we fight bloody wars over land, culture, language and faith.

Each lie is a tear that further diminishes the possibility of a safe and kind future. Changing this demands acute reflection, selflessness, kindness, grace, patience and sacrifice. But to even move away from our perversions, we first need a baseline. An idea that we can adhere to, a promise we will keep. Truth—a non-parochial ideal—is probably a good starting point. With truth come courage, love and comradery.

The Mundaka Upanishad does not dwell upon the truths that we have been struggling with. Using many analogies—such as the sparks that emanate from the fire, the spider that weaves its web only to take it all back in, rivers that flow into the sea giving up their identities, and two birds seated on the tree, one of them embodying universal consciousness and the other the personality-centric conscience—the Upanishad tries to unpack the truth about existence. It attempts to shed light on the illogical separation between the creator and all of creation. We do not come from anywhere, neither are we going anywhere.

'Satyam eva jayate' is one part of a phrase that appears in the third and last chapter (Khanda One) of the Mundaka Upanishad, which is believed to be for ascetics. Mundaka means shaven-headed.

> *satyam eva jayate nanrtam,*
> *satyena pantha vitato devayanah*
> *yenakramanty rsayo hy aptakama,*
> yatra tat satyasya paramam nidhanom
>
> Truth alone conquers, not untruth.
> By truth is laid out the path leading to the gods
> by which the sages who have their desires fulfilled
> travelled to where is that supreme abode of truth.[44]

Until now, we have gone with the widely used translation of the phrase 'satyam eva jayate': truth alone triumphs. If we include the last word in that line, 'nanrtam', the translation would read: truth alone triumphs, not falsehood. Some translators have used the word 'conquers' or 'prevails' instead of 'triumphs', but the import remains the same. And yet, if we make a few changes to the way we comprehend this line, its import transforms dramatically.

In most interpretations, 'satyam' is taken to be the subject of the line. Scholars such as M.A. Mehendale and Patrick Olivelle have suggested that 'satyam' is the object and not the subject. The subject, they affirm, is a person, in this case, a rishi or sage. The issue is grammatical, yet with a philosophical underpinning. Atmanepadas are verb endings which are reflexive, meaning the benefit of an action goes to oneself. Parasmaipadas are verb endings with an active voice, where the benefit accrues to another. In this case, 'jayati' is a parasmaipada verb, and 'jayate' an atmanepada verb. If 'satyam' is taken to be the subject, then the verb expression has to be 'jayati' because 'satyam' cannot triumph for itself. At the same time, triumph of the truth is a temporal event, and hence there needs to be a recipient of the triumph. This quagmire is resolved when we understand the subject as the sage, the beneficiary of the triumph. Such a sage is victorious because they follow the truth: satyam eva jayate.

This shift resolves the jayate vs jayati debate. It also makes the motto even more relevant—not merely the disincarnate 'truth' that triumphs, but embracing all humans who unabashedly seek the truth. Mehendale and Olivelle explain that, in this context, the 'real' and the 'truth' are synonymous and refer to the ultimate reality, not truth in an everyday sense. This once again shifts its meaning. Mehendale translates the line as: 'The sage only obtains the real, and not the unreal.'

The real is revealed by a reflective way of living, the unreal becoming irrelevant. Much like truth in Kamban's imagined Kosala, the real here is the natural state. As a thought experiment, if we imagine the subject to be all people and not a select few, the line would then read: everyone only obtains the real, and not the unreal.

4

Jana Gana Mana

A Song and an Anthem

In the Karnatik music tradition, composers occupy a unique position. A composer is described as vaggeyakara—one who has ideated what is said (vak, the lyrics) and sung (geya, the music). For someone to be recognised as a vaggeyakara, mastery in these two primary aspects of the song is a prerequisite. In addition, the verses also need to follow certain pre-established rules of prosody, rhyme and alliteration. Traditionally, vaggeyakaras had limited social exposure, but within their context, they observed the world and gave expression to it in musical verse—the masters among them did so with elan.

But a composition does not come alive unless it is sung over and over. Through repeated renderings by artists across generations, it acquires musical and social meanings. In some sense, the 'original' is just the first layer. The song comes into its own when other dimensions are added by musicians who are captivated by its beauty and potential, that is, its inherent capacity to expand meaning both in music and word. Only when this last prospect is robust in the composition's internal structure does it transcend specificities.

Some songs seem captivating at first, but turn out to be temporary crushes. Neither in lyrical structure nor in musicality do they allow for a new and dynamic imagination. Art is not the display of an end product emanating from one artist. On the contrary, art is the gift of imagination offered to the receiver by artists.

In Karnatik music, the business of attribution is messy. We learn that a song was composed by a vaggeyakara who lived a few hundred years ago. The name of the raga (melodic framework) and tala (rhythmic structure) in which the song was originally composed is documented in a manuscript or etching. But the actual music—delineated in notations or carried forward through the oral tradition—does not exist. It is lost in the sands of time. In such a situation, musicians do one of two things. Either they tune the lyrics in the specific raga and tala mentioned in the document or reimagine the song in a raga and tala of their own choosing. The musician is free to choose either route—yet, the song is still entirely attributed to the 'original' vaggeyakara. This is the case with all the songs of Purandara Dasa (fourteenth to fifteenth century), though the music for his compositions may have been created later, in the nineteenth or twentieth century. Since Purandara Dasa was a person of eminence, the song is endowed with ancient authority. And the contribution of the contemporary tunesmith who gave the words their modern life goes unrecognised.

A very different situation arises when the poetry of a non-vaggeyakara is put to music by someone else. Irrespective of whether the poem was conceived as a song or not, it transforms into one. The tunesmith enters the mind of the poet and suffuses the words with musical fragrance. An arduous task, but one that can at times elevate even ordinary poetry. The great Tamil scholar and teacher Meenakshi Sundaram Pillai sternly directed his student—the legendary Tamil researcher and scholar U.V. Svaminatha Iyer, who lived in the nineteenth century—to choose between learning music and Tamil. The former, he believed, contained low-grade Tamil that would adversely affect his pupil's linguistic education. To the linguistic snob, musical literature is lowbrow. At the same time, music has been known to add lustre to the most exquisite literary work. In such cases, surely the song is a product of both the lyricist and the tunesmith? Unlike film music, where the contribution of both individuals is acknowledged, in Karnatik music, the poet is referred to as the vaggeyakara, even though they only wrote the words. For example, most people do not know that the popular tune for the Tamil poet C. Subramania Bharati's lilting poem *Chinnanjiru Kiliye* was composed by C.R. Subbaraman. Programme sheets just say 'Composer: Subramania Bharati'.

When a song written 200 years ago is brought to life in a different world by another person, its meaning is altered. The music moves the meaning in a direction that caters to the social and aesthetic sensibilities of its time. When we receive this composite song—a creation of different times and emotional spaces—where does the meaning lie and what is the meaning that is sought to be communicated? The song activates many registers. Impressions form both at an individual level and, as shared notions, at the level of communities.

A song is not static; it ambles through the societies it lives in. Songs can also, for no clear reason, fade out of those spaces. *Saare Jahan se Achcha*, written by Mohammad Iqbal, is rarely heard today. Yet other songs find their way back. Faiz Ahmad Faiz's *Hum Dekhenge*, written in 1979 as a protest against Pakistani dictator Zia-ul-Haq, circulated largely within left circles in Pakistan and India, particularly in Iqbal Bano's fantastic rendition of 1986. In 2019, though, the song gave aesthetic life to the anti-CAA movement in India. It now embodies meanings that even Faiz could not have envisaged. That is the quality of art. It doesn't belong to the first creator alone, and is destined to change hands and travel unforeseen paths.

The trigger in this case was a complaint filed by a faculty member of IIT Kanpur, who claimed that portions of the song were anti-Hindu. That single act brought the song to life. A new generation that never knew of the song now owns it. It has been translated into more languages than Faiz would have imagined in his time. As much as *Hum Dekhenge* is a powerful protest call, it also disturbs the establishment. Its aesthetic pliability, as well as the possibilities that it opens up, make the powerful uncomfortable.

There appears to be a larger social agreement that some songs should be set in stone and evoke only certain sentiments, no matter who sings it and when. Every culture has songs that fulfill this need, but every country has only one such song. We call it the national anthem.

Singing the national anthem evokes a sense of pride. Even in those among us who are not card-carrying nationalists, it stirs something. There is a remembrance that stimulates our emotional and sensorial palette. Musically, anthems may not possess any spectacular facet, yet the melody and rhythm urge us to respond with respect. *Jana Gana Mana* evokes in me a strange feeling, of being indebted, and I feel overwhelmed and teary-eyed, as it connects me with this ambiguous idea that is the nation. My mind insists that it is not ambiguous, that the affiliation is definite and unquestionable. I've pondered this for so long, but I am still unable to understand why I feel this bond. The nation is not merely our location on the world map; it is something more—a feeling. Memories of the freedom struggle, names of leaders, borders, cultures and wars are no doubt links that establish the bond, but these only substantiate the feeling. Whether we need to create such identities is an existential question, and beyond the scope of this essay. Even if we accept that the feeling exists, we still need to reflect on what it is and why we feel it.

All nations are a creation of the mind, the consolidation of a set of chosen imageries and notions. They are political extensions of the need to create groups of similar people. Similarity is subjective, and established by the dominant through the systematic creation of power structures. We build a set of unifying indicators, connect disparate ways of life, design symbols and knit a binding storyline. The physical extent of the land is demarcated by political borders, and there you have it—nationhood. To establish this artificially constructed reality as the truth, it is essential to define the insider and the outsider.

For the insider, the nation is home. As the aeroplane levels off in the air just before landing in the construct we call 'India', I feel a sense of lightness, a smile coming on. The landscape, colours, buildings, streets, bustling traffic become clearer as the plane descends. When we touch down, I fall into the lap of safety. Home is warmth; I can even smell it in the air. But does every Indian citizen feel this way? Does everyone belong as I do? The answer is an unequivocal no. Those who do not tick one or the other box of 'Indianness' are pushed to the brink. These identification marks do not come from the constitution; they are socially and culturally positioned, picked up selectively and arbitrarily. There are many Muslims, dalits, transgender people, the residents of the Northeast and of Kashmir, who are angered by our favoured idea of India.

The struggle for freedom from the British gave us a readymade design for nationhood. The outsider was obvious, but the identity of the insider tenuous. It was inevitable that a land ridden with caste inequalities, religious differences and many princely states would struggle to find something that kept it together. Political leaders, philosophers and theorists came up with their own ideas of togetherness, each prioritising different times of history and reinterpreting texts to formulate a new present.

Perhaps it was inevitable that a Hindu-majority country would have demands for a nationhood based on Hinduness. Yet, even within this sphere, there were divergent opinions, ranging from utmost tolerance to unabashed fascism. The nervousness generated by these interpretations is evident in the counter movements that emerged, especially from among the Muslim and dalit communities. Without delving into the details of these historical tugs of war, it is important to keep the various ideological struggles in mind to understand the fissures in our nation.

Since nationhood has no physical reality, it needs representation by something that is seen as unsullied and pure, and can evoke intimacy, like parenthood. Parenthood denotes emotional constancy and dependency, and its near sanctification is unique. It is no surprise then that most countries refer to their territory as fatherland or motherland. Not knowing the identity of one's parents is seen as not having an identity, a lack of antecedents. The weightage placed on parenthood is found on every application form. The response to 'Who are you?' includes the names of one's parents (or at least that of the father), the place of birth and present dominion. Here, too, not everyone is equal. If a person belongs to a marginalised community or lives in a stigmatised suburb, they run the risk of being ostracised or otherwise disadvantaged. Motherland and fatherland are only extensions of a dominant social construct, which means they only include a select group. Even so, fatherland and motherland are, to my mind, very different registers.

In most societies, social ancestry is confirmed via the father. A 'bastard' does not have a 'legitimate' father—the mother not being enough to confer social respectability and ancestry. Often, in order to receive a tribal community certificate, only proof of the father's tribal identity is accepted. Hence, it is the fatherland that links citizens with their nation's old or original inhabitants. This originality is determined by ethnicity, language, religion, race, colour and culture, among other things. Defining such a homogenous beginning is like chasing a mirage, yet, a certain era is chosen as the dawn of the nation's history. The fatherland is a unifying symbol that gives citizens a glorious past to hold on to—a past that is established through folklore and tales, both historical and fantastical, and passed down from one generation to another. These stories crystalise into the physical, social and cultural qualities that the fatherland is then said to embody. Citizens see themselves as the carriers of that legacy.

The motherland, on the other hand, is a tender, compassionate caregiver to everyone who lives within her realm. Legitimacy is sought through the idea of one common mother—not an individual woman, but an obscure idea of womanhood constructed by men. People buy into this abstract and glorified idea of a mother who stands beyond and above all real women. Motherland is evocative because motherhood represents creation. Despite our modern, scientific understanding of conception and childbirth, the enigma associated with it has not dissipated. Even the contemporary discourse on essentialising motherhood has been unable to dismantle its distinct resonance. This idea of maternity is superimposed on the relationship between citizens and the nation.

Seen like this, motherland seeks an umbilical unification, while fatherland looks for social congruence via a homogenous genesis.

If we are truly seeking a motherland or fatherland for humanity, then there is only one place to go: Africa.

The United States of America steers clear of ascribing a gender to the nation. It has, over the years, used the term 'homeland', one that possibly fits a country of immigrants. But 'homeland' is not a congenial expression. For who is accepted as a homelander? In 2002, a year after 9/11, the US Department of Homeland Security was established. A coming together of different federal departments, it became a supremely powerful arm of the federal government, endowed with sweeping powers. In the recent past, we have witnessed the arrest and deportation of many allegedly 'illegal' immigrants from the US. The prescriptions for how the US government expects an immigrant to behave are only getting more and more stringent and invasive.

Most problematically, the term 'homeland' does not recognise Native Americans as the original residents of the land. The US came into being as part of what the white man called the 'New World'—one of the places they plundered and then went on to call homeland, the land of opportunity.

The Indian motherland was constructed in the later part of the nineteenth century, embodied as Bharat Mata. The idea of a mother goddess who secures and protects a specific region has long been present in various cultures. Fisherfolk, forest dwellers and many other communities have had protective goddesses. But the idea of a specific goddess to represent what was then undivided India was new. She was conceived of as strong, beautiful and protective; a reminder to Indians of her glorious past. And a visual cue to fight all those destroying her, the evil outsiders. If she regained her rightful place in the minds and hearts of the people, the result would be freedom for all of them. Bharat Mata became a deity who gathered everyone together for a mission: Indian independence.

Bharat Mata was probably first articulated in the satirical piece 'Unabimsa Purana' by Bhudeb Mukhopadhyay, published anonymously in 1866.[1] Her visual origins may have been non-confrontational, but by the early twentieth century, she started becoming a physical symbol of the Indian subcontinent and a stanch Hindu figurine.

The most common image of Bharat Mata today is of a bejewelled and crowned goddess Durga standing in front of a lion. She holds the Indian flag in her left hand, the right raised in a blessing. In the background is a map of India. The demarcation of Indian territory on that map varies, depending on the date of the print or painting. In the more fanatical Hindu adaptations, the Indian flag is replaced with a saffron one and a political region that extends from Afghanistan in the northwest up to Indonesia in the southwest is coloured in saffron. Sometimes her saree drapes this entire region, which is referred to as 'Akhand Bharat', a claim to a continuous, unbroken, larger India on the basis of the various Hindu kingdoms that ruled these regions at different times in history.

Sometime between 1904 and 1905, Abanindranath Tagore gave Bharat Mata a matchless visual form.[2] It is the work of great artists to create a little doubt in rigid minds. They do not demand change, instead inviting us to pause and reflect. Abanindranath's Mother India is not a decked-up goddess. No roaring lion waits for her to climb on and vanquish the foe. There is, in fact, no enemy in sight. She does not lay claim to any piece of land. Dressed in ochre, she stands looking slightly to our left, her feet placed as though she's about to take a step towards someone. She isn't raging or angry, not smiling or upset, neither is she asking for help. She stands in peace. In her four hands are a piece of white cloth, prayer beads, sheafs of grain and a manuscript, representing shelter, faith, food and learning. Bharat Mata stands before us as a carrier of goodness. She may be a Hindu ascetic, but do true ascetics belong to any one religion?

Tagore's Mother India is a renunciate, asking everyone who looks upon her to give up anger, hate and division. She is addressing the schisms in Indian society as much as she is urging a coming together. Since there is no claim to land, there is no outsider.

What prompted Abanindranath Tagore to create her? It was a time of turmoil and separation, with Bengal having been split by the British government in 1905. Was Tagore asking questions of the kind of nationalism that was emerging even in the early 1900s, especially in Bengal? I am not a historian, but his Bharat Mata makes me think about what and for whom I am fighting. And to ask: who is the enemy?

Yet, this pictorial metaphor, too, was open to parochial sentiments. It is hard to deny that even this representation of Bharat Mata could be seen as representing the all-embracing Hindu sentiment—and isn't that quite often placed in opposition to Islamic bigotry? This painting was part of the larger artistic response to the partitioning of Bengal by Her Majesty's Government, which included songs, poems, flag designs and slogans, and is, therefore, not just another art object.

Though the British were the primary opponents, there was at the time one other target for the majority community: Muslims. The relationship between Hindus and Muslims had long been fragile. Depending on the region, its weave varied. Phases of bonhomie and discomfort followed each other very closely. There were always those who systemically and culturally aggravated the hate and others who sought to bring people back to their senses. Peace depended on the balance of power between these groups.

Symbols allow for consolidations within resistance movements, and Bharat Mata became an inner mechanism for powering the Hindu community. From the beginning, this image of Bharat Mata and the slogan 'Vande Mataram' were coupled.

'Vande Mataram' was a cry for freedom against the tyranny of the British in Bengal, a rallying slogan during the anti–Bengal Partition movement. Aurobindo Ghosh and Rabindranath Tagore adopted that phrase, with Ghosh calling it a mantra. The slogan spread like wildfire across the land, bringing Indians together, but simultaneously seeding separation.

The slogan was borrowed from the first line of a song written by Bankim Chandra Chatterjee. Historian Sabyasachi Bhattacharya dates the song to between 1872 and 1875. Some other narrations place it between a tighter time period of 1874-

75. When we say 'the song', what do we mean? The first two stanzas were penned in this period. The rest seems to have been written later, when Bankim wrote his novel *Anandamath*, which was published in 1881. Should we treat *Vande Mataram* as one song? An idea worth exploring, especially because the remaining stanzas were religiously charged, and by the late 1930s, leaders of the Muslim League were reacting to the song with angry discomfort. Unlike the brilliant phrase 'Jai Hind', devised in the early 1940s by Abid Hasan of the Indian National Army (INA), the result of a conscious effort to create an inclusive greeting, 'Vande Mataram' the slogan that emerged from the song, carried a lot of baggage.

Before we go on, I'd like to clarify that the stanza divide of *Vande Mataram* in this book is based on Aurobindo's translation and Bhattacharya's definitive book on the song. Here is the first stanza in Aurobindo's well-known translation:

Vande Mataram
I bow to thee, Mother,
Sujalam suphalam
richly watered, richly fruited,
Malayajashitalam
cool with the winds of the south,
Shasyashyamalam
dark with the crops of the harvests
Mataram.
the Mother!
Subhrajyotsana pulakita yaminim
Her nights rejoicing in the glory of the moonlight,
Phullakusumita drumadalashobhinim
Her lands clothed beautifully with her trees in flowering bloom,
Suhasinim sumadhurabhashinim
Sweet of laughter, sweet of speech,
Sukhadam varadam mataram.
The Mother, giver of boons, giver of bliss.

This stanza, like many songs or anthems, describes the natural beauty and bounty of the motherland. It also has an inherent aural softness. This comes from the wonderful use of the consonants 'sa' and 'sha' in the prosody. These consonants evoke a feeling of softness especially among people who speak languages that have a close connection with Sanskrit: sujalam, suphalam, shitalam, shasyashyamalam, shubhrajyotsana, suhasinim, sumadhura, sukhadam.

The descriptive warmth of these words is striking. In the very last line of the first stanza, anthropomorphism kicks in. Motherland becomes a person: the mother who is endowed with sweet speech and laughter: suhasinim, sumadhurabhashinim. She is a person of love, compassion. One could interpret this as a reference to the multitudes of languages and dialects in the country, and the beauty in all those who consider India their home. But this interpretation needs to be tempered.

Saptakotikantha kala kala ninadakarale
Terrible with the clamorous shout of seventy
million throats,
Dvisaptakoti bhujaidhrita kharakaravale
and the sharpness of the swords raised in twice
seventy million hands,
Ke bale ma tumi abale![3]
Who sayeth to thee, Mother, that thou art weak
Bahubaladharinim
Holder of multitudinous strength
Namami tarinim
I bow to her who saves,
Ripudalavarinim
to her who drives from her the armies of her forearm
Mataram.
the Mother!

In the second stanza, Bankim is frontally nationalistic. Bharat Mata is a fierce protector of her land and children. Another significant move away from the first stanza is in its materiality, a sharp shift in imagination. Bankim identifies the mother in a geographical and political location and even enumerates her children. Bankim's geographical and political radius was limited to the Bangla spectrum, so her population is only seven crore—based on the population of the Bengal Province. Though strength and valour are attributed to Bharat Mata, Bankim might be alluding to the people as the true, fearless warriors. They have raised their swords and are ready for battle, so do not underestimate them. This is a stanza of self-belief. Quite brilliantly, the mother is an external device used to urge strength from within every person in the land. This fluidity allows for understandings from both directions. Every individual can garner strength from the mother as much as they can from their compatriots.

There is, however, some linguistic jerkiness in this movement away from the voice of the first stanza. The change in intentionality and content affects the acoustic nature of the poetry, and this is perceptible especially when the poem is heard as a song, even by non-Bengali and non-Sanskrit speakers.

In his letter to Jawaharlal Nehru on 26 October 1937, Tagore wrote,

> I am reminded that the privilege of originally setting its first stanza to the tune was mine when the author was still alive and I was the first person to sing it before a gathering of the Calcutta Congress. To me the spirit of tenderness and devotion expressed in its first portion, the emphasis it gave to beautiful and beneficent aspects of our motherland made special appeal so much so that I found no difficulty in dissociating it from the rest of the poem and from those portions of the book of which it is a part, with all sentiments of which, brought up as I was in the monotheistic ideals of my father, I could have no sympathy.[4]

Most scholars point to the year 1896 as possibly the first time *Vande Mataram* was rendered at a Congress session in Calcutta, and suggest that Tagore may have been the singer.

Tagore had been present at previous Congress sessions too. He attended the reception that followed the 1890 Calcutta session, for instance, and rendered the song *Jai Bharater Jai, Gao Bharater Jai*, written by his brother Satyendranath. It is said that Tagore also attended and sang at the 1886 Congress session. Indeed, it is a peculiar fact that the only time Tagore is mentioned in a creative role in the Congress session reports is when he opened the 1917 session in Calcutta with an invocation in English, 'Thou hast given us to live'.

Two very significant points emerge from that letter to Nehru. Firstly, Tagore had set to tune only the first verse. Secondly, he was bowled over by its poetic elegance. But his claim that he was the first to set music for *Vande Mataram* is questionable.

The song may have been first set to music and sung sometime between 1876 and 1881. According to Bankim's biographer Amitrasudan Bhattacharya, when Bankim was in Hooghly, a government official named Kshetranath Mukhopadhyay composed a tune for the song. Bhattacharya even goes on to say that Bankim had to alter the lyrics slightly in order to accommodate the tune. So, that might have been the first attempt. The tune was set in Raga Malhar. There is also a record of the song being rendered at a public meeting in 1882.

There is yet another claim: that the first tune was composed by the respected musician Jadunath Bhattacharya from Bishnupur. Bhattacharya had given Bankim some music lessons and was a music tutor to members of the Tagore family. Jadunath seems to have been a musician of great ability who died young, in his early forties. Rabindranath and Jyotirindranath apparently composed a few Bengali songs based on his tunes. Before Jadunath, the musician Priyonath Kathak is said to have also tried his hand at setting the song to tune, but Bankim was apparently not pleased with the outcome. He preferred Jadunath's tune. Unfortunately, no notation of his version remains. From these accounts, we gather that Bankim was highly invested in the musicality of the poem. It is said that Bankim did not have a pleasant voice, but he played the harmonium very well and his sense of rhythm was impeccable. It would be fair then to assume that the first musical rendition was in Raga Malhar, and that is how Bankim wanted it.

Why Raga Malhar, though? *Anandamath* contains a reference relevant to this discussion: 'At that moment, Bhavananda said, "We have got to jump in this deadly current, brothers, which of you dare? Now come let us sing 'Bande Mataram!'" Then in full throated chorus in loud Megha-mallar tune keeping time with the boom of cannons the Santan army sang "Hail Mother!"'[5]

Nares Chandra Sengupta renders it thus: '"Into this fire have the children to jump today." Said Bhavananda, "Comrades sing now, who can 'Hail Mother'." Then thousands of Children sang aloud "Hail Mother" in the deep strains of the Meghmallar tune and to the time of the Canon's roar.'[6]

The choice of Malhar must have originated from Bankim's mention of the raga in the novel. When musicians speak of Raga Malhar, they usually mean Miya Malhar or Megh Malhar. Unfortunately, the original tunes are unavailable.

In November 1905, a version of *Vande Mataram* in Raga Malhar and set to Kawwali Tala (eight-beat cycle) attributed to Raicharan Mukherjee was published in Jogendranath Sharma's book *Swadesh Sangeet*. A study of this notation which was republished in *Ranbindrasangeete Swadeshchetana* in the year 1986[7] reveals that, though the raga mentioned is Malhar, its phraseology is not that of Malhar. There is a small possibility that it represented some obscure version or variant of the raga, but that seems quite unlikely. Even a reinterpretation of some of the notation does not yield Malhar. At times it strays into Raga Desh's melodic territory. The mention of a raga as a verse's melodic identity is not always musically true. When a tune is different from the attributed raga or melodic designation, its historical value and impact are altered. The change in aural identity is not merely misinformation, but a factor that impacts the song's very value, import and impact at a certain point in history. Hence, it is important that an attempt be made to reconstruct the song, and actually hear it. Similarly, though Kawwali is mentioned as the tala, the composition feels rhythmically loose and might have been rendered in an unregimented manner. Despite these technical anomalies, I must say that the tune is indeed melodious. It was much later that *Vande Mataram* was imbued with the fragrance of Malhar. In 1951, Pannalal Ghosh composed a tune based on Mia Ki Malhar for the film *Andolan*.

In 1885, *Balak* magazine published a tune for *Vande Mataram*, with the melody based on Raga Desh. Just a year later, in 1886, a collection of songs, *Sangeet Kalpataru*, compiled by Baishnabcharan Basak and Narendranath Datta mentioned raga Raga Tilak Kamod for *Vande Mataram*. Narendranath Datta, of course, is none other than Swami Vivekananda. According to Devajit Bandyopadhyay, a theatre activist who is deeply involved in the revival of Bengali art music, in the year 1883 *Anandamath* was staged at Grand National Theatre in Kolkata. The music for *Vande Mataram* was composed by the music director of the play, Debakantha Bagchi. He set it in Raga Tilak Kamod. The notation was published in *Surer Roop*, a book of Debakantha Bagchi's compositions.

Sima Bandyopadhyay, in her publication *Ranbindrasangeete Swadeshchetana*, says she has published what is most probably the same tune as the one published in *Balak* in 1885, and attributes the music to Pratibhasundari Devi of the Tagore family. But this was the work of Rabindranath Tagore. In 1900, a nearly identical notation was published in the book *Shotogan*, published by Rajagopal Chakroborty for the Adi Brahmo Samaj of Kolkata.[8] That notation is attributed to Tagore and Sarala Devi Chaudhurani, his niece and a political activist. The *Balak* notation has only the first stanza of *Vande Mataram*, while the *Shotogan* version has all the four stanzas in music. A study of the melody of the first stanza in both publications reveals that they are foundationally the same, though there are differences in a few notes and variations in embellishments. There is, though, one major shift: in the way the lyrics are spread across the rhythm. In both notations, the rhythm for the opening lines and the first stanza is a four-beat cycle. But the *Shotogan* version allows for more pauses and a slightly wider spread of the words, making the song slower in pace. A further slowing down is heard in Tagore's own vocal rendition which is now available for listening thanks to the internet.

Tagore's singing of the first stanza was published in 1906 by Pathephone, the gramophone company. The recording that one can listen to online does not present Tagore as a great singer. In fact, he eschews some of the faster and slightly complicated melodic phrases notated in *Balak* and *Shotogan*. This is a staid version sung by an untrained singer. Yet, I feel that, beyond the fact that he employs the aural terrain of Rabindra Sangeet, which is uncomplicated and languorous, there is something to Tagore's rendition that is truly expansive. He begins with 'Vande' at the Shadja (Sa) in the upper octave and then gradually descends, gently cajoles 'mataram' as he ascends a few svaras before finally settling on the Rishabha (Ri) in the middle octave. It is a yearning, a cry of desperation, not a battle cry. Tagore's *Vande Mataram* feels like it is being rendered from the foothills of the grand Himalayas as he stretches his hands forward, uninhibited, welcoming his mother into his arms. This intimacy is ever present in the sound. His singing has the quality of an azaan asking everyone to surrender to god.

Tagore was in his early forties when the song was recorded, but his voice sounds like that of an older man. It has an otherworldly quality, like an ashariri, the disembodied conscience that guides us when all seems lost. This is Tagore's *Vande Mataram*, perhaps even at a remove from Bankim's. Poems and songs are merely readings until they are sung. When they glide in tune, each syllable blossoms, taking in greater space than language accorded them. In these melodically moving vowel extensions, the motherland's tenderness lingers—an experience Tagore adds to by singing in a non-rhythmic, free style. The gaps between words and lines are open-ended and unequal. It is as though he does not care whether anyone is listening; we are just privileged to have been allowed to listen. It is obvious that Tagore had initially composed music only for the first stanza. I think it would be fair to assume that, sometime in the last decade of the nineteenth century, he and Sarala Devi put to music the rest of the song.

Sarala Devi herself sang *Vande Mataram* in 1905 at the Indian National Congress session in Banaras. The session report mentions the rendition by Mrs Dutt Chowdhury (Rambhuj Dutt Chowdhury was her husband) along with other ladies. She replaced the word 'saptakoti' (seven crore) with 'tringshakoti' (thirty crore) since that was the population of India.

Sarala Devi described the event in her own words.

> After my marriage, at the Banaras Congress presided over by Gokhale, I was seated on the ladies' stage on the second floor of the pandal. Lady Abala Bose was by my side. Suddenly a request came from the audience to Gokhale for me to sing 'Bande Mataram'. Gokhale was in a quandary. Earlier, the magistrates had banned the singing of 'Bande Mataram' in meetings in some parts of Bengal. Gokhale followed the path of caution. He wanted to work in line with the government and not against them. But what could he do? But he had no option. He could not ignore the desire of the delegates from all over India to listen to the song 'Bande Mataram'. Then Gokhale sent me a short note requesting me to sing and also instructed me that as time was short I should not sing the whole of the long song, but just a part of it. I don't know what

> part he intended to cut, I cut a little from the middle and said 'thirty crores' instead of 'seven crores' and presented the rest of the whole song to the audience, and the hearts of listeners were in turmoil. Those who are still alive among the patriots from all over India who were gathered on that day have not forgotten the song of that day.

Even before this lyrical change was introduced by Sarala Devi, other grammatical alterations had been made to the song.

The Visva-Bharati chorus rendition of 1945 has only the first two stanzas. But there are some significant differences between the *Shotogan* version of the second stanza and the Visva-Bharati chorus rendition.

It is most likely that Bankim wrote the third and fourth stanzas when he decided to bring the song into his novel *Anandamath*. In 1937, at the height of the debate regarding *Vande Mataram* and its status as a national song, Tagore wrote to Nehru. The first two stanzas were entirely acceptable to him, he said, but he disassociated himself from the rest of the song. He said he could understand why they might hurt Muslim sensibilities given the context, '... but a national song though derived from it which has spontaneously come to consist only of the first two stanzas of the original poem need not remind us every time of the whole of it, much less of the story with which it was accidentally associated'.[9]

Nehru said something similar in turn to Ali Sardar Jafri in his letter of 1 September 1937: 'Nor are we concerned with the idea that the author of the book, which contains this song, had in his mind when he wrote it, because the public does not think on those lines.' He also felt that the song as a whole and its words were 'harmless' and 'nobody can take exception to their meaning'.[10]

Tagore's attribution of accidentality to the song's role in the novel *Anandamath* is inaccurate because the song did play an important role within the narrative.

I have been unable to find any commentary by Tagore on the lyrical content beyond the first stanza, but yet surmise that when he refers to the song's 'tenderness', he meant only that one stanza. It is clear that Tagore's fascination for the song, besides its historic catalytic role, lay in the magic of that stanza.

Vande Mataram in *Anandamath* was a political device that necessitated the writing of the new stanzas. But Tagore's personal affiliation with *Vande Mataram* and admiration for Bankim made it difficult for him to accuse the author of weaponising his own song. Sabyasachi Bhattacharya has observed that the song comes in at crucial moments in the story: 'Below the surface of the novel there is this moral core and this is where the song marks the moment of significance. If we analyze the narrative in this way, it may explain the centrality of the song in the novel, apart from the obvious didactic function of the song.'[11]

It can be hypothesised that Bankim saw in the second stanza a possibility to turn the song into a Hindu nationalistic outcry, a sensibility that *Anandamath* cradled. Oral history[12] suggests that Ramchandra Bandopadhyay, who proofread *Bangadarshan*, a literary magazine started by Bankim, came to him asking for matter to fill up a page in the magazine. He saw a piece of paper lying on the desk and read it. It was *Vande Mataram*. Bandopadhyay felt the song was not bad and could be used. Bankim, who is said to have been annoyed with this suggestion, put the manuscript away, replying that the value of the song would be realised only later and that he might not even be alive when that happened. Another version of the same story has Bankim prophesying that the significance of the song would be realised twenty-five years hence, and that the song would become the Bengali anthem. One more account of the story has Bankim quickly writing the first two stanzas just to fill up space in a forthcoming issue.

Anandamath is set in the late eighteenth century, during the Bengal famine. In the story, Bankim frames the issue around one primary evil: the tyrannical Islamic ruler Mir Jafar. But the revolutionists who call themselves 'children of the motherland' are not only fighting an oppressive power. The entire Muslim community is their enemy, and the intention is to get rid of them. They attack and kill Muslims, pillaging and setting fire to their homes and villages. Some scholars have suggested that the conflict is political rather than religious in nature. But the words and actions of the characters make it very difficult to accept such an explanation. *Vande Mataram* is the symbolic, aesthetic and emotional cog that drives an angry religious fervour. It is the song of initiation for new volunteers joining the band of Hindu sanyasin warriors. Without a doubt, it is a call to preserve 'Hindu' culture—a violent, anti-Muslim war cry. There is nothing congenial about its role in the novel. Within this context, the song's direction changes, its invocatory affection is lost. The British are accused of allying with the Muslims and are treated as something akin to collateral damage. Ironically, the novel ends with the hope that the British will continue to rule. In other words, the British traders (East India Company) need to become administrators. In the final scene, a mystical saint explains that it is only through the reign of the British that Indians can educate themselves and gain material knowledge. This, he says, can then lead to the acquisition of interior knowledge and the establishment of the one true Hindu religion.

One translation states it thus: 'The Santan rebellion has come only to put the British on the throne.'[13] Another thus: 'The rebellion was raised only that the English might be initiated into sovereignty.'[14]

According to Sureshchandra Samajpati, when he asked Bakim which of his novels he loved the most, he did not name *Anandamath*. 'I said to him, "as a patriotic work *Anandamath* is superb". He replied, "In that sense it could be said that the novel is good, but there is little art in that."'[15]

This observation says something about how Bankim viewed his novel after many years had passed.

In a letter to Subhas Chandra Bose on 20 October 1937, Nehru said, 'I have managed to get an English translation of Ananda Math and I am reading it at present to get the background of the song. It does seem that this background is likely to irritate the Muslims.'[16]

This letter was sent about a month and a half after his letter to Jafri. A change in opinion after having read the book is evident, even if 'irritate' seems too mild an admonishment of the song's new context.

Despite his obvious love for *Vande Mataram*, Tagore certainly recognised the problem with the song. In response to Bose, he wrote in October 1937, 'It is so evident that Bande Mataram is in praise of goddess Durga that it cannot be up for debate. Although Bankim has tried to portray Goddess Durga as symbolic of Bengal, no Muslim will accept the ten-handed idol of goddess Durga as a symbol of their country.'[17]

At the same time, he was upset with the attitude of both Muslims and Hindus. He went on to say, 'Witnessing stubborn fundamentalism from a certain section of Muslim Bengalis has become unbearable to us. Similarly, when we become stubborn with our immoral demands, it is a matter of embarrassment and shame. In this is our defeat.'[18]

And finally, in a postscript, he struck an advisory tone. 'Bengali Hindus are agitated about this, but the matter is not limited to them. Wherever the anger is deepest on both sides, there is need for objective judgement. In the service of our country, we need peace, unity, and good wishes—we do not need endless competition around victory or loss against the stubbornness of either side.'[19]

The impact of the novel and the later emergence of 'Vande Mataram' as a galvanising slogan must not be underestimated. Even those who read the novel may not have immediately recognised its potency. In his book *Banglay Biplab Prachesta*, Hemchandra Das Kanungo attributes the birth of his own revolutionary sentiments to *Anandamath*. He does not remember when he first read the book, but recalls watching its performance sometime before 1902. When he read it again, it 'unknowingly' left a 'lively and intense' effect on his mind. He goes on to say: 'Many years later when the history of the Indian freedom movement will be written, this attempt at revolution, enacted in imitation of Bankimchandra's *Anandamath* may or may not be worthy of mention, and even if it is, it may be dismissed as being laughable; but the works of Bankimchandra "Bande Mataram" will be inscribed in the brightest of letters.'[20]

The impact of the slogan remained. *Ananda Bazar Patrika* used 'Vande Mataram' on the masthead of the opinion page right from its inaugural issue in 13 March 1922.

To me, as a musician who views *Vande Mataram* as a musical object, the aesthetic incongruence between the first two verses and the added stanzas is clear as day and night. Fundamentally, there is no musical continuity between the stanzas. When I use the word 'musical', I am not referring to the melody, but the musicality in the lyrics. If we listen to the cinematic version of *Vande Mataram* composed by Hemant Kumar for the 1952 movie *Anandamath*, it is obvious that some words of the second stanza are left hanging, while others are rushed through. This cannot be explained away as a stylistic phenomenon. There are innumerable film songs from that period which are poetically and musically in sync.

The second stanza of *Vande Mataram* does not even flow in the manner of the first. It is the change in the lyrical structuring of the second stanza that opened the gates for what followed in the third and fourth stanzas some years later. They are aesthetically further removed from the opening stanza. The use of Bangla lines that have their own independent inner rhythm in between the Sanskrit also makes it a song with too many starts and stutters. Right through, especially in the second, third and a large portion of the last stanza, the song remains unsettled.

I have heard some fifteen-odd versions of *Vande Mataram* in different tunes and genres ranging from the classical to the cinematic, and choral to instrumental music. Some renditions contained only the first stanza, some the first two, others the entire song. It is my opinion that all attempts to render the four stanzas together as one composition have musically failed. They do not fit or move together. Each stanza works on its own, but when put together, it is disjointed and the song falls apart. One can quite literally hear the tunesmiths struggling to present it as one cohesive aesthetic creation.

The inconsistencies in the syllabic length of the lines also do not help. There are dense lines, some far less wordy, some long and others very short. These variances can only work within a musical form if they come together cohesively; in this case, they do not. This makes it very hard to place the entire song comfortably in one rhythmic structure, or even place it elegantly across a few different rhythmic structures. The tala designated by Tagore and Sarala Devi is pherta, which indicates that the song is set to multiple tala structures within the composition. In other words, the tala shifts according to the measure of the lyrics. As an aesthetic possibility, this is not necessarily wrong.

In the Karnatik tradition, we have a set of poetic songs called the Tiruppugazh. When rendered as music, the tala is structured to match the length of each word individually and of the line as a whole. But there is consistency between the lines. Each line comfortably falls into some rhythmic structure, which allows for easy transitions between each of the rhythmic frames. The problem with *Vande Mataram* is that, except for the first stanza and a few later lines, the lyrics do not naturally fit into any rhythmic framework. They need to be artificially placed in position, and all movement between stanzas is forced.

The Tamil nationalist poet Subramania Bharati translated the song twice—first in 1905, and then again in 1909 with a note that said, 'I had earlier translated this in a poetic form called

Akaval. But I realised that was not conducive to be performed as a song and hence I have now retranslated it in this form.'[21]

On 23 November 1907, the journalist Henry Wood Nevinson was witness to the Tamil rendition of *Vande Mataram* by a small boy on the sands of Madras's Marina Beach. The song was sung at a meeting organised to celebrate the release of Lala Lajpat Rai and Ajit Singh.[22] The rendition must have been that of Bharati's first translation of *Vande Mataram*.

That Bharati took a second shot at translating *Vande Mataram* seems uncharacteristic. Bharati's own poetry oozes musicality. You could pick any of his poems and it would be singable. There is no struggle with lyrical prosody, flow or measure, and you could adapt his words to any genre of music. This is not true of all great poetry. There are deeply impactful poems that collapse as musical creations. It would appear that Bharati was unhappy with his first attempt and recognised that it needed constructional changes. He had used many old Tamil words in the first translation, which he minimised in his second version. We also have to keep in mind that Bharati himself used the phrase 'vande mataram' in his songs that paid homage to 'Mother India' such as the composition *Vandemataram Enbom*. One has to wonder then if this redrafting of the Tamil translation of *Vande Mataram* by Bharati says something about Bankim's original. Or was it just a problem with the translated text? At any rate, I can't help but feel that Bharati returning to his translation with dissatisfaction is more than just proof of his diligence.

Dilip Kumar Roy gave us two musical versions of the song, one rendered on his own and the other a duet with M.S. Subbulakshmi. Let us analyse the latter carefully. The four stanzas could have been rendered as four different songs because nothing binds them together. The metre in the second stanza shifts uneasily and is then interspersed with '*ke bale ma tumi abale*', which obviously does not fit within the chosen rhythmic form. Hence it is sung loosely. The next lines follow in a semi-rhythmic set-up. Roy has tried to connect this stanza with the refrain 'vande mataram', but the transition is abrupt. The next stanza settles into a lovely gait with a wonderful change of raga, but every third line needs adjustment because the poetic metre is uneven. By the time we get to '*Twam hi Durga dashapraharana dharini*', the song has lost form. One could argue that the divergence in melodic and rhythmic texture in each stanza is tactical. If that was the case, when brought together as one song, there should have been bridges that allowed for crossovers and returns. There is none here. I do not believe this was Roy's fault. Sometimes musicians feel compelled to bring into musical form songs that have a socio-political significance. It is very difficult for them to say in such a situation that the song or poem does not work. I fear that *Vande Mataram* in its full form is one such entity. All said, the rendering is captivating because of its two singers.

It is probably for the best that most people only know the first stanza of the song: the section that is free of social burden and is aesthetically splendorous. The Desh version of that stanza, now ubiquitous, is definitely based on Tagore's tune, but the music for the phrase 'vande mataram' was melodically inversed and a few other changes were brought in. The first line of Tagore's version descends from the Shadja in the upper octave; in the popular version, the song rises to the Shadja in the upper octave, albeit with a repetition of 'vande mataram' because of an interim stop at the middle octave Panchama (Pa).

If we recognise *Vande Mataram* as only a cog in the *Anandamath* narrative, our perception of its musical incongruity is altered. The act of reading and visual picturisation turns it into a part of a theatrical performance or a dance ballet. In this form, the song responds to theatrical possibilities in ways that a standalone song would not (and need not). A song can be written as a social, spiritual or political response, or as part of a story or dance composition. Each of these intentions gives the composition its form, structure and spirit. Once *Vande Mataram* became the voice of the Hindu sanyasins in *Anandamath*, it became a different beast, both in political import and aesthetic form.

I speculate that the first stanza was an instantaneous outpouring. The second stanza, consciously constructed, finalised the song's political, social and historical direction. In the first stanza, Bharat Mata was closer to what Abanindranath imagined her to be. But there are hints in the second stanza that she might transform into a different goddess. As the song progressed, she became the populist Bharat Mata, the mother goddess with the country's map in the background and the lion as her vahana. It is possible Bankim recognised the song's storytelling potential and waited for the story to emerge. If this is true, it would make sense that he placed the song within a novel. In fact, that is where it belongs if we are to consider the entire song as one piece. The moment I recognise it as one aspect of a telling, my criticisms of literary style and musical inconsistency vanish. The constant shifts between styles, languages, syllabic content, emotional direction and meaning make sense.

Dilip Kumar Roy and M.S. Subbulakshmi also directed my attention to something I had missed in my earlier reading of the song, which was that the last line of the fourth stanza flows beautifully into the refrain. The music, language and mood in the line '*Namami kamalam amalam athulam sujalam suphalam mataram*' matches perfectly the first stanza. Bankim may have written these last lines keeping in mind the need to turn back to the primary refrain. Hence this sudden emotional, linguistic and ideological flip back to the old.

By the 1930s, Bharat Mata had become Durga, a goddess in a temple holding ten weapons. The motherland had become a deity.

For Muslim leaders, the song became unacceptable as a national song because of the monotheistic nature of Islam. Combined with the plot of the novel and the use of the slogan 'Vande Mataram' by Hindu nationalists, it had become a loaded cultural object. Poet and writer Harivansh Rai Bachchan remembers seeing special issues of Bengali magazines around Durga Puja where the song was printed next to the picture of the goddess. He noticed Muslims leaving when the song was played, which he felt was understandable. *Vande Mataram* had travelled the length and breadth of the country, and had been translated into several other languages. It had become much more than a Bengali nationalistic song serving the cause of the anti–Bengal Partition movement. In this new position of musical power, *Vande Mataram* was a peg on which the already developing fissures between the Hindu and Muslim communities were accentuated.

In the early days of the twentieth century, all anti-colonial activists, whether Hindu or Muslim, despite areas of discomfort, were largely united in their opposition to the partition of Bengal. By the early 1920s, communal tensions had become overt, blowing up in the 1930s. Meanwhile, the independence movement had gained enormous traction and was rapidly moving towards the final act. In the Indian National Congress session of 1927 held in Madras, the issue of Hindus holding processions and singing in front of mosques and Muslims slaughtering cows were seen as serious enough to be slotted for discussion. A resolution was passed calling on both communities to not resort to violence and to desist from such provocative actions.

In an essay titled 'Our National Anthem',[23] published in 1948, Harivansh Rai Bachchan speaks about what *Vande Mataram* meant to him as a twelve-year-old. Until a few years earlier, he had been trained by his school teachers to sing and listen to the song *Bhagwan, Hamare George Pancham Ko Chirayu Keejiye* (God, please give long life to our George V) with respect and admiration. Bachchan blamed it on a slave mentality. In 1919, when he joined a Kayasth pathashala, he heard *Vande Mataram*, which was sung every day before school work began. On one occasion, when he was humming its tune at home, his uncle said, 'By singing *Vande Mataram* this way, do you want us to get caught?' This reaction told him it was a song that needed to be taken seriously. Slowly he comprehended the Vande Mataram movement, an inference probably to it being a symbol of rebellion against the Raj. Bachchan, in fact, thought it was the national anthem.

In 1939, Gandhi, too, recalled the unifying history of the song:

> No matter what its source was and how and when it was composed, it had become a most powerful battle-cry among Hindus and Mussalmans of Bengal during the partition days. It was an anti-imperialist cry. As a lad, when I knew nothing of *Anandmath* or even Bankim, its immortal author, *Vandemataram* had gripped me, and when I first heard it sung, it had enthralled me. I associated the purest national spirit with it. It never occurred to me that it was a Hindu song or meant only for Hindus.[24]

Gandhi used 'bande mataram' or 'vande mataram' as a sign off in some of his letters from around 1911 until nearly the very end of his life. It might have been Gopal Krishna Gokhale, with whom Gandhi had been corresponding since the late nineteenth century, who brought him close to this phrase. Gandhi's earliest reference to *Vande Mataram* the song is in an article titled 'The Heroic Song of Bengal'. This is what he said:

> The song, it is said, has proved so popular that it has come to be our national anthem. It is nobler in sentiment and sweeter than the songs of other nations. While other anthems contain sentiments that are derogatory to others, Bande Mataram is quite free from such faults. Its only aim is to arouse in us a sense of patriotism. It regards India as the mother and sings

> her praises. The poet attributes to Mother India all the good qualities one finds in one's own mother. Just as we worship our mother, so is this song a passionate prayer to India.[25]

Gandhi remained passionate about the song until the very end. At a discussion with political workers in Sodepur on 23 December 1945, when asked if a new song such as *Qadam Qadam* could replace *Vande Mataram*, he said, '... a song that carried such glorious associations of sacrifice as "Vandemataram" could never be given up. It would be like discarding one's mother. But they could certainly add a new song or songs like the one mentioned to their repertoire of national songs after due thought and discrimination.'[26]

In January 1946, when Gandhi arrived at a prayer meeting, a girl greeted him with 'Jai Hind'. At the meeting, Gandhi made it a point to say that 'Jai Hind' should not replace 'Vande Mataram' as the greeting. He was worried the latter would be forgotten. When asked a few days later about whether 'Jai Hind' could be adopted for non-violent action, since it was created as a war cry, Gandhi responded by saying that if that was the logic, even 'Vande Mataram' may need to be eschewed since people have indulged in violence with 'this cry on their lips'.[27] But to him, 'Vande Mataram' was 'obeisance to Mother India' while 'Jai Hind' only wished her victory. The former took precedence.

The universal appeal of *Vande Mataram* is a reflection of the allure that Mother India in her human form has for our people. This is also reflected in the way we situate the mother in Indian cultures. In colloquial Tamil film lingua, there is the expression 'amma sentiment'. Every movie that hopes to be commercially viable is expected to have a scene or segment that taps into the 'motherly love' sentiment. This could be a teary song sequence between the mother and the protagonist (male), where he is being fed a meal or there is a show of motherly sacrifice, which may mean tolerating an abusive husband for the sake of the son, covering up for the son or even losing her life for him. For the viewer, this translates into an expression of unconditional love or protectiveness towards her child (especially the son). The transformation of *Vande Mataram*, the song, symbol and slogan, into the most popular nationalistic theme during the struggle for independence is understandable when seen in this context.

In *The Historical Record of the Imperial Visit of 1911*, published in 1914, the opening chapter describes Queen Victoria's 1858 declaration of 'direct supremacy' of the British Crown over India.

> The proclamation of the direct supremacy of the British Crown, simple and natural enough as it appears at the present day in the light of what has followed, was a stroke of genius at the time. 'It sealed the unity of Indian government and opened a new era.' It was the act of a great Sovereign mother which appealed to oriental sentiment as nothing could have done. An entirely new keynote was struck. Her Majesty directed her Minister to issue the great announcement, 'bearing in mind that it is a female Sovereign who speaks to more than a hundred millions of Eastern people on assuming the direct government over them and, after a bloody war, giving them pledges which her future reign is to redeem and explaining the principles of her government.' 'Such a document,' said Her Majesty, 'should breathe feelings of generosity, benevolence, and religious toleration and point out the privileges which the Indians will receive in being placed on an equality with the subjects of the British Crown.'[28]

Whether or not this observation comes from ground reality, the specific reference to 'a great Sovereign mother which appealed to oriental sentiment as nothing could have done' is perceptive and gives us an understanding of how well the British administrators knew their subjects. Considering that this was the late nineteenth century, one would have to conclude that these 'subjects' were visualised as men.

Dinabandhu Mitra, author of the novel *Nil Darpan*, which was based on the Indigo revolt of 1859, made this observation about Queen Victoria taking direct charge of India: 'The most kind hearted Queen Victoria, the mother of the people, thinking it unadvisable to suckle her children through maid-servants, has now taken them on her own lap to nourish them.'[29]

In the late nineteenth century, at the Indian National Congress sessions, on more than one occasion, Surendranath Banerjea, the senior Congressman, referred to Britain as 'the august mother of free nations'.

Hindu nationalism was dovetailing with the freedom struggle. Muslim nationalism was not far behind, and conflicts over the song only aggravated mutual suspicion. By the late 1930s, *Vande Mataram* was a fiery issue within the Congress. After the 1937 provincial elections, the party was in power in many provinces, and so it became imperative that it deal with the issue. The party tried to find a via media. The Congress Working Committee issued a statement on 28 October 1937 to the effect that *Vande Mataram* was a historical song and represented the sacrifices of so many who had these words on their lips. It was a symbol, the statement said, of 'national resistance to British imperialism'. The British had, in fact, tried to suppress the very utterance of those words. The Lyon circular in November 1905 explicitly said that 'shouting the cry Bande Mataram on the streets' should be stopped. Public political meetings were banned and there could be no music during processions. The circular ridiculously stated that even 'sankirtan parties' had to follow these norms!

In the 1906 Congress session held in Calcutta, Rash Behari Ghosh spoke of the 'Russian methods' being employed by the British. He said,

> The singing of national songs and even the cry of *Bande Mataram* were forbidden under severe penalties. This ordinance was fittingly succeeded by the prosecution of school boys, the quartering of military and punitive police, the prohibition and forcible dispersion of public meetings and these high-handed proceedings attained their crown and completion in the tragedy at Barisal, when the Provincial Conference was dispersed by the Police who Wantonly broke the peace in order, I imagine, to keep the peace.[30]

The Congress Committee in 1937 acknowledged the validity of the objections raised but felt that 'the modern evolution of the use of the song as part of National life is of infinitely greater importance than its setting in a historical novel before the national movement had taken shape'.

In a letter to Subhas Chandra Bose, on 20 October 1937, Nehru had said,

> There is no doubt that the present outcry against Bande Mataram is to a large extent a manufactured one by the communalists. At the same time there does seem some substance in it and people who are communalistically inclined have been affected. Whatever we do cannot be to pander to communalists' feelings but to meet real grievances where they exist.[31]

The Congress Working Committee came to the conciliatory conclusion that only the first two stanzas of *Vande Mataram* would be sung in 'national gatherings', if it was sung at all. Other songs of an 'unobjectionable character' could replace *Vande Mataram* or be added to the programme.

The very next day after the statement was published, Nehru explained in the All India Congress Committee meeting that he was 'personally opposed to the last two stanzas and, therefore, urged the deletion of the same'.

None of this satisfied people like Jinnah, who were worried that the song could become the national anthem of India. He and others in the Muslim League wanted the song expunged from nationalist culture. Nehru tried explaining that *Vande Mataram* was not the national anthem adopted by the Congress, and that, in any case, the two recommended stanzas had no objectionable words. In another context, he referred to the statement made by the Minister of Education of Bihar, Dr Syed Mahmud, who concurred with the view that there was nothing objectionable about the first two stanzas. Nehru tried explaining its popularity sociologically. He said, 'Popular songs are not made to order, nor can they be successfully imposed. They grow out of public sentiment.'[32] I consider this a somewhat slippery argument since it sanctifies a piece of art on the basis of mass acceptance. In any case, Jinnah did not budge. *Vande Mataram* had no place in public institutions or mixed gatherings and was an assault on Muslim culture, sensibilities and faith, he argued. A tool that the Congress was using to target Muslims.

There were complaints that it was being sung in legislatures and those who protested were looked at suspiciously. In government schools too, Muslim children were being compelled to sing the song. Gandhi tried addressing these concerns in a confidential draft that he placed before the Congress Working Committee in late 1938. He suggested that the song be sung only at Congress gatherings and not at local board and Assembly meetings. And even at the Congress meetings, it should be left to people to decide whether they wanted to stand or not.

The Hindu Mahasabha and the Democratic Swaraj Party declared 26 October 1937 as Vande Mataram Day. On the other side, in early 1938, the Cuttack chapter of the Muslim League published a pamphlet that said Hindus wanted to destroy the houses of Muslims, demolish mosques and erect temples instead. They said the Congress's message was that India was for Hindus and Muslims were foreigners. The Inspector General of Crime wrote to the Chief Secretary of Orissa saying that the pamphlet was divisive, but so were the actions of certain provincial politicians.

The battlelines between the Congress and the Muslim League were now sharply drawn. Talk of an Islamic Quam and a Hindu Rashtra was gathering strength too. The effect of these hostilities would prove to be long-lasting. Even when the Constitution of India was being framed, there was tremendous pressure from Hindu conservatives. This is why *Vande Mataram* remained an important peg even in 1947-48.

The song had by now metamorphosed in musical form and in political intent. What began as a sensitive and vivid description of a shared land became the carrier of a form of Hindu cultism that was promoted by people with caste privilege and filled with puritanical ritualism. This *Vande Mataram* was not a celebration of all of the nation's people and their common mother. The song was now an assertion that symbolically put Muslims 'in their place'. Tracing the changes in the language of each verse is like a journey through the transformations in the socio-political landscape of the then emerging India. Some meanings hardened, others were ignored. Even the beautiful land described with grace in the first few lines was now not for sharing. Whether Bankim intended it or not, his poem became *Anandamath*'s *Vande Mataram* and there was no way to extricate it from the story.

Between 1920 and 1948, many classical musicians, especially from conservative Hindu communities, tuned, performed and released recordings of this song. It was as though they were making a socio-political statement, participating in the ongoing debate and even goading politicians to adopt it as our national anthem. We noticed the very same trend recently. In the weeks before 22 January 2024, when the pranpratishta of the Rama temple in Ayodhya was scheduled, many classical musicians began sharing songs in praise of Rama, even if they all had different levels of association with the impending event. Some directly pointed to the inauguration and expressed their happiness at what was being touted as a civilisational moment. Others just used the moment to share their renditions, informing or assuring their audience of their religious probity.

There are many stories associated with classical musicians and the song. As a student at Professor Deodhar's School of Indian Music, an eighteen-year-old Kumar Gandharva sang *Vande Mataram* with other students at Gowalia Tank in Bombay on 14 August 1942 in the presence of Mahatma Gandhi. They were marking the first session of the Bharat Chhodo Andolan. Omkarnath Thakur apparently refused to sing the truncated version at Congress sessions. He had sung the song (presumably all four verses) at the 1934 session in Bombay, and he finally rendered the full version on 15 August 1947. Master Krishna Rao Phulambrikar composed a tune for *Vande Mataram*. It is said that he refused to sing on air for the period that the song was banned on radio. His version of *Vande Mataram*, which was of the first two verses alone, is one of the best I have heard, with a bewitching tune for the first line. I would argue, however, that even in this version, the second verse struggles to find musical stability due to its lyrical structure. The maestro Faiyaz Khan gave Krishna Rao a letter of commendation for his tune. He said, 'The famous singer of Maharashtra and disciple of Pandit Bhaskarbuwa Bakhle, Sangeet Kalanidhi Master Krishnarao, has awarded the rashtra-geet a tune that is simple, sweet and serious, and easily singable by a chorus of people. It is my opinion that this tune is more appropriate than any other.'

So did Ustad Alladiya Khan: '... Chi Master is deserving of this praise. About the tune, I feel it is a very simple and serious [gambhir] tune, and is one that everyone will easily be able to sing. This was clear from today's experience. I pray that the lord gives his work complete success.'

What Faiyaz Khan or Alladiya Khan thought of the song's history is not known, so we can only speculate. Perhaps it is that, in a musician's mind, when poetry becomes music, everything else dissolves into the background. Or maybe these men, like Abul Kalam Azad, believed that *Vande Mataram* was an amalgam of Vedantic vision and Islamic thoughts of unity of religion and universal peace. There could also be a far simpler explanation. Krishna Rao was Bhaskarbuwa Bakhale's student. And Bhaskarbuwa, in turn, was a very dear student of Alladiya Khan. Hence, this note of appreciation could have just been encouragement for an emerging student from his lineage. For Faiyaz Khan, perhaps it was just a show of courtesy.

As our prospective constitution was being debated, the spirit of *Vande Mataram* hovered within the precincts of the Central Hall. Though secular democrats in the Constituent Assembly consistently resisted parochial pressures, they had to occasionally give in to *Vande Mataram*-like demands. Uncomfortable compromises were reached, some etched permanently in our constitution. The confused collection of articles under Part IV of the constitution is a case in point. Even liberals do not know how to deal with the Directive Principles because, along with so much that is wise and just and forward-looking, certain 'principles' that do not sit well with our Fundamental Rights have been written into them. On the face of it, the Directive Principles are an assurance by the State that it will do whatever it can to secure the promises we have given ourselves in the Preamble. The Directive Principles lay these out as possible action plans. Legalists tell us that Part III (Fundamental Rights) and Part IV (Directive Principles) need to be read together. If the State makes a law to accomplish an article laid down in Part IV and such legislation violates Part III, it needs to be struck down. But this is easier said than done because the Supreme Court tells us that Part IV is meant to be harmonised with our Fundamental Rights.

There are two articles in the Directive Principles that echo the melody of *Vande Mataram*. Article 44 states, 'Uniform civil code for the citizens.—The State shall endeavour to secure for the citizens a uniform civil code throughout the territory of India.'

It seems logical that all citizens, irrespective of their social identifications, live by the same civil code. One cannot argue with this in principle. In the Constituent Assembly, legalists such as Ananthasayanam Ayyangar, Alladi Krishnaswamy Iyer and Bhimrao Ambedkar were votaries for a uniform civil code and resisted attempts at amendments. These suggested changes came mainly from the Muslim members of the Constituent Assembly, who hoped to protect themselves from the State if it chose to meddle in their personal law. Hussain Imam made the point that safeguards were needed for the minorities and not the majority, since the majority would always have the numbers to push through any bill or amendment they sought. On the face of it, this is a defensive argument, a resistance to change. But the numbers have proved him right. Since Independence, there have never been more than forty-nine (in 1980) Muslim members of the Lok Sabha. The tally was twenty-seven after the 2019 elections, which was an increase of four members from the previous Parliament. But the BJP (the single largest party) did not have a single Muslim member of Parliament.

The Rajya Sabha is said to balance out the anomalies of how candidates are selected by political parties in the Lok Sabha elections. But if the formula for political success is based on marginalising a specific community, this balance will not materialise. Therefore, Imam's unease turned out to be legitimate. Who was making laws for whom? Even Ayyangar, while arguing for the possibility of a uniform civil code and rebutting the many arguments against it, said, 'This is only an enabling provision. Without the consent of the minority that is affected, no such law will be framed.'[33]

Ambedkar went a step further. He said,

> We must all remember—including Members of the Muslim community who have spoken on this subject, though one can appreciate their feelings very well—that sovereignty is always limited, no matter even if you assert that it is unlimited, because sovereignty in the exercise of that power must reconcile itself to the sentiments of different communities. No Government can exercise its power in such a manner as to provoke the Muslim community to rise in rebellion. I think it would be a mad Government if it did so. But that is a matter which relates to the exercise of the power and not to the power itself.[34]

Ambedkar believed in a consultatory approach that included easing citizens into the idea of a uniform civil code. He said that a future Parliament might even provide for a time period when citizens would abide by it on a 'purely voluntary' basis. He was convinced about the need for change, but was deeply sensitive to how it would be brought about and implemented. His position was that the influence of religion on people's lives must be limited to ritualistic ceremonial requirements. Unfortunately, this idealistic stance did not have enough takers. There cannot be a powerful pushback, let alone revolution, if the majority consolidates within the house and on the streets, poisoned by the belief that members of certain communities are 'enemies' of the State.

In this context, Pocker Sahib Bahadur of the Muslim League asked a question in the Constituent Assembly that squarely hit the mark: 'By uniform, I ask, what do you mean and which particular law, of which community are you going to take as the standard?'[35]

This question, asked over seventy years ago, has been answered in the recent past. Declarations have been made by the Gujarat and Haryana state governments that they would implement a uniform civil code. The Uttarakhand legislative assembly has even passed a bill. A code that has homogenised succession laws in a manner that may affect vulnerable members of Muslim families and places onerous conditions on those who want to be in live-in relationships. It is also not really uniform because Scheduled Tribes are exempted. Politically, the demand for a uniform civil code is a dog whistle that galvanises Muslim hate and makes suspect any suggestion of sympathy for the position of the community. The call for such a code does not germinate from an acceptance that all religion-based personal laws are inherently unequal. As many have suggested, what is needed is reformation of all personal laws and not a uniform civil code. The promotion of a uniform civil code cannot be seen in isolation. It is part of a series of actions that include criminalising religious conversions, propagating the bogus term 'Love Jihad' and the targeted demolishing of homes inhabited by people of the Islamic faith. Anti-conversion bills brought in by various state governments are a result of this Islamophobic mindset and specifically target inter-faith marriages.

During all the discussions, Mohammad Ismail Khan made a sharp point regarding respecting one another's religio-cultural practices. He said,

> This House will remember that on another question, which is really a religious question—I mean the question of cow-slaughter—an obligation has been placed upon other communities than the one which considers the prohibition of cow-slaughter as a religious matter. But then, Sir, respecting the views and feelings of our friends, the minority communities who have got the right and privilege of slaughtering and eating the flesh of cows have agreed to the proposal put before the House, though that is going beyond affecting one particular community alone.[36]

Thus, we come to the second article in the Directive Principles that echoes the *Vande Mataram*—Article 48, which finally read as: 'Organisation of agriculture and animal husbandry.—The state shall endeavour to organize agriculture and animal husbandry on modern and scientific lines and shall, in particular, take steps for preserving and improving the breeds, and prohibiting the slaughter, of cows and calves and other milch and draught cattle.'

The existence of this article has led to violence against dalits and Muslims across India over the past three or four years. State governments have often regulated the slaughter of cows, but we are now seeing outright bans and the criminalisation of cattle trade and consumption of beef. About twenty states have brought forth legislations banning or regulating cow slaughter and sale. Knowing full well that most Indians who work at abattoirs or transport meat are dalits and Muslims, some states have passed stringent laws restricting cattle trade. Coupled with religious hatred and casteism, this has allowed caste Hindus to unleash violence in the name of faith and purity. The scale of this violence has been unprecedented—what used to be localised, occasional flare-ups has become a nationwide phenomenon. Cow protection armies are on the prowl, assaulting marginalised citizens without an iota of fear and often without consequence.

Lawyers will argue that such laws can be challenged in courts as contravening sub-clause (g) of the Right to Freedom. While the hearings go on in the courts, people continue to get hurt. Judges do not always help. Recently, Justice Shekhar Yadav of the Allahabad High Court had much to say on cow protection.[37] He demanded that cow protection be made a Fundamental Right and went on to use the cow issue to make insidious remarks against the Muslim community. He said, 'Whenever we forgot our culture, foreigners attacked us and enslaved us and if we are not warned, we should not forget the unbridled attack on and capture of Afghanistan by Taliban.' He wanted Parliament to declare the cow a national animal and 'make strict laws against people who talk of harming cows'.

The sensitivity of Hindus who worship the cow is respected when they have the right to live their lives as per this belief.

Muslims have every right to eat only halal meat and abjure pork. But neither has the right to stop others from doing what they please or force them to behave in a manner that tallies with one way of living. Our sensitivities need to remain in our personal spaces and cannot be turned into aggressive ideologies that are forced upon others. Vegans find the consumption of milk products unacceptable, pointing to the harm this brings upon the cow. Cows are stuffed into tiny pens, injected with antibiotics and hormones, forced to lactate for ten months a year and rarely allowed to feed their calves. This is the reality of milk production. I don't hear conservative Hindus who demand a ban on cow slaughter express their willingness to give up milk, curd, ghee and stop the use of dairy products in their 'cleansing' homas and yagnas. There can never be an absolute position on such matters. It has to be left to individuals to decide where they stand on an issue and then act accordingly in their personal life. This cow protection frenzy originated in the brahmin community and then percolated to aspirational caste groups. The communities who are in fact affected by it, socially and economically, are dalits and Muslims.

It is in this same spirit that the slogans 'Vande Mataram' and 'Bharat Mata ki Jai' have been weaponised against Muslims and dalits by those who dream of a monolithic Hindu Rashtra.

Every once in a while, there is some brouhaha from the Hindu Right around *Vande Mataram*. For all this chest thumping, no one knows who composed the now popular tune of the song etched in our minds by its constant relay on All India Radio (AIR). According to record collector Suresh Chandvankar, the renowned vocalist from the Agra gharana, Dinkar Kaikini, informed him that it was he and Sumati Mutatkar, from the same gharana, who rendered the AIR version. Mutatkar also confirmed this. Kaikini often sang this version at official gatherings. Some people credit sitar maestro Ravi Shankar for this moving melody based on Raga Desh. Given the fact that Kaikini collaborated with Shankar on the *Discovery of India* ballet, there is a greater likelihood of Shankar having composed the music. If this is indeed true, then two of India's best-known songs of patriotism have been rendered in the melody composed by Ravi Shankar, the other one being *Saare Jahan se Achcha*.

The anomalies surrounding *Vande Mataram* don't stop there. The Publications Division of the Ministry of Information and Broadcasting published a book titled *National Songs* in November 1951, multiple revised editions of which have been issued since. When I filed an RTI application asking for the original notation of the national anthem, I was directed by the Ministry of Home Affairs to the digital scan of this book available on the Publications Division website. In it is contained a brief contextual history of *Vande Mataram*, Gandhi's thoughts on the song, the text of all four stanzas in English and Devanagari, and Aurobindo Ghosh's English translation of the first stanza. The musical notation for the first stanza published in Appendix K is attributed to Rabindranath Tagore, while the music for the second stanza in Appendix L is attributed to Indira Devi Chaudhurani. However, this is nearly the same notation published in *Shotogan* in 1900, where credit for the music was given to Tagore and Sarala Devi, not Indira Devi Chaudhurani.

The only real difference between the two notations is caused by a change in the lyrics. '*Ke bale ma tumi abala*' becomes '*Abala kena eta bala*', a change that was made in the fifth edition of *Anandamath*.

Also, 'tringshakoti' had come to stay. But by placing each verse of the song under a different appendix and attributing the notation to two different people, the publication suggests that the melody for the second verse was not composed by Tagore.

What is startling is that the popular, unattributable tune that we have all been singing and humming for the past seven decades is not the one published by the Government of India.

Though *Vande Mataram* is considered the national song and is to be given equal status[38] as the national anthem, unlike the anthem, its form and performance were not regulated by officialdom.

Where lies the patriotism or jingoism that a song triggers? It is not situated in the words or the song's history. The music carries the spirit that we imbue the text with and the past that we wish to tap into. If we sang *Vande Mataram* in Tagore's tune, would it be less othering—or, dare I say, welcoming? To my ears, Tagore's tune is filled with compassion. It transforms *Vande Mataram* into a descriptive conversation with the idea of India. The standard tune that all of us sing evokes a blind servitude to power through higher-octave emphasis and military-style melodic ascendancies. But it was probably Tagore's tune that was popularly rendered in the early twentieth century when the song was heard as offensive by the Islamic community. Maybe I am missing another piece in this puzzle: the singers. Adding to the text, the tune and its past is the nature and intention of the singers. If we sing to offend and hurt, even the most docile words (or, indeed, music) can turn violent.

In the early part of the twentieth century, when *Vande Mataram* dominated the nationalist's musical mindscape, another song quietly emerged, eventually pipping its predecessor to the exalted post of the national anthem of India. Once again, Rabindranath Tagore—the only individual other than Ashoka to so intensely influence democratic India's symbolic imagination—was at the epicentre. In the case of *Vande Mataram*, Tagore was one of the early tunesmiths and propagators. The song was, and is spoken of, only as Bankim's composition, but as a composition in the national imagination, it has always been a collaborative composition. According to the record collector Chandvankar, over 125 different versions of *Vande Mataram* have been recorded. This means over 125 different musicians have given Bankim's words a musical life. But we don't know, or speak of, most of them. There is no such problem with the national anthem, though. It was entirely created by the polymath vaggeyakara Rabindranath Tagore.

In May 1910, Edward VII died and his son George became 'King-Emperor'. On 23 March 2011, the king-emperor proclaimed his 'royal intention' of holding an Imperial Darbar in Delhi on 12 December 1911. This would be the first time that the monarch would be personally present at the darbar. The first darbar in 1877 was held 'to celebrate the passing of India under the Imperial rule'. The Queen became the Qaisar-i-Hind, the 'Empress of India'. The previous darbar in 1903 was attended by the Duke of Connaught, the brother of King Edward VII. This was the first time that his Indian subjects would see the emperor in flesh and blood. When King Edward VII did not himself attend the durbar in 1903, Lord Curzon had said in disappointment: 'Some day we may hope that, as time and distance continue to dwindle under the magic finger of science, it may be found possible for the Viceroy on some future occasion like the present to be eliminated as a superfluous phantom and for the real figure to appear on the scene.'[39]

Curzon's wish became reality in 1911.

George V disembarked in Bombay on 2 December 1911. Other than the grand darbar in Delhi, his itinerary included visits to Nepal, Rajputana and Calcutta. The maiden visit by the king-emperor and queen empress was a momentous occasion for the Raj. Among the Indians, too, the kings of princely states and all those who were loyal to the crown either happily or obediently accepted their role in welcoming the almighty emperor.

Many scholars have written about how India's national anthem came into being and addressed the misunderstandings surrounding its creation. Yet, I will take the reader through its conception and first performance, in an attempt to bring back to life all that might have transpired and, at the same time, dispel the untruths that still linger, a century later.

Tagore was approached by a friend, 'well established and devoted in His Majesty's Service', to write a eulogy for the emperor of India. We are not certain of the identity of this friend. In his book *Bharat Borsher Jatiyo Sangeet*,[40] Probodh Chandra Sen suggests that it may have been the barrister Asutosh Chaudhuri. However, in *Rabijibani*,[41] Prashanta Kumar Pal refutes this on the grounds that Asutosh Chaudhuri was closely associated with the Swadeshi Movement and was appointed a judge in Calcutta High Court only on 5 February 1912 and knighted in 1921. Pal posits that the individual must have been Sir Prodyot Tagore, who was knighted in 1906 and declared maharaja in 1908. This seems plausible. Pal also quotes a letter Rabindranath Tagore wrote in 1937 to Pulin Bihari Sen, his erstwhile student at Visva-Bharati, explaining the circumstances of the composition.

> That year when preparations were being made for the Emperor's visit to India, a friend of mine, well established and devoted in His Majesty's Service, had requested me to write a song in eulogy to the Emperor of India. I was stunned hearing this, at the same time I felt indignation rising in me. So in a flood of reaction from my heart, I hailed the Decider of the fate of our country in my song Jana Gana Mana—the one who has always been there as a companion in the path of life that is full of ups and downs, the one who knows what the hearts of the people of our country want, the one who has for eons been the navigator of human fate. The fact that such a person can never be a 'George V' or a 'George VI' or for that matter any emperor, even my friend understood. It goes without saying that, no matter how devoted to the British Raj, he had no dearth of common sense.

Was *Jana Gana Mana* rendered at the darbar in Delhi or when the royals visited Calcutta? At the Delhi Darbar on 12

December 1911, and the events and celebrations that took place around it, there was no music of any significance. Regiments played band music and English marching songs and 'stately' music. In a Hindu religious procession in Delhi after the darbar, songs of benediction and specially composed hymns were sung and instrumental music was played. There is no way a song composed by Rabindranath Tagore would have gone unnoticed or unreported.

The only other possibility is that the song was rendered in Calcutta. The royal entourage arrived in Calcutta on 30 December 1911. On the afternoon of 5 January 1912, a pageant in their honour was held at the military parade grounds. *The Historical Record of the Imperial Visit of 1911* has this to say about the pageant: 'A short procession was formed to the Thrones, which were beneath a crimson canopy, decorated with golden peacocks and Stars of India. In this procession Maharaja Sir Prodyot Tagore bore the state umbrella, Maharaja Jagadindra Nath Ray of Natore the suraj-mukhi, and the Maharaj Kumar of Moharbhanj and the Murshidzada Waris Ali Mirza of Murshidabad the morchals.'[42]

And then it goes on to specify,

> An Indian band organized by Maharaja Sir Prodyot Tagore, and trained by Professor Dakshina Sen, a well-known Indian musician, advanced before the dais and played during the processions on a hundred instruments that were special reproductions of the best ancient models. The programme included some Indian pieces and marches composed respectively by Sir Prodyot Tagore and Professor Sen. It also contained the Flag of Britain and the National Anthem specially set to Indian instruments.

Maharaja Sir Prodyot Tagore was loyal to the crown and a central figure in organising this musical performance. This increases the probability that he was indeed the 'friend' who approached Rabindranath Tagore. But it is clear that the song that Rabindranath might have given him was not rendered in Calcutta. Prodyot Tagore would not have been happy with *Jana Gana Mana*. He had composed new songs along with the eminent musician Dakshinacharan Sen for the occasion. This is further established by the following story, which comes to us in a rather roundabout fashion. A friend of Rabindranath's tells W.B. Yeats in London, who in turns narrates the story to the American poet Ezra Pound, who then goes on to share it with his father in a letter. She calls it a joke 'worthy of Voltaire'.

> The national committee came to Mr. Tagore and asked him to write something for the (Delhi Darbar). And as you know, Mr. Tagore is very obliging. And all that afternoon he tried to write them a poem, and he could not. And that evening the poet as usual retired to his meditation. And in the morning he descended with a sheet of paper. He said, 'Here is a poem I have written. It is addressed to the deity. But you may give it to the national committee. Perhaps it will content them.'[43]

This may not be exactly how things transpired before the song came to be written. Retold stories are always ornamented, especially when conveyed by a friend some years later. But if we place this telling alongside Rabindranath Tagore's own narration, it is clear that Tagore was disturbed by the suggestion that he write a paean to the British monarch. The story of great poets and musicians refusing to write a commissioned song in honour of a king is a narrative that runs right through our cultural history. These examples are recurring exceptions, for it was, and remains, normal for artists to succumb to such requests from people with political and social power. A similar story is told of the great composer Tyagaraja. When he was approached by the Tanjore court to sing paeans to the king in exchange for substantial money, his response in song was,

nidhi stala sukhama
ramuni sannidhi seva sukhama
nijamuga balku manasa

O mind, tell me truthfully, does wealth or being at the feet of Rama give you comfort

Tagore seems to have been in a similar predicament. Agitated and unable to respond immediately with his characteristic poetic eloquence, he retires for the night. But, at some point in that night or in the wee hours of the morning, he crafts a subtle and subversive song. He couldn't have known then that, in a few weeks, the song would debut elsewhere and go on to become the voice of millions.

Let me now wind the clock back to December 1911, and using multiple sources, reconstruct the possible flow of events that led to the first-ever rendition of *Jana Gana Mana*.

In *Rabijibani*, Pal cites the *Calcutta Municipal Gazette* as saying, '[I]n December (1911) Rabindranath composed, at the request of Asutosh Chaudhuri, for the twenty-sixth session of the Indian National Congress in Calcutta, his famous national song Jana-gana-manaadhinayaka ...'

Pal asserts that Tagore did not compose this song for the Congress session, the report got that wrong. It is likely that Tagore gave this song, which he had already composed, to Asutosh Chaudhuri, who was a bar-at-law and zamindar and a delegate representing Calcutta at the Congress session.

The song reached Dr Nilratan Sircar via his associate Gyananjan Niyogi and a rehearsal was organised at Sircar's house in Harrison Road. Sircar and his family had long been associated with the music presented at Congress sessions. He and his wife had supported Jyotirindranath Tagore, who trained thirty young girls to sing national songs at the Calcutta session of 1906. In 1914, at the Madras session, the ladies of the Sircar family had sung *Vande Mataram*. Hence, it is not surprising that the practice sessions took place at the Sircar residence.

Knowing how essential practice sessions are for group renditions, especially when it is a new song, I postulate that this rehearsal must have happened in early December and was possibly one of many. We know from a few sources that Amal Holm and Chitralekha Siddhanta (the wife of the scholar Nirmal Kumar Siddhanta) were among the principal singers. The leader of the group seems to have been Dinendranath Tagore (Rabindranath Tagore's grandnephew). It is likely that Dinendranath provided the tune for the song—he wrote the musical notation for *Jana Gana Mana* when it was published in the book *Gita Panchashika* in 1918. But I am tempted to speculate that the larger-than-life Tagore himself came for at least one of those rehearsals and helped the singers get it just right.

The twenty-sixth session of the Indian National Congress was held in Calcutta between 26 and 28 December 1911. In the same year and the same city, the Brahmo Samaj Conference was held between 26 and 29 December. We do not know whether Tagore attended the Congress session at all. There is no mention of him having done so. But he presented a lecture on the 'religious education of young people' on the evening of 27 December at the Brahmo Samaj Conference.

That same day, when the Indian National Congress session began at noon, 'the proceedings commenced with a patriotic song composed by Babu Rabindranath Tagore'. We can confirm this was a reference to *Jana Gana Mana* because of a news report in the *Bengalee* on 28 December 2011: 'The proceeding commenced with a patriotic song composed by Babu Rabindranath Tagore, the leading poet of Bengal ("Jana gano mano adhinayak") of which we give an English translation.'[44] A translation of all the five stanzas was provided in the publication. The author of the translation is unknown.

Two reports state that Sarala Devi Chaudhurani might have led the choir. She had already led the *Vande Mataram* chorus on the first day of the session. Dinendranath Tagore was also an important singer. According to the session report, the first day ended with the 'singing of another song'. Sarala Devi's composition *Atita gourababahini mama bani* was sung at the conference. But it is not clear whether this was that 'another song' because it may well have been sung on another day.

But let us return to the afternoon of 27 December 1911.

Immediately after the rendition of *Jana Gana Mana*, there was a reading of a letter from Ramsay MacDonald (the Labour leader and future prime minister of Great Britain) and other letters from 'European and Indian gentlemen expressing their sympathy with the Congress and regret for their unavoidable absence'.[45] The first resolution moved by the president of the Congress was 'Welcome to Their Majesties' for which 'Three hearty cheers for the King-Emperor and three more for the Queen-Empress were given'. It was then announced that the president would send His Majesty a copy of the resolution. This was followed by the choir rendering a song to welcome their Imperial Majesties, which had been composed for the occasion. According to the *Bengalee*, it was a Hindi song 'paying a heartfelt homage to their Imperial Majesties'. There is some discrepancy between the order of the events published in the *Bengalee* on 28 December and the Congress's own report.

Coinciding with the king-emperor's visit, His Majesty's Government announced that the seat of government would be moved from Calcutta to Delhi. Importantly for Bengalis, the partition of Bengal was rescinded. This was a huge victory and the gushing declarations in the Congress session may have been born out of this decision. There were shouts of 'God Save the King' and 'God Save the Queen' after the passing of the first resolution. The second resolution passed by the Congress was an expression of gratitude to the king-emperor for the annulment of the partition of Bengal. Even without such a momentous turn of events, praising, cheering and expressing loyalty towards the king-emperor or the queen-empress were regular occurrences in the early Congress sessions.

Two songs with very different intentions were sung before and after the resolution that welcomed Their Majesties. Because the choir rendered *Jana Gana Mana* before the resolution was read and then sang another song that extolled the emperor after the reading, English newspapers reported the happenings with varying degrees of inaccuracy. The publication *Englishman* recognised that two songs were sung, but stated that both, the Bengali song specially composed by Tagore and a Hindi song, welcomed the king-emperor.[46] *Reuters* reported the rendition of just one Bengali song, specially composed to welcome the king,[47] The *Statesman* reported that two Bengali songs were rendered, but did not give any details of the first one, which was *Jana Gana Mana*. Instead, it mentioned the second song that was rendered after the passing of the resolution as a Bengali song that welcomed the king, specially composed by Tagore.[48] Bengali journalists wrote with greater clarity, and hence reports published in *Amrita Bazar Patrika* and the *Bengalee* referred to *Jana Gana Mana* as a 'Bengali song of benediction or a patriotic song'. *Amrita Bazar Patrika* said another song 'in honour of their Majesties' visit to India' was rendered.

The identity of the mystery song that praised their majesties is uncovered in a footnote published in Prabhat Kumar Mukhopadhyay's *Rabindrajiban*. It refers to a letter written by Chitralekha Siddhanta. This is what she has to say:

> I am also a living witness of the 1911 Congress. I was also in the singing party. Actually we also sang an imperial eulogy. That song was composed by the late Rambhuj Dutt Chaudhuri, husband of the late Sarala Devi. The first line was 'Yug jiv

mera badshah, chahun dis raj saraya'. I don't remember all the words, but the tune is still in my ears.

The erroneous reporting in the British press along with the fact that the song was Tagore's subversive response to someone having the gumption to ask him to compose a song in praise of the king gave rise to, and has sustained, the false assumption that 'adhinayaka' in the lyrics refers to King George. Since the coronation of King George, other poets had written songs in his honour. It is quite possible that this general trend also affected the way people interpreted songs and events.

There can be absolutely no doubt that Tagore was not referring to George V. In fact, his musical response to the request for a song in honour of King George was an act of inspired patriotism that rose above provincialism. The song was sung again in January 1912 at the Brahmo Samaj Maghotsava. As members of the governing body of Visva-Bharati noted in their statement published in the *Visva-Bharati News* in December 1948: 'It is evident that a song composed in praise of the English king could not be sung by a congregation assembled to sing the praise of god "the king of kings".'[49]

Tagore, probably in response to all the misinformation that had begun floating around, published *Jana Gana Mana* as 'Bharat-Bidhata/Brahmo-sangeet' in the January 1912 issue of the Brahmo Samaj's *Tatwabodhini*.

In the late 1930s, when the *Vande Mataram* debate was most volatile, Tagore reiterated the point more than once. He said in 1937: 'In this song I have proclaimed the victory of the "Eternal Charioteer" who has man's destiny along the road rugged with rises and falls of nations. The dispenser of human destiny through the ages could never be George Fifth, George the Sixth, or for that matter, any other George.'[50]

Again in 1939, he said: 'I should only insult myself if I cared to answer those who consider me capable of as unbound stupidity as to worship George the Fourth or Fifth as the Eternal Charioteer leading the pilgrims on their journey through ages of the timeless history of mankind.'[51]

There is one more piece of information which confirms that all the adverse chatter about *Jana Gana Mana* is false. On 26 January 1912, the *Bengalee* published a secret circular[52] issued by the Director of Public Instruction of Eastern Bengal and Assam, declaring Santiniketan or Brahmacharyasrama as 'altogether unsuitable for the education of the sons of Government Servants'. The circular asked them to remove their children and advise others to do so. It went on to warn government servants that, if any of their children continued at the institution, it would affect their future. It is unlikely that the government would have issued such an overt stricture against an institution founded by the individual who just a few months ago had extolled the king!

Jana Gana Mana came alive at an Indian National Congress session, while *Vande Mataram* was an integral part of most meetings. These two songs were among the many that were shared on the Congress stage since its first annual session in 1885. How many and what kind of music was heard under those large tents that were erected for the Congress gatherings?

In the reports of the initial years, no specific song is noted; only generic phrases such as 'music playing'. No doubt there were invocatory songs, some solo renditions and bands playing with gusto to induce national consciousness. Though music was present, it was not considered an integral part of the sessions; it did not warrant specific detailing in the notes.

The first instance of a song being specifically printed as part of the Congress session report can be found in the 1901 Calcutta session publication. The lyrics are given in Bengali and a translation in English of a song composed and led by Sarala Devi Ghoshal (later Chaudhurani). She was joined by fifty-eight men and boys from different parts of India. It was an 'ode to the Mother country'. Among the singers were Hindus, Muslims,

Jains, Parsis, Sikhs and Christians. They were joined in chorus by around 400 volunteers. On what had inspired this song, Sarala Devi said:

> Having lived for a year outside Bengal and having come in touch with the people of Maharashtra and Southern India, the boundaries of my love for my country expanded a great deal. The India that Shankaracharya had unified from North to South and East to West by enclosing it in the bonds of four pilgrim sites held sway over my heart. I became aware of the whole of that India—which had Bengal on its eastern edge. Bengal should stand in line with the rest of the states holding the head high; however, the other states should not be ignored. So when the Congress convened under Wacha's presidentship at Beadon Street, this song came forth from me churning my whole being.

Given the sheer number of people who joined in the chorus, one imagines that it would have been an evocative, large rendition.

The song was Sarala Devi's *Atita gourababahini mama bani*. Below is the translation published in the Congress report:

> Sing, O my Muse, recall our ancient glory
> Sing thou, sing Hindustan
> Inspire this throng with soul bestirring story,
> Sing now, sing Hindustan!
> Let valour bright breathe in the very name
> Instil into thy song past wealth and fame
>
> (Chorus)
> Orissa, Behar, Bengal, Oudh, Punjab, Nepal,
> Madras, Bombay, and Rajputan!
> Hindu, Parsee, and Jain, Sikh, Christian, Mussulman!
> Let every voice, in concord ring,
> In every tongue the burden sing,
> All hail to Hindustan!

Hara, Hara, Hara—hail Hindustan!
Dadar Hormuzd—Hindustan!
Elahi Akbar—Hindustan!
All hail to Hindustan!

Sing, O my Muse, defeat all party-strife,
Sing thou, sing Hindustan!
Giver of strength and power, giver of life,
Sing now, sing, Hindustan!
In joy and sorrow let us not be parted,
In aim and effort make us single hearted

(Chorus)
Orissa, Behar, Bengal, Oudh, Punjab, Nepal,
Madras, Bombay, and Rajputan!
Hindu, Parsee, and Jain, Sikh, Christian, Mussulman!
Let every voice, in concord ring,
In every tongue the burden sing,
All hail to Hindustan!
Hari, Hari, Hari—hail Hindustan!
Jay Jihova—Hindustan!
Elahi Akbar—Hindustan!
All hail to Hindustan!

Sing, O my Muse, arouse the people's heart,
Sing thou, sing Hindustan
Maker of mighty nation that thou art
Sing now, sing Hindustan!
Uplift the flag of *Energy* on high,
And let stern *Duty* sound her bugle-cry.

(Chorus)
Orissa, Behar, Bengal, Oudh, Punjab, Nepal,
Madras, Bombay, and Rajputan!
Hindu, Parsee, and Jain, Sikh, Christian, Mussulman!
Let every voice, in concord ring,
In every tongue the burden sing,

All hail to Hindustan!
Jay Brahman—hail Hindustan!
Alakha Niranjan—Hindustan!
Jay Jihova—Hindustan!
Dadar Hormuz—Hindustan!
All hail to Hindustan!

There is unmistakable similarity in the religious and regional universality that this song celebrates and which Tagore's *Jana Gana Mana* elegantly postulates. In an essay penned in the early twentieth century, Tagore spoke about the coming together of Hindus, Muslims, Christians and Buddhists to vanquish the British.

The report of the eighteenth Indian National Congress session (1902) in Ahmedabad published a 'National Congress Anthem' in Hindi and Gujarati, along with an English translation. This song, too, asks all Indians to come together and usher in a new dawn. It speaks to people of different faiths and regions, including Burma, and describes the beauty of India's landscape. The song goes beyond the land and even hails Congress leaders! This song is set to Raga Khamaj. The 'anthem' was rendered again on the opening day in 1904. The second day's report calls it the 'usual Congress Anthem'. Unusual as it might be for us now, the song refers to India as a 'fatherland'. In fact, in the Congress sessions held in the late nineteenth century, there are a few references to India as a fatherland. But by the time we come to 1905, when the partition of Bengal is the political catalyst for revolution, India has undisputedly become a motherland.

It is in these years that singing became an important political tool at the Congress sessions. This can be attributed to the emergence of one song, one slogan—*Vande Mataram*—which from then on became a fixture at these events.

India has an interesting musical tradition wherein the same tune is used for different sets of lyrics in different periods of time. A tune could have been first composed for a specific poem, but is later used for other poems and lyrics. In fact, taking into account the popularity of a tune, song writers will compose verses that fit the well-established melody. A similar practice can also be noticed in the case of some European and American tunes. We see this happening at the 1908 session.

> On the President arriving on the platform, 'India's National Anthem' was sung by a number of delegates to the tune of 'God Save the King' and the accompaniment of a piano and violin, the audience standing.

Bharat of holy fame,
Motherland mine!
Teach me to know thy worth,
O, Land of Sacred Birth,
Thou Soul of All the Earth,
My heart is thine!

Land where the Sages walk,
Where Saints and Prophets talk,
Blest be thy clime!
The glory of thy past
Awakes to life at last,
In all the splendour vast
of that bright time.

Where'er my feet may roam,
Thou art my well-loved home,
My country dear!
The Magic of thy air
And all thy beauties rare
But haunt me everywhere,
Both far and near.

Bharata's sons arise
And sing unto the skies
Fair India's praise.

Her ideals are not dead
For which her children bled,
She proudly rears her head
To greet new days.

Then let her watchword be
That word of harmony,
Peace, blessed Peace!
Its potency shall sway,
All that obstructs the way,
To bring the perfect day,
When strife shall cease.

Nations arise and fall,
But thou dost stand through all,
Unchanged by time.
So shall it ever be,
Child of Eternity,
The Gods do favour thee
With grace sublime.

The storm may beat thy brow,
But strong in faith art thou,
The calm to see.
The heritage divine
To save all worlds is thine,
For eons shall it shine
Their light to be.[53]

This was not the first time, either. A hundred years earlier, Karnatik composer Muthusvami Dikshitar had written Sanskrit lyrics praising goddess Sarasvati to this very tune:

santatam pahimam sangita shyamale
sarvadhare janani sarvadhare
chintitartha prade chidrupini shive
shri guruguha sevite shivamoha kare

Neither were the Congress writers the last to try their hand at it. Sometime later, Annie Besant wrote another set of lyrics to chime with this tune, and it was printed on one side of the Home Rule League membership card.

A few years after Queen Victoria declared herself the 'Empress of India', some Englishmen seriously considered making 'God Save the Queen' the country's national anthem. This was a private citizens' initiative with official blessing. One of the proponents of this project was Reverent Frederick K. Harford, who was also a poet, song writer and musician. He wrote an essay expounding the benefits of such an endeavour. The premise was that Indians were incapable of creating a unifying anthem since they had never been one nation. They were divided by race, religion, languages, customs and habits. In other words, only the British could achieve something so momentous.

To the question of how establishing the British anthem in India was a project for the good, he provided many reasons. It would be a 'gift from the people of England'. Such a gesture could improve the Britain–India relationship. He went on to explain that the 'veneration for the person of the reigning sovereign was an unusually strong characteristic of natives of India'. The anthem would only heighten this feeling and help them connect with the queen. He suggested that their sovereign being a woman would have a positive effect on the status of women in Indian society:

> The fact that the most illustrious woman upon earth—their Empress—the embodiment in their minds of all power and grace, has placed the record of her domestic life before the eyes of all persons in the world who wish to learn it, would tend with an indirect force, slowly but surely, and far more efficiently than any direct persuasions of argument, to kindle a desire for more social expansiveness in many a home where the beauty and holiness which consecrate the union of the good is now shut out from the sight of others.[54]

He explained that Indians (read Hindus) believed that god is one, even if worshiped in different forms and under various names. The establishment of the anthem would confirm the truth of 'One Supreme Heavenly Ruler'. This monotheism was, according to him, the foundation of the Vedas. Harford also made the point that many priests had given their support to this idea.

Finally, he proposed a musical reason. Though there was a lot of musical talent in India, it was in a depressed state and practised by 'wandering minstrels and dancing women'. Changing this would 'steadily raise the moral tone of the people'. He felt Indians were ignorant of harmonisation and hence their music was inferior. Such a project would uplift the state of their music.

The project began in June 1882. At a meeting held in London at Grosvenor House on 11 July 1883, a resolution was passed:

> That this meeting views with decided approval the project of tendering to Her Majesty's subjects in India, the hymn, God Save the Queen, as a National Anthem for that country, believing that it will form a new and valuable means of binding together in stronger because more sympathetic allegiance to Her Majesty the inhabitants of India, with all the other subjects of the Crown throughout the British Dominions and Colonies.[55]

The detailed minutes of the meeting reveal that many leading members of British society, elite Indians and some from even across the Atlantic supported the anthem project. Among those present were also Indians who were ambivalent and satiric about British rule and policies. One such individual was P.V. Ramaswami Raju, a playwright, essayist, poet and translator who was then at University College London, where he taught Sanskrit and Telugu. At this meeting, he was an active votary of the anthem movement, even penning an extra verse to a poem written by Alfred Henry Louis that celebrated 'Sending the National Anthem to India'. Also attending the meeting was

Shyamji Krishnavarma, who later became a staunch anti-colonist and was closely monitored by the British government.

The chief music consultant was Sourindro Mohun Tagore, a loyalist of the Crown, well-respected musicologist and author of many books on Indian classical music. After much thought, he came to the conclusion that there was no need to change the tune of the anthem to suit Indian ears. He also expressed difficulty in identifying one raga that all Indians would accept:

> Some may like the Bibhasha, some the Bhairavi, some the Saranga, and so forth. Under these circumstances it would be, I fear, difficult to fix a melody which will address itself to the musical proclivities of the Indian people in general. It is, therefore, politic that the original English melody, which I have declared in previous correspondence is not repugnant to Indian notions of music, should be adopted.[56]

It was agreed that the anthem would be translated into twenty languages. This gave Indians the opportunity to express their loyalty in their own languages. Among the twenty were Malay, Arabic, Pashto, Sinhala and Hebrew. Many leading scholars and poets, including Monier Williams, Max Müller, William Muir and poet and writer Bharatendu Harishchandra, who is often referred to as the 'Father of modern Hindi literature', participated in this process. Support also came from various rulers and people in powerful positions. Some sent translations in their respective languages. At this meeting, the anthem was presented in different languages and with varied musical arrangements. A supplementary stanza was also added to the anthem specially for India.

Concerns were expressed about the lack of financial support from the people of Britain. It was not only a question of writing these songs in different languages. To make sure that the anthem reached the people of India, propagation was required. The committee decided that they would popularise the song through government and private schools, colleges and pathashalas. Although this would only reach a very small percentage of the total population, it would be a start. The cost to print and distribute was calculated as £4,166 for a million copies, and the target was £8 million.

A few months earlier, at a meeting in Bombay, the Gujarati version of the anthem had been performed. Kaikhosro N. Kabraji, a prolific Parsi writer and editor of the journal *Stri Bodh*, was at the centre of this effort. Bombay's Governor J. Fergusson, who had convened the meeting, had this to say: 'These are some of the blessings which we enjoy by British law and British rule, which we typify by the name Queen. Therefore, in singing the prayer, "God Save the Queen", we mean "God save all that the Queen loves, all that the Queen represents, and all that the Queen guards".'[57]

It is evident that behind this very daunting symbolic effort was political nervousness, and this was expressed at the London gathering. There was a feeling that the British needed to show greater care for Indians. It was a moment for reconciliation and cooperation. The British had to change their rather standoffish and inexpressive nature. Law, freedom and order were more important than loyalty.

One speaker at the London gathering said, 'If we have erred in any way in our relationship with our Indian fellow-subjects, it has been in a want of sympathy, with them, or, at any rate, in failing to make them feel that they do command our sympathy.'[58]

The future, they said, depended on this change of attitude.

If we go by the Congress session reports, the attention to music in each session varied, but the songs were all filled with patriotism and woven through with religious diversity and togetherness. They were rendered either at the beginning or at the end of a day's proceedings, or after a mid-day break.

Not all reports detail the songs. Nor do they publish their lyrics or translations. But there were certain years when the

Congress session report overflowed with musical content. In 1912, at Bankipore (Patna), musician Raghubir Narayan sang five songs. Not only were the lyrics of all of these published, so were the rag/dhun and tala for every song.[59] Over the years, songs in ragas such as Poorvi, Pahadi, Kalyan and Khamaj were rendered at Congress sessions. Most of these songs were written in Hindustani.

In the report of the 1915 Bombay session, when different factions within the Congress were on the verge of reconciling and the Muslim League and the Congress were trying to come closer to each other, the scribe made it a point to mention the coming together of singers from various communities. They apparently opened every day's session with a 'concord of sweet sounds' and enthralled the gathering with 'patriotic fervour and soul-stirring music'.

The 1916 Lucknow session was also musically interesting because the Indian Muslim League joined in. This rapprochement between the two big political outfits was musically marked by the rendition of an 'Urdu poem by a Muslim youth' and another Urdu poem by poet Pandit Brij Narain Chakbast. The report notes, 'The songs were well received and repeatedly cheered, where there was reference to the country, the motherland of Hindus and Muslims alike.'[60]

From the way the songs are described in the Congress session reports, it is abundantly clear that no single song was considered to be representative of all Indians, or one that everyone had to pay obeisance to. Words such as 'national anthem', 'patriotic song', 'patriotic poem' and 'rashtra geet' were used interchangeably. All the musical renderings spoke of a unified search for justice, freedom and betterment. At times, there were non-Hindustani songs too. At the Belgaum session in 1924, there were three Kannada songs. On the first day of the session, two welcome songs were presented. The first was *Swagatavu Swagatavu Sakalajana Sankulake* composed by Betageri Krishna Sharma. The other was a nationalistic composition titled *Bharata Rastrageethe* composed by Shanthakavi. The Karnatik ragas in which these two songs were composed, Shri and Mukhari respectively, are mentioned.

The second day of the Congress session opened with the 'Karnataka rashtra gite', *Udayavagali namma cheluva Kannada nadu*. Composed by Huyilagola Narayana Rao and sung, on that day, by Gavayyi Subbaraya. At a time when the state of Karnataka had not yet been actively imagined, this song written in the future tense said, 'Let my beautiful Kannada land rise and shine.'

In the Kannada-speaking districts, including Belgaum, that were part of Bombay Presidency, this song and *Rakshisu Kannada Devi* by Shantakavi were referred to as the 'nada gite' or state anthems. In some other parts of Karnataka, Manjeshwara Govinda Pai's song *Taayi Baare Mogava Tore Kannadiagara Matheye* was sung as nada gite. There is an inherent plurality in accepting different songs, and by inference different ideas of the land, as being equally representative of a region.

Regional empowerment was not seen as contesting the idea of a nation. Differences and distinctness added to the multiplicity of voices, debates and resistance. Therefore, depending on the location of the session, songs in the local language celebrating that particular geography and culture were sung. The 1924 report states as much: 'Prominence was given to Kannad raags and tunes.'

And yet, rarely did significant cultural crossovers take place, with the sounds of the South reverberating in the North. The two exceptions are the rendition of a poem by Balamba from Madras at the Amritsar session in 1919 and a Kathakali performance at the Lucknow session in 1936. Otherwise, beyond the intellectual and political, there seems to have been little cultural interaction. The North–South divide was definitely in place even then.

There can be no doubt that the Congress sessions were dominated by Bengali singers, both individuals and groups.

Bengali ladies, boys and girls are mentioned on multiple occasions. A friend and well-known Tamil historian has often complained that too much of India's modern aesthetic imagination is Brahmo Bengali. I am inclined to agree.

Among the lead singers, a few stand out for their repeated appearance. Sarala Devi Chaudhurani was an old-timer at the Congress sessions. Vishnu Digambar Paluskar became an integral part of them from around 1913. Either he or his students from Gandharva Mahavidyalaya were always present. They most probably sang *Vande Mataram* in his tune set to Raga Kafi. Paluskar also composed patriotic songs in Hindi.

Another woman who sang at the sessions was Raihana Tyabji, the granddaughter of Badruddin Tyabji, a barrister and judge in the Bombay High Court and president of the 1887 Congress session. Raihana was close to Gandhi, and taught him to speak and read Urdu. She was also some sort of a mystic who lived austerely, and went on to write *The Heart of a Gopi*, a book that spoke of her experiences in Krishna bhakti. Her name appears as a singer for the first time in the 1921 session report.

Beyond the socio-political need for music, organisers of the Congress sessions also had to give their delegates a flavour of the local culture and, importantly, something to do in the evenings. The solution: organise performances! Not all reports mention these events, but I suspect they must have been the norm. At times a music committee was constituted, with leading classical musicians and poets helping in the curation. The Kakinada session report of 1923 is rich with information. There was Vedic chanting, the recitation of verses from the Quoran and multi-religious songs in many languages, though Telugu did dominate. Besides these renditions during the day, there were musical concerts held at night. Revenue from concert ticket sales at the Kakinada conference was Rs 1,235 and 9 annas, which was considerably more than the Rs 383 collected the following year at the Belgaum session. The 1927 Congress session balance sheet has a specific mention of the All-India Music Conference that was organised along with the political event.

With Congress sessions moving from city to city amidst much political turmoil, only one thing remained constant: *Vande Mataram*. Irrespective of where they gathered, the song was sung and the slogan sounded. The report of the 1931 session at Karachi says, 'The proceedings commenced with the singing, all standing, of the Indian National Anthem ...'[61]

It is highly probable that, in 1931, *Vande Mataram* was inferred to be the Indian national anthem. If this is true, then Nehru's argument that *Vande Mataram* had not been formally adopted by the Congress as the national anthem becomes a technicality. *Jana Gana Mana* is not mentioned in the reports published by the Congress until later in the 1930s. It may have been one of the 'patriotic songs', but it was not specifically named.

A January 1918 special report in *New India* titled 'Songs Sung at the Calcutta Session' gives the English translation of the songs that were rendered at the 1917 session, which opened with Rabindranath Tagore reciting an English invocation. First, a hymn from the Rigveda is printed. Following this chant is Aurobindo's translation of *Vande Mataram*. Curiously, the translation provided in the paper is Aurobindo's earlier, more interpretative translation of the song and not the literal, line by line translation from November 1909. The former is more suggestive of the independence struggle in which he was actively participating. Aurobindo uses words such as 'lord', 'lady' and 'queen' to address the goddess!

Sarala Devi's *Atita gourababahini mama bani*, a song written by Satyendranath Tagore and two songs of Rabindranath are also given. All translations are credited to Indira Devi. The first Rabindranath song is *Desh Desh Nandit Kari*. In his book *India's National Anthem*, Probodh Chandra Sen has pointed to similarities between this song and *Jana Gana Mana*. The last song in the news article is indeed *Jana Gana Mana*, presented as an English abridgement of the five-verse song. This could mean a couple of things. It is possible that a shortened version was sung at the session, or the more likely explanation, *New India* chose to publish a condensed translation.

In his address at the session, Chittaranjan Das had this to say: 'Brother delegates, at the very outset I desire to refer to the song to which you have just listened. It is a song of the glory and victory of India.'[62]

It must be noted that Rabindranath was yet to publish his own translation of the song. Hence, Indira Devi's translation may have been the first.

It would be fair to say that *Jana Gana Mana* had not yet caught the people's fancy; it had not become an earworm, a tuneful memory. If not for the controversy of the 1930s, *Vande Mataram* would have become our national anthem because the dominant Congress leaders do not seem to have understood why the song was unacceptable. They only made the necessary philosophical shift later, in order to ensure religious harmony.

There is a curious incident in Tagore's own life that Krishna Dutta and Andrew Robinson have documented in their biography of the poet.[63] In 1913, just a few years after he had composed *Jana Gana Mana*, Tagore was asked to sing *Vande Mataram* at a private dinner hosted by William Rothenstein and W.B. Yeats. The poet apparently hummed the tune, but could not remember more than a few words. Rather unusual, one would think.

Much later, on 31 August 1927, in a letter written when he was travelling in Java, Tagore had this to say:

> At one point in our history India (bharatavarsha) was deeply conscious of its geographical identity; at that time it internalised its physical image by meditating on its rivers and mountains. The places of pilgrimage are thus accordingly organised. Kanyakumari to the South, Manas Sarovar to the North, Dwaraka on the Western Sea coast, and Ganga

> Sangam on the Eastern seas. Thus through pilgrimage the whole image of India can be gathered with due reverence in the mind. There can be no better way of knowing India. At that time travel was conducted on foot, and so through pilgrimage not only could the geography of India be known, but also there was close contact with the diverse inhabitants of the country. As at that time self-realisation of India was a quest for truth, the method of self-recognition also became one of truth by itself. True respect never looks for shortcuts. That is to say, the pretence of a fleeting meeting on the stage of nationhood is not paraded as (true) union. Quest for union at that time was one of unfeigned devotion.[64]

Even if *Jana Gana Mana* had not been selected as the national anthem, it would remain one of Tagore's great compositions. His India is poetic, abundant, vulnerable, all-encompassing, in need of an awakening. Tagore was never prosaic. Reality did not stand in front and explain itself. It shone by unravelling the imaginative. There was also never one reality that everyone needed to comprehend identically. Tagore dealt in possibilities, leaving it to the reader or singer to realise the unseen and unsaid within his words. He was willing to greet uncertainty.

Indians have been unnecessarily obsessed with the word 'adhinayaka' for decades when the song actually lives in its first three words, which precede the allegorical charioteer: 'Jana Gana Mana'.

In these three words of equal syllabic measure, Tagore brings the people of India together. Everything that follows is an elucidation. 'Jana' is every individual of this land, 'gana' are collections of people and communities and 'mana' is the heart and mind of each individual as well as their collective identities. The Preamble to our constitution begins with the words 'We, the people', an idea encapsulated in 'jana gana mana'. Tagore recognises individual free will and spirit, but does not forget that we live as groups. Who we are is defined by the exchange between the inner and the outer, the self and its myriad reflections. In placing 'mana' after the psychological markers of the individual and the collective, Tagore expresses his hope for fraternity. The coming together of the hearts of individuals and all their chosen and unchosen identifications is India. In just three words, our entire social and political consciousness is covered.

In his 1919 translation of the song, Tagore speaks of 'adhinayaka' as the ruler, dispenser of India's destiny, the Eternal Charioteer. But the first time that Tagore translated *Jana Gana Mana* was in 1918. The translation was published in the February issue of *Modern Review*. He translated the song once again, more than a decade later, in 1931. The note above this translation mentions that 'The Proceedings of the last Karachi session of the Indian National Congress began with the singing of three stanzas of Rabindranath Tagore's Bengali national anthem Janaganamana—Adhinayaka jaya he Bharata-Bhagyavidhata.' Rather oddly, it also states that 'The poet recently translated all the five verses of the song into English and sent the translation to us for publication in the *Modern Review*.' It was published in the May issue with no reference to the 1918 publication.

This version is a recall of the 1919 translation, but contains memories of his first attempt in 1918. I am tempted to speculate that the author wanted it published because it might have been the translation that he considered final. But we have to keep in mind that though we refer to them as translations, they are closer to interpretative trans-lingual imaginations.

In Tagore's 1918 English interpretation, 'adhinayaka' is the Eternal Charioteer but not the dispenser of India's destiny. He titled the song 'Victory to Thee, Builder of India's Destiny'. By 1919, the 'builder' becomes the 'dispenser'. 'Dispenser', apart from being closer to the word 'vidhata', also refers to a larger, decisive, even metaphysical being who determines our destiny. On the other hand, 'builder' brings down the universal guide to the domain of materiality and transactions. Someone who works on a concrete, step-by-step process.

Tagore was a poet, musician and painter. He seemed to be always tapping into an interior intangible spirit. Much like Baul singers or whirling dervishes, Tagore's realisations were aesthetic experiences from which he constructed philosophical pathways. This is not to say that his literary output was airy-fairy wordplay. He sought to understand social and political realities, and knew that reasoning can only evolve by uncaging the human mind.

Some construe that the Eternal Charioteer that Tagore references is Lord Krishna. The question is, what or who rules over our minds? The direct answer would be an all-powerful being, god, a universal power or consciousness. But 'adhinayaka' could simply mean untampered and non-judgemental reflection, from which goodness emerges. I realise that this is a bit of a leap, but I urge you to let the possibility rest in your mind for some time. These different expositions need not contest each other. Neither is this a battle between theists and atheists. If there is an all-pervading power that is the dispenser of our destiny, where does it reside? Tagore tells us that this power brings people together, hopes to end our sorrows, points us to the righteous path and accompanies us on the rugged journey towards freedom. It is a resident of our hearts and minds. Appayya Dikshitar, a sixteenth-century Vedantin, expressed this confluence of the external and the internal in a descriptive verse. He describes Siva as a person surrounded by all things cold. Ganga, the moon, snakes, sandal paste, and the daughter of the snow-clad mountains who is his consort. He then asks a rhetorical question: how does Nataraja (Siva) bear all this cold? He answers: unless the lord resides forever in the devotee's heart that is burning with desire for him, he cannot withstand the cold.

Tagore appeals to the Charioteer to awaken within our manas. The song proceeds to hug the borders and the coast of India. It comes down from Punjab and Sindh, through the Konkan coast, only to go up the Coromandel coastline on the other side and finally reach Bengal. After the partition of India, the word 'Sind' became a point of contention. On 21 May 1948, in his Note to the Cabinet which stated that *Jana Gana Mana* would be provisionally used as the anthem, Nehru wrote, 'It has also been suggested that instead of Sind, Assam might be included in the list of provinces mentioned in it.'[65]

In fact, versions of the anthem with the lyrics altered were being sung in places across the country. From a series of letters written in early 1953 by All India Educational Supply Co. (the government-approved publishers of educational maps and charts), it is clear that there was much confusion. Though the company copied the lyrics from the book *Our National Songs*, published by the Government of India, it had received a letter from the Director of Education, Sourashtra, claiming that the lyrics on the charts were the 'old one, which is not to be used, now'. The company also mentioned that the government of Uttar Pradesh had published the wrong lyrics. It repeatedly wrote to the secretary of education, Government of India, requesting a clarification.[66]

In a handwritten letter from the Government High School in Dharam Jaigarh, Raigarh district, addressed to the under-secretary, Ministry of Education, Government of India, the head master says,

> I shall be highly obliged if you kindly enlighten me at your earliest convenience if the following line in the national anthem is correct or its alternative quoted below. Kamrup Gujarat Maratha Dravida Utkala Banga.
>
> The objector who is a local official said the line should be

> Panjab Sindh Gujarat Maratha Dravida Utkala Banga because although Punjab and Sindh have gone into Pakistan the people of those parts have migrated to India.[67]

Questions about whether 'Sindh' should remain in the national anthem have been periodically raised. In 2005, the issue came up before the Supreme Court of India.

The court observed:

> 'Sindh' is not just a geographical region. It refers to the place and to its people. Sindhis are spread throughout the country and they derive their such name as having originated and migrated from Sindh. 'Sindh' also refers to the river 'Sindhu' or 'Indus'. It also refers to a culture, one of the oldest in the world and even modern India feels proud of its having inherited the Indus Valley Civilisation as an inalienable part of its heritage. River Indus (Sindhu) finds numerous references in the Indian Classical Literature including Rig Veda.[68]

The Union government was categorical. 'The song is a literary creation which cannot be changed.' The Attorney General for India, Milon Banerjee, then went beyond staid legalities and made aesthetic observations on poetry, form and import.

> Every word placed therein is carefully in position in the whole composition. A suggestion seeking a substitution of words in the National Anthem would be 'a bid to rob Tagore of his greatness' ... in any poetry the structure has some purpose other than to clarify the content ... It is the structure which forces the author to be more creative; to find ways of saying things which do not disrupt the flow ... The fabric of words is the creation of the author. A poem once popular, more so if adopted as a National Anthem, becomes symbolic of the feelings, ideas and images that have come to be associated in our minds with the words used by the author in structuring

> the poem and then the meaning of a word or a group of words reaches far beyond its dictionary definition.[69]

What if 'Sindh' is representative of all those who do not have states or regions named after them? They are Indian because they are one among us. As are the Siddi Damamis who trace their origin to Africa centuries ago. Tibetans living in India for decades may or may not have taken Indian citizenship, but they are one among us. This deeply inclusive notion dismantles the chest-thumping nationalism that is dependent on religious and ethnic antecedents.

Sindh must then be seen as our answer to the kind of bigotry that masks itself as nationalism and reclaims a selective past. Sindhis are people who came here looking for a home or have been here because it is home. Their Indianness is not defined by a piece of paper. An Indian is anyone who belongs, and this belonging comes from within. Acceptance of all such people is not tolerance; it is just how it should be because we are human beings sharing this earth. The Tamils from Sri Lanka and the Rohingyas from Myanmar belong to Sindh. Their religion, language, culture does not matter. When the Government of India provides special provisions for citizenship only for non-Muslims from neighbouring countries, it ruptures that shared humanity.

Tagore realised at one point that he had not mentioned every province of India in his song. In his letter from Java, he added,

> In the victory song of the controller of India's destiny that I composed a few years ago, I have stitched together the names of the provinces of India, and the names of the Vindhyas, the Himalaya, Ganga, Yamuna are also there. But today I think the names of all the provinces of India and the seas and mountains should be put together in rhythm in a song of recognition of our country, to implant it in the minds of our people. Patriotism is a word that is much bandied around

> these days, but how can patriotism come where the true knowledge of our country is lacking.

Tagore did not see India as a unified monolith that required citizens to shed their regional, ethnic or even religious identities. His India was built on a national consciousness that was receptive of differences and built on dialogue.

Tagore concludes his letter with another observation. He attempts to provide reasoning as to why the lands around the five rivers (Punjab) and Brahmaputra in India's west and east never really became part of our cultural consciousness. He reasons that Punjab is missing from the overarching cultural ambit because the region was 'repeatedly disturbed and colonised'. The easternmost province, he believes, 'had not been fully assimilated into Hindu India'. Knowing Tagore's sense of this nation, I do not believe his observations are assertions of a monolithic Hindu India, but are rather an objective reasoning for why religious and historical contradictions, erasures and hatred continue to haunt us. If anything, he is making the critical point that the 'geographical memory' of India has been traditionally constructed only on the basis of a Hindu India. Tagore's thoughts on country, nationalism and identity underwent a sea change over time, and it is likely that if he had been around when the national anthem was being finalised, he would not have suggested *Jana Gana Mana*. In the introduction to the Rabindranath Tagore Centenary volume published in 1961, Nehru said that he had asked Tagore to compose a 'National Anthem for the new India'. Tagore did not immediately suggest *Jana Gana Mana*. In Nehru's words, Tagore 'partly agreed' to write a song. What would he have written? Historian Rudrangshu Mukherjee has speculated that Tagore would have moved away from making any reference to divinity.[70] His song would have taken in the magnitude of the moment, yet recognised the tragedies of the recent past.

The poet Harivansh Rai Bachchan was critical of *Jana Gana Mana*. He thought the mention of religions and regions divided people and allowed 'regionalism and communalism to gain ground'. He subscribed to the One India and One Indian theory. In my opinion, this is a dangerous paradigm.

When Tagore used the word 'Dravida', Periyar had yet to make it a potent political force in the Tamil region. Tagore's Dravida was not limited to Tamil-speaking people. It encompassed the lands where the major Dravidian languages were spoken, and built on interconnections. We now know that Dravidian languages flourish in pockets of Pakistan and other countries in minuscule numbers. Languages of Dravidian origin are also found in Jharkhand, Orissa and West Bengal. The imagination born from this understanding allows us to expand the physical horizons of that expression. Language is a conduit for cultural ties. Dravida is not just a place south of the Vindhyas, it is every place where people of Dravida ancestry reside and celebrate life. Thol Thirumavalavan, Member of Parliament and leader of the political party Viduthalai Chiruthaigal Katchi (VCK), has pushed the frontiers of Dravida further. He speaks of Dravida as a stand against religious parochialism, casteism and all forms of repression—an altogether new terrain that is not limited by identity or geography.

In one of his speeches, Thirumavalavan expanded this thought even further, equating the ideology of Dravida with democracy itself. He said the Dravidian ideology is not owned by any one political party; it belongs to everyone, and represents social justice, equality, upliftment of the marginalised, feminism, cultural freedom and human rights.[71] And then he suggested, 'You can also understand it as democracy.'

Tagore speaks of the seas, the Himalayas and the rivers. Again, this is not an exhaustive list. He mentions the Yamuna and Ganga. Ganga is not just the legendary river that came down from the heavens; she is the lifeline of existence, water.

While speaking about the anthem at a public meeting, I was asked by a young person why the Northeast finds no mention. It gave me pause. Some people have suggested that 'Uttarpurva' must replace 'Sindh' in the text. But did Tagore really forget the Northeast, a region where he had spent many moons? It is unfortunate that we only sing the first stanza of the song as our anthem. For, in the last stanza, Tagore describes the light breaking from *over the peaks of the Eastern Hills*.

An anthem needs to be concise and representative, so compromises are made with regard to what can be included. But if we were to learn the entire song, we could fill our rendition of the anthem with the spirit of the song. If we knew and felt the second stanza of the song when Tagore asks Hindus, Muslims, Sikhs, Jains, Buddhists, Christians and Parsis to come together in love and harmony, and pray to the dispenser of India's destiny, we would not allow the anthem to become an excuse to abuse or attack people. The song's emotional landscape lies in the unsung stanzas. Tagore sees darkness all around, people are weighed down by sorrow; they are terrified, yearning for comfort, protection and affection. They need to be lifted out of this state of despair.

Exquisitely, for a large part of the song Tagore does not specify whether the Eternal Charioteer, the protector, is male or female. Much like Tiruvalluvar's 'adi bhagavan' in the first verse of the *Tirukural*, the creator is not a singular deity and remains gender neutral. Only in the penultimate stanza does Tagore refer to the 'mother' in the phrase 'snehomayi tumi mata'. Yet, the artist in me is not convinced that it is a gendered identification.

This is Tagore's translation of the stanza:

> The darkness was dense and deep was the night. My country lay in a deathlike silence of swoon. But thy mother's arms were round her and thin eyes gazed upon her troubled face in sleepless love through her hours of ghastly dreams. Thou art

the companion and the saviour of the people in their sorrow,
thou dispenser of India's destiny![72]

He is reaching for that feeling of a mother's love, that unreserved embrace, the female spirit, the primal force of creation. A significant difference between this and previous imaginations of the nation is that 'she' is not Mother India. The song carries no such reference. The feminine spirit comforts the people, the country, but she herself is not the country. And this spirit is plural, manifesting according to the imagination of the people who live on this land, referred to and revered by them in innumerable ways. Depending on how you want to recognise her, she is either a Supreme Being or the untainted compassion buried within all of us. This is a song about the people, their attributes and state of mind. Their experience defines the country.

Tagore's description of the topography and geographic spread of India brings it alive. He achieves a unification of cultures without resorting to any convenient nationalistic cliché. Nor is this a status quo composition. In the last stanza, Tagore infuses the song with a dream, the kind of dream that eclipses reality. He hears the birds chirping and feels the morning breeze while the sun rises over the eastern hills, and the dispenser of India's destiny becomes 'the king of kings'. Just as the mother is not a woman, the king is not a man. Drawing from Tagore's play *Raja* (*The King of the Dark Chamber*), written a year before *Jana Gana Mana* was composed, Rudrangshu Mukherjee explains the last line of the song as 'the victory of the rajeswar in every sovereign individual's heart and consciousness'.[73]

Tagore's English renditions of the song in 1918 and 1919 are different in style and description, though the import does not shift. Maybe one should not even compare the two translations.

Professor Sukanta Chaudhuri suggested to me, 'Tagore's English versions of his Bengali poems and songs are often very free versions ... they do not seem guided by any wish to render the original closely, but rather to achieve an independent poetic effect, and/or keep things simple for non-Indian readers.'

Still, I cannot help but be fascinated by his differing translations and interpretations.

The 1918 translation of the first line in the third stanza reads: 'Pilgrims pass from age to age on the road of Time uneven with the rise and fall of *races*'. (emphasis mine)

In 1919, this became: 'The procession of pilgrims passes over the endless road rugged with the rise and fall of *nations*'. (emphasis mine)

The word used by Tagore in the poem is 'jatri', a traveller on an inhospitable road that rises and falls. But he translates it first as 'races' and then changes it to 'nations'. Neither word is connected literally to 'jatri'. But with this change in its translation, the song addresses nationalistic jingoism directly. All forms of nationalism draw strength from racial, religious, caste, gender, ethnic or sexual parochialism. When Tagore writes 'nations' instead of 'races', he is referring not only to the white man's rule, but also to all kinds of parochialism. Tagore's use of the term 'nation' in 1919 is interesting also because he was opposed to the Western construct of nationalism. His idea of the nation was a coming together of many 'samajs'. Tagore's nation was not limited by political boundaries. His India was permanently in a fluid state, allowing itself to be enriched by the flow of peoples and cultures from across the world.

He also seems to be echoing Gandhi's idea of a creative swarajya. Tagore asks the Eternal Charioteer to lead people beyond death—death of the mind, heart and body—to the righteous path of self-discovery and undemarcated love.

But why did he send this song to the Congress? It was 1911, and Indians were primarily fighting for a place within the British government. They were demanding that they be treated in every manner as 'full subjects'. Poorna Swaraj had not yet been envisaged. Was the dreamer in the poet looking into the crystal ball and telling the Congress that they needed to think beyond and get their act together?

Tagore also replaced a word in stanza four.

The 1918 translation: 'Victory to thee who leadest people across their *insult* into triumph.' (emphasis mine)

In 1919: 'Thou art compassion and saviour of the people in their *sorrows*.' (emphasis mine)

Sorrow is most definitely closer to 'dukkha', the word used in the poem. An insult points to a third person, an external power that has violated us. Here, it must mean the British and their draconian rule. An anti-colonial stance, then. When Tagore changed 'insult' to 'sorrow', his imagination was not limited to the British alone. Sorrow is not necessarily induced by external oppression; it can be a result of circumstances, personal loss, lack of self-worth, and socio-cultural conditioning. Though sorrow is a feeling of emptiness, it is not entrapped in blame. The feeling of being insulted can be momentarily transcended by retaliation, but sorrow cannot. Dukkha in Buddhism is not the opposite of 'sukha', or happiness, peace. It refers to a state of life, an inevitable reality unless human beings free themselves of its causes.

Tagore began with 'jana' and 'gana', so the sorrows he addresses are of the collective and the individual. The dispenser of India's destiny is not just a force for British eviction, but also a moral compass and guide for personal and common happiness and altruism.

He wrote *Jana Gana Mana* in response to a request that annoyed him and then handed it over for rendition at a Congress session. Two distinctly political acts from the poet. We have to wonder if he was sending messages to both the British Raj and the Indian National Congress. Asked to honour the king-emperor, Tagore insinuates that, under the Raj, people are fearful, living in gloom, hoping that the Eternal Charioteer will show them the way. 'The sun never sets on the British Empire' was the arrogant British maxim. Was Tagore telling them that their sun was about to set, and that an Indian sun was rising from behind the eastern hills?

Coincidentally, at the 1911 session, the Congress applauded Gandhi for his work in Transvaal, South Africa.

> Resolution
>
> XXIX. INDIANS IN THE COLONIES
>
> (a) That this Congress, anticipating the forthcoming legislation of the provincial settlement recently arrived at, cordially congratulates Mr. Gandhi and the Transvaal Indian community upon the repeal of the anti-Asiatic legislation of the Province regarding registration and immigration, and expresses its high admiration of the intense patriotism, courage and self-sacrifice with which they—Mahomedan and Hindu, Zoroastrian and Christian—have suffered persecution in the interest of their countrymen during their peaceful and selfless struggle for elementary civil rights against overwhelming odds.
>
> 'The motion was put and carried by acclamation, with three hearty and ringing cheers for Gandhi.'[74]

Jana Gana Mana did not echo through the countryside with the speed and spirit of *Vande Mataram*. It was not directly attached to any specific movement, nor did it express a sloganeering form of nationalism that could attract crowds and kindle mythical memories. *Jana Gana Mana* was a poetic mural that required meditation. Gandhi recognised the potential of the song before most others. Narayan Moreshwar Khare, a disciple of Vishnu Digambar Paluskar, joined the Sabarmati Ashram as a music teacher and guide on a salary of Rs 20 per month in 1915. Under his guidance, Gandhi began publishing the *Bhajanavali*, a collection of songs that were part of the ashram's musical oeuvre. Much before *Jana Gana Mana* emerged as a song of national significance, a prescient Gandhi included it in the first edition of the *Bhajanavali* published in 1922. In that edition, he also included *Vande Mataram* and *Saare Jahan se Achcha*.

At 11 p.m. on 14 August 1947, the fifth session of the Constituent Assembly of India commenced in the Constitution Hall, New Delhi. It opened with a rendition of the first verse of *Vande Mataram* by Sucheta Kripalani. What followed is, of course, unforgettable: Nehru's spine-tingling 'Tryst with Destiny' oration. He ended by moving a resolution that the representatives of the people of India take a pledge dedicating themselves 'to the service of India and her people to the end that this ancient land attain her rightful and honoured place in the world and make her full and willing contribution to the promotion of world peace and the welfare of mankind'.[75] This was supported by Chaudhari Khaliquzzaman and S. Radhakrishnan. At the stroke of midnight, all the members took the pledge.

At the very end, after the presentation of the national flag and just before the assembly dispersed for a short break of a few hours, Kripalani sang the other national songs. 'Mr. President: The next item is the singing of the first few lines of *Saare Jahan se Achcha Hindustan Hamara* and the first verse of *Janaganamana Adhinayaka Jaya He*.'

Jana Gana Mana pipped *Vande Mataram* to the post, to become the national anthem. Long before this constitutional acceptance, Subhas Chandra Bose had named *Jana Gana Mana* the national anthem. If he had not given the song this top-drawer status and drawn everyone's attention to its magnificence, who knows if it would have become our national anthem. Even for Bose, this was a striking decision because, in 1937, he had defended *Vande Mataram* even as he was instrumental in helping to defuse the political confrontation that was building around it. Bose was a member of the sub-committee appointed by the

Congress Working Committee in October 1937, which included Maulana Abul Kalam Azad, Jawaharlal Nehru and Narendra Dev. The committee had a musical mandate: to examine all current songs that may be sent to them, and to submit a collection that they thought was 'worthy', 'have rousing and inspiring tune'. They were also asked to accept only songs that were written in 'simple Hindustani or can be adapted to it'. The committee was also told to 'consult and take advice' from Tagore. We do not know what happened next, or if a set of songs was even finalised. But, in January 1938, Bose became president of the Indian National Congress and remained in that position until 29 April 1939, when he resigned amid disagreements with the organisation. In any case, by 1941, Bose had gravitated towards *Jana Gana Mana*. He was forming the INA, and recognised the need to forge Hindu–Muslim unity. Symbols—aural, visual and literary—would play a crucial role in this.

After discussions with Abid Hasan and others, in which *Saare Jahan se Achcha* and *Vande Mataram* were probably also considered, Bose announced *Jana Gana Mana* as the national anthem at the inauguration of the Free India Centre in Berlin on 2 November 1941. On 11 September 1942, a Chamber Orchestra of Hamburg Radio performed it at the inauguration of the Deutsche-Indische Gesellschaft, under the auspices of Hamburg Rathaus. The conductor was Eigel Krutge, and the orchestration was done at a cost of 750 Reichsmarks. This was the first orchestration of the song. It was played again on 26 January 1943 by the Berlin Radio Orchestra and broadcast on Azad Hind Radio after Bose's Independence Day speech in Berlin. We do not know if the same orchestration was reproduced or another musical arrangement was designed. This was Bose's last public appearance before he embarked on his great crossing to Asia on 9 February 1943.

When the Draft Constitution was introduced in the Constituent Assembly on 4 November 1948, it did not carry any mention of a national anthem. Members began urging the assembly that the national anthem and the national flag needed to find mention in the constitution. There were requests from members such as Seth Govind Das, B.A. Mandlo, Madhav Rao and Shibban Lal Saxena, asking for a decision on this matter. The national anthem was not a standalone issue of concern. It was often coupled with the need for a decision on a national language, national script, national dress and cow slaughter. At least some of the protagonists who raised these issues also believed that *Vande Mataram* was the ideal choice. This affirms my earlier point that the issue of cow slaughter, a uniform civil code and *Vande Mataram* cannot be disassociated from one another.

At the Constituent Assembly, the national anthem was never discussed in any detail. But in October 1949, the president of the Constituent Assembly, Rajendra Prasad, made it clear that the anthem, like the national flag, would be passed by a resolution.[76]

Nehru said nothing on this matter in the Constituent Assembly. But he made his position obvious in a Cabinet Note in May 1948.[77] He believed that there was an urgent need for at least 'some temporary arrangements' to be made regarding the national anthem. This was not only an internal issue but also concerned embassies and foreign authorities who needed an anthem that could be played on official occasions. According to him, except for the governor of the Central Provinces, who preferred *Vande Mataram*, there was unanimous support for *Jana Gana Mana*.

A month later, in June 1948, in a letter to B.C. Roy, who was then the chief minister of Bengal, Nehru said that, when it was played in New York in October 1947, *Jana Gana Mana* 'produced a sensation' and representatives of many countries loved the anthem. After that, army bands were asked to practise the song, and *Jana Gana Mana* was regularly played by the Indian Army, Navy and Air Force. It was also recommended that AIR be 'requested to broadcast some brief rendering of *Jana Gana*

Mana frequently so as to popularise it'.[78] The song was being pushed within official circles and its rendition made a habit. People were getting used to the song even before it was provided official status. This decision of the Cabinet did not go down well with everybody. Syama Prasad Mookerjee maintained that, since there were strong opinions with regard to the adoption of *Jana Gana Mana* as the provisional national anthem, the government must issue a statement that made its position on the matter clear. But Nehru did not feel the need to do any such thing. Until the Constituent Assembly decided on the national anthem, *Jana Gana Mana* would do just fine.

By the end of 1949, *Jana Gana Mana* had become the default national anthem. On 13 October 1949, Rajendra Prasad said in the Constituent Assembly, 'The Government have already adopted a particular song as the National Anthem, but the Constituent Assembly has not yet accepted that. So we have not taken any steps in that direction yet; I do not know what to do, but we may have to consider that point also.'

The reasons that Nehru provided for rejecting *Vande Mataram* as the national anthem in 1948 were different from his criticism of it in 1937. Back then, he found the lyrics difficult to comprehend and felt that its ideas were 'out of keeping with modern notions of nationalism and progress'.[79] In 1948, he shifted focus to the music of the song.[80] He now said that the music of the anthem must be 'full of life', have 'dignity' and should be suitable for small and big orchestras as well as military bands and pipes. *Vande Mataram* was too 'plaintive', 'mournful' and 'repetitive', and not suitable for orchestral presentations. He had consulted many musicians and orchestra conductors from foreign countries and they concurred with the view that *Vande Mataram* was not good for orchestral or military renditions. In various letters and notes, he stressed the fact that the music mattered more than the words in a national anthem. He even said it was 'a form of words, but it is even more so a tune, or a musical score' and 'chiefly music and not words.' All disagreements around the song so far had been about its lyrical import, and in cleverly presenting a strong musical opposition, Nehru side-stepped the communal conversation. He wrote in his letter to B.C. Roy, 'There is no question of some Muslims objecting to *Vande Mataram*. That has not influenced many people here, but many of us and I feel strongly about it, think that in the present context *Vande Mataram* is completely unsuited as a National Anthem.'[81]

Nehru felt that *Jana Gana Mana* was distinctive and had 'an ideal lilt'. In his view, *Vande Mataram* was a 'flop' from the point of view of how it would sound or be received by foreign countries. Nehru was also making a philosophical argument to explain his tilt towards *Jana Gana Mana*. He said *Vande Mataram* represented a longing for freedom, while *Jana Gana Mana* was a song of its attainment, and hence the more suitable choice. Nehru also wanted to standardise the tune of *Jana Gana Mana* and its words changed to simple Hindustani.

In his Note for the Cabinet, Nehru judged the version of *Jana Gana Mana* played by the Patiala State Military Band as the best in the country. The London Philharmonic was asked to record three versions with the full orchestra, string orchestra and military band. There was, however, some concern that the anthem would become too Westernised, and hence an expert Indian musician was asked to advise them. I have not been able to trace the identity of this mystery expert. Rudrangshu Mukherjee had this to say on the possible identity of the 'expert': 'My own guess is that the concerned Indian musician could have been Timir Baran who worked very closely with GOI after independence.'

It does seem probable that Baran was the consultant because he was one of the pioneers of orchestration in Indian music.

It was not so easy to come up with standardised recordings of *Jana Gana Mana*. In fact, the project took many years. The first hurdle was the issue of copyright, which had to be obtained from Rathindranath Tagore and Visva-Bharati, which held the rights to his works, and from the composers Herbert Murrill and Norman Richardson, who had arranged the music. I could not get much information on how and when the copyrights were received from the music composers, but there is substantial material on the rights to the song itself, in the letters exchanged between the ministries of Home Affairs, Education, Information and Broadcasting and the Director General, AIR.

Rathindranath Tagore and Visva-Bharati appear to have been dragging their feet, and this irritated the government. In one of his letters, the Director General, AIR wrote, 'Vishwabharati people have been procrastinating for several months now.' Despite multiple personal discussions with Rathindranath, and the involvement of senior Supreme Court judge S.R. Das, who was one of Rabindranath Tagore's early students and went on to become Chief Justice of India, the issue was not resolved.

Rathindranath was concerned about the use of the text and tune of *Jana Gana Mana*. He wanted a guarantee that no changes would be made in either. The Director General made it clear to him that this was not an acceptable condition. The best he could do was to write to the Government of India expressing the hope that nothing would be changed in the text or the tune.

All India Radio was only concerned that the approved musical rendering be as close to the Visva-Bharati tune as possible. Decisions on textual change had to be taken by the Ministry of Home Affairs. Rathindranath wrote to the Ministry of Home Affairs on 23 March 1951, offering to assign copyright to the song to the Government of India. Though I have not seen that letter, it is safe to assume that he included his request regarding the tune and text. In response, the Ministry of Home Affairs said that, though no alterations to the text had so far been authorised, the government could not assure him that no change to the text or music would be made in the future. All they were willing to say was, 'your wish that the original text and tune should be preserved will be kept in mind'. Following these exchanges, on 2

May 1951, the Ministry of Home Affairs informed the country through a press communique that Visva-Bharati and the heirs of Rabindranath Tagore had agreed to the 'government authorising the public to use freely the song and its tune'.[82]

After some back and forth, and more red tapism (because Visva-Bharati became a university in 1951), the copyright transfer deed dated 28 September 1951 was signed by Visva-Bharati and Rathindranath on 3 October 1951. Visva-Bharati held the rights for the words of the song, while Rathindranath kept the musical recording and broadcasting rights. What is not clear is whether the entire song with all its five verses was signed over to the Government of India or only the first verse. Since the verses were not printed as part of the agreement, and the agreement just says 'the said song Jana Gana Mana Adhinayaka', my reading is that the copyright for the entire song was given to the Government of India.

In his essay 'Our National Anthem', Harivansh Rai Bachchan agreed with Nehru's comparative analysis.[83] He felt *Vande Mataram* induced excitement and admiration, but was static. On the other hand, *Jana Gana Mana* was a song of rebellion, the first dream of freedom. In *Jana Gana Mana*, Bharat Mata had moved to defeat the enemy. He believed that it had emerged among people as a symbol of their solidarity with the dream of 'Azad Hind' because of Bose's investment in the song. Bachchan felt this was the reason Nehru was inclined to choose *Jana Gana Mana*. By establishing this connection, Bachchan gave the song a context that had been largely missing from public discourse.

However, Nehru's musical insights need investigation. His emotional differentiation of the two contending songs is subjective, but his obsession with a specific orchestral aural arch is dictated by what he was accustomed to thinking of as ideal anthem music. Nehru did not consider that orchestral music could be reimagined. He believed that orchestral and military renditions of anthems necessitated that the song should have a certain tone, tune and rhythmic forcefulness. To him, these qualities reflected positivity, self-respect and fulfilment. A meandering, slow raga melody did not fit the bill. I consider this a lack of understanding of Indian music and its emotional expanse—which is not to say that *Jana Gana Mana* is a Western tune or any less Indian, of course.

In 1952, when Ravi Shankar became the director of music at AIR, he created an instrumental orchestra called the Vadya Vrinda. Shankar was one of the earliest musicians to conceive of a confluence of Hindustani and Karnatik music, and in creating the Vadya Vrinda he put this idea into practice. His assistant conductor was T.K. Jayarama Iyer, a scholarly Karnatik musician. They did not play Western-style orchestral music; instead, they used Indian ragas as the base for their orchestra.

Despite my criticism of the various attempts to present the four *Vande Mataram* stanzas together as one song, it has to be said that the music of the first stanza—based on Tagore's tune—would have suited any musical presentation, vocal or instrumental, solo or group. Nehru possibly did not have the ability to comprehend this musical canvas. The musicians he consulted either failed him or just decided to agree with the prime minister of India.

In 1972, Bangladesh chose as its anthem a song that is quite far from what Nehru described as the ideal resonance for an anthem. They chose yet another song by Rabindranath Tagore. A song that was also associated with the Swadeshi Movement, and was sung at the Town Hall gathering on 7 August 1905, when the boycott resolution was adopted.

The music of *Amar Shonar Bangla* is deeply grounded in the sounds of the Bangla land. It is a stunning piece of music. One can almost imagine the song being sung by people working in the fields or by ordinary citizens on the street. Orchestras and bands around the world have also been playing it with finesse. I am certain those musicians would have had to imbibe an entirely new musical sensibility to play the anthem. This is a true aesthetic assertion of a country's identity. The melody moves slowly; it is gentle, passionate and tugs at our heart, with no room for any rhythmic vigorousness. Even when the Bangladesh Army band adds beats and emphasis, the anthem remains tranquil. Most other anthems convey some measure of haughtiness, not *Amar Shonar Bangla*. The anthem does not end on a high note of victory but with tenderness, as the poet tells his motherland:[84]

> If sadness, Oh mother mine, casts a gloom on your face,
> My eyes are filled with tears!

Another neighbour, Bhutan, aesthetically demolishes all anthem-related musical predispositions. When I listen to *Druk Tsendhen* without knowing the meaning of the lyrics, it sounds like a Buddhist chant.

My intention is not to say that *Jana Gana Mana* is musically unrepresentative of India, but that the musical grounds articulated by Nehru don't hold water. *Vande Mataram* was unacceptable because of its lyrical import and historical baggage. If I was to give Nehru the benefit of the doubt, I would argue that he was being sensitive to religious sentiments, especially in the wake of Partition, and did not want to reopen wounds. This entire argument of musical inappropriateness was to distract from the communal tensions *Vande Mataram* could potentially trigger, and also probably the reason why the anthem was hardly debated in the Constituent Assembly.

Jana Gana Mana was announced as the national anthem on 24 January 1950 without a debate. According to the *Hindu*'s news report dated 21 January,[85] the steering committee of the Constituent Assembly had approved *Jana Gana Mana* as the national anthem after a 'long discussion' on the previous day. The committee did consider other options, such as creating a new anthem or adopting a Hindi version of *Jana Gana Mana* introduced by Subhas Chandra Bose in the INA, but finally settled on the original version of Tagore's *Jana Gana Mana.* Another news report said that the version composed (arranged) by Herbert Murrill had the approval of Prime Minister Nehru and a number of members of the Constituent Assembly, and *Vande Mataram*, considering its association with the freedom struggle, would be given the 'same honoured place'. All India Radio said it had supplied copies of the score to provincial governments, states and foreign embassies to have it played on 26 January. The report claimed that the approved version was not only the best, but also reflected 'faithfully' the Indian tune. Interestingly, the notation was also sent to well-known hotels and clubs.

The *Hindu* report also recalled that, during earlier discussions in the steering committee, *Vande Mataram* had considerable support, and suggested that the equalisation of the status of the two songs was an accommodation of that viewpoint.

By 1950, Nehru had diplomatically laid the groundwork for the acceptance of *Jana Gana Mana*. Rajendra Prasad's remarks on 24 January 1950 said it all.

> There is one matter which has been pending for discussion, namely the question of the National Anthem. At one time it was thought that the matter might be brought up before the House and a decision taken by the House by way of a resolution. But it has been felt that, instead of taking a formal decision by means of a resolution, it is better if I make a statement with regard to the National Anthem. Accordingly, I make this statement.[86]

After declaring *Jana Gana Mana* as the national anthem, he stated that *Vande Mataram* would be 'honoured equally' and have 'equal status'. He did not call it the national song. It was Nehru, on 25 August 1948, while reiterating the reasons for preferring *Jana Gana Mana* as the national anthem in the Constituent Assembly (Legislative), who said that *Vande Mataram* should continue as 'the national song Par Excellence in India'.[87]

That would have been a political compulsion. However, his placing of *Vande Mataram* on an equal footing with *Jana Gana Mana*, the official national anthem, created confusion in the minds of people. Even members of Parliament were not sure what the status of each was. Two such members, Satish Chandra Samanta and Balwant Sinha Mehta (the latter also a member of the Constituent Assembly), raised different questions regarding the national anthem in early 1950 and mid-1951 respectively.[88] But both enquired about the 'national anthems' in plural. Samanta, in fact, wanted to know if the government had issued any directions to the states on 'which are to be sung on what occasions'.

The government responded to Samanta by first clarifying that India had only one national anthem. In the pre-Independence era, many songs had occupied centre stage as national songs and anthems, so Samanta and Mehta's confusion is understandable. The conflation between the two songs could also be due to the lack of a clear and assertive announcement that *Jana Gana Mana* was the national anthem—the only musical representation of the republic.

Naturally, this lack of clarity was not limited to government circles. In 1950, the Ministry of Education wanted to ensure that all students in schools and colleges across the country sang the national anthem correctly in the official tune as a chorus. However, before considering the steps that needed to be taken in this direction, it sought responses from the Education ministries of the states on the current practice and their suggestions in this regard. Delhi wanted clarity about the 'position of the song Bande Mataram'.[89] School headmasters and mistresses were using either *Vande Mataram* or *Jana Gana Mana*, based on personal preference. I suspect this might have been the case in many other schools across the country. In the state of Madhya Bharat, *Vande Mataram* was treated as a prayer, so all functions began with it. *Jana Gana Mana* was sung at the conclusion.[90] Madras State's response contains an order issued by the secretary to government in 1948, which is a response to some exchanges between the special officer, District Board, South Kanara and the director of public instruction. The secretary says that *Vande Mataram* and *Jana Gana Mana* (mentioned in that order) should be treated as national songs by schools. And then, in the next paragraph, he says: 'The Special Officer, District Board, South Kanara, is informed that "Vande Mataram" is considered as a national song in schools and that Muslim teachers must also learn to respect it and stand by it. Persons who are against the singing of this song should be dealt with severely.'[91]

Clearly, the threat of violence associated with not singing *Vande Mataram* is not a new phenomenon. *Vande Mataram* and *Jana Gana Mana* represent two ideas of India. And the truth is, we never entirely gave up the former. The initial and continued coupling of the two songs symbolises the ever-present tensions in our attempt to reconcile or find balance between the two.

There were other linguistic, regional and ethnic assertions. In the same order, the secretary to the government said that, in Tamilnad (which at that time was part of Madras State), *Vazhiya Sentamizh*, written by Subramania Bharati, should also be considered a national song.[92]

In September 1949, this order was changed, and *Jana Gana Mana* was referred to as the national anthem and given pride of place as the song that should be sung at the end of public events. The singing of no other song was to be considered 'compulsory' in morning assemblies, and all else was left to 'the discretion of headmaster of the school concerned'.

The letter received from the prime minister's secretariat of the Government of Jammu and Kashmir in December 1950 strikes a distinct note.[93] The officer writes that no national songs are sung in schools, but of late, a few songs about the flag of the National Conference and some patriotic songs were being rendered in mufassil schools. The letter also states that, in

Jammu, *Dogra Desh Hamara* had gained popularity. This gives us a glimpse into the cultural distinctions between Jammu and Kashmir. The region's government felt there was a need for a state song—the emphasis on a state identity is notable. The letter subtly communicates its position vis-à-vis Delhi. In stark contrast, the Government of Hyderabad proclaimed that *Jana Gana Mana* had already replaced *Tarana-e-Deccan*.[94] But, even in Hyderabad, the officials were either not clear on the matter or were just continuing pre-annexation habits. When the president of India visited Hyderabad in August 1951, the Nizam, who was also the rajpramukh, called on him. On that occasion, instead of *Jana Gana Mana*, the band played 'God Bless the Nizam'.[95] The coming together of a land with many provinces and states, each with different and well-entrenched official practices, made the instituting of a common rendition ritual difficult.

How then to popularise the anthem among the citizens of this new nation? The primary hurdle was the lack of a standardised version. Many responses from the states in 1950 point to this, as also the need for a gramophone recording and for music teachers who knew the words and the tune correctly. *Jana Gana Mana* was not part of a collective cultural memory; it would take a determined effort to popularise it. It is obvious from the letters between the Union government and state governments that this was discussed extensively, and a sustained effort was made to popularise the national anthem among school students, ensuring that they sang it correctly, right through the 1950s. There were many suggestions that came their way, including printing the anthem inside the front covers of notebooks and on the front page of all school and college textbooks. The Union government suggested that prizes be given for the best rendition of the national anthem at schools.

In September 1951, the principal of Gudivada College in Andhra Pradesh wrote to the Ministry of Education and provided a mindful reason for students not singing the anthem. He said,

'Our countrymen are not used to community singing and seem to be averse to it. They much prefer listening to the anthem, sung as a solo, to joining in the singing themselves.'[96]

The principal was unwittingly referring to the divisive nature of Indian society. Indians certainly do sing collectively, but predominantly within caste communities.

The Government of India asked every state government to include the national anthem in the language textbooks in their primary and secondary schools.[97] Every state was also doing its bit to popularise the anthem. In an interesting 'secret letter' addressed to the president of India, the governor of Assam complained about the lack of participation in the singing of the national anthem among the youth, and urged that a concerted effort be made 'to make every school boy and girl sing the national anthem with accuracy, enthusiasm and vigour'.

Meanwhile, rules were being framed regarding protocol for the anthem. Once ready, these orders were to be sent to Indian missions abroad and to the various Indian states.

A word that we encounter in discussions about where and when the anthem must be rendered is 'cheap'. Like with the national flag, a puritanical protectiveness, as well as the fear of desecration, lingered.

The May 1951 press communique from the government of India also stated that the government had standardised the orchestral and vocal versions of *Jana Gana Mana*. Further, the government had in its possession the approved version of the text, the tune in Indian notation and its orchestral rendition with score in staff notation in three formats: symphony orchestra, military band and piano. Gramophone companies and publishers were asked to procure the approved version from the government and publish it.

In late 1949, when *Jana Gana Mana* was still the provisional anthem, AIR had sent out the first copies of an approved version to be played on 26 January 1950 by police and military bands, as well as to various diplomatic posts. This would have been the military band version, the version that was played for a while at official and ceremonial events. There is no information on which band recorded this version—possibly the Patiala State Military Band, since Nehru himself had high praise for their rendition.

Herbert Murrill and Norman Richardson must have finished composing the military version by 1949. I am convinced of this because, until September 1950, only the military version was being played at official and ceremonial events. Murrill and Richardson also completed the orchestral and piano reduction scores around the same time. This is confirmed by the fact that in 1950 the Indian government was discussing copyright transfer for the orchestral and vocal versions from the composers. When Visva-Bharati and Rathindranath Tagore publicly announced that they would transfer the rights for the song in May 1951, the Government of India decided to release notations for the various versions of the anthem. A task that proved to be arduous.

By mid-1951, the government published the first stanza of *Jana Gana Mana* in the Devanagari script, with a transliteration in Roman script and musical notation in Devanagari. In November 1951, it released the booklet *National Songs*, which contained historical details about the song, the text in Devanagari and English, the piano reduction score of the song and the Indian music notation.

But it was only in March 1952 that the government signed up with a publishing house to publish the military version (instrumental) of the notation. It was the United Kingdom–based publishers Boosey and Hawkes. They were and remain well-known publishers of Western classical music. On the pages of the notation, it is clearly stated that this was 'published by authority' of the Government of India. The copyright (1952) is attributed to All India Radio, New Delhi. Once the military version score was ready, the government made it available at a cost of Rs 6/Rs 8 in Pune. State governments also began procuring this notation from Boosey and Hawkes. The Orissa government, for example, ordered copies that were to be sent directly to various colleges and schools.[98] But the Ministry of Home Affairs was careful to say that the arrangement with Boosey and Hawkes did not affect the general permission for free reproduction.

The Ministry of Defence was also deliberating on a full and a short version of the anthem. After considering various options, it narrowed down on a long version (52 seconds approximately) and a short version (20 seconds approximately). This was also approved by the prime minister. Sometime in late 1953, the recording of the full military version was prepared and sent to all state governments, government institutions and diplomatic missions. It was decided that the shorter version would not be recorded since it was meant for military bands and they could just use the score.

Interestingly, in a 1951 letter, the Directorate of AIR stated that, as far as they were concerned, the authorised version referred to the musical rendering and not the text. This was despite the fact that AIR was planning to publish a vocal recording of the anthem, lasting a duration of three minutes, so that it would 'fill one side of a gramophone record'. In its response, the Ministry of Education stated that the text was equally important if the song was to be taught and sung at schools. This debate also makes the larger point that the tune alone can evoke the sensations we seek as long as the performance is strong enough. But in the case of *Jana Gana Mana*, this is a curious assertion because its music was not yet on the lips of a majority of Indians.

Nehru's personal investment in the anthem is evident—there are mentions in government papers that the versions of the anthem were finalised after Nehru's approval along with that of senior ministers and even the president.[99] Despite this high-level intervention, the national anthem continued to be rendered poorly, and gramophone records were being played at functions. At least on one occasion, Nehru himself was present. At an engineers' conference in the Central Hall of Parliament in 1953, Nehru sat through a gramophone recording of the anthem. The cabinet secretary had this to say: 'The Prime Minister feels that this gramophone version is most painful to hear. The words are not correct, the singing bad and has no dignity at all about it, and the thing lasts much too long, as the whole of the song is sung. To listen to it is an ordeal ...'[100]

Curiously, a few years earlier, on the advice of AIR, recording companies had been asked to stop production of the song. There were apparently a dozen versions of *Jana Gana Mana* in the market. In a letter dated October 1950, the Ministry of Home Affairs stated that there was no authorised version, but that Record No. 27829 published by HMV came closest to the authorised tune based on the Visva-Bharati version.

Nehru did not stop pushing for standardisation and quality presentation of the anthem. He wanted every Indian to have the song in their heart and mind. This was part of his nation-building exercise. So, at the end of 1954, we see him stressing once again on the importance of singing the national songs in chorus, correctly, without being ashamed.

Between 1952 and 1954, the government tried getting the notation for the orchestral and piano versions of the anthem published professionally, like they had for the military band version. In 1953, they entrusted the government's Photo Litho Press in New Delhi with this task. However, on receiving the proofs, the Ministry of Information and Broadcasting expressed dissatisfaction.[101] In a letter dated 15 December 1953, the ministry said that it had asked a firm in the UK to publish the notation and was waiting for their acceptance.[102] It is likely that they went back to Boosey and Hawkes, but I haven't been able to confirm this, one way or the other.

Though Nehru had said in 1948 that the London Philharmonic had been asked to record three versions—full orchestra, string orchestra and military band—this doesn't seem to have happened, at least not immediately. It is not clear who conducted, played or recorded the military version that the Ministry of Defence had approved. The full orchestra and string orchestra recordings were yet to be commissioned. Perhaps it was expedited after the gramophone incident at the engineers' conference?

The mention of 'London Philharmonic' by Nehru is also confusing. There was the then century-old Royal Philharmonic Society, as also the London Philharmonic Orchestra established in the 1930s. As it turned out, the orchestra that recorded the anthem was neither. A recording of the symphonic/orchestral version was prepared by the BBC Symphony Orchestra, conducted by the much-acclaimed Sir Malcolm Sargent. Herbert Murrill was assistant head of music at BBC Symphony Orchestra in 1948 and became head of music in 1950. Sargent became chief conductor in the same year. The relationship between Sargent and Murrill was acrimonious right until Murrill's death in 1952. Though Murrill along with Richardson had composed the orchestration for the anthem, the recording conducted by Sargent probably happened only after Murrill's passing. A few copies were sent to AIR, and approval for large-scale production was being awaited as on 9 February 1954.[103] The government was happy with the quality and were planning to have the rendering printed on gramophone discs. It was also looking to produce an abridged version (20 seconds) under the conductorship of Sir Malcolm Sargent. The cost estimated for this exercise was between £500 and £800 for the full version and about £200 for the short version.[104] All India Radio's Vadya Vrinda were also asked to produce three instrumental versions of the anthem.

A choral rendering prepared by Santiniketan was tentatively approved (with some modifications).[105] Finalising the Indian versions, instrumental and choral, was considered urgent, because the government wanted to publish them on discs as soon as possible. A handwritten note dated 31 August 1954 states that the Director General of AIR had received all the recordings of the national anthem sometime back and was waiting for time with the minister to play them back for him.

Now we must return to the music of *Jana Gana Mana*. For the people of Tamil Nadu, Tagore is the Subramania Bharati of the East. Both of them wrote musically. Their works seem to suggest that they did not have to think about prosody, search for melodically appropriate consonant–vowel forms, forcefully construct a pause in the vowel extensions, count the syllabic length of each line or stanza. There's an ease to their writing, as though everything just fell into place—every word encapsulates not just its semantic meaning but also its sonic curvature. Other poets may sometimes use an expression that is technically accurate but still inappropriate because its sound conveys a divergent emotion in that given context. It may also be in discord with a neighbouring word. This causes an aural dissonance that could be contraindicative to the desired symbolism. Something we never find in Bharati or Tagore. On occasion, Bharati provided the raga in which he imagined his song. Tagore was closer to the music because he was the vaggeyakara. His songs came to life in his music and voice. This is more than evident in *Jana Gana Mana*.

The music, lyrics and meaning are never at odds. The syllabic, melodic and rhythmic measures are perfect. The melody is tantalising because it is not on expected lines, except for the 'jaya he' at the end of the stanza. Until then, it is difficult to predict the melody's progress. A reader may disagree. But if they had never heard the song, would they be able to foresee the melodic direction? That said, the song is not jumpy, nor is it unnecessarily complicated, unnaturally broken up. All the lines hover around the lower regions of the middle octave, circling around the Pa and settling at the middle octave Sa. There are two perceivable leaps. The first one at 'Punjab' indicates a shift in lyrical import because the two following lines explore the extent of the land. The second and larger jump is a one-octave vault. This is to hail the 'adhinayaka'. There is always a temptation to end a stanza that announces victory on a high note. Tagore defies the norm, and so the victory changes colour. It does not generate patriotism of the flag-planting kind or the announcement that our god or country is unparalleled. The 'victory to thee' in the last line is inward-looking. If I were to describe the emotional graph of *Jana Gana Mana*, I would say that it begins with a mellow appeal to the 'adhinayaka'. After having sought the Eternal Charioteer's blessing, Tagore introduces us to this 'adhinayaka'. An introduction requires description, which he provides in fluent rhyme. This is followed by salutation and proclamation, which begins as a burst of energy, only to descend into a peaceful rest on the middle octave Ma (madhyama). Tagore's own rendition of *Jana Gana Mana* sounds more like a mantra.

It takes a genius to make a new tune appear comfortable and familiar. Tagore found a new sound within the Indian aural palette that was not stiffly encased in the traditional raga mould. The music of Rabindra Sangeet is national. Melodies from all parts of the country as well as the West found their way into Tagore's songs. But once taken in, they came into their own, not mere imitations of their source. It is very difficult to recognise the song that may have inspired a Tagore composition. Rabindra Sangeet is a seamless fabric of India's rural, Hindustani and Karnatik music combined with influences from the West. The so-called classical forms are so overburdened with sacrality that the common person feels unworthy of participating. Tagore gave these 'elite' forms a connection to real life. He did not simplify them; instead, he imbued them with an enlarged soundscape of listenability. This new form was an early experiment in aesthetic socialism. Tagore's politics did not involve straightforward activism; it was born from inward experience and inspired the same in the receiver, be it through his stories, poems or songs. You may like or dislike his work, but its seriousness is beyond question.

Since every stanza in *Jana Gana Mana* is identical in intra- and inter-syllabic measure, the same tune works for all the stanzas. There is no need for any uncomfortable musical or lyrical adjustments. Look at how wonderfully Tagore plays with a couple of descriptive words in the penultimate line of every stanza.

In the anthem stanza, he says (all emphases mine):

> Jana Gana *mangala dayaka* jaya he
>
> The saving of all people waits in thy hand

And then, ever so masterfully, he changes the phrase without affecting the form:

> Jana Gana *aikya vidhayaka* jaya he
>
> Thou bringest the hearts of all people into the harmony of one life
>
> Jana Gana *patha parichayaka* jaya he
>
> Thy finger points the path to all people
>
> Jana Gana *duhkhatrayaka* jaya he
>
> Thou art the companion and the saviour of the people in their sorrows.

Finally, after having delineated the 'adhinayaka' in so many ways, he crowns the Eternal Charioteer with a title:

> Jana jaya *jaya he, jaya rajesvara*
>
> Victory to the king of kings, victory to thee.

In early 1919, Tagore toured South India. In February, he headed to Madanapalli to spend time with James H. Cousins and

Margaret E. Cousins. A theosophist writer and teacher, James was principal of the Theosophical Society College. An otherwise nondescript spot on the Indian map, Madanapalli was important to Theosophists because it was the birthplace of J. Krishnamurti, whom Annie Besant was grooming as a 'world teacher'.

According to James, when Tagore arrived in Madanapalli, he was 'tired and sick and disturbed by the sight of fabulous wealth stored away in temples when it might be put to the education of the young'.[106]

Tagore joined the post-dinner Wednesday night informal song and fun gathering in the art room. They were playing the 'hot potato game' when he entered. Those gathered sang in chorus and James also sang an Irish number. By singing solo a song that was not part of the group renditions, James was conveying the message that individuals could sing other songs. And Tagore responded. James H. Cousins notes,

> Rabindranath asked if he might sing one of his Bengali songs. Leave was granted. In a voice surprisingly light for so large a man he sang something like a piece of geography giving a list of countries, mountains and rivers, and in a second verse a list of the religions of India. The refrain to the first verse made us prick up our ears. The refrain to the second verse made us clear our throats. We asked for it again and again, and before long we were singing it with gusto: 'Jaya hai, jaya hai, jaya hai, jaya jaya jaya jaya hai.' (Victory, victory, victory to thee)[107]

They were obviously enchanted by the song. The next day, Tagore gave Margaret the musical notes (svaras) for it. A clarification here: many news articles have misinterpreted this incident and given Margaret the credit for tuning or giving final musical shape to the song. This is untrue. Tagore provided Margaret with the svaras so that the song could be recorded accurately. This was not the first time the song was notated. The notation for *Jana Gana Mana* was first published by Brajendralal Ganguli in *Ananda Sangeet Patrika* in May 1915.

This visit to Madanapalli is significant because it was here that Tagore titled it the 'Morning Song of India' and wrote what was to become the most widely used translation of the song. This is James's own recollection:

> Next day Rabindranath gave the swarams (notes) of 'Jana gana' to Mrs. Cousins so that the melody should have accurate permanent record. He also made a translation of the song into English as the 'Morning Song of India'. That night under the peepul tree at the back of our home, he went over the song line by line in Bengali, with its English equivalent for understanding, until we could sing it with assurance. It took its place in the 'daily dedication' of the combined School and College in the great Besant Hall, and through students and visitors was carried to the borders of India.[108]

Even before Bose declared *Jana Gana Mana* India's national anthem in Berlin in 1941, the song had made its international debut. James Cousins and Rukmini Devi Arundale sang it on 26 August 1929 at the Theosophical Congress in Chicago, USA. Annie Besant asked Rukmini Devi 'why there was no Indian Anthem', and then requested her and James to sing *Jana Gana Mana*. In 1930, James sang the first stanza and read out Tagore's English translation when he delivered a talk on Gandhi, Bose and Tagore under the auspices of University Men's Club in Washington. He later remembered:

> Then flashed into my mind what must have been one of the earliest hints of 'Jana gana mana' as the national anthem of India, though at the time months of civil disobedience had been met by extreme brutality, and freedom for India seemed as far off as ever. In the reverent silence that followed I ended my address: 'I offer you this "Morning Song of India" not as the national anthem of one nation as opposed to others, but

as the international anthem of humanity.' The larger offer has not been fulfilled; but after much controversy it became the national anthem of free India.[109]

It can be said that, though *Jana Gana Mana* was not gaining popularity among the people, the intelligentsia was taking note of its potential.

Being a musician, I feel compelled to discuss the music of the song. Dinendranath Tagore published the song and its svaralipi in 1918. His notated tune is nearly the same as the anthem that we sing today. But the first notation published by Brajendralal Ganguli in 1915 has some minor and one major difference. The melody for the lines *tava shubha name jage / tava shubha ashisha mage* is not what we are used to. 'Tava' begins at the Sa in the middle octave, moving upwards during the rendering of the word 'jage', settling on Ri. The 'tava' of the next phrase, beginning on the same Ri, once again moves upwards when 'mage' is sung, finally resting on the Gandhara (Ga). The tune we are familiar with begins on the Ga in the middle octave and is different in movement. To Brajendralal Ganguli's credit, he designated the raga for the song as 'mishra' meaning 'a mixture'.

The emotive quality that the two melodies give rise to is also different. To my ear, the former is imbued with a greater degree of 'plea', while the latter is stronger. Every time the tune of a song changes ever so slightly, the sensibility it carries undergoes a revision.

Once *Jana Gana Mana* was designated as the national anthem, it transformed into a multi-layered harmony-laden musical composition. This journey began on 11 September 1942 in Berlin, a recording of which performance is available online. Though the authenticity of this recording has not been confirmed, I will venture into an aesthetic analysis of the rendition on the assumption that it is the original recording. In places such as 'Bharata bhagya vidhata', 'Vindhya Himachala' and 'uchhala jaladhi taranga', there are differences in the tune. The Chamber Orchestra of Hamburg Radio version is string-dominated, with the brass section providing backing and body. No woodwind instruments are audible. The arrangement is heavily orchestrated and exudes a feeling of heightened pride, even bordering on pomposity. Maybe there are reasons for this kind of an interpretation. It was the first time ever that *Jana Gana Mana* was being played as the national anthem—and it was being done on foreign soil when all the odds were packed against Bose. The song needed to galvanise people to fight as a military force, which meant it needed to be imposing and monumental. Also, it was to be played alongside the German national anthem, which meant it needed to stand shoulder-to-shoulder with its counterpart in musical grandiosity.

Herbert Murrill and Norman Richardson's arrangement—the military band notation that Boosey and Hawkes published in 1952—provides an interesting contrast to that first attempt. In their arrangement, the main melody is carried by the woodwinds. Instruments include the flute, piccolo, clarinet, oboe, bassoons, cornet, horns, trombone, saxophone, euphonium and basses. The brass arrangement backs the woodwinds entirely in the lower octaves. The two percussion instruments are the side drum and the base drum. The arrangement is gentle and mellow though it is meant for the military band. In this musical voice, the nation is not a haughty dominator. Since we know Nehru was deeply involved in the choice and arrangement of the anthem, one wonders whether he provided any emotional pointers to Murrill and Richardson.

Jana Gana Mana was written in heavily Sanskritised Bangla. In fact, both the national anthem and the national song were written in Sanskritised Bangla. Bose realised the need to attend to the Hindi-dominated political scene, and translated *Jana Gana Mana* into Hindustani. Having adopted it as the national anthem in 1941, he could have just continued to sing the song.

However, Bose was a man of constant learning. On 21 October 1943, in Singapore, he announced the creation of the provisional government of Azad Hind. Leading up to that announcement, he had asked Abid Hasan, his companion on the submarine journey from Keil in Germany to Sabang in Indonesia, to translate *Jana Gana Mana* into Hindustani. South-East Asia was a different theatre, and Bose was acutely aware of the larger picture and the specific needs of his movement. It was not only a question of structure and mechanism but also about recreating symbols. His speeches were now in Hindustani, with a strong leaning towards Urdu. Bose was consciously fostering Hindu–Muslim comradery. Though most of his professional soldiers were Punjabi or Pathan, the newer recruits were South Indians, mainly Tamil, and hence his speeches were translated into Tamil for their understanding.

Mumtaz Hussain, the lyricist from Lyallpur in Punjab who had written songs such as *Kadam Kadam Badhaye Ja*, and Abid Hasan, by then a Major in the INA, translated three of the five stanzas of *Jana Gana Mana*. Bose himself is said to have explained the meaning of the song. The *Hind Qaumi Tarana* began with the words *Shubh Sukh Chain*. The song was used between 21 October 1943 and 14 August 1945 by the INA. On that last day, Bose himself sang it along with 3,000 men and women of the army in an open-air theatre in Singapore. The song continued to be heard during the INA trials in the winter of 1945-46. Unfortunately, it was soon lost in the shadow of its more prominent sibling.

shubh sukh chain ki barkha barase
bharat bhaag hai jaaga
punjab sindh gujarat maratha dravid utkal banga
chanchal saagar vindhya himala neela jamuna ganga
tere nit gun gayein tujh se jeevan payein
sab tan payein asha
suraj bankar jag par chamke bharat naam subhaaga
jaya ho, jaya ho, jaya ho,

jaya jaya jaya ho
bharat naam subhaaga

sab ke dil mein preet bhashaein
teri meethi baani
har subeh ke rahne waale har mazhab ke praani
sab bhed aur farq mitake sab god mein teri aake
gundhein prem ki maala.
suraj bankar jag par chamke bharat naam subhaaga
jaya ho, jaya ho, jaya ho,
jaya jaya jaya ho
bharat naam subhaaga

subah savere pankh pakheru
tere hi gun gaayein
baas bhari bharpoor havaayein jeevan mein rut laayein
sab milkar hind pukare jai azad hind ke naare
pyaara desh hamaara
suraj bankar jag par chamke bharat naam subhaaga
jaya ho, jaya ho, jaya ho,
jaya jaya jaya ho
bharat naam subhaaga

Shubh Sukh Chain is not a straightforward translation of *Jana Gana Mana*. It is a retelling. This was the song that Bose wanted his multi-religious marching army to draw courage and inspiration from. Tagore's larger-than-life, moving imagination had to acquire an everyday resonance. *Jana Gana Mana* lyrically traverses many emotional registers—pain, agony, dismay, supplication, and then a shift to hope, faith and beatitude as the sun rises from behind the eastern hills. Melodically, it is regal and towering. On the other hand, *Shubh Sukh Chain* gives us a musical glimpse of an everyday morning on an Indian street, where necessities and playfulness come together in an aural portrait. This India is a star that brightens the world and asserts its faith in the 'Bharat bhaag'.

Mumtaz Hussain's language allows the colloquial to coexist with the literary. Some scholars may frown at this mix, which at times may not be linguistically ironed out, yet remains musically compatible. To me, these anomalies are ideal, for the song's inner voice is one of multiplicity. The celebration of diversity comes through radiantly. We know that these lyrics were written to match Tagore's linguistic and musical metre. Yet, *Shubh Sukh Chain* has its own life.

As Gopalkrishna Gandhi poetically said in a note to me, 'Netaji's song ever so subtly moves from orbiting around the mould of Tagore's song into its own orbit, but also drawing tincts from Bankim's *Vande Mataram* and—quite distinctly—from Iqbal's Tarana-e-Hind (Song of Hind) *Saare Jahan se Achcha*.'

The words 'teri meethi baani' (your sweet voice) and 'baas bhari bharpoor havaaein' (fragrant, redolent breeze) in *Shubh Sukh Chain* resonate with 'sumadhura bhaashini' and 'malayaja sheetalam' in *Vande Mataram*. And Iqbal's 'mazhab nahin sikhata' in *Saare Jahan se Achcha* is lodged within these phrases:

har subeh ke rahne waale

people of every habitation

har mazhab ke praani

followers of every faith

sab bhed aur farq mitaake

erasing all divisions and every difference

sab god mein teri aake

cradling in your lap

gundhein prem ki mala

string the garland of love

Shubh Sukh Chain was part of the corpus of songs that came from the Azad Hind movement. All of them extol a united and secular India in which all religions thrive with confidence and all Indians respect the faiths of this country. It is a political song with patriotism at its heart.

With the help of Subhas Chandra Bose's grandnephew, the historian Sugata Bose, I was able to access an early (1943-44) staff notation of *Shubh Sukh Chain* from the Netaji Research Bureau. Published in Malaya and written for the voice with piano arrangement, the notation belonged to the Indian National School in Ipoh. A picture of a woman is printed on the cover, which carries the title *Hind Kaumi Tarana, National Anthem, Qaumi Gana.*[110] I can only infer that the woman might have been the conductor of the choir and a member of the Azad Hind Fauj.

My students and I reconstructed the notation believing that it would be identical to *Jana Gana Mana*. But we were in for a surprise. There are subtle but emphatic differences that appear in the most unusual places. Melodic parts of *Jana Gana Mana* that are monotonic are treated with ingenious fine movements. An undeviated note landing is replaced by a graceful angular approach. Equi-paced melodic lines have been reconstructed to accommodate a more fluid flow. It is impossible to say whether the changes in language, semantic gait and spirit induced those melodic novelties or whether Tagore's musicality inspired *Shubh Sukh Chain*'s poetics segues. *Shubh Sukh Chain* is its own song even musically, with a musical ambience very different from that of its parent.

Jana Gana Mana and *Shubh Sukh Chain* are not two contesting ideas. Instead, they inspire a conversation between two diverse, but elevated, sensibilities. They churn in me both passion for this land and the need to live within it in love. Yet, they do not come from the same sonic comprehension of India. Melodies too carry meaning. Whether or not a person understands Tagore's or Hussain's words, the aurality of their songs alone can evoke feelings.

Harivansh Rai Bachchan also proposed a new Hindi song as the anthem (with some suggested lyrical changes), which was a retelling of *Jana Gana Mana*. Written by the Education minister of the Central Provinces, Dwarka Prasad Mishra, who went by the pen name 'Krishnayan', this song began with the words 'Jana Gana Mana Adhi Vasini Jay'. Bachchan argued that this song was a blend of *Jana Gana Mana* and *Vande Mataram*: a song that retained lyrical proximity to *Jana Gana Mana* and could be sung in the same tune, and also brought Bharat Mata back to the forefront.

The need to have an anthem that could inspire all members of the INA made Hindustani the choice of language. It was considered the lowest common denominator. Yet, keeping aside Bose's immediate symbolic requirement for the march towards Delhi, we have to wonder if 'Hindi' or 'Hindustani' is really the answer when faced with the question of India's linguistic diversity. Does this language choice undermine the federalism that Tagore wrote into *Jana Gana Mana*? Even in 1937, the sub-committee appointed by the Congress Working Committee[111] was only looking for songs composed in simple Hindustani or those that could be adapted into Hindustani. Therefore, it is no surprise that nothing else was even considered 'national'.

There are two types of language nationalists. One set believes that Hindi and its cousins are spoken and understood by most Indians, and hence it should be our national language. Some among them even subscribe to the idea that it is superior to other languages. Within this group, there are the rabid proponents of a Hindi cleansed of Urdu words. Progressive Hindi nationalists, too, obsess over the language and its place in the country. They recognise the need for liberty to prioritise one's mother tongue, but believe that an overemphasis on linguistic diversity could create instability, and that there should be a unifying language for the country. (And, no, they don't think English should do that job.) Hindustani, which is Urdu-inflected, is a no-brainer choice to foster togetherness, they believe. National symbols tend to be viewed from this one lens: togetherness.

During the framing of the Constitution of India, the issue of creating states on a linguistic basis became a knotty matter. Nehru, Vallabhbhai Patel, Rajendra Prasad and Maulana Azad did not approve of the idea. How much of this came from a fear of separatism and how much was governance-related centralisation is hard to tell. But there definitely was the fear that India might disintegrate even before it came together. Inevitably, though, in 1953, Andhra Pradesh was created, followed by the States Reorganisation Act in 1956.

However, the formation of states along language lines did not dampen the push for Hindi. It kept coming back in different shapes, and continues to do so. Anti-Hindi agitations periodically raise their head in Tamil Nadu. In the Indian context, it is hard to separate federalism and linguistic and cultural identity. The suppression or empowerment of one affects the other. The fight for state rights is intertwined with the insistence on linguistic independence. The jallikattu protests in Tamil Nadu in reaction to a court-imposed ban on a traditional sport are an example of how intertwined cultural roots and linguistic pride are with constitutional rights. These are emotional ownerships that do not demolish national unity. Such sub-nationalisms are not cowed down by a majoritarian pressure to conform. They are locally rooted emotions felt in the hundreds of languages that inhabit our land. Understanding this diversity keeps us together.

Unitarian nationalists continue to propose One Nation One Language. Astonishingly, even today, many Indians believe that Hindi is our national language.

The National Education Policy (NEP) released by the Government of India in 2020 perpetuates this imposition in an insidious way.[112] Using the argument that all school children must learn three languages, Hindi is pushed southwards. On the face of it, saying every child should learn three languages seems fine, even if the necessity for it is debatable. It is argued that no language is being imposed, and that the third language could be any Indian language. But most schools will only offer Hindi as the third language because any other would be a fraught choice. There is also no way of justifying why one language has been chosen over another. Equally, schools in states such as Bihar and Uttar Pradesh will not teach Tamil or Malayalam as the third language because of a lack of resources.

The NEP also blatantly pushes Sanskrit over all other classical languages. Tamil Nadu has resisted the Hindi invasion for long. There are cultural and linguistic reasons as to why Tamils oppose such a measure. The Tamils are extremely proud of their linguistic ancestry and independence. So much so that, from the early twentieth century, there was a movement (Tani Tamil Iyakkam) to replace all Sanskrit and English words that had become part of Tamil. But it is also true that Sanskrit words used in Tamil often undergo such a dramatic sonic metamorphosis that it is difficult to recognise their Sanskrit origin. The grammar of the language is distinct, making it that much harder for a Tamil speaker to learn Hindi. There is also a caste angle to this resistance. Very often, those who learn Hindi with ease belong to brahminical castes, where Sanskrit is already a part of the cultural milieu. The state of Tamil Nadu hosts lakhs of migrant workers from Bihar, Jharkhand, West Bengal and Uttar Pradesh. People on both sides find a way to communicate and live together. Similarly, contractors from Tamil Nadu can be found in the Hindi belt. They learn Hindi without complaining.

The question is, why do people learn a language? It is need, environment and an emotional bond that makes language learning natural and even pleasurable. Therefore, forcing Hindi merely as a nationalistic policy is insensitivity.

It is, therefore, no surprise that it was never considered desirable to have the national anthem sung in translation. Today, as per the Eighth Schedule of the Indian constitution, there are twenty-two official languages, but we are not allowed to sing the anthem officially in any of them. It could even be considered an insult. To understand the difficulty that the people of India face in trying to pronounce the words of the anthem, one just needs to go to schools across the country and listen. The children stand and sing with utmost respect and diligence, their entire body involved. But the sound of the words and the combinations are tongue twisters. In Tamil Nadu, for example, '*uchhala jaladhi taranga*' becomes '*uchala jalasitha ranga*'! In the 1950s, one T. Neelakantan from Madras wrote letters to the Minister of Education, Maulana Azad, complaining that students were not singing the anthem correctly, they did not know the words or they seemed uninterested. The problem then, and now, is not one of unfamiliarity. The song is simply in a language that is alien to many.

There are countries that have diverse languages within their anthem, like South Africa's anthem with five stanzas in five languages. New Zealand's anthem can be rendered in English and Maori. Closer to home, the Sri Lankan anthem, though originally written in Sinhala, has been translated into Tamil. The anthem is sung in one of these two languages. Its story is one of intrigue, linguistic nationalism and contestation. And a song that has an Indian connection.

Namo Namo Matha was written by Ananda Samarakoon, who travelled to India in 1936 and spent some time at Santiniketan. He returned to Sri Lanka in 1937, deeply influenced by Tagore. The popular story in Sri Lanka, as told to me by Ravibandu Vidyapathy, the Kandyan dancer, scholar and choreographer, goes something like this: 'In the 1940s when Samarakoon was the music teacher in Mahinda College in Galle, suddenly one night, he was inspired to write this patriotic song. The song was written in 1940, and was recorded in 1946 by HMV.' There's a prequel to this story too. Samarakoon was returning from India one time, his first ever aeroplane trip. He looked down at his country from the sky and wrote down a few words. Those few words turned into the song *Nama Namo Matha* that night. Samarakoon was its vaggeyakara, though there are some who believe Tagore composed the tune for his favourite student.

In *Nama Namo Matha*, Sri Lanka is feminine. The song is a salutation to the beautiful land of wisdom, abundance, joy and love. A land that smudges inequalities and leads the people to freedom and victory.

Ravibandhu feels that *Namo Namo Matha* was inspired by *Vande Mataram* rather than a Tagore song. Here are some commonalities he mentions.

Vande Mataram: Namo Namo Matha
tumi vidya: oba ve apa vidya
tumi dharma: obamaya apa satya
bahute tumi ma shakti: oba ve apa shakti
hrdaya tumi ma bhakti: apa hada tula bhakti

If I were to assume that Samarakoon learnt *Vande Mataram* during his stay in Santiniketan, the year would have been 1936-37, around the time the song was a religio-political flashpoint in India. The music for *Namo Namo Matha* is undoubtedly Bangla-influenced. Unlike its Indian counterpart *Vande Mataram, Namo Namo Matha* was free of literary baggage and accepted by all.

Interestingly, in 1939, Samarakoon wrote another song, *Sama Jana Mana Adhipatiyani Tuti We*, set to the tune of *Jana Gana Mana*. Between these two songs, there are also many similarities in the choice of words and lyrical import.

Here are some lines that remind us of *Jana Gana Mana*:

Hara jati vansa agam kula bheda-ruduvam hama apavitra ...
Discard the discriminations of caste, creed and religions, those unclean foes
Navajeevana rasa demine—avadi karan lak manee

Give us a taste of the new life, Awake mother Lanka

Uda karan nava surya ...

Give us the light of a new sun

Sita oba sihasuna sevane-kiyamu me gee sadarine ...

Under the shade of thy throne, we sing songs of love

Jaya jaya mangala ve jaya mangala, mangala ve apa mata

Blessed be our motherland

Namo Namo Matha became very popular in Sri Lanka. Also contributing to its popularity was the great Kandyan dancer Chitrasena, who ensured that the song was sung by the entire cast of his troupe at all their performances, which included dance items, songs and instrumental music. Despite wide public acceptance, *Namo Namo Matha* was not automatically selected as the national anthem of Sri Lanka. The committee that was to make the selection chose *Sri Lanka Matha, Yasa Mahima*, written by Illengesinghe and set to music by Edirisinghe. Since both these individuals were members of the selection committee, a controversy inevitably followed.

To cut a long story short, in 1951, due to public pressure, *Namo Namo Matha* was adopted as the national anthem with some minor changes to the lyrics, which Samarakoon accepted. Sri Lanka being a country with a large minority Tamil population, the song was also translated into Tamil by the poet Nallathambi from Vaddukoddai in the Jaffna peninsula. By the mid-1950s, the Tamil version of the anthem was being used by the state. The first official broadcast by Radio Ceylon was in 1955.

The tale of this anthem does not end there. After 1956, there was a demand for changing the opening words 'namo namo'. It was believed that the great difficulties the nation was going through, including the economic downturn, the accidental death of D.S. Senanayake, the first prime minister of Sri Lanka, and the assassination of S.W.R.D. Bandaranaike were caused by the placement of the inauspicious syllables 'namo namo' at the beginning of the anthem. For this bizarre reason, the opening line was changed to 'Sri Lanka Matha'. Samarakoon's permission was not sought, and even until his suicide in 1962, he never got over the hurt. Formal constitutional recognition for 'Sri Lanka Matha' came in 1978 in Sri Lanka's second autochthonous constitution. The Tamil translation was not officialised in this manner.

As we saw earlier, Rathidranath Tagore's primary concern when asked to transfer the copyright of *Jana Gana Mana* was also the matter of lyrical authenticity. Questions about changing a poem or song without the permission of the writer or after their demise have been raised even with state songs. In 2003, at the inauguration of the centenary celebrations of Karnataka's most revered and influential writer Kuvempu, his song *Jaya Bharata Jananiya Tanujate*—inspired by *Jana Gana Mana*—was chosen as the state song. As expected, there were objections. Some argued that there were other songs that could have been chosen. There were also whispers about an underlying angle of caste and region. The main bone of contention, though, was a missing name. Kuvempu had not included the name of the twelfth- or thirteenth-century philosopher and spiritual teacher Madhvacharya, whereas Shankaracharya and Ramanuja, not from Kannada-speaking regions, were included. This irked the pontiff of the powerful Pejawar Mutt and some intellectuals. Matters were further complicated by the fact that Madhvacharya's name was included in the song sometime in the 1970s. Whether Kuvempu accepted such an inclusion is questionable. H.R. Leelavathi rendered this song first in 1957. In 1987, when Kuvempu received the Karnataka state literary award, she was asked to sing the song. When she asked Kuvempu, he told her to sing it without Madhvacharya's name. Kuvempu's son argued that his father did not include Madhvacharya's name because his philosophy was not socially inclusive, whereas Shankaracharya and Ramanuja, despite their brahminical foundations, gave space for the 'shudras' to attain salvation and professed the oneness of humanity. There were also those who pointed to the fact that no women were mentioned in the song. The Karnataka state government finally officialised the edited version that included Madhvacharya's name.

To return to the Sri Lankan anthem, Ravibandu had a musical critique of it. Unlike *Jana Gana Mana*, whose melody moves upwards, he observed that the *Sri Lanka Matha* melody descends. He made a sociological correlation between musical ascent and moving forward, of growth as opposed to descent and moving backwards or remaining static. Similarly, he also felt that *Jana Gana Mana*'s ending on the Ma, the note before the resting note Pa (the perfect fifth), signifies progress and mobility. It is fascinating to study how associations are made between melodic trajectory, octaves, notes and human aspirations, hope and positivity. The answer to the mystery possibly lies at the intersection of psychology, evolutionary habits and social aesthetics.

In any case, until 1956, the Sinhala version was sung at official events in Sinhala-dominated areas and the Tamil one in Tamil-dominated areas. In 1956, the 'Sinhala Only Act' was passed, and it is believed that the Tamil version was slowly phased out of official events in the south of the country. Tamil itself got the status of an official language only in 1987 via the thirteenth amendment to the Sri Lankan constitution, born out of the Indo–Lanka Accord. That amendment included many provisions with regard to devolution of powers to the provinces, and is one that remains unfulfilled and contentious. Coincidentally, the thirteenth amendment of the Constitution of India was also related to empowering a minority community. The amendment gave the Nagas a separate state, Nagaland. Yet, the Naga issue remains volatile.

Ethnic tension and the twenty-six-year-long civil war changed everything in Sri Lanka. Inevitably, the Tamil version of *Sri Lanka Matha* disappeared from Tamil memory at least in the regions controlled by the LTTE. It was the Eelam anthem that reverberated in these areas. In 2010, soon after the civil war ended, President Mahinda Rajapaksa's government expressed its displeasure at the singing of the Tamil version. In a reversal, in 2015, President Maithripala Sirisena's government encouraged the singing of the anthem in Tamil. It was then sung during the Independence Day celebrations in 2016. The dispensation under President Gotabaya Rajapaksa turned the clock back and dropped the Tamil anthem from the Independence Day celebrations in 2020. It made a comeback in 2023. These flip-flops only exemplify the simmering tensions and the power of symbolism in the battle for national identity.

The tough questions remain. Do the Tamils, especially in the North and East of Sri Lanka, feel connected to the words and music of the anthem? Does it inspire in them a sense of patriotism as it does in the people of the South?

One argument against a Tamil anthem uses India as an example: '... even in neighbouring India, where around 300 languages were used, the national anthem was only in Hindi'.

But the real question is: should India have only one version of the anthem? In the grind of daily life, music often passes unnoticed. But tunes, words and lines remain in our heads. We hum them silently as we cycle, walk, drink or eat. The associations we build with these songs shape our inner life, both as individuals and as citizens. When we fixate on one song in one language that speaks for and to us, we forget that such a choice silences many other songs.

Would a national anthem that can be sung in all our languages become a vehicle for many expressions of belonging?

Though most Indians have accepted *Jana Gana Mana* as the national anthem, loyalty to the song, and in turn to the country, is questioned, sometimes violently. In the past decade, we have witnessed incidents of people being beaten up for not standing when the anthem was played in theatres. In more than one case, the assaulted person was differently abled.[113] Legal cases have been filed for disrespecting the anthem. The question arises: should the anthem be played in a cinema hall? Nehru answered this question in 1948 when he said, 'I think it is undesirable for the anthem to be played after every cinema performance when people are shuffling out and little respect is shown to the anthem.'[114] Though Nehru was uncomfortable with the anthem being played in cinema theatres, *Jana Gana Mana* made its appearance on the silver screen a decade before it became the national anthem. According to the film historian Randor Guy, the film *Bhama Vijayam*, which was released in the year 1934, was not only the debut film of the trailblazing Karnatik musician G.N. Balasubramaniam, it was also the first time *Jana Gana Mana* was sung as part of a film. Foretelling the future status of this Tagore creation, it was sung in chorus at the very end of the film by all the characters. It is said that many in the audience were moved and stood up when the song played.

In 2016, the Supreme Court in its wisdom asked the government to make it mandatory for the anthem to be played in theatres before the screening of a film. Luckily, that order was changed in 2018 to 'not mandatory, but optional or directory'. Court orders apart, this aggressive demand for allegiance has only been escalating.

I faced an uncomfortable situation when, just before a concert, the anthem was played in a government auditorium. I was in the green room tuning my tambura, trying to remain still and centred, when the anthem blared through the speakers. This disturbed me, displaced my concentration. Instead of evoking a feeling of respect, the anthem on that occasion disconcerted me.

We already have rules regarding where, when and how the anthem can be played. Of all the conditions, the most unmusical is the one about time. It is said the rendition of the anthem in its entirety should be approximately fifty-two seconds. I am not aware how the Government of India chose this peculiar time barrier. As long as the melody and lyrics are not mutilated, an artist must have the right to render it for a longer duration. It is obvious that this rule was put in by a musically ignorant bureaucrat or politician. In the past, the government has been flexible about this rule. A.R. Rahman's interpretation of the national anthem produced by Bharat Bala went on for nearly two minutes. In that rendition, which featured some of India's greatest musicians, the melody was caressed, with the singers deviating ever so slightly from the original fixed path. This gave new life to the song. Thankfully, no one asked for it to be banned. Standing at attention is another demand. Does a military posture confirm respect? In many Indian traditions, musicians sing and play instruments while seated cross-legged. They offer us music with deep reverence. Why cannot the anthem be rendered in the same manner? I can understand the trepidation in allowing seated renditions because it might result in a disrespectful casualness. But we must find a solution that accommodates our musico-cultural practices.

To stand for the anthem out of love and respect is different from standing out of fear that somebody will pull us up. Respect cannot be demanded, made to order. The anthem is too lofty to be let loose on people as a patriotism-monitoring patrol. It is to be felt within, and the experience must be shared, celebrated—and interrogated.

5

The Preamble

A Vision for the Republic

WE, THE PEOPLE OF INDIA, having solemnly resolved to constitute India into a SOVEREIGN SOCIALIST SECULAR DEMOCRATIC REPUBLIC and to secure to all its citizens:

JUSTICE, social, economic and political;

LIBERTY of thought, expression, belief, faith and worship;

EQUALITY of status and of opportunity,

and to promote among them all,

FRATERNITY assuring the dignity of the individual and the unity and integrity of the Nation;

IN OUR CONSTITUENT ASSEMBLY this 26th day of November 1949, do HEREBY ADOPT, ENACT AND GIVE TO OURSELVES THIS CONSTITUTION.

According to the website *Constitute*,[1] over 80 per cent of all national constitutions begin with a preamble. A study by Vladan Kutlesic of Belgrade Business School, Serbia, does not agree, stating that, out of the 194 constitutions studied, fifty-four do not have preambles.[2] Whatever the reason for this discrepancy, this much at least is clear: all preambles are not created equal. Some have little substance and do not affect or influence the constitution. They are just declarations emphasising the relevance of the constitution, past histories or just the method of its passing. The preambles of the constitutions enacted by Liechtenstein, Peru, Nauru, Vietnam and New Zealand are examples.

But in the constitutions of countries such as Angola, Guatemala and Tajikistan, where a preambular statement of purpose is meant to capture the spirit of the constitution and act as a guide for the functioning of society, principles such as freedom, liberty, human rights, equality and equal opportunity are articulated. Justice, rights and dignity are mentioned in some form or the other in over a hundred preambles. While some of these principles may not have found a place in a country's preamble, they do register in its fundamental rights or other constitutional principles.

There are other differences between preambles. While god or the divine are present in about seventy preambles, others are silent about a supreme being. In the constitutions of countries such as Colombia, Marshall Islands and Bahrain, concepts of liberty and justice mingle with scriptural precepts in an attempt to reconcile social ethics and religious doctrine. Some countries, Trinidad and Tobago and Turkey among them, are also interested in spiritual values and well-being. In cases where the constitution was written after years of ethnic or religious conflict, there is an emphasis on social diversity. Though secularism finds very few takers, co-existence, harmony, pluralism or religious tolerance as a conceptual framework for society finds a place in over sixty preambles. The welfare and well-being of citizens is also stressed in the preambles of Panama, Niger, Nigeria and Argentina.

Many preambles also deal with the history of the country and communicate the map for the future. Some speak directly about the country's political struggles for freedom and begin with a specific mention of its tumultuous past. The preamble to the Rwandan constitution displays great political courage and historical honesty in mentioning the country's genocidal past: 'CONSCIOUS of the genocide committed against Tutsi that decimated more than a million sons and daughters of Rwanda, and conscious of the tragic history of our country ...'

Many preambles speak of good international relations as a general principle. Several African countries also make a specific mention of African unity and cooperation. The African Charter of Rights of Man and Peoples is as important to these countries as the United Nations' Universal Declaration of Human Rights. This assertion of continental identity is significant in the light of Africa's horrific colonial past.

Yet other countries just put the past behind them, much like India has done. Though all preambles are a statement of hope for a better future, some countries, like Chile and Poland, have made it a point to use the phrase 'future generations'. In others, it is understood that those who are to come are very much on the minds of the constitution-makers.

Other social and political values—such as gender equality, environmental conservation and explicit anti-dictatorship, anti-corruption or anti-discrimination stances, or disapproval of undemocratic means to attain power—are also at times articulated. The Slovakian preamble uses the expression 'free life', which might be a product of translation; nevertheless, it is a profound comment on freedom and liberty.

Only about twenty countries in the world have actually used the expression 'fraternity' in their preambles—a large number of them belong to the African continent. Cuba and Morocco use fraternity in relation to international cooperation and not as a precept for their own citizenry.

The most arresting line in the Preamble of the Constitution of India is: 'FRATERNITY assuring the dignity of the individual and the unity and integrity of the Nation.'

Much has been said and written about the exquisite structuring of the Preamble to the Indian constitution, its emphasis on the 'dignity of the individual' and the gentle reminder that this is a prerequisite for keeping the nation together. In the discussions that led up to the finalisation of this line, there were suggestions that it needed to be inverted, with unity of the nation taking precedence over the dignity of the individual. But this was not accepted. In this, we followed a precedent: the preamble to the Irish constitution. 'And seeking to promote the common good, with due observance of Prudence, Justice and Charity, so that the dignity and freedom of the individual may be assured, true social order attained, the unity of our country restored, and concord established with other nations ...'

Importantly, the fraternity clause found its way into the Preamble only in the later stages of its formulation. It is not in the Swarajya Resolution of 1931 postulated at the forty-fifth session of the Indian National Congress in Karachi, nor was it a part of the Objectives Resolution presented by Jawaharlal Nehru to the Constituent Assembly on 13 December 1946.

On 6 February 1948, the Drafting Committee decided to substitute the older, simpler preamble formulated by the constitutional advisor B.N. Rau in May 1947 with a more ambitious one.

Rau's brief preamble read: 'We, the people of India, seek to promote the common good, do hereby, through our chosen representatives, enact, adopt and give to ourselves this constitution.'

Clearly, this was meant to be a holding clause to be replaced once a wholesome preamble was formulated.

In the Draft Constitution prepared by the Drafting Committee and submitted to the president of the Constituent Assembly, it was replaced with this text:

> WE, THE PEOPLE OF INDIA, having solemnly resolved to constitute India into a SOVEREIGN INDEPENDENT STATE, and to secure to, or promote among, all its citizens:

> JUSTICE social, economic and political;
> LIBERTY of thought, expression, belief, faith, worship, vocation, association and action;
> EQUALITY of status, and of opportunity; and
> FRATERNITY assuring the dignity of every individual without distinction of caste or creed,
> IN OUR CONSTITUENT ASSEMBLY this ... of ... (... day of May, 1948 AD) do HEREBY ADOPT, ENACT AND GIVE TO OURSELVES THIS CONSTITUTION.

In his book, *Ambedkar's Preamble*, Aakash Singh Rathore argues that this new Preamble had to have been Babasaheb Ambedkar's own draft, and the inclusion of the word 'fraternity' his choice and decision.[3] While submitting the Draft Constitution to the president of the Constituent Assembly, Dr Rajendra Prasad, on 21 February 1948, Ambedkar wrote in his accompanying letter, 'The committee has added a clause about fraternity in the preamble, although it does not occur in the Objectives Resolution. The committee felt that the need for fraternal concord and goodwill in India was never greater than now and that this particular aim of the new Constitution should be emphasised by special mention in the preamble.'[4]

Interestingly, adopting the Preamble was one of the final acts of the Constituent Assembly. The Preamble was a vision statement, but was also considered a philosophical summation of all that the constitution had envisaged for Indian citizens. Adopting it at the very end ensured that it accurately captured the spirit of the constitution; it was the culmination of the work that the Constituent Assembly had set out to accomplish. On the final day, 26 November 1949, Rajendra Prasad said: 'The method which the Constituent Assembly adopted in connection with the Constitution was first to lay down its "terms of reference" as it were in the form of an Objectives Resolution which was moved by Pandit Jawaharlal Nehru in [an] inspiring speech and which constitutes now the Preamble to our Constitution.'

Prasad attributed the Preamble to the Objectives Resolution

To understand how we got to the adoption of the Preamble on 26 November 1949, we need to wind the clock back a little.

In its opening paragraph, the 1931 Swarajya Resolution had emphasised economic freedom, which it argued was necessary to end exploitation. This was followed by a wide-ranging list of Fundamental Rights that the Swaraj government would guarantee its people. The list covered freedom of speech, press, profession and practice of religion, and equal rights to all citizens; it stated that religion, caste or creed should not affect public employment, office of power or honour or any trade; it promised religious neutrality on the part of the State and limited work hours of labour, as well as the right to form labour unions and progressive income tax for agriculture. There was one right—to bear arms in accordance with the law—that ultimately did not find a place in our constitution.[5] The resolution also declared that expenditure on defence would be reduced by half, that there would be no duty on salt (the Salt Satyagraha movement was in 1930) and that the State would control certain industries and resources. Mahatma Gandhi's abhorrence of alcohol found place in the form of a call for total prohibition. This Gandhian commandment was reframed and retained in our constitution under Article 47 as a Directive Principle. The Swarajya Resolution was, in short, an amalgam of what would eventually take shape as fundamental rights, directive principles and policy statements.

Much of what made it to the resolution can be traced back to the Nehru Report of 1928.[6]

Before we get to that, allow me to take you on a musical detour to a month that changed the course of things for Karnatik music. The forty-second session of the Indian National Congress took place in Madras in December 1927, and an All-India Music Conference was organised on the sidelines. The success of the music conference led to an annual music festival in Madras, now known as the December, or Margazhi, Music Festival, and the establishment of the Music Academy, Madras—the premier classical music and dance organisation in South India. Patrons of the All-India Music Conference and the various office-bearers of the reception committee for this conference included prominent members of the Indian National Congress, theosophists and other prominent members of society. The public appeal[7] for support issued by the reception committee of the music conference before December 1927 makes for interesting reading. The agenda for the festival was: 'To bring together musicians, music lovers and scholars in the art and to consider the various problems concerning the theory and practice of Indian Music in its various systems ...' The goal was to standardise, innovate, preserve, publish and improve Indian music. The appeal also said this was the first time that such a conference was being held in South India, where Karnatik and Hindustani musicians could confer and develop a 'common National Heritage of Music'. Vishnu Digambar Paluskar, the music man of the Congress sessions, was going to 'cooperate' and help make the conference a 'success'.

At the end of the conference, the festival committee published a report which reveals that over a hundred musicians participated in the performances and over forty papers were presented. There was an exhibition of instruments, photographs, personal collections, books and manuscripts. At the end of the conference, a set of music-related resolutions were passed, and it was decided that the Music Academy, Madras would be formed.

The music festival shared purpose with the Indian National Congress's own agenda, only the domains varied. Both were a coming together of diverse Indians to tell the British that the people of this land came from a sophisticated ancestry and had the ability to intellectualise and draw up their social, political and aesthetic future in cohesion. But there was one difference. Political freedom was largely a participatory exercise. The music festival and the planned musical initiative cared only about the 'classical' universe and those who belonged to it. It also epitomised the attitude of the caste-elite towards India's culture. While democratic values mattered legally, in matters of art and culture, privileged sensibilities were prioritised.

In any case, it was at this 1927 session held in Madras that the Congress resolved to boycott the Simon Commission which was deciding the future of India, stripping Indians of their right to determine their own future. The Congress decided to propose its own draft Swaraj constitution on the basis of a declaration of rights. This was to be prepared in consultation with the representatives of various political, labour, commercial and communal formations and elected members of the central and provincial legislatures. Under the chairmanship of Motilal Nehru, the report was prepared in 1928.

The Objectives Resolution that Jawaharlal Nehru read out a decade and a half later was a more definitive, well formulated, succinct document. It crystallised the ideas that were acceptable to most political influencers.

The fourth, fifth, sixth and seventh paragraphs of the resolution are the ones that relate to our discussion here.

> (4) WHEREIN all power and authority of the Sovereign Independent India, its constituent parts and organs of government, are derived from the people; and
> (5) WHEREIN shall be guaranteed and secured to all the people of India justice, social, economic and political; equality of status, of opportunity, and before the law; freedom of thought, expression, belief, faith, worship, vocation, association and action, subject to law and public morality; and
> (6) WHEREIN adequate safeguards shall be provided for minorities, backward and tribal areas, and depressed and other backward classes; and

(7) WHEREBY shall be maintained the integrity of the territory of the Republic and its sovereign rights on land, sea and air according to Justice and the law of civilised nations ...

The continuity of thought between this resolution and the Preamble—and thus in the principles that guided the dreamers of a free India—is obvious. The fourth paragraph makes it clear that our entire political edifice would rest on the will of the people. In a manner of speaking, 'we, the people' was implied. The phrase had already been used in the preamble to the US constitution and pluralised elegantly in the United Nations Charter in 1945 as 'We, the Peoples of the United Nations'.

The Objectives Resolution did not include an explicit intention to live as a fraternity. But the understanding that a country is prosperous and well-meaning only when people come together out of respect and love was something we needed to express. Unless all of us showed a willingness to learn and unlearn together, no other right had any meaning. It was the later inclusion of fraternity that brought into the Preamble this qualitative element describing and defining the nature of the community we were dreaming of building. At the same time, it was a confession of the lack of a fraternal instinct among the people of India. The inclusion of fraternity in the Preamble intended to make the nurturing of mutual affection a necessity.

Fraternity was not a new idea—it had primacy in French political thought, for instance. But our Preamble delineates its intent: 'assuring the dignity of the individual and the unity and integrity of the Nation'. This description gives direction to our relationship with each other and our country. For this reason, above all, Rathore's argument that the word came from Ambedkar is compelling. Ambedkar knew better than anyone that all Indians would never be treated equally and with love unless it was an imperative in the new nation. This was a word

Ambedkar used many times, often in conjecture with liberty and equality in his monumental *Annihilation of Caste*.

> An ideal society should be mobile, should be full of channels for conveying a change taking place in one part to other parts. In an ideal society there should be many interests consciously communicated and shared. There should be varied and free points of contact with other modes of association. In other words there must be social endosmosis. This is fraternity, which is only another name for democracy.[8]

In present-day India, this line in the Preamble assumes more significance than ever. The deeply philosophical promise of fraternity is one that we cannot afford to forget or ignore for it is what, as the makers of our constitution clearly understood, glues this diverse and messy nation into a cohesive whole. It also means that we must be willing to converse with people who hold an opinion opposed to our own. But I will readily concede that I do not know how to have a dialogue with those who believe that fraternity itself is unnecessary. Is the promise to live as a fraternity untenable? We have to find a way out of this chakravyuh, this labyrinth, of the impossibility of conversation. Fraternity shows us the way. Whether or not another person will engage with me, I must be willing to do so. When every individual waits for someone else to realise the error of their argument, we all remain where we are. Much to the delight of the conspirators and the hate-filled, this only breeds resentment and dislike.

Ambedkar's fraternity was not anthropocentric. Sounding much like the emperor Ashoka, he gave us this interpretation of a section in Buddha's first sermon:

> Love is not enough; what is required is Maitri. It is wider than love. It means fellowship not merely with human beings but with all living beings. It is not confined to human beings. Is not such Maitri necessary? What else can give to all living beings the same happiness which one seeks for one's own self,

to keep the mind impartial, open to all, with affection for every one and hatred for none?[9]

To truly understand what 'fraternity' signifies in the Preamble, let us meditate on the word 'dignity'. Like most abstract ideas, dignity is something we instinctively understand but struggle to easily describe. What we do instead is provide examples that extrapolate the experience of dignity or its opposite, debasement. We reach out to associated feelings to comprehend its character.

Dignity is a sense of self-worth, self-respect and rightful honour. It is about one's place under the sun. It is a positive affirmation that does not need its validity attested by another. An individual senses both the presence and deprivation of it.

While the Preamble asserts that every individual must feel 'dignified', it is a fact that social interactions are expressed in unsaid, even unseen, ways. So, merely ensuring material and expressed rights cannot ensure dignity. The unsaid emotional exchanges in society could grant an individual the strength to express themselves or cause them to live in subjugated silence. The lack of dignity is the playground for fear. Inversely, the presence of dignity is the absence of fear. In his oft-quoted poem, Rabindranath Tagore said,

Chitto jetha bhoyshunyo, uchcho jetha shir
Where the mind is without fear and the head is held high

Holding one's head high as a symbol of fearlessness is salient because it points to the servitude and indignity associated with the opposite: compulsion and bowing down. No law can ensure that we treat each other with respect. But if dignity is an uncompromisable vision, we embolden ourselves in the journey towards equitability.

When we look each other in the eye, it is an expression of mutual freedom that stems from dignity. This is the country that we, the people promised to build for ourselves.

Dignity goes beyond justiciable rights and non-justiciable promises to the subtle emotional well-being of every individual. In a just society, dignity must always be present, in every space, among all people, even when we are all alone, fulfilled by our own being. When there is a lack of dignity, we are never alone; other people's voices clutter our mind. We see ourselves as the diminished individual that others aver we are. The atomising experience of the reduction of individual worth, the lack of dignity, is systematically ingrained in us. The Tamil poet Subramania Bharati captured this in a line:

Endru madiyum engal adimaiyin moham
When will we stop yearning to remain enslaved

Bharati wrote this in the context of the freedom struggle, asking Indians to break out of habitual subservience. But it applies to all socially discriminative practices. The perpetual lack of dignity results in the acceptance—even romanticisation—of abuse and allows abusers to continue the perpetration unquestioned. The oppressed remain trapped in the vortex of suppression. If they manage to free themselves, it is perceived as a transgression.

As a musician, it is also my experience that creativity thrives in the presence of dignity. I sit in solitude, imagining songs, cadences and rhythmic sequences. There is no audience before me, I am not pleasing anyone, it is just me and the music. The music permeates every part of my body, I smile, cry in joy, struggle with a raga and express myself to the fullest without any external burden. I flower when I am not worried about being watched; I am not worried about whether my music and I have value. It is impossible for me to inhabit this limitless space in music unless I treasure my own self, and feel present as a complete person. This is no mystical experience—it is real, and the society we construct will offer or deny us the possibility of achieving it.

Privacy, dignity and freedom are inextricably intertwined; at the loss of one, the rest disintegrate. In the *Justice K.S. Puttaswamy (Retd) v. Union of India* judgment of 26 September 2018, the Aadhaar-related case, the Supreme Court stated that 'privacy is a postulate of dignity', and further that 'privacy and liberty are intertwined, privacy is necessary for the exercise of liberty'.[10]

Earlier, in *Justice K.S. Puttaswamy (Retd) v. Union of India*, the right to privacy case of 2017, the Supreme Court had already stated: 'The expression "Dignity" carried with it moral and spiritual imports. It also implied an obligation on the part of the Union to respect the personality of every citizen and create the conditions in which every citizen would be left free to find himself/herself and attain self-fulfilment.'[11]This fulfilment is only possible when privacy of mind and body are enshrined in our way of life. The Constitution of India does not explicitly codify the Right to Privacy. It has been read into Article 21, Right to Life and Personal Liberty. The court also recognised that the dignity of the individual is a prime constituent of fraternity. It said, 'The incorporation of expression "Dignity of the individual" in the Preamble was aimed essentially to show explicit repudiation of what people of this Country had inherited from the past. Dignity of the individual was, therefore, always considered the prime constituent of the fraternity, which assures the dignity to every individual. Both expressions are interdependent and intertwined.'[12]

This is a very important observation. We cannot live together harmoniously, sharing a land, different ideas and cultures, unless every individual is able to feel worthy, and can freely celebrate the physical, social, economic, political and psychological environment. I sing my song to the open skies only when dignity is an inherent state and my privacy is secured.

The popular discourse in India appears to confuse privacy with secrecy, consequently leading to the mistaken belief that only those who have something to hide make a demand for privacy. There is also the impression that privacy is the preoccupation of the Westernised urban elite. The older generation often reminiscences about joint families, about a time when everyone knew everything. 'What is all this talk of privacy, we are an open society, we helped each other,' they say. Naturally, in those joint families, there were weaker members who were unable to express discomfort. They could do nothing when they felt violated, and their dreams and private moments were analysed openly by everyone else. After their passing, perhaps they are remembered as quiet, gentle beings.

Privacy is not only about data safety, information or surveillance cameras, but also about being able to live unsecretively, if I may coin a word for a certain shade of freedom. The expression of freedom ought not to be a celebrated act of bravado. It has to be the natural mode of living—no citizen, however vulnerable, should have to look over their shoulder or second guess their thoughts and actions. No one should feel ashamed of the clothes they wear, the food they eat, their language, customs, occupation, physical appearance, gender or sexual orientation. There should be no need to hide who you are or what you want to be. This is privacy. Privacy is not about being away from the public glare. Privacy needs to exist everywhere, but especially in a crowded street, in the public sphere. I need to know that I will not be judged or prosecuted for the person I am.

In the *Navtej Singh Johar v. Union of India* judgment that decriminalised queer sexual activity, the Supreme Court stated: 'Section 377 is an anathema to the concept of fraternity as enshrined in the Preamble to our Constitution and the Indian Constitution mandates that we must promote fraternity amongst the citizens sans which unity shall remain a distant dream.'[13]

This long overdue ruling took its lead from the right to privacy judgment of 2017. The reading down of Section 377 is just one step in a battle that is far from won. I know people who provide examples from mythology, sculptures and texts to claim that there was a time when Indians (read: Hindus) were open-minded and all-embracing. Quite aside from the highly shaky foundations of such portrayals, the argument does nothing to change the fact that the conditioning of gender and sexual conformity is deeply entrenched in Indian (including Hindu) society today. I distinctly remember the shock of hearing an audience member ask a trans person how they have sex and why they overdress. Not a question any cis-heterosexual man has had to face, I'm sure. Laws and judgments can be regressive or forward-looking depending on the judges on the bench, but for us to discard the crud in our minds—which, unfortunately, we pass on to the next generation—education is needed. Conversations on the body, sexual desire, gender, love need to be uncensored. Justice Anand Venkatesh of the Madras High Court acknowledged his own limitations in understanding homosexuality and the need to get rid of his prejudices. He put himself through learning sessions with a psychologist and members of the LGBTQ+ community before ruling in a case relating to the harassment of a gay couple by their families and the police.

Sadly, judges who acknowledge their ignorance and educate themselves are very much the exception.

A test to confirm the existence of freedom in any society is looking at its members' ability to say 'no'. The rejection must be heard and respected. This is only possible if society recognises individual dignity as a basic right. When a woman says 'no' to advances by men, her voice is not heard. In India, on the streets and in the courts, callous arguments that strip women of all dignity are made without any consideration of their impact. Judges are still divided on whether marital rape should be considered a crime. Rape is in itself an extension of a socially sanctioned belief system that diminishes women.

In homes and schools, in the media and in advertisements, women are reduced to objects of sexual desire. Boys are trained at home to treat women as lesser, as vehicles for procreation. Feminism and the constitution are what push back against this patriarchy. Unlike other democracies, adult suffrage in India was never closed to women. The Nehru Report of 1928 and the Swarajya Resolution of 1931 had already asserted both universal adult suffrage and equality. Then again, in 1950, when most Indians would have been uneducated, casteist and patriarchal, we declared emphatically in our constitution that every person, irrespective of their sex or identity, had a right to vote and participate in our democracy. The Fundamental Right to Equality under Articles 14, 15 and 16 assured every woman dignity and equality. But in the Constituent Assembly that took these brave steps, women numbered only fifteen among a total of 389 members! From then onwards, cutting across party lines, women have been demanding reservations in the legislature, but the men have been consistently scuttling that demand. Changes to the law are only possible when people change; at the same time, for people to transform, progressive laws need to be in place. This is the circular trap that has resulted in stagnation.

Nearly sixteen years after the Supreme Court of India's observations in the *Vishaka and Others v. State of Rajasthan and Others* case, on 22 April 2013, the Sexual Harassment of Women at Workplace (Prevention, Prohibition and Redressal) (POSH) Act, 2013, which stipulates mechanisms for the prevention and redressal of complaints of sexual harassment, was enacted. The expressions 'sexual harassment' and 'workplace' were defined with a view to ensuring that no women or place of work could be considered outside its purview. Yet, the law has not always been equal to the task, and accountability remains a serious problem.

The larger issue lies in us. I was told by a woman politician that her male counterparts do not understand the issue of sexual harassment. A serious impediment to finding justice is the power imbalance. Women often have no choice but to keep quiet for years, even continue professional contact with abusers. The protest by India's star wrestlers, and the lack of impact it has had, is an instance of this.[14] When professions are men's clubs, any challenge to a member is taken as an affront to the entire membership. Therefore, legal and administrative mechanisms are vital, but not enough. Society needs to become a safe place for women. This can only happen if men change. Until then, dignity is a right denied.

I think, too, of communities—transpersons, dalits and others—who are fighting to be treated as human among humans, and then all my philosophical musings sound hollow.

Dignity is a complicated terrain to navigate.

Photojournalist Dorothea Lange's work is acknowledged to have unveiled the human cost of the Great Depression in the US. Her iconic photo *Migrant Mother*, taken in California in 1936, became the symbol of that era. At its centre was Florence Owens Thompson (her name was unknown when the picture was published), a woman visibly worried about her difficult present and uncertain future. In the picture, leaning on her shoulders with their faces looking away from the camera are her daughters. Unless you look closely, you may miss the little baby wrapped in a cloth and snuggled in her arms. During the Great Depression, this photograph became a symbol of both abject poverty and resilience in the face of it. It continues to convey a story of struggle and hardship. Beyond these immediate feelings, Thompson exudes a calm dignity and inner strength that still resonate all these decades later.

To Lange, Thompson was just a subject, one of many who symbolised the dark times. We know that she did not ask for her subject's name or story. Is the dignity we observe in Thompson a projection of our own reading of her situation? We access the feeling not only from the picture but also from the matter-of-fact caption (*Destitute pea pickers in California. Mother of seven children. Age thirty-two. Nipomo, California*) and historical context—together, they suggest a resoluteness that offsets the depressing context and Thompson's personal burden. She may have been a fighter who, despite all the challenges life threw at her, trudged along, doing the best she could for her children.

But what did she actually feel at the moment the picture was taken? So powerful is the image of her that the individual in the frame becomes irrelevant. In capturing Thompson at that vulnerable moment, did Lange invade her privacy, ignore her right to dignity? These are not constitutional questions but ethical ones. By portraying Thompson in a manner that suited the visualiser's narrative, was her dignity erased? Could she have refused to be photographed? Did she have the freedom of mind for that thought to have even occurred? These are all important questions.

Years later, this is what Lange had to say about the event: 'I saw and approached the hungry and desperate mother, as if drawn by a magnet. I do not remember how I explained my presence or my camera to her, but I do remember she asked me no questions. I made five exposures, working closer and closer from the same direction.'[15]

In the 1970s, Thompson, the 'subject', finally spoke. 'I wish she hadn't taken my picture,' she declared. 'I can't get a penny out of it. [Lange] didn't ask my name. She said she wouldn't sell the pictures. She said she'd send me a copy. She never did.'[16] Thompson felt exploited.

Photographs continue to be published and names revealed without permission. If the individual in the frame is a 'nobody', their indignation does not matter. This feeling of being nobody is the absence of dignity, and the observer's disdain is the violence unleashed on the observed.

After the publication of Lange's photograph, the migrant farm workers in that camp received support from the US federal government. However, Thompson and her family, who had only stopped temporarily at the camp, had left by the time aid came. They were not migrant workers. But it is their image that gave life to the many migrants in the camp. Not only was Thompson not a migrant worker, she was Cherokee, not white. If that had been known and revealed at the time of publication, it is fairly certain that her face would not have been accepted as representative of migrant white people nor would the legacy of a resilient woman have arisen from that image.

The story does not end there. Many decades later, after the identity of the 'Migrant Mother' was publicly known, Thompson's family were able to crowdfund the money needed for her healthcare. The letters they received revealed that many people had derived strength and dignity from the picture. Does that mitigate the loss of Thompson's dignity? There is probably no correct answer to the Migrant Mother conundrum, but it does give us a glimpse into the moral dilemma of ruminating about dignity in an inherently unequal society.

That said, whatever good may come of it, or however well-intentioned an action may have been, if someone is deprived of their right to say 'no', there can be no denying the loss of dignity. Intention or impact is no excuse for denying a person agency. The lack of agency is the lack of dignity, which is why Thompson could not say no.

The Migrant Mother image inevitably reminds us of the thousands of migrant workers in India who were dislocated and forced to return to their homes due to the Union government's unplanned lockdown, announced with only a four-hour notice in March 2020. After ignoring many warnings, the government suddenly woke up to the reality of the pandemic. With Covid-19 finally acknowledged as a health crisis, Prime Minister Narendra Modi decided that the nation had to be shut down, literally overnight. 'Stay at home' was his order to all of us. Modi and his cabinet colleagues obviously forgot that many citizens were far away from their homes, in distant places, helping build an 'Atmanirbhar Bharat', a self-reliant India. With no earnings they could depend on to get them through the lockdown, no time to organise their return, no public transport, food or shelter, migrant workers walked or cycled thousands of kilometres to reach their homes. Not all of them managed to complete the journey. Even those who did were not always assured of reaching their home, as fellow villagers, fearing the virus, would not allow them to enter the village. They were dispossessed of every form of dignity, mere machine parts in the factory of production. They too were photographed, sometimes with context, even empathy. But were they asked if their images could be splashed in newspapers across the country? We don't know. The conflict between wanting to inform citizens of the unravelling tragedy and the rights of the workers must have haunted at least a few journalists. At the same time, it is possible that many workers never considered the fact that they could refuse to be photographed. Much like the story from 1936, as a result of the published stories and photographs, support poured in—not from the government but from civil society.

How are right and wrong placed here? It is hard to say, but this much seems undeniable, that we need to be shown the naked distress of people in a manner that deprives them of their dignity to move us to a humane response.

This must be said about dignity: it does not gain from another's loss. And it is not to be confused with pride. Pride is the symbol of the victor, and the lack of it that of the vanquished. In dignity, no one is defeated, no one wins. Dignity does not result from comparison, nor does it depend on what another feels. It is internal and individual. Pride, on the other hand, is the result of looking outward. When someone is proud of their country, they are looking at the opposite state somewhere else.

The Preamble does not mention pride, in the nation or our culture; it speaks of dignity. Until that line, it grapples directly with social inequalities. Then, in a spectacular leap of faith, the Preamble speaks of a dream, the hope that we will become a fraternity that assures the dignity of every individual.

Within the framework of the Preamble, this dream follows our resolve to secure for ourselves justice, equality and liberty. It can be inferred that, when these three rights are secured, fraternity that enables dignity for every individual is attainable. This is a partial truth. Dignity, though closely intertwined with justice, equality and liberty, is its own being. The latter three are legally enforceable, but dignity is an intangible, unquantifiable quality. Yet, when justice, equality and liberty are suffused with dignity, a Rubicon is crossed. But have we reached that point yet? In India, dalits are forced to physically enter and clean sewers and drains, usually without safety equipment. Even though it is outlawed, manual scavenging is a reality. India dances around technical terms and denies the existence of this practice and takes no responsibility for the deaths it causes. The manual scavengers are stripped of dignity in their lives, and then again in their death and in our memories. When dignity is not the norm, liberty, equality and justice can be manipulated. And fraternity remains an ever-receding ideal.

The Preamble is a clarifier, an interpretative tool, our conscience, a lodestar. On the other hand, Part III of the constitution articulates our Fundamental Rights, which are justiciable and inextricably connected to the declaratory promises we made to ourselves as citizens of this country. It is the legal detailing of the philosophical assurances in the Preamble. Our life as Indian citizens is (or would be) free, just, equitable and enabling only to the extent that these Fundamental Rights permit and limit our thoughts and actions.

In 1929, at its Lahore session, the Congress redefined 'swaraj' to mean complete independence, the absolute severance of India's sovereign relationship with the British. The reasons for this call were further explained in a Congress Committee resolution that declared 26 January 1930 as Swaraj Day. The Congress described India's condition as one of economic, cultural, political and spiritual ruin, with its people politically reduced and bound to an education system that had detached them from their 'moorings' and furthered servitude. The spirit of resistance had been crushed, it said, and compulsory disarmament had made them 'unmanly'. Right to Freedom was the inalienable right of all Indians so they might receive all the benefits from their own work and grow. The resolution declared, 'We hold it to be a crime against man and God to submit any longer to a rule that has caused this fourfold disaster to our country.' But it also unequivocally stated that violence could not be used to attain this end. In pointing out all that had been lost under the British, the Congress was saying that Indians were bereft of dignity in their own land.

The use of the terms 'cultural' and 'spiritual' signify a deeper understanding of dignity—that is, emotional dignity. How does one explain the state of being emotionally secure? I propose that it is a state in which our mind is cleared of all unnecessary doubt, allowing us to receive life in all its colours. From this inner well-being materialises a diverse and rich culture. Poems, melodies, cuisines, rituals and theatre, indeed, an entire way of life, with all its furrows and value systems, emerges.

Unfortunately, this can also work the other way. Manipulation that deprives others of their dignity is also hailed as culture. What then is the connection between culture and emotional dignity? Dignity must be at the core of the evolution of culture. Not just the dignity of human beings, but of all beings and the natural environment we inhabit. This is the culture I speak of, not of something brandished violently as a sign of superiority. Calling that culture is an abomination.

Bureaucrats, politicians and corporate honchos believe culture must wait until bathrooms, schools and roads have been built and jobs provided. I have been told that, 'at that level', culture does not matter, intellectual conversations do not exist. Food, shelter and clothes take precedence over all else. Those who hold power and privilege, and I do not absolve myself of responsibility here, treat the materially deprived as people who cannot think or feel beyond the spectrum of necessity, as if it is from our munificence alone that they might tomorrow advance to emotional sophistication. This is deeply offensive. It presumes that those who live on the precipice have no immediate need for aesthetic pleasure, beauty or their own way of life and death. What about the culture that gives those removed from power their sense of self? We are told that only economic upliftment matters. But the economy is itself a sphere of cultural activity. Every thought and action is drenched in accepted notions of culture. Financial management is culturally driven. Knowledge is passed on through culture. The natural life that surrounds us is interwoven with our culture. It is from, and as a result of, these relationships that imagination is born. If there is no imagination, there can be no life. Yet, this is the kind of existence that we want to assign to those who are less fortunate.

A good meal or a job does not complete the imagination; it takes songs, faith and expressions of love to do that. We need money to feed the child so they can sleep undisturbed by nightmares. Yet, it is a lullaby that puts the child to sleep even when there is no food on the table. If culture were just top dressing, there would be no rangolis outside huts, no songs of the fisherfolk, no theatre among the dalits. It is insulting when policymakers force the oppressed among us to also forgo their 'unnecessary' culture. This prioritising of money over everything else is an erasure of dignity.

In the Indian context, the cultural and the spiritual are cohabitants of the same enclave. There are emotional crossovers between culture, religion, faith and spirituality. Our thoughts and practices belong to more than one of these categories. Spirituality, though described as a way to 'realise the self', is always stuck between belief, ritual and purity. More often than not, societal condescension and disregard of certain cultures is a judgement of their spiritual status.

For long I have refrained from using this word to describe my musical experience. I was afraid that it would be highjacked by the religious and filed in the Religion rack. Clouded by that fear, I forgot that it could be the open door needed for the conservative faithful to join in a larger, catholic conversation. My musical experiences are spiritual; they are deeply moving philosophical dives that cannot be explained in words. But they are not otherworldly, nor are they transcendent or inaccessible to everyone else. And they most definitely do not place me at a higher level of consciousness.

They are moments of reflection, when I am able to observe all the sensory inputs I receive sans pre-conceived judgement. This also means I am able to offer music without blocks or suspicion. Music breaks down the walls that isolate me. I stand before you with no protective gear. But there is one question that remains with me once I return from these enlightening musical voyages: Why am I not such a human being in my everyday life?

For believers, perhaps this experience might arise when they stand before their lord—a state in which the disturbing voices of oppressors don't haunt the oppressed. If that fleeting moment of uncluttered solitude exists for someone, no one has the right to snatch it away from them.

I am reminded of an old woman I met when a few of us were trekking up Parvathamalai, a hill near the town of Tiruvannamalai in Tamil Nadu. It is a three-hour trek that includes a few tough stretches, a series of cement steps and finally, a precarious climb on and over a rock face. Waiting for us on the other side was lord Siva in the form of a linga. The weather in the month of May was blistering and dehydrating. As we neared the steps section, I noticed an old lady panting and scrambling over the steps. Every move was a herculean task. I was concerned for her well-being. Her son kept providing her water to drink as she stumbled along. Every few moments, she called out the name of the lord with whatever energy she had, pushing herself ever closer to the top. As she neared the temple, her voice got louder, she raised her arms in obeisance to Siva and her body suddenly moved with greater ease. It was as though god had given her new strength. On reaching the top, she stood up and walked towards the temple with an evident sense of expectation, like a lover would rush towards her beloved. She entered the temple in a state of thrall. She did not look around for validation, neither did she act as though the trek was an achievement. Tears rolled down her cheeks as her eyes remained transfixed on him, her god!

The legend of Kannappa Nayanar is an evocative reminder that the relationship between god and devotee needs to be unhindered. Kannappan, a hunter, fed his Siva the meat from his hunts. He collected water in his mouth and spat it on the linga to bathe his Siva. Siva was decorated with the flowers that Kannappan plucked and carried in his own hair. Kannapan did not know that his every action threw brahminical rules of ritual to the wind. This was his offering, his personal relationship with his lord. The lord had no right to refuse. One day, Kannappan found that his Siva was bleeding from one eye. Unable to stop the bleeding, Kannappan gouged out his own eye and placed it on the lord's. Soon, the linga's other eye began to bleed. The only way to remove his own remaining eye and offer it to Siva was to use his foot as a place-marker on the linga as he gouged his eye out with an arrow. In the tale, Siva is testing the devotee. An elucidation of bhakti, this is also a story about being free, free from the fear of judgement. Kannappan decided how he would pray; that right was not just freedom, it was dignity. This dignity was born from devotion. Every religion has stories of society shunning people who surrender to god in the manner of their choosing. And one need not be a saint to have this right.

The Sabarimala temple case, dealing with the denial of worshiping rights to women who menstruate, is about the dignity of the bhakta. When a specific class of women are systemically refused the right to experience the joy of meeting their god, it is a humiliation.

Ritualistic traditions and mythological explanations are no defence for such discrimination. According to Hindu ritualistic practice, when the 'eyes' of a sculpted idol are opened, the deity comes alive. Once we attribute this quality to the idol, we can use scriptures related to the temple (sthala puranas) to argue that the deity has made certain demands or issued regulations. In India, such a deity is a juristic person, and lawyers have argued that the ban is justified because the deity enjoys fundamental rights, just as other citizens do.[17] In the Sabarimala case, Indira Jaising argued against such an equalisation: '[T]here is difference between juristic person, and citizens ... deity being juristic person is nothing but right to sue and be sued. Deity has no other rights ... conscience doesn't reside in institutions, but in living beings.'[18]

It is said that the eternally celibate Ayyappa wishes to maintain a fair distance from fertile women. Even if we are to accept that these are the wishes of the deity himself and they need to be respected, one question still needs addressing: do his wishes supersede the yearning of a devotee?

The power equation between Ayyappa and his devotees is skewed in his favour. But if he is the benevolent and loving god I sing about, then he does not dominate. He comes to the rescue of the weak. In a poem, Perumal Murugan asks Siva whether it is right that he closes his eyes and the doors of his abode, the sanctum sanctorum, while the ignorant and malicious attack his devotee. I ask Ayyappa the same question. Why does he not respond? Has Ayyappa placed his personal principle above the bhakti of a devotee? Is not the burden of enduring the presence of the bhakta the god's rather than the women's? For the Sabarimala Ayyappa to refuse darshan on the basis of gender to a devotee who, in order to worship him, is willing to perform the required rituals and follow the mandated abstentions, is discriminative.

Theologically, the only test that a woman devotee can be put through is the test that gauges her bhakti, even if that's a test we don't ask of male devotees. Importantly, if mythology is to be believed, Ayyappa will find his own way of assessing each devotee. It is not something for us to be concerned about. But then, the problem is not the god's, is it? The problem is the male-constructed notion of purity.

Privacy, or the right to the private conduct of affairs—though I cannot see how it applies to Ayyappa—cannot be used as an excuse for practising a form of untouchability. As Jaising stated in her written submission to the Supreme Court:

> [T]he practice of considering women impure between the ages of 10-50, must thus be considered the practice of 'untouchability'. The word 'untouchability' has not been defined and there can be multiple forms of 'untouchability' which are not based on caste but based on notions of impurity. The present case is one of this kind ...
>
> It is submitted that untouchables and menstruating women are similarly situated in relation to temple entry. Therefore, the ban on entry of women from age group of 10 to 50 amounts to 'untouchability'.[19]

The argument that there are so many other Ayyappa temples that allow all women does not take away the unfairness of the exclusionary rule at Sabarimala. Neither does the whataboutery that there are other temples where some other group is denied permission justify this rule. No god can be kept beyond the reach of a devotee. This is both a religious and constitutional right.

Belief in its truest sense is an inner luminescence born from unabashedly believing in oneself or something higher. And doing so without being trapped within a belief system or ideology. Its partner expression 'faith' lies very close by, yet distinct, imbued as it is with fragility and doubt. One could say 'faith' yearns for 'belief'. Bhakti is a confluence of these sensibilities and much more. Bhakti transforms the fragility in faith into a vulnerability to despair and even disappointment. When the doubt that faith embodies confluences with the freedom that belief offers, it can lead to critical thought.

Uncritically accepting the primacy of practices in any shrine is where we must draw the line. If discriminatory practices can be justified by scriptural tradition and further explained as the wish of the deity, what stops someone from saying that a specific dalit community belonging to one village cannot enter a designated temple? Theoretically, there could be scriptures that tell a legend in which the lord fought a battle against these specific people and hence took a vow to never set eyes on them.

Any conversation on dignity today must bring forth the memory of Stan Swamy, the eighty-four-year-old social worker and human rights activist who was arrested in October 2020 under the draconian Unlawful Activities (Prevention) Act (UAPA), 1967. Not only was he unjustly arrested and held without trial for nine months, he was denied dignity. Even though the State knew he was a Parkinson's patient, he was refused a sipper-cup for weeks. The courts remained silent—a proclivity about which constitutional scholar Gautam Bhatia said, 'the harm in judicial evasion lies in how it effectively "decides without deciding" in favour of the executive'.[20] When Swamy was finally given medical support, it was too late. He passed away on 5 July 2021. Some call it a case of judicial murder.[21] After his death, many retired Supreme Court judges condemned the UAPA. But none were willing to go as far as questioning the following clauses under Article 22 of the constitution which enable the promulgation of such punitive laws.[22]

> 3) Nothing in clauses (1) and (2) shall apply—
>
> (a) to any person who for the time being is an enemy alien; or
>
> (b) to any person who is arrested or detained under any law providing for preventive detention.
>
> (4) No law providing for preventive detention shall authorise the detention of a person for a longer period than three months unless—
>
> (a) an Advisory Board consisting of persons who are, or have been, or are qualified to be appointed as, Judges of a High Court has reported before the expiration of the said period of three months that there is in its opinion sufficient cause for such detention:
>
> Provided that nothing in this sub-clause shall authorise the detention of any person beyond the maximum period prescribed by any law made by Parliament under sub-clause (b) of clause (7); or
>
> (b) such person is detained in accordance with the provisions of any law made by Parliament under subclauses (a) and (b) of clause (7).
>
> (5) When any person is detained in pursuance of an order made under any law providing for preventive detention, the authority making the order shall, as soon as may be, communicate to such person the grounds on which the order has been made and shall afford him the earliest opportunity of making a representation against the order.

(6) Nothing in clause (5) shall require the authority making any such order as is referred to in that clause to disclose facts which such authority considers to be against the public interest to disclose.

(7) Parliament may by law prescribe—

(a) the circumstances under which, and the class or classes of cases in which, a person may be detained for a period longer than three months under any law providing for preventive detention without obtaining the opinion of an Advisory Board in accordance with the provisions of sub-clause (a) of clause (4);

(b) the maximum period for which any person may in any class or classes of cases be detained under any law providing for preventive detention; and

(c) the procedure to be followed by an Advisory Board in an inquiry under sub-clause (a) of clause (4).

As we boldly call out the innumerable human rights violations that have occurred under laws that draw their right to exist from these clauses, we must also have the courage to demand the removal of 'preventive detention' from our Fundamental Rights. It is no mere restriction that the Fundamental Rights section enables the denial of freedom. Nor ought it to be considered 'reasonable' in law when the UAPA allows the State to declare any association as unlawful—indeed, 'terrorist'—even before a trial is held. The burden of proving innocence shifts to the accused—a reversal of the fundamental principle of natural justice. Further, irrespective of what the court may finally say, the damage is done, with the stigma permanently attaching to the accused. Most crucially, the process itself is the punishment. With extremely low conviction rates under UAPA (less than 3 per cent according to a study), it has proven to be chiefly a method to keep individuals in prison without any means of getting to a speedy trial.[23]

Politicians, judges, police officers and bureaucrats want to keep this provision in place, exactly as it is. Preventive custody, by its very nature, is also tacit permission to abuse the detainee. The message to every person who wields power is that guilt is presumed.

Prevention is a convenient word that gives citizens the feeling that something has been or will be averted. But what systems exist to judge whether officials actually acted in the best interests of citizens in an enforcement and legal system as opaque as ours? The Terrorist and Disruptive Activities (Prevention) Act (TADA), 1987, another avatar of the UAPA, too gave the State unbridled powers. A.G. Perarivalan was arrested under this law as a conspirator in the Rajiv Gandhi murder case. He was only nineteen years old then. He languished in jail for three decades. The only evidence against him was his own so-called confession, which was not recorded in its entirety and conveniently left out portions where he stated that he had no idea about the use of the two nine-volt batteries he had been asked to buy.

This was confirmed to the courts in 2017, in an affidavit submitted by the investigating Central Bureau of Investigation (CBI) officer. In 2015 Perarivalan filed a remission petition with the Tamil Nadu governor. Governors came and went, but the file remained on the desk. The Supreme Court and the Government of India also played pass-the-parcel with his life for a while. The enormous ego of the State prevented it from taking responsibility for the loss of Perarivalan's freedom, life and personal liberty. He was eventually released in 2022 by the Supreme Court invoking its extraordinary powers under Article 142.[24] Humility does not come easily to the State, which is why a loophole such as the one in our constitution is dangerous.

The UAPA was first passed in 1967, but India's constitutional history is dotted with innumerable acronyms enforcing preventive detention, such as the Armed Forces (Special Powers) Act (AFSPA), 1958, Maintenance of Internal Security Act (MISA), 1971, National Security Act (NSA), 1980, TADA, 1987 and Prevention of Terrorism Act (POTA), 2002, and others in specific regions and states, each one more crushing than the other.

It is hard to argue that the makers of the constitution did not know what they were doing when they introduced preventive detention into the Fundamental Rights clause. After all, many of them had been arrested under preventive detention, a provision that had been in operation in various parts of British India, beginning with the Bengal State Prisoners Regulation III of 1818. Why our freedom fighters and Constituent Assembly members thought it fit to keep this provision alive in independent India is baffling. Historians explain it as the psychological impact of Partition and the innumerable pulls and pushes that the government was dealing with in various parts of the country.

Without diminishing the impact these epochal events would have had on the decision-makers of the day, I argue that this provision directly contradicts every principle that these very people espoused during the Constituent Assembly debates.

Dr B.R. Ambedkar, head of the Drafting Committee, in his final speech in the Constituent Assembly on 25 November 1949, averred that the nature of the people in power would decide the quality of the constitution: 'However good a Constitution may be, it is sure to turn out bad because those who are called to work it, happen to be a bad lot. However bad a Constitution may be, it may turn out to be good if those who are called to work it, happen to be a good lot.'[25]

It is astonishing then that Ambedkar was a votary of preventive detention. He must have known that the clause would be used to deny the oppressed their dignity. The marginalised and oppressed—the very people Ambedkar fought tooth and nail to protect—are disproportionately impacted by preventive detention laws.[26] Ambedkar's support to this clause is indefensible, although, to be fair, there was an across-the-board consensus on the matter in the Assembly. Equally, Ambedkar was worried about misuse and exercised about the question of due process. On 15 September 1949, he said in the Constituent Assembly:

> [T]hose who believe in the absolute personal liberty of the individual will recognise that this power of preventive detention has been helped by two limitations: one is that the Government shall have power to detain a person in custody under the provisions of clause (3) only for three months. If they want to detain him beyond three months, they must be in possession of a report made by an advisory board which will examine the papers submitted by the executive and will probably also give an opportunity to the accused to represent his case and come to the conclusion that the detention is justifiable. It is only under that that the executive will be able to detain him for more than three months. Secondly, detention may be extended beyond three months if Parliament makes a general law laying down in what class of cases the detention may exceed three months and state the period of such detention.[27]

Did he expect the Indian government to behave any better than the British? I don't know, but he was uncertain about how Indian citizens would behave.

> Now I come to the question of three months' detention without enquiry or trial. Some Members have said that it should not be more than 15 days and others have suggested some other period and so on ... We do not know how the situation in this country will develop, what would be the circumstances which would face the country when the Constitution comes into operation, whether the people, and parties in this country would behave in a constitutional manner in the matter of getting hold of power, or whether they would resort to unconstitutional methods for carrying out their purposes. If all of us follow purely constitutional methods to achieve our objective I think the situation would

> have been different and probably the necessity of having preventive detention might not be there at all.[28]

Ambedkar defended the clause by saying that preventive detention was already present in both the Union and Concurrent lists (List I and III respectively) of the Seventh Schedule. This article, he claimed, limited its use, otherwise both Union and state governments could abuse it and 'there would be no liberty left'.

> My submission is that if their attitude was as expressed today, that we ought to have no such provision, then what they ought to have done was to have objected to those entries in List I and List III. We are trying to rescue the thing. We have given power to the Legislatures of the State and Parliament to make laws regarding preventive detention. What I am trying to do is to curtail that power and put a limitation upon it. I am not doing worse. You have done worse.[29]

When asked about who had made those lists, Ambedkar said he had, and the house had passed them. He also added that, even then, 'I had these limitations in mind.'[30] He also backed T.T. Krishnamachari's amendment, which he proposed at the fag end of the Constituent Assembly's sittings, allowing Parliament to decide on the categories for preventive detention and increase the duration of detention without any oversight. This is Article 22, Clause (7).

Ambedkar believed that a State born out of a liberal constitution was the best mechanism for change. He was probably wary of socio-cultural movements, and this suspicion was a result of his lived experience. Such movements were more often than not dictated, controlled and perpetuated by the caste-privileged, and kept the marginalised at the fringes or as receivers of largesse. If the people on the edges took to the streets of their own will, with demands of their own, they were squashed or ignored. To Ambedkar, the solution lay in what we guaranteed and made enforceable in the constitution. He was a State-constitutionalist. Ambedkar did not, and rightfully so, trust the upper-castes and elites. In my opinion, this led him to place unbridled trust in the establishment in this particular case. An establishment which was also elite.

On 17 December 1946, Ambedkar criticised Nehru's Objectives Resolution on the grounds that it did not speak of remedies. He said, 'All of us are aware of the fact that rights are nothing unless remedies are provided whereby people can seek to obtain redress when rights are invaded. I find a complete absence of remedies.'[31] It is clear then, that Ambedkar was aware of the dangers of an oppressive State. He also said in that same speech: 'Obviously, what is law, what is morality, will be determined by the executive of the day, and when the executive may take one view, another executive may take another view and we do not know what exactly would be the position with regard to fundamental rights if this matter is left to the executive of the day.'[32]

Yet, in the case of preventive detention, he left too much in the hands of the executive, and in hindsight, it is clear that his proscriptions on the matter were not good enough. At the very end, he did warn us: 'If hereafter things go wrong, we will have nobody to blame except ourselves.'[33]

He was right. In *A.K. Gopalan v. State of Madras* (1950), the Supreme Court in a majority judgment upheld the communist leader AKG's detention under the Preventive Detention Act, 1950. This ruling set the tone for independent India. Between 2015 and 2019, 5,102 individuals were arrested and cases were registered against 3,902 persons under the UAPA. The conviction rate is a meagre 2.8 per cent.[34] No surer proof is needed for the argument that these cases were motivated by reasons other than the rule of law.

A constitutional clause needs to be a safeguard against the worst excesses of the people in power. In a world where terrorism looms large, many feel the need for a legal armoury to prevent horrific crimes. Even in such situations, the State must only be able to bring in a very limited, narrowly tailored, tightly woven law, restricted to extraordinary situations and subject still to the supervision of the court. What we have today is a trivialisation of democracy.

The bogeymen used to scare the people of India are the possible splintering of our country and the ever-present rumour that anti-Indian forces are conniving to destroy this nation. Within three months of Gandhi's assassination, at a meeting in Sevagram on 13 March 1948, Nehru said: '*Desh ke do tukre to ho gaye, lekin aage chalkar aur bhi tukre-tukre ho jaane ka dar hai.*' (The country has split into two—that is an established fact. But the danger is of further fragmentation in the future.) Eerily, this expression reminds me of the 'tukde-tukde gang' spook that is used today to scare us about exactly the same thing.

Unlike the false alarms of today, in 1947, these fears were real and would have gripped the minds of the constitution-makers. British India was being partitioned into India and Pakistan. And as a union, we were unusual—a coming together of former provinces, princely states and centrally administered areas. A reflection of this need for cohesion is evident in this expression in the Preamble:

> and to promote among them all,
> FRATERNITY assuring the dignity of the individual and the unity of the Nation;

There is nothing wrong with this. But in 1976, a second condition was added: 'unity of the nation' became 'unity and integrity of the nation'.

Was it merely a further emphasis on the idea of unity, a reaffirmation of territorial integrity? The word was introduced by the Government of India during the Emergency and passed as a part of the 42nd Amendment. It is an innocuous-sounding word, 'integrity', but I am not entirely convinced of its innocence.

The word, coming so soon after unity, in my opinion, shifts the balance in the statement.

Though 'dignity of the individual' is given first place, now it is the entity that is the nation that has a much larger presence. The dignity of the individual is crushed under its weight. This was a pushback from the State, an intention that is evident from the context in which the word 'integrity' was inserted. The legitimacy of Indira Gandhi's government had been challenged in the courts and she was convicted of electoral malpractice in the Raj Narain case. Led by Jayaprakash Narayan, citizens across the country were protesting. To crush this dissent, Indira Gandhi declared an 'Emergency', innumerable politicians were incarcerated and the press was heavily censored. It was in such a stifling environment that the State decided to add the word 'integrity' and a powerless Parliament passed it. We can debate the difference between the nation and the State, but to most citizens, the State always seems to speak as the nation.

Allow me to take the creative liberty to reframe the fraternity line in the Preamble for a thought exercise: FRATERNITY assuring the dignity of the individual and the integrity and unity of the Nation.

In such a formulation, 'integrity' can be reinterpreted because it is freed from the 'unity and integrity' conjoint phraseology we are used to. Now, the line can be understood as the promotion of fraternity to assure the honesty and unity of the nation. The reader may argue that 'integrity of the nation' cannot refer to honesty because the nation is not a living entity. But it is. The nation is its people, and we have made a promise to ourselves that we will strive towards becoming honest people—all of us, the legislature, judiciary, executive and every citizen. Dignity is then extended from being an assurance to each individual to a collective promise. This would be synchronous with Justice, Equality and Liberty. The unity that binds us is common dignity and compassion, not the fear of territorial disintegration.

Despite the insertion of 'integrity', the intent of the line remains strong. That is because fraternity is based on mutual respect and love. Neither respect nor love can exist without the acceptance that we must make room for one another. We may disagree and argue, but we remain together. Such a bond develops from the attributes that society cultivates in individuals—attributes that must be taught and reiterated in every home, street, school and institution. That way, a society uncompromisingly negates any institution that forefronts hate and disdain. This is substantiated in the way Justice, Equality and Liberty are delineated, not just in the Preamble, but even more so in the Fundamental Rights. We have not taken any of them for granted. Instead, we have made a promise to ourselves to strive towards the fulfilment of their interconnected yet respective ideal states.

Unlike the Fundamental Rights, fraternity is not a tangible target. It is a cultural construct that cannot be translated into rights and laws. Recognising this limitation, the Preamble only promises to promote fraternity among Indians. But the very nature of fraternity is its limitation—it needs to be nurtured, not forced. Our failure lies not in the constitution, but in the lack of integration of fraternity into our schooling of young people. Irrespective of whether they are run by governments or private organisations, our schools have churned out generations of individuals who live by illiberal and undemocratic commandments, taught primarily to adhere to rules and precepts. Such an environment cannot possibly foster fraternity.

Equality, on the other hand, cannot be achieved by suggestion alone; it needs to be insisted upon. Education and enforcement need to work in tandem to achieve it. Those in positions of dominance, comfort and privilege will have to give up things they have become used to. They will have to learn to stand in queue, rub shoulders with everyone else, step aside, listen, respect and welcome those whom they have marginalised. As a nation, we need to put in place enabling structures to allow the oppressed to catch up with their past and present oppressors. The oppressed must be empowered to think, feel and act freely, overcome generational psychological trauma and develop equal relationships with the hereditarily privileged. These shifts are unlikely to be smooth. They are bound to ruffle many feathers and cause social contestations. How then is fraternity to be achieved? Ambedkar said, 'Without fraternity, liberty and equality could not become a natural course of things.'[35]

But fraternity is not our natural way of being. We are trained to see people as members of groups, of communities, and the individual is viewed as a representative of the qualities that society has assigned to a group. This is also how we view our own selves: that the things I cherish or detest about myself are reflections of my various identities. Some claim that social limitations do not matter, that we must treat each person as a human being with their own individual value. That is escapism, which allows the privileged to retain their generational advantages.

The phrase 'dignity of the individual' inverts our programmed observation technique: looking at the social location rather than the individual. If we accept dignity as a non-negotiable core value, the socio-cultural outer shell ceases to be our route to understanding people. Rather, social, political and cultural norms are evaluated on the basis of respect for individual dignity. We are thus released from identity-seeking. Equality and Liberty become accessible because they are a shared passageway that ensures individual dignity. This is a transformative possibility.

By focusing on individual dignity, the Preamble presents us with a profound possibility. Constitutions and legislations are large-scale constructional interventions, and philosophers argue that, by themselves, they make limited difference. However, the conceptual framework of 'individual dignity' brings together the individual and the collective: equality and fraternity. By seeking to inculcate this thinking in citizens, the Preamble attempts to temper the battle between those who want to hold on to their privileges and those who demand access. The establishment of individual dignity is, after all, Equality.

There is another argument that the preambular phrase 'dignity of the individual' can resolve. Political theorists position Equality and Liberty as opposing ideas. Equality includes affirmative action and State policy aimed at achieving social, economic and political equality. Equality is plural and layered, while Liberty is singular and specific. The striving for Equality necessitates placing restraints on personal liberty understood in its simplest sense. However, if we position the 'dignity of the individual' as the nucleus of Liberty and Equality, the tension between these two ideas is minimised.

When each individual's dignity is paramount, actions aiming to deliver social, economic or political equality cannot be seen as dampening individual expression. If anything, it ensures that the argument 'for the larger good' does not suppress individual rights. Irrespective of the status of the person, the dignity of the individual will need to be preserved. If the centrality of dignity is internalised, the necessary curtailment of personal liberty will not be an uncomfortable compromise.

Justice, equality, liberty and fraternity are the anchors that we have given ourselves. It was these words that gave me the courage to explore the inner resonances of the Preamble. I have no legal training, but the Preamble is not just a legal document. Its words are as much mine as they are any judge's. As citizens, we not only own the right to justice but are also obliged to give justice to others.

It was this sensibility that brought hundreds of students and protestors together at Shaheen Bagh. They read the Preamble, reminding us of the promises we are yet to keep. These anti-

Citizenship Amendment Act (CAA) protests brought back into the public imagination the introductory words of our constitution. People who had never heard them did so for the first time. Meanings began to emerge for those who had merely memorised the lines as an examination requirement.

Some claimed that it was a catalytic moment, while others thought of it as romanticisation. The Indian constitution is not a perfect document and not entirely consistent with the vision laid out in the Preamble. Yet, it is something we need to hold close to our hearts, work with, and take into the future. During the anti-CAA protests, we witnessed something that has rarely happened in independent India. Young people discovered in the Preamble the power to question the government. The fraternity expressed in the Preamble blossomed. Citizens demanded justice, not just for Indians, but for anyone who wanted to become a part of our experiment called democracy. It was something this country had not seen for decades.

The Preamble is a sophisticated-sounding declaration with an aural finish that makes it sonically intimidating. Irrespective of the medium of instruction in our schools, unfortunately, most of us learnt the Preamble in English. The sound was disconnecting and the dry meaning that was explained seemed like an import from the white man's country or 'seemai', as they used to say in Tamil. We have rarely heard the Preamble in our respective mother tongues.[36]

The meaning is the same in every language, yet each language's tonality changes the music in the Preamble. What is this music in the Preamble's unsung words? It is its speaking melody, its breath, the subtle meanings we share and receive. It is symbolic of our country, our people, our minds, songs, dances, stories and struggles. When we say 'we, the people', it encapsulates everyone, especially those who live beyond our eyeline. And sovereignty lies with each and every person who is a part of this 'we'. It is a deep affirmation of individual *sovereignty* that our Preamble conveys in the phrase 'assuring the dignity of the individual'.

We, the people of India
Eikhoi Bharat ki meeyamna
Hum Hind ki aavaam
Vayam Bharatasya janaah
Bhaaratattile janangal aaya naam
Aamra Bharater janagan
Amhi, Bharatache lok
...

Notes

Introduction

1. The Constituent Assembly Debates, Vol. XI, 25 November 1949, https://www.constitutionofindia.net/debates/25-nov-1949/.

1. The National Flag: A Symbol of Freedom

1. The Constituent Assembly Debates, Vol. IV, 22 July 1947, https://www.constitutionofindia.net/debates/22-jul-1947/.
2. The Constituent Assembly Debates, Vol. IV, 22 July 1947, https://www.constitutionofindia.net/debates/22-jul-1947/.
3. C. Rajagopalachari, *India's Flag*, Ganesh & Co, Madras, p. 4.
4. The Constituent Assembly Debates, Vol. IV, 22 July 1947, https://www.constitutionofindia.net/debates/22-jul-1947/.
5. P. Venkayya, *A National Flag for India*, self-published, Masulipatam, 1916, p. 37.
6. Venkayya, *A National Flag for India*, p. 34.
7. M.K. Gandhi, *The Collected Works of Mahatma Gandhi* (*CWMG*), Vol. 19, p. 561, gandhiheritageportal.org.
8. 'A National Flag for India', *New India*, 14 August 1917. p. 9.
9. Gandhi, *CWMG*, Vol. 69, p. 379, gandhiheritageportal.org.
10. Gandhi, *CWMG*, Vol. 45, p. 232.
11. British Library, File Pol 6552/48, Flag of the Last Viceroy, India Office Records and Private Papers, IOR/L/PJ/7/13479.
12. Report of the sixteenth session of the Indian National Congress held in Lahore, 1900, p. 46.

13. Report of the thirtieth session of the Indian National Congress held in Bombay, 1915, p. xxvii.
14. Report of the thirtieth session of the Indian National Congress held in Bombay, p. 10.
15. Report of the thirtieth session of the Indian National Congress held in Bombay, p. 66.
16. M.K. Gandhi, 'Chapter 4: What Is Swaraj', *Hind Swaraj or Indian Home Rule*, https://www.gandhiashramsevagram.org/pdf-books/hind-swaraj.pdf.
17. Gandhi, 'Chapter 14: How Can India Become Free', *Hind Swaraj or Indian Home Rule*.
18. Rajagopalachari, *India's Flag*.
19. Poulomi Saha, 'President Signs Off on Farm Laws Repeal Bill', *India Today*, 1 December 2021.
20. Shabbir Ahmed, 'RSS Stage-managed Anna Hazare Movement, Says Ex-India Against Corruption Team Member', *The News Minute*, 30 July 2023, https://www.thenewsminute.com/news/rss-stage-managed-anna-hazare-movement-says-ex-india-against-corruption-team-member-180413.
21. 'The National Flag', *Young India*, 11 December 1924.
22. Gandhi, *CWMG*, Vol. 59, pp. 10–11, gandhiheritageportal.org.
23. See, for instance, Laila Tyabji, 'Polyester Flags? Gandhi Would Have Protested This Desecration of His Beloved Khadi', *The Hindu*, 1 October 2022.
24. There were even disturbing reports such as this one: Sanjay K. Jha, 'Centre Accused of Tying Food for Poor to Flag Purchase', *The Telegraph*, 11 August 2022.
25. Report of the forty-second session of the Indian National Congress, held at Madras, 1927, p. 15.
26. S. Gopal, *Jawaharlal Nehru: A Biography*, Vol. 1, Oxford University Press, 1976, p. 138.
27. S.A.I. Tirmizi (ed.), *Paradoxes of Partition (1937–47): Vol. 1 (1937-1939)*, Hamdard University, New Delhi, p. 541.
28. Tirmizi (ed.), *Paradoxes of Partition (1937–47)*, p. 326.
29. Tirmizi (ed.), *Paradoxes of Partition (1937–47)*, p. 242.
30. Tirmizi (ed.), *Paradoxes of Partition (1937–47)*, pp. 357–358.

31. Tirmizi (ed.), *Paradoxes of Partition (1937–47)*, pp. 301–302, 330–332, 368–375, 607, 620–621.
32. Tirmizi (ed.), *Paradoxes of Partition (1937–47)*, pp. 330–331.
33. Tirmizi (ed.), *Paradoxes of Partition (1937–47)*, pp. 301–302.
34. Tirmizi (ed.), *Paradoxes of Partition (1937–47)*, p. 949.
35. Angelina E. Theodorou, '64 Countries Have Religious Symbols on Their National Flags', Pew Research Center, https://www.pewresearch.org/short-reads/2014/11/25/64-countries-have-religious-symbols-on-their-national-flags/.
36. 'The Religion-State Relationship and the Right to Freedom of Religion or Belief: A Comparative Textual Analysis of the Constitutions of Majority Muslim Countries and Other OIC Members', United States Commission on International Religious Freedom, https://www.uscirf.gov/sites/default/files/resources/USCIRF%20Constitution%20Study%202012%20(full%20Text(2)).pdf.
37. Ibn Majah, *Kitab al-Tahaara*.
38. Imam Bukhari, *al-Adab al-Mufrad: Kitab al -i'tinaa'a bid duniya*.
39. Al-Muwatta, *Kitab al-Jihad*.
40. Constitution of the Republic of South Africa, 1996, Chapter 2: Bill of Rights, Article 24, https://www.gov.za/documents/constitution/chapter-2-bill-rights.
41. Translated by Rajesh Garga.
42. Jacqui James, 'Dark and Light, Light and Dark', https://www.uua.org/worship/words/reading/5934.shtml.
43. Commonwealth Human Rights Initiative has this Hall of Shame map, http://attacksonrtiusers.org.
44. The Constituent Assembly Debates, Vol. 4, 22 July 1947, https://www.constitutionofindia.net/debates/22-jul-1947/.
45. The Constituent Assembly Debates, Vol. 4, 22 July 1947, https://www.constitutionofindia.net/debates/22-jul-1947/.
46. Naresh Keerthi, 'Spring Blossoms and Forgotten Poetry', *The Hindu*, 15 April 2017, https://www.thehindu.com/books/spring-blossoms-and-forgotten-poetry/article18059973.ece.
47. Simon Brodbeck, *Krishna's Lineage: The Harivamsha of Vyasa's Mahabharata*, Oxford University Press, New York, 2019, p. 354.

48. Brodbeck, *Krishna's Lineage*, pp. 353–358.
49. Translated by Professor Naresh Keerthi, Sanskritist.
50. All India Congress Committee, *Indian National Congress, 1920–1923: Being a Collection of the Resolutions of the Congress and of the All-India Congress Committee and of the Working Committee of the Congress from September 1920 to December 1923*, Allahabad: Allahabad Journal Press, 1924.
51. Sabyasachi Bhattacharya (compiled and edited with an introduction), *The Mahatma and the Poet: Letters and Debates Between Gandhi and Tagore, 1915–1941*, National Book Trust of India, 1997.
52. The Constituent Assembly Debates, Vol. IV, 1947, 22 July 1947, https://www.constitutionofindia.net/debates/22-jul-1947/.
53. Ananya Vajpeyi, *Righteous Republic*, Harvard University Press, 2012, pp. 184–185.
54. B. Shiva Rao, *The Framing of India's Constitution: Selected Documents*, Vol. 1, p. 496.
55. Rao, *The Framing of India's Constitution*, p. 497.
56. The Constituent Assembly Debates, Vol. IV, 22 July 1947, https://www.constitutionofindia.net/debates/22-jul-1947/.
57. Laila Tyabji, 'How the Tricolour and Lion Emblem Really Came to Be', *The Wire*, 14 August 2018, https://thewire.in/history/india-national-flag-emblem-suraiya-badruddin-tyabji.
58. Subhas Bhattacharya, 'The Indigo Revolt of Bengal', *Social Scientist*, Vol. 5, No. 12, July 1977, pp. 13–23.
59. M.K. Gandhi, *An Autobiography*, Critical Edition, Introduced with Notes by Tridip Suhrud, Hamish Hamilton, 2019, pp. 637–638.
60. B.R. Ambedkar, 'Riddle No. 16: The Four Varnas—Are the Brahmins Sure of Their Origin': Riddles of Hinduism: An Exposition to Enlighten the Masses, *Dr. Babasaheb Ambedkar: Writings and Speeches*, https://baws.in/books/baws/EN/Volume_04/pdf/200.
61. Nick Allen, 'Varnas, Colours and Functions: Extending Dumézil's Schema', *Zeitschrift für Religionswissenschaft*, Vol. 6, pp. 163–177.

62. See, for instance, Michael Kelly, 'France's Laïcité: Why the Rest of the World Struggles to Understand It', *The Conversation*, 20 November 2020, https://theconversation.com/frances-la-cite-why-the-rest-of-the-world-struggles-to-understand-it-149943.
63. The Constituent Assembly Debates, Vol. 4, 22 July 1947, https://www.constitutionofindia.net/debates/22-jul-1947/.
64. B. Shiva Rao, *The Framing of India's Constitution: A Study*, The Indian Institute of Public Administration, New Delhi, p. 131.
65. See, for instance, 'Addition of "Socialism", "Secularism" to Preamble of Constitution Is Sacrilege to Spirit of "Sanatana": Vice President Dhankhar', *The Hindu*, 28 June 2025; '"Socialist", "Secular" Don't Reflect India's Core Cultural Values: Chouhan', *Hindustan Times*, 28 June 2025; '"Golden Time to Remove Socialism, Secularism from Constitution": Himanta Joins Debate on Preamble', *The Indian Express*, 29 June 2025.
66. Khorshed Adi Sethna, *Madame Bhikhaiji Rustom Cama*, Publications Division, Ministry of Information and Broadcasting, Government of India, pp. 69–70.
67. 'Indian Independence and the International Congress of Socialists', *The Indian Sociologist*, August 1907, London, p. 32.
68. 'Stuttgart Congress: Socialism in Colonies—An Angry Debate', *Manchester Guardian*, 22 August 1907.
69. Hemchandra Kanungo, *Banglay Biplab Prachesta*, Kolkata, 1928, pp. 204–205.
70. Translated from the Bengali by Amlan Das Gupta.
71. Translated from the Bengali by Amlan Das Gupta.
72. Kamar, 'Die Kolonialfrage', In *Internationaler Sozialisten-Kongreß, Stuttgart 18. bis 24.* August 1907. Berlin: 1907, p. 38.
73. Translated from the German by P. Seralathan.
74. Kamar, 'Die Kolonialfrage', p. 38.
75. Translated from the German by P. Seralathan.
76. 'India at the International Socialist Congress, the Indian National Flag Unfurled', *The Indian Sociologist*, September 1907, London, p. 35.
77. Dr Bhupendranath Dutta, *Bharater Dwitiya Swadhinata Sangram*, Kolkata, 1928, reprint 1983, pp. 220–232.

78. Sir Surendranath Banerjea, *A Nation in Making: Being the Reminiscences of Fifty Years of Public Life*, Oxford University Press, first published 1925, reset and reprinted 1963, p. 180.
79. 'Seventh of August Celebration', *The Bengalee*, 8 August 1906, pp. 3, 6.
80. Dutta, *Bharater Dwitiya Swadhinata Sangram*, pp. 220–232.
81. The *Amrita Bazar Patrika* (Sree Bimal Ghosh, 'Our National Flag', 22 January 1945) has this interesting nugget about Mitra: 'At this time, *Sanjibani* journal, edited by the late popular leader Krishnakumar Mitra, used as their signature a flag inscribed with "liberte, equalite, fraternite" published on the front page. This journal was at the forefront of the protest against partition and the wider freedom struggle. The youth and employees of the Anti-Circular Society, located at 4 College Square near the *Sanjibani* offices, were highly influenced by this journal.'
82. 'The Vajra as a National Flag', *The Modern Review*, November, 1909, pp. 443–447.
83. Mrs Besant's Address, New India, 10 May 1916, Gokhale Memorial Society.
84. 'The HR Flag Case: Examination of Witnesses', *New India*, 4 September 1917; 'The HR Flag Case: In the Court of the District Magistrate', *New India*, 5 September 1917.
85. 'Sudandira Naalaa?', *Viduthalai*, 20 August 1972. (Quoting from a report in *Kudiyarasu* in August 1947.)
86. 'Sundandira Naal', *Viduthalai*, 15 August 1972.
87. In the Supreme Court of India Criminal Appellate Jurisdiction, Criminal Appeal No. 1545 of 2025, *Imran Pratapgarhi, Appellant, v. State of Gujarat & Anr, Respondents.*
88. K. Tirunavukarasu, *DMK Varalaru, Vol. 3: 1949–1969*, Nakkheeran Pathippagam, third edition, pp. 1374–1382.
89. Judgement available here: https://main.sci.gov.in/judgment/judis/25781.pdf.
90. Judgement available here: https://indiankanoon.org/doc/104833120/.

91. Judgement available here: https://indiankanoon.org/doc/783849/.
92. Judgement available here: In the High Court of Bombay (Nagpur Bench), Writ Petition No. 268 of 2015, Decided On: 29.11.2018, *President, Municipal Council, Achalpur and Ors. Vs. The Additional Commissioner, Amravati Division and Ors.*
93. Judgement available here: https://indiankanoon.org/doc/78121118/.

2. The Lion Capital: An Emblem for Justice

1. Excerpted from the translation of the Rupnath Rock inscription: E. Hultzch, *Corpus Inscriptionum Indicarum, Vol. 1: Inscriptions of Asoka*, printed for the Government of India, Clarendon Press, Oxford, 1925, p. 168.
2. Hultzch, *Corpus Inscriptionum Indicarum, Vol. I*, p. 58. Excerpted from the translation of the VI rock edict at Shahbazgarhi.
3. Hultzch, *Corpus Inscriptionum Indicarum, Vol. I*, p. 130. Excerpted from the translation of the VI pillar edict at Delhi-Topra.
4. Hultzch, *Corpus Inscriptionum Indicarum, Vol. I*, p. 114. Excerpted from the translation of the first separate rock edict at Jaugada.
5. Hultzch, *Corpus Inscriptionum Indicarum, Vol. I*, p. 114. Excerpted from the translation of the first separate rock edict at Jaugada.
6. Hultzch, *Corpus Inscriptionum Indicarum, Vol. I*, p. 115. Excerpted from the translation of the first separate rock edict at Jaugada.
7. Nayanjot Lahiri, *Ashoka in Ancient India*, Permanent Black, Ranikhet, 2020, pp. 99–101.
8. Hultzch, *Corpus Inscriptionum Indicarum, Vol. I*, pp. 68, 69. Excerpted from the translation of the XIII rock edict at Shahbazgarhi.
9. Hultzch, *Corpus Inscriptionum Indicarum, Vol. I*, p. 69. Excerpted from the translation of the XIII rock edict at Shahbazgarhi.

10. Hultzch, *Corpus Inscriptionum Indicarum, Vol. I*, p. 71. Excerpted from the translation of the XIV rock edict at Shahbazgarhi.
11. Hultzch, *Corpus Inscriptionum Indicarum, Vol. I*, p. 137. Excerpted from the translation of the VII pillar edict at Delhi-Topra.
12. Office of Secretary to President, General Branch, File No. 25/56, 1956, National Archives of India.
13. Government of India, Ministry of W.M.P., Filed and Indexed, File No.A763(77), 1950, National Archives of India.
14. Durrant's Press Clippings, *The Illustrated London News*, 26 January 1948; The British Library, 10122: State Emblems of India and Pakistan, India Office Records and Private Papers, IOR/L/PJ/7/12487, October 1947–February 1948.
15. The British Library, File Pol 11752/49, Questions Asked in the Constituent Assembly of India (Legislative) concerning the substitution of the Crown Emblem by the Emblem of the Indian Dominion by the High Courts, and..., India Office Records and Private Papers, IOR/L/PJ/7/14912, March 1949; The British Library, 10122: State Emblems of India and Pakistan, India Office Records and Private Papers, IOR/L/PJ/7/12487, October 1947–February 1948.
16. The Constituent Assembly Debates, Vol. VII, 15 November 1948, https://www.constitutionofindia.net/debates/15-nov-1948/.
17. Essential Service and Values & Banga, Dr U.V. Biswas, IPS (Retd) PhD, Edited by Jitendra K.R. Roy WBCS (Exec), Administrative training Institute, Government of West Bengal, pp. 50–55.
18. State Emblem, The Honourable Shri R.R. Diwakar's article on Dharmachakra, File No 170/51, 1951, National Archives of India.
19. 'Mahāhaṁsajātaka—Mahāsaṅgīti Tipiṭaka Buddhavasse 2500', translated by Amarasiri Bhikkhu, https://suttacentral.net/ja534/pli/ms.
20. Akeel Bilgrami, 'Gandhi and Liberal Modernity: The Vexed Question of Caste', *The India Forum*, 2 August 2023; Sujay Biswas, 'Gandhi's Approach to Caste and Untouchability', *Social Scientist*, Vol. 46, September–October 2018, pp. 71–

90; Anil Nauriya, 'Gandhi's Little-Known Critique of Varna', *Economic & Political Weekly*, Vol. 41, No. 19, 13–19 May 2006, pp. 1835–1838; Rajmohan Gandhi, *The Good Boatman*, Penguin Books, 1997, pp. 225–264.

21. M.K. Gandhi, *The Collected Works of Mahatma Gandhi* (*CWMG*), Vol. 62, p. 121, gandhiheritageportal.org.
22. Gandhi, *CWMG*, Vol. 48, pp. 161, 179, 258, 297.
23. Gandhi, *CWMG*, Vol. 48, p. 160.
24. Gandhi, *CWMG*, Vol. 62, p. 231.
25. Gandhi, *CWMG*, Vol. 84, p. 247.
26. Gandhi, *CWMG*, Vol. 84, p. 334.
27. Dr Babasaheb Ambedkar, *Writings and Speeches*, compiled by Vasant Moon, Vol. 1, reprint edition, Dr Ambedkar Foundation, 2014, p. 31, https://www.mea.gov.in/Images/CPV/Volume1.pdf.
28. Ambedkar, *Writings and Speeches*, pp. 27–28.
29. Gandhi, *CWMG*, Vol. 63, pp. 225–226.
30. Gandhi, *CWMG*, Vol. 63, p. 225.
31. B.R. Ambedkar, *Annihilation of Caste in Writings and Speeches*, compiled by Vasant Moon, Vol. 1, reprint edition, Dr Ambedkar Foundation, p. 77.
32. Gandhi, *CWMG*, Vol. 26, p. 323.
33. Gandhi, *CWMG*, Vol. 26, p. 540.
34. P.K. Balakrishnan, *Narayanaguru*, DC Books, 2008, pp. 168–170 (first published in 1954); M.K. Sanu, *Narayanaguruswamy*, National Book Stall, pp. 339–341, translated by S. Gopalakrishnan at the author's request.
35. Gandhi, *CWMG*, Vol. 57, p. 6.
36. Balakrishnan, *Narayanaguru*, pp. 168–170, translated by S. Gopalakrishnan at the author's request.
37. Gandhi, *CWMG*, Vol. 57, p. 90.
38. Rudrangshu Mukherjee, 'Dharma and Caste in the Mahabharata', 1 February 2021, https://www.theindiaforum.in/article/dharma-and-caste-mahabharata.
39. See, for instance, Dakshayani Velayudhan's criticism of Gandhi: https://www.constitutionofindia.net/debates/29-nov-1948/.

40. The Constituent Assembly Debates, Vol. XI, 21 November 1949, https://www.constitutionofindia.net/debates/21-nov-1949/
41. 'Rolling Forth the Wheel of Dhamma', translated by Bhikkhu Sujato, https://suttacentral.net/sn56.11/en/sujato.
42. 'Rolling Forth the Wheel of Dhamma', translated by Bhikkhu Sujato.
43. Hultzch, *Corpus Inscriptionum Indicarum, Vol. 1*, p. 162. Excerpted from the translation of the Sarnath Pillar inscription.

3. Satyameva Jayate: An Old Truth for a New Motto

1. Translated by Naresh Keerthi.
2. 'Truth Alone Will Triumph, Sardar Patel's Message to Gujarat', *The Hindu*, 18 July 1934.
3. Gopalkrishna Gandhi and Tridip Suhrud, *Scorching Love: Letters from Mohandas Karamchand Gandhi to His Son, Devdas*, Oxford University Press, 2022, pp. 301–302.
4. Jairam Ramesh, *A Chequered Brilliance: The Many Lives of V.K. Krishna Menon*, Penguin Random House, 2019, pp. 335–336.
5. 'Jawaharlal Nehru's First TV Appearance | Archives', BBC India, https://www.youtube.com/watch?v=y6XeUjU3giY.
6. https://youtu.be/PXEYaI40wr8.
7. B. Tilak Chandar, 'Sattankulam Custodial Deaths | Police Tortured Jayaraj and Benicks Knowing It Will Result in Death, Says CBI Charge Sheet', *The Hindu*, 28 October 2020.
8. Sambavi Parthasarathy, Devyanshi Bihani and Vignesh Radhakrishnan, 'Custodial Deaths: Police Convictions Remain Zero in Tamil Nadu and Beyond', *The Hindu*, 3 July 2025.
9. S. Sundar, 'Assistant Superintendent of Police in Ambasamudram Accused of Breaking the Teeth of Suspects; Tirunelveli District SP Recommends Inquiry', *The Hindu*, 11 April 2023.
10. Parthasarathy, et al., 'Custodial Deaths: Police Convictions Remain Zero in Tamil Nadu and Beyond'.
11. Parthasarathy, et al., 'Custodial Deaths: Police Convictions Remain Zero in Tamil Nadu and Beyond'.

12. Parthasarathy, et al., 'Custodial Deaths: Police Convictions Remain Zero in Tamil Nadu and Beyond'.
13. Bureau, 'After Peace Talks, Scheduled Caste Devotees Enter Temple in Gummidipoondi', *The Hindu*, 17 September 2024.
14. Bureau, 'Caste Hindus Object to Dalits Using Main Road for Funeral Procession in Tiruvannamalai', *The Hindu*, 2 October 2024; D. Karthikeyan, 'Separate Cemeteries for Dalits', *The Hindu*, 4 June 2011.
15. Bureau, 'Tirunelveli "Honour" Killing Case: Victim Kavin's Mother, Teachers Express Shock', *The Hindu*, 29 July 2025.
16. Bureau, 'Tirunelveli "Honour" Killing Case: Victim Kavin's Mother, Teachers Express Shock'.
17. T.M. Krishna, 'Periyar Urged Change at Personal Level, Nanguneri Shows It Hasn't Happened', Deccan Herald, 27 August 2023.
18. The response to the RTI application carried a photocopy of a letter with this notation on it: Ministry of Home Affairs, Government of India, No. 13/07/72, Pub. II.
19. 'The National Emblem', *The Hindu*, 26 January 1950.
20. 'India's Emblem and Seal', *The Hindu*, 15 December 1947; 'India Government's Emblem', *The Hindu*, 30 December 1947.
21. State Emblem, The Hon'ble R.R. Diwakar's Article on Dharma-chakra, File No. 170/51, 1951, National Archives of India.
22. Ramesh, *A Chequered Brilliance*, pp. 335–336.
23. Government of India, Ministry of W.M.P, Filed and Indexed, File No. A763 (77), 1950, National Archives of India.
24. Amitabh Sinha, 'What New Govt Data Reveals on the Extent of Undercount of Covid-19 Deaths in India', *The Indian Express*, 10 May 2025; Bindu Shajan Perappadan, 'Excess Deaths in 2020 and 2021 Not Equal to Deaths by Covid-19, Increase Attributable to Several Reasons', *The Hindu*, 10 May 2025; Pooja Prasanna, 'How India Hid Its Covid Death Numbers | LME 74', *The News Minute*, 17 May 2025.
25. See K. Deepalakshmi and Anirudh Parthasarathy, 'Fact Check: "The Kashmir Files" and the Disinformation Surrounding It', *The Hindu*, 2 April 2022; Astha Rajvanshi, 'How a Low-Budget

Hindi Film Ignited Deadly Religious Tension', *Time*, 18 May 2023.

26. Samuel Beal, *Si-yu-ki, Buddhist Records of the Western World*, translation from the Chinese of Hiutn Tsiang, Vol. I, 2003, Asian Educational Services, New Delhi, Chennai, 2003 (First published by Kegan Paul, Trench, Trübner & Co., London, 1884), p. 150.
27. M.A. Stein, *Kalhana's Rajatarangini: A Chronicle of the Kings of Kashmir*, Vol. I, First Book, Motilal Banarasidas Publishers, Delhi, 1900 (reprint edition 1989), pp. 19, 20.
28. Translated by Naresh Keerthi.
29. Dániel Balogh and Ezster Somogyi, *Mālavikā and Agnimitra*, New York University Press, JJC Foundation, The Clay Sanskrit Library, first edition, New York, 2009, https://annas-archive.org/md5/2ada33e5bd9ad9e075449f53777a3e69.
30. Mundaka Upanishad, verse 2.1.10, from Patrick Olivelle, *Upanisads*, Oxford World's Classics, Oxford University Press, 1998, p. 272.
31. Translated by Gopalkrishna Gandhi.
32. 'Abolition of the Death Penalty in Sub-Saharan Africa', https://www.fiacat.org/en/our-actions/project-for-the-abolition-of-the-death-penalty-in-subsaharan-africa.
33. 'Abolitionist and Retentionist Countries as of December 2024', https://www.amnesty.org/en/documents/act50/9240/2025/en/.
34. Himanshi Dhavan, 'President Pratibha Patil Goes On Mercy Overdrive', *The Times of India*, 22 June 2022, https://timesofindia.indiatimes.com/india/President-Pratibha-Patil-goes-on-mercy-overdrive/articleshow/14330594.cms.
35. 'Outgoing President Ram Nath Kovind Turned Down Six Mercy Petitions', *The Economic Times*, 7 July 2022, https://economictimes.indiatimes.com/news/india/outgoing-president-ram-nath-kovind-turned-down-six-mercy-petitions/articleshow/92709277.cms?from=mdr.
36. *Death Penalty India Report*, National Law University, Delhi, 2016, pp. 20, 21, 23.

37. Arthur Koestler and Albert Camus, 'Reflections on the Guillotine', in *Resistance, Rebellion and Death*, translated by Justin O. Brian, The Modern Library, New York, p. 136.
38. Amrit Dhillon, '"Free Pass for Mobs": India Urged to Stem Vigilante Violence Against Minorities', *The Guardian*, 19 February 2019.
39. John Curtis, Nigel Walker and Tim Robinson, 'Research Briefing for the UK Parliament: Persecution of Christians and Religious Minorities in India', 22 February 2022, https://commonslibrary.parliament.uk/research-briefings/cdp-2022-0042/.
40. Ratna Singh and Areeb Uddin Ahmed, 'Demolitions as Collective, Illegal Punishment, with Mainly Muslim Properties Destroyed After Riots', *Article 14*, 25 April 2022.
41. Soutik Biswas, Vikas Pandey, 'Atiq Ahmed: The Life of India's Gangster-Politician Killed on Live TV', *BBC.com*, 15 May 2023.
42. Prabha Sridevan, 'Take These Men off Death Row', *The Hindu*, 6 July 2012.
43. 'Botched Executions', https://deathpenaltyinfo.org/executions/botched-executions.
44. S. Radhakrishnan, *The Principal Upanishads*, George Allen and Unwin Ltd, London, first published in 1953, second impression 1968, p. 688.

4. Jana Gana Mana: A Song and an Anthem

1. Sadan Jha, 'A History of Bharat Mata and Why We Need to Draw a Parallel with the National Anthem', *The Indian Express*, 18 March 2016.
2. Sumathi Ramaswamy, *The Goddess and the Nation: Mapping Mother India*, Duke University Press, 2010, pp. 15, 16.
3. This line was changed to *'Abala kena ma eta bale!'* in the fifth edition of *Anandamath*. However, Aurobindo's translation followed the first edition.
4. Prabhat Kumar Mukhopadhyay, *Rabindra Jiban Katha*, Ananda Publishers, 1991, pp. 110–111.

5. Bankim Chandra Chatterjee, *Anandamath*, translated by Aurobindo Ghosh and Barindra Kumar Ghosh, Auro e-Books (based on Ashir Prakashan's 2010 edition), 2016, p. 123.
6. Bankim Chandra Chatterjee, *Anandamath: The Abbey of Bliss*, translated by Nares Chandra Sengupta, Padmini Mohan Neogi, 1906, fifth edition, p. 152.
7. Sima Bandyopadhyay, *Rabindrasangeete Swadeshchetana*, National Book Agency, Kolkata, 1986. Quoted in Sumit Sarkar, *The Swadeshi Movement in Bengal, 1903-1908*, Permanent Black, 2011 (first published 1973), p. 246.
8. Sarala Devi, *Shotogan*, published by Rangopal Chakroborty for Adi Brahmo Samaj, Kolkata.
9. Prabhat Kumar Mukhopadhyay, *Rabindrajibani*, Visva-Bharati, 1936, pp. 110–111.
10. Jawaharlal Nehru, *Selected Works of Jawaharlal Nehru*, Series 1, Vol. 8, p. 435; available at Jawaharlal Nehru Memorial Fund, https://nehruselectedworks.com.
11. Sabyasachi Bhattacharya, *Vande Mataram*, revised edition, 2015, p. 74.
12. Sureshchandra Samajpati, *Bankim Prasanga*, pp. 287–289, https://archive.org/details/dli.bengal.10689.5420.
13. Chatterjee, *Anandamath*, p. 162.
14. Chatterjee, *Anandamath: The Abbey of Bliss*, p. 199.
15. Samajpati, *Bankim Prasanga*, pp. 287–289, https://archive.org/details/dli.bengal.10689.5420.
16. Nehru, *Selected Works of Jawaharlal Nehru*, Series 1, Vol. 8, pp. 186–187; available at Jawaharlal Nehru Memorial Fund, https://nehruselectedworks.com.
17. Nepal Majumder, *Rabindranath O Subhashchandra*, Saraswat Library, 1969, pp. 72–73.
18. Majumder, *Rabindranath O Subhashchandra*, pp. 72–73.
19. Majumder, *Rabindranath O Subhashchandra*, pp. 72–73.
20. Hemchandra Kanungo, *Banglay Biplab Prachesta*, Kolkata, 1928, p. 76.
21. Seeni Viswanathan, *Kaala Varisayil Bharati Padalgal*, Seeni Viswanathan, Chennai, 2012, pp. 101, 102, 292, 293.

22. A.R. Venkatachalapthy, 'A British Journalist & The Tamil Poet', *The Hindu*, 4 December 2021.
23. Bachchan, 'Hamara Rastriya Geet', pp. 37–43, 52 (originally published in *Navneet*).
24. Mahatma Gandhi, *Collected Works of Mahatma Gandhi* (*CWMG*), Vol. 69, p. 380, gandhiheritageportal.org.
25. Mahatma Gandhi, 'The Heroic Song of Bengal', translated from the Gujarati, *Indian Opinion*, 2 December 1905; Gandhi, *CWMG*, Vol. 5, p. 156, gandhiheritageportal.org.
26. Gandhi, *CWMG*, Vol. 82, p. 265, gandhiheritageportal.org.
27. Gandhi, *CWMG*, Vol. 82, pp. 391, 415 gandhiheritageportal.org.
28. John Murray, *The Historical Record of the Imperial Visit of 1911*, for the Government of India, London, p. 5.
29. *Nil Durpan, or The Indigo Planting Mirror: A Drama*, translated from the Bengali by A Native, Calcutta, 1860, p. 2.
30. Report of the twenty-second session of the Indian National Congress, Calcutta, 1906, p. 7.
31. Nehru, *Selected Works of Jawaharlal Nehru*, Series 1, Vol. 8, p. 186; available at Jawaharlal Nehru Memorial Fund, https://nehruselectedworks.com.
32. S.A.I. Tirmizi (ed.), *Paradoxes of Partition (1937–47): Vol. 1 (1937–1939)*, Hamdard University, New Delhi, p. 371.
33. The Constituent Assembly Debates, Vol. 7, 2 December 1948, https://www.constitutionofindia.net/debates/02-dec-1948/.
34. The Constituent Assembly Debates, Vol. 7, 2 December 1948, https://www.constitutionofindia.net/debates/02-dec-1948/.
35. The Constituent Assembly Debates, Vol. 7, 23 November 1948, https://www.constitutionofindia.net/debates/23-nov-1948/.
36. The Constituent Assembly Debates, Vol. 7, 1 December 1948, https://www.constitutionofindia.net/debates/01-dec-1948/.
37. Rajesh Kumar Pandey, 'Judge Backing UCC at VHP Event Wanted Cow as "National Animal"', *The Times of India*, 10 December 2024.
38. '[A]nd the song *Vande Mataram*, which has played a historic part in the struggle for Indian freedom, shall be honoured

equally with *Jana Gana Mana* and shall have equal status with it.': Rajendra Prasad. See Constituent Assembly Debates, Vol. 12, 24 January 1950, https://www.constitutionofindia.net/debates/24-jan-1950/.

39. *The Historical Record of the Imperial Visit of 1911*, for the Government of India, John Murray, London, p. 13.
40. Probodh Chandra Sen, *Bharat Borsher Jatiyo Sangeet*, Purbasha Ltd, Kolkata, 1949, p. 2.
41. Prashanta Kumar Pal, *Rabijibani*, Vol. 6, Ananda Publishers, Kolkata.
42. *The Historical Record of the Imperial Visit of 1911*, for the Government of India, John Murray, London, p. 257.
43. Krishna Dutta and Andrew Robinson, *Rabindranath Tagore: The Myriad-Minded Man*, St. Martin's Press, New York, 1996, p. 161.
44. 'Indian National Congress: Twenty Sixth Session in Calcutta, Wednesday Sitting', *The Bengalee*, 28 December 1911.
45. Report of the twenty-sixth session of the Indian National Congress, Calcutta, 1911, p. 38.
46. 'Indian National Congress: Mr S.N. Banerjee on Partition, The Swadeshi Movement to Be Continued, Reconstitution of the Congress', Second Day's Proceedings, *The Englishman*, 28 December 1911.
47. 'Indian National Congress: The Change of the Capital, New Conditions in Bengal', Leicester Daily Report, *Reuters*, 28 December 1911, p. 8.
48. 'National Congress: The Transfer to Delhi, Interesting Arguments', *The Stateman*, 4 January 1912, p. 18.
49. 'Jana Gana Mana, Its Occasion and Date', *Visva Bharati News*, December 1948, p. 41.
50. 'Jana Gana Mana, Its Occasion and Date', pp. 40– 41.
51. 'Jana Gana Mana, Its Occasion and Date', p. 41.
52. 'The Bolepur Brahmacharyasrama and D.P.I., New Province', *The Bengalee*, 26 January 1912, p. 4.
53. Report of the twenty-third session of the Indian National Congress, Madras, p. 24.

54. Frederick Kill Harford, *The National Anthem for India: Verbatim Report of the Meeting at Grosvenor House, on Wednesday, July 11, by Kind Permission of His Grace the Duke of Westminster, K.G. To Which Is Added Extract from the Times of India Report of a Meeting Held at Bombay under the Presidency of H.E. Sir James Fergusson, the Governor. London*, W.H. Allen & Co., 1883, p. 7; British Library.
55. Harford, *The National Anthem for India*, p. 19.
56. Harford, *The National Anthem for India*, p. 9
57. Harford, *The National Anthem for India*, p. 31.
58. Harford, *The National Anthem for India*, p. 19.
59. Report of the twenty-seventh session of the Indian National Congress, Bankipore, pp. 151–153.
60. Report of the thirty-first session of the Indian National Congress, Benares, p. 70.
61. Report of the forty-fifth session of the Indian National Congress, Karachi, p. 28.
62. Report of the thirty-second session of the Indian National Congress, Calcutta, 1917, p. 108.
63. Dutta and Robinson, *Rabindranath Tagore*, p. 179.
64. Javayatrir Patra, letter 10, dated 31 August 1927, p. 54. Translated by Amlan Das Gupta.
65. *Selected Works of Jawahar Lal Nehru, Second Series*, Vol. 6 , p. 279, https://nehruportal.nic.in/selected-works-jawahar-lal-nehru-second-series-6#page/326/mode/2up.
66. Education, Education (D III), 1950, File No. 49-111/50-D.III, National Archives of India.
67. Education, Education (D III), 1950, File No. 49-111/50-D.III, National Archives of India.
68. https://api.sci.gov.in/jonew/judis/27027.pdf.
69. https://api.sci.gov.in/jonew/judis/27027.pdf.
70. Rudrangshu Mukherjee, *Song of India: A Study of the National Anthem*, Essential India editions, Aleph, 2025, pp. 65–70.
71. V. Geetha, 'Can Powerful Words and Unfettered Love Help Shape the Future of Politics These Dark Times?', *Scroll.in*, 18 March 2023, https://scroll.in/article/1045530/can-

powerful-words-and-unfettered-love-help-shape-the-future-of-politics-these-dark-times. Also see the video of the speech (in Tamil, from 20:00–24:00) at https://www.youtube.com/watch?v=hkdkEEMlidc&t=1461s.

72. Rabindranath Tagore, 1919, Madanapalle.
73. Mukherjee, *Song of India*, p. 47.
74. Report of the twenty-sixth session of the Indian National Congress, 1911, p. 110.
75. *Constituent Assembly of India Debates (Proceedings)*, Vol. V, https://www.constitutionofindia.net/debates/14-aug-1947/.
76. *The Constituent Assembly Debates*, Vol. X, 13 October 1949, https://www.constitutionofindia.net/debates/13-oct-1949/.
77. Nehru, 'The Music of the National Anthem', *Selected Works of Jawaharlal Nehru*, Series 2, Vol. 6, April–June 1948, p. 277; available at Jawaharlal Nehru Memorial Fund, https://nehruselectedworks.com.
78. Nehru, 'The Music of the National Anthem', p. 281.
79. Nehru, 'To Ali Sardar Jafri', *Selected Works of Jawaharlal Nehru*, Series 1, Vol. 8, p. 435.
80. Nehru, 'The Music of the National Anthem', *Selected Works of Jawaharlal Nehru*, Series 2, Vol. 6, p. 278.
81. Nehru, 'The Music of the National Anthem', p. 282.
82. Education Ministry, Government of India, A2 Section, F 15-6 /51- A2, Subject: Transfer of Copyright in Jana Gana Mana from Visva Bharati to Government of India, National Archives of India.
83. Bachchan, 'Hamara Rastriya Geet', pp. 37–43, 52.
84. *Visva-Bharati Quarterly*, November 1942–January 1943; translated by Amiya Chakravarty.
85. 'Indian National Anthem, Jana Gana Mana to Be Chosen', *The Hindu*, 21 January 1950.
86. The Constituent Assembly Debates, Vol. XII, 24 January 1950, https://www.constitutionofindia.net/debates/24-jan-1950/.
87. The Constituent Assembly of India (Legislative) Debates, Official Report, Vol. VI, 1948, 9 August to 31 August 1948, p. 549,

https://eparlib.sansad.in/bitstream/123456789/760463/1/cald_03_25-08-1948.pdf.

88. Home Affairs, Public Section, 1950, File No. 12/25/50-public; Home Affairs, Public Section, 1951, File No. 15/112/51-public, National Archives of India.
89. Education, Education (D III), 1950, File No. 49-111/50-D.III, National Archives of India.
90. Education, Education (D III), 1950, File No. 49-111/50-D.III, National Archives of India.
91. Education, Education (D III), 1950, File No. 49-111/50-D.III, National Archives of India.
92. Education, Education (D III), 1950, File No. 49-111/50-D.III, National Archives of India.
93. Education, Education (D III), 1950, File No. 49-111/50-D.III, National Archives of India.
94. Education, Education (D III), 1950, File No. 49-111/50-D.III, National Archives of India.
95. States, Ministry of States, 1952, File No. F1(4)-H/52, National Archives of India.
96. Education, Education (D III), 1950, File No. 49-111/50-D.III, National Archives of India.
97. Education, Education, File No. F-22-5/57-B.5 (B.3); Education, Education (D III), 1950, File No. 49-111/50-D.III; Education, Education, File No. F-8-51/5407, (Section D-7), National Archives of India.
98. Education, Education (D III), 1950, File No. 49-111/50-D.III, National Archives of India.
99. Home, Home Ministry, 1950, File No. 40/08/53-Public, National Archives of India.
100. Home, Home Ministry, 1950, File No. 40/08/53-Public, National Archives of India.
101. Education, Education (D III), 1950, File No. 49-111/50-D.III, National Archives of India.
102. Education, Education (D III), 1950, File No. 49-111/50-D.III, National Archives of India.

103. Home, Home Ministry, 1950, File No. 40/08/53-Public, National Archives of India.
104. Home, Home Ministry, 1950, File No. 40/08/53-Public, National Archives of India.
105. Home, Home Ministry, 1950, File No. 40/08/53-Public, National Archives of India.
106. James H. Cousins and Margaret E. Cousins, *We Two Together*, Ganesh and Company, Madras, 1950, pp. 341–342.
107. Cousins and Cousins, *We Two Together*, pp. 341–342.
108. Cousins and Cousins, *We Two Together*, p. 342.
109. Cousins and Cousins, *We Two Together*, p. 519.
110. Archives of Netaji Research Bureau, Hindi Qaumi Tarana, Indian National Anthem, Qaumi Gana.
111. All India Congress Committee, *Indian National Congress 1936-37, Being the Resolutions Passed by the Congress, the All-India Congress Committee and the Working Committee During the Period Between April 1936 to January 1938*, Allahabad: Allahabad Journal Press, 1951, p. 77.
112. K.V. Prasad, 'Is Learning Hindi as a Third Language Necessary?', *The Hindu*, 14 March 2025.
113. See, for instance, 'Writer and Disability Campaigner Thrashed in Goa Theatre for Not Standing Up During National Anthem', *The Indian Express*, 20 October 2016 and 'Disabled Man Abused for Not Standing Up During National Anthem', *The Times of India*, 2 October 2017.
114. Nehru, 'The Music of the National Anthem', *Selected Works of Jawaharlal Nehru*, Series 2, Vol. 6, p. 279; available at Jawaharlal Nehru Memorial Fund, https://nehruselectedworks.com.

5. The Preamble: A Vision for the Republic

1. See www.constituteproject.org. *Constitute* was developed by the Comparative Constitutions Project at the University of Texas at Austin and the University of Chicago.
2. 'Preambles of Constitutions: A Comparative Study of 194 Current Constitutions', https://www.constitutional-change.

com/preambles-of-constitutions-a-comparative-study-of-194-current-constitutions/.

3. Aakash Singh Rathore, *Ambedkar's Preamble: A Secret History of the Constitution of India*, Penguin Random House, 2020, pp. 89–118.
4. B. Shiva Rao, *The Framing of Indian Constitution, Select Documents, Vol. III*, The Indian Institute of Public Administration, 1967, p. 510.
5. See the discussion on it here: Constituent Assembly Debates, Vol. 7, 2 December 1948, https://www.constitutionofindia.net/debates/02-dec-1948/.
6. Nehru Report (Motilal Nehru, 1928), https://www.constitutionofindia.net/historical-constitution/nehru-report-motilal-nehru1928/.
7. Public appeal; author's personal archive.
8. B.R. Ambedkar, 'Annihilation of Caste' in Vasant Moon (compiler), *Dr Babasaheb Ambedkar: Writings and Speeches*, reprint by Dr Ambedkar Foundation, Vol. 1, p. 57.
9. Vasant Moon (compiler), *Dr Babasaheb Ambedkar: Writings and Speeches*, Vol. 11, p. 129.
10. https://indiankanoon.org/doc/127517806/.
11. https://indiankanoon.org/doc/91938676/.
12. https://indiankanoon.org/doc/91938676/.
13. https://indiankanoon.org/doc/168671544/.
14. Asim Ali, 'Citizen Activism That Is Missing from the Wrestling Ring', *The Hindu*, 5 June 2023. Also see 'Court Accepts Closure Report to Cancel Sexual Harassment Case Against Brij Bhushan', *The Hindu*, 26 May 2025.
15. 'Dorothea Lange's "Migrant Mother" Photographs in the Farm Security Administration Collection', Library of Congress, https://guides.loc.gov/migrant-mother.
16. Geoffrey Dunn, 'Photographic License', https://www.newtimesslo.com/archive/2003-12-03/archives/cov_stories_2002/cov_01172002.html.
17. Shishir Tripathi, 'A Lawyer for Lord Ayyappa: Advocate Sai Deepak Turns Heads in SC Arguing for Sabarimala Deity's Right

to Celibacy', *Firstpost*, 31 July 2018, https://www.firstpost.com/india/a-lawyer-for-lord-ayyappa-advocate-sai-deepak-turns-heads-in-supreme-court-arguing-for-sabarimala-deitys-right-to-celibacy-4859291.html.

18. https://x.com/TheLeaflet_in/status/1024584202610794497.
19. https://images.assettype.com/barandbench/import/2018/08/Indira-Jaising-written-submissions.pdf.
20. Gautam Bhatia, 'A Banquet of Scraps: On the Legacy of Chief Justice Sanjiv Khanna', 13 May 2025, https://indconlawphil.wordpress.com/2025/05/13/a-banquet-of-scraps-on-the-legacy-of-chief-justice-sanjiv-khanna/.
21. See, for instance, this video of reactions by two legal experts: https://www.thequint.com/news/law/the-judicial-murder-of-stan-swamy.
22. Article 22 of the Constitution was amended by the 44th Amendment, 1978, but the amendment is yet to be brought into force by successive governments: John Sebastian and Faiza Rahman, 'Improving Preventive Detention Laws', *The India Forum*, 15 May 2023.
23. See 'Less Than 3% Arrests Under UAPA Led to Conviction Between 2015 and 2020, Shows PUCL Draft Report', *Scroll.in*, 16 September 2022, https://scroll.in/latest/1033009/less-than-3-arrests-under-uapa-resulted-in-conviction-between-2015-and-2020-shows-report.
24. Krishnadas Rajagopal, 'Perarivalan, Rajiv Gandhi Case Convict, Released by Supreme Court Citing Extraordinary Powers', *The Hindu*, 18 May 2022: 'The court held that the Tamil Nadu Council of Ministers' advice on September 9, 2018 to pardon Perarivalan was binding on the Governor under Article 161 (Governor's power of clemency) of the Constitution.'
25. Constituent Assembly Debates, Vol. 11, 24 November 1949, https://www.constitutionofindia.net/debates/24-nov-1949/.
26. Suraj Yengde, 'State Attacks Dalits via Anti-Left Rhetoric, as Directly Attacking Them Would Cost It Heavily', *The Indian Express*, 3 May 2020.

27. Constituent Assembly Debates, Vol. 9, 15 September 1949, https://www.constitutionofindia.net/debates/15-sep-1949/.
28. Constituent Assembly Debates, Vol. 9, 16 September 1949, https://www.constitutionofindia.net/debates/16-sep-1949/.
29. Constituent Assembly Debates, Vol. 9, 16 September 1949, https://www.constitutionofindia.net/debates/16-sep-1949/.
30. Constituent Assembly Debates, Vol. 9, 16 September 1949, https://www.constitutionofindia.net/debates/16-sep-1949/.
31. https://www.constitutionofindia.net/debate_paragraphs/395043/.
32. https://www.constitutionofindia.net/debate_paragraphs/395043/.
33. Constituent Assembly Debates, Vol. 11, 25 November 1949, https://www.constitutionofindia.net/debates/25-nov-1949/.
34. 'Less Than 3% Arrests Under UAPA Led to Conviction Between 2015 and 2020, Shows PUCL Draft Report', *Scroll.in*, 16 September 2022, https://scroll.in/latest/1033009/less-than-3-arrests-under-uapa-resulted-in-conviction-between-2015-and-2020-shows-report.
35. Constituent Assembly Debates, Vol. 11, 25 November 1949, https://www.constitutionofindia.net/debates/25-nov-1949/.
36. Translations here, although not all twenty-two are available: https://legislative.gov.in/document-category/preamble-to-constitution-of-india/.

Select Bibliography

BOOKS

Abū'l-Faẓl 'Allāmī. *Ā'īn-i-Akbarī, Vol. 2.* Translated by H.S. Jarrett. 2nd edition. Corrected and further annotated by Jadunath Sarkar. Calcutta: Royal Asiatic Society of Bengal, 1949.

Agrawala, Vasudeva S. *The Wheel Flag of India: Chakra-Dhvaja* [चक्रध्वज]. Varanasi: Pethen Prakashan, 1964.

al-Bukhārī, Muhammad. *Al-Adab al-Mufrad: Kitāb al-I'tinā' bi-d-Dunyā.*

All-India Music Conference. *Report of the All-India Music Conference (1927, Madras) Held at Madras During the Last Week of December 1927.* Madras, 1928.

Ambedkar, B.R., *Dr. Babasaheb Ambedkar: Writings and Speeches.* 17 vols. Edited by Vasant Moon et al. Bombay/Mumbai: Education Department, Government of Maharashtra, 1979–1995; New Delhi: Dr. Ambedkar Foundation, Ministry of Social Justice and Empowerment, reprint editions, 2014–present.

Amin, Shahin, Tridip Suhrud and Megha Todi (eds). *Thumb Printed: Champaran Indigo Peasents Speak to Gandhi,* Volume I. New Delhi: National Archives of India; Ahmedabad: Navajivan Trust, 2022.

Amnesty International. *Abolitionist and Retentionist Countries as of December 2024.* Report ACT 50/9240/2025. London: Amnesty International, 2025.

Ansari, Iqbal A., *Political Representation of Muslims in India (1952–2004).* New Delhi: Manak Publications Pvt. Ltd, 2006.

Archaeological Survey of India. *Ancient India: Bulletin of the*

Archaeological Survey of India, No. 4. New Delhi: Archaeological Survey of India, 1948.

Archives of Netaji Research Bureau. Hindi Qaumi Tarana: Indian National Anthem, Qaumi Gana.

Austin, Granville. *The Indian Constitution: Cornerstone of a Nation*. Thirty-sixth reprint edition. New Delhi: Oxford University Press, 2019.

Austin, Granville. *Working a Democratic Constitution: A History of the Indian Experience*. Thirty-fourth reprint edition. New Delhi: Oxford University Press, 2023.

Bachchan, Harivansh Rai. 'Hamara Rastriya Geet'. *Sangeet*, December 2011. (Originally published in *Navneet*.)

Balakrishnan, P.K. *Narayana Guru*. Kottayam: DC Books, 2008.

Bandyopadhyay, Sima. *Rabindrasangeete Swadeshchetana*. Kolkata: National Book Agency, 1986.

Banerjea, Surendranath. *A Nation in Making: Being the Reminiscences of Fifty Years of Public Life*. Reprint edition. Oxford: Oxford University Press, 1963. (First published in 1925.)

Beal, Samuel, *Buddhist Records of the Western World, Vol. 1*. Translated by Si-Yu-Ki. New Delhi: Asian Educational Services, 2003. (Originally published in 1884.)

Beal, Samuel, *Buddhist Records of the Western World, Vol. 2*. Translated by Si-Yu-Ki. London: Trübner & Co., 1884.

Beverley, H. *Report on the Census of Bengal, 1872*. Calcutta: Bengal Secretariat Press, 1874.

Bhagwat A.K. and G.P. Pradhan, *Lokamanya Tilak: A Biography*. Seventh reprint edition. Mumbai: Jaico Publishing House, 2016.

Bhatia, Gautam. 'A Banquet of Scraps: On the Legacy of Chief Justice Sanjiv Khanna'. *Constitutional Law & Philosophy Blog*, 13 May 2025.

Bhattacharya, Amitrasudan. *Bankimchandra Jībani*. Kolkata: Ananda Publishers, 1991.

Bhattacharya, Sabyasachi (ed.). *The Mahatma and the Poet: Letters and Debates Between Gandhi and Tagore, 1915–1941*. New Delhi: National Book Trust of India, 1997.

Bhattacharya, Sabyasachi. *Vande Mataram: The Biography of a Song*. Revised edition, reprint. Delhi: Primus Books, 2015.

Bhikkhu, Amarasiri (trans.). 'Mahāhaṃsajātaka' in *Mahāsaṅgīti Tipiṭaka Buddhavasse 2500*. Sutta Central.

Biswas, Soutik and Vikas Pandey. 'Atiq Ahmed: The Life of India's Gangster-Politician Killed on Live TV'. BBC.com, 15 May 2023.

Biswas, U.N. *Essential Service Values & Banga*. Edited by Jitendra Kr. Roy. Kolkata: Administrative Training Institute, Government of West Bengal, 2009.

Bose, Phanindranath. *Life of Sris Chandra Basu*. Calcutta: R. Chatterjee, 1932.

Bose, Sugata. *His Majesty's Opponent: Subhas Chandra Bose and India's Struggle Against Empire*, Gurgaon: Penguin Random House India, 2019.

British Library. Royal Philharmonic Society Archive (c. 1792–1990). London: British Library, 2021.

Brodbeck, Simon. *Krishna's Lineage: The Harivamsha of Vyasa's Mahabharata*. Oxford: Oxford University Press, 2009.

Camus, Albert. *Resistance, Rebellion, and Death: Essays*. Translated by Justin O'Brien; with an introduction by Arthur Koestler. New York: The Modern Library, 1960.

Camus, Albert. 'Reflections on the Guillotine', in *Resistance, Rebellion, and Death*. Translated by Justin O'Brien; with an introduction by Arthur Koestler. New York: The Modern Library, 1960, pp. 115–165.

Charles Allen, *Ashoka: The Search for India's Lost Emperor*, Abacus, Great Britain, 2012.

Chatterjee, Bankim Chandra. *Anandamath*. Translated by Aurobindo Ghosh and Barindra Kumar Ghosh. Auro e-Books, 2016. (Based on the 2010 Ashir Prakashan edition.)

Chatterjee, Bankim Chandra. *Bande Mataram*. Translation and Introduction by Sri Aurobindo. Tamil Nadu: Auroville Press, 2000. (First published in 1907.)

Chatterjee, Bankim Chandra. *Anandamath: The Abbey of Bliss*. Translated by Nares Chandra Sengupta. Fifth edition. Kolkata: Padmini Mohan Neogi, 1906.

Chatterjee, Ramananda (ed.). *The Modern Review*, Vol. 49 (May 1931). Calcutta: The Modern Review Office, 1931.

Chatterjee, Ramananda (ed.). *The Modern Review*, Vol. XLVIII, Nos. 1–6 (July–December 1930). Calcutta: The Modern Review Office, 1930.

Chaudhrani, Sarala Devi. *Jibaner Jharapata*. Kolkata: Sahitya Samsad, 1973.

Chaudhrani, Sarala Devi. *Shotogan*. Kolkata: Rangopal Chakroborty for Adi Brahmo Samaj, n.d.

Cousins, James H. and Margaret E. Cousins. *We Two Together*. Madras: Ganesh and Company, 1950.

Craske, Oliver. *Indian Sun: The Life and Music of Ravi Shankar*. United Kingdom: Faber & Faber, 2020.

Cunningham, Alexander. *Inscriptions of Asoka*. Vol. 1 of Corpus Inscriptionum Indicarum. Reprint edition. Varanasi: Indological Book House, 1961. (Originally published in 1877.)

Das, Bhagavan. *The Science of Peace*. Adyar: Theosophical Publishing House, 1903.

Das Gupta, Rabindra Kumar, *Our National Anthem*, Tagore Research Institute, Kolkata: Second Printing, 2020.

Dhammika, Ven. S. *The Edicts of King Ashoka: An English Rendering*. The Wheel Publication No. 386/387. Kandy: Buddhist Publication Society, 1993.

Dutta, Bhupendranath. *Bharater Dwitiya Swadhinata Sangram*. Reprint edition. Kolkata, 1983. (First published in 1928.)

Dutta, Krishna and Andrew Robinson. *Rabindranath Tagore: The Myriad-Minded Man*. New York: St. Martin's Press, 1996.

Fischer-Tine, Harald. *Shyamji Krishnavarma: Sanskrit, Sociology, and Anti-Imperialism*. Reprint edition. New Delhi: Routledge, 2019.

France. *Constitution of October 4, 1958*. English translation. Paris: Government of France, 2009.

Gandhi, Gopalkrishna. *The Undying Light: A Personal History of Independent India*, New Delhi: Aleph Book Company, 2025.

Gandhi, Gopalkrishna and Tridip Suhrud (eds). *Scorching Love: Letters from Mohandas Karamchand Gandhi to His Son Devadas*. New Delhi: Oxford University Press, 2022.

Gandhi Heritage Portal. *Collected Works of Mahatma Gandhi*. All volumes. New Delhi: Publications Division, Ministry of Information and Broadcasting, Government of India.

Gandhi, M.K. *Hind Swaraj or Indian Home Rule*. Ahmedabad: Navajivan Publishing House, 1921.

Gandhi M.K. *An Autobiography, or The Story of My Experiments with Truth*. Critical Edition, Gurgaon: Penguin Random House India, 2019.

Gandhi, M.K. *Restless as Mercury: My Life as a Young Man*. Edited by Gopalkrishna Gandhi. New Delhi: Aleph Book Company, 2021.

Gandhi, Rajmohan. *Patel: A Life*. Ahmedabad: Navajivan Publishing House, 1990.

Gandhi, Rajmohan. *The Good Boatman: A Portrait of Gandhi*. New Delhi: Penguin Books, 1997.

Gandhi, Rajmohan. *Mohandas: A True Story of a Man, His People and an Empire*. New Delhi: Penguin Books, 2006.

Gopal, Ashok, *A Part Apart: The Life and Thought of B.R. Ambedkar*. New Delhi: Navayana Publishing Pvt. Ltd, 2023.

Gopal, Sarvepalli. *Jawaharlal Nehru: A Biography, Vol. 1: 1889–1947*. Oxford: Oxford University Press, 1976.

Gopal, Sarvepalli. *Jawaharlal Nehru: A Biography, Vol. 3: 1956–1964.* Second reprint edition. Bombay: Oxford University Press, 1985. (First published in 1984.)

Government of India, Ministry of Information and Broadcasting, Publications Division. *Our National Songs*. New Delhi: Publications Division, 1988. (First published in 1951; revised edition, 1962.)

Guha, Ramachandra. *Gandhi Before India*. New Delhi: Penguin India, 2013.

Guha, Ramachandra. *Gandhi: The Years That Changed the World, 1914–1948*. London: Allen Lane (Penguin), 2018.

Guruge, Ananda W.P. *Buddhism and the Race Question*; *The Race Question and Modern Thought*. Paris: UNESCO, 1958.

Harford, Frederick Kill. *The National Anthem for India: Verbatim Report of the Meeting at Grosvenor House, July 11*. London: W.H. Allen & Co., 1883.

Hultzsch, E. *Corpus Inscriptionum Indicarum*. Vol. I: Inscriptions of Asoka. Oxford: Clarendon Press, 1925.

Ibn Majah. *Kitab al-Tahaara*.

Internationaler Sozialisten-Kongreß zu Amsterdam, 14. bin 20. August 1904. Berlin: Buchhandlung Vorwärts, 1904.

Isaka, Riho. *Language, Identity, and Power in Modern India: Gujarat, c. 1850–1960*. London and New York: Routledge, 2022.

Jha, Sadan. *Reverence, Resistance, and Politics of Seeing the Indian National Flag*. Delhi: Cambridge University Press, 2016.

Joll, James. *The Second International, 1889–1914*. New York: Frederick A. Praeger, 1956.

Kachru, Sonam. 'Ashoka's Moral Empire'. *Aeon*, 19 September 2022.

Kalam, A.P.J. *Turning Points: A Journey Through Challenges*. New Delhi: HarperCollins Publishers India, 2012.

Kalidasa. *Mālavikā and Agnimitra*. Translated by Dániel Balogh and Eszter Somogyi. The Clay Sanskrit Library. First edition. New York: New York University Press; JJC Foundation, 2009.

Kanungo, Hemchandra. *Banglay Biplab Prachesta*. Kolkata: 1928.

Lahiri, Nayanjot, *Ashoka in Ancient India*. Third reprint edition. Ranikhet: Permanent Black in association with Ashoka University, 2020.

Lahiri, Nayanjot, *Searching for Ashoka: Questing for a Buddhist King from India to Thailand*. Ranikhet: Permanent Black in association with Ashoka University, 2022.

Lelyveld, Joseph. *Great Soul: Mahatma Gandhi and His Struggle with India*. New York: Alfred A. Knopf, 2011.

Lenin, V.I. *Collected Works, Vol. 13, June 1907–April 1908*. Translated by Bernard Isaacs. Edited by Clemens Dutt. Moscow: Progress Publishers, 1978.

Majumder, Nepal. *Rabindranath O Subhashchandra*. Kolkata: Saraswat Library, 1969.

Marshall, John and Alfred Foucher. *The Monuments of Sānchi, Vol. 1.* Edited and annotated by N.G. Majumdar. Delhi: Swati Publications, 1983. (First published in 1982.)

Mitra, Dinabandhu. *Nil Darpan; or, The Indigo Planting Mirror.*

Translated by 'A Native'. Calcutta: C.H. Manuel, Calcutta Printing and Publishing Press, 1861.

Mitra, Nripendra Nath (ed.). *The Indian Annual Register: An Annual Digest of Public Affairs of India, Vol. II, July–December 1937.* Calcutta: The Annual Register Office, 1938.

Muir, John. *Original Sanskrit Texts on the Origin and History of the People of India, Their Religion and Institutions, Vol. 1: Mythical and Legendary Accounts of the Origin of Caste, with an Enquiry into Its Existence in the Vedic Age.* Second edition. Rewritten and greatly enlarged. London: Trübner & Co., 1868.

Mukherjee, Rudrangshu, *Song of India: A Study of the National Anthem*. New Delhi: Aleph Book Company, 2025.

Mukherjee, Rudrangshu, *Tagore & Gandhi: Walking Alone, Walking Together*. New Delhi: Aleph Book Company, 2021.

Mukhopadhyay, Prabhat Kumar. *Rabindra Jiban Katha*. Kolkata: Ananda Publishers, 1991.

Mukhopadhyay, Prabhat Kumar. *Rabindra-Jībani, Vol. 1*. Calcutta: Visva-Bharati, 1933.

Murray, John. *The Historical Record of the Imperial Visit of 1911*. London: John Murray, for the Government of India.

Nehru, Jawaharlal. *An Autobiography, with Musings on Recent Events in India*. Reprint edition. London: Jane Lane The Bodley Head, 1947. (First published in 1936.)

Nehru, Jawaharlal. *Selected Works of Jawaharlal Nehru*. New Delhi: Jawaharlal Nehru Memorial Fund.

Olivelle, Patrick (trans.). *Upanisads*. Oxford: Oxford University Press, 1998.

Pal, Prashanta Kumar. *Rabijibani, Vol. 6*. Kolkata: Ananda Publishers, 1988.

Periyar, *Periyar Kalanjiyam, Kudi Arasu, Collected Works of Thanthai Periyar E.V. Ramasamy*. Chennai: The Periyar Self-Respect Propaganda Institution, 2011.

Radhakrishnan, S. *The Principal Upanishads*. London: George Allen and Unwin, 1953.

Rajagopalachari, C. *India's Flag*. Madras: Ganesh & Co., 1923.

Ramaswamy, Sumathi. *The Goddess and the Nation: Mapping Mother India*. New Delhi: Zubaan, 2011.

Ramesh, Jairam. *A Chequered Brilliance: The Many Lives of V.K. Krishna Menon*. Gurgaon: Penguin Random House, 2019.

Rao, B. Shiva (ed.). *The Framing of India's Constitution: A Study*. 4 vols. New Delhi: Indian Institute of Public Administration; printed at Government of India Press, Nasik, 1968.

Rathore, Aakash Singh. *Ambedkar's Preamble: A Secret History of the Constitution of India*. Gurgaon: Penguin Random House, 2020.

Sahni, Daya Ram. *Catalogue of the Museum of Archaeology at Sarnath*. With an introduction by J. Ph. Vogel. Calcutta: Superintendent Government Printing, India, 1914.

Samajpati, Sureshchandra. *Bankim Prasanga*. Kolkata: Mukherjee, Bose & Co., 1893.

Śaṅkara. *The Upanishads and Śrī Śaṅkara's Commentary*. Translated by S. Sitarama Sastri. Vol. 1. Madras: V.C. Seshacharri, 1905; reprint by Madras: G.A. Natesan & Co.

Sarkar, Sumit. *The Swadeshi Movement in Bengal, 1903–1908*. New edition; sixth reprint. Ranikhet: Permanent Black in association with Ashoka University, 2020.

Sen, Amulyachandra. *Asoka's Edicts*. With a Preface by Suniti Kumar Chatterji. Calcutta: The Indian Publicity Society for the Institute of Indology, 1956.

Sen, Probodh Chandra. *Bharat Borsher Jatiyo Sangeet*. Kolkata: Purbasha Ltd, 1949.

Sethna, Khorshed Adi. *Madame Bhikhaiji Rustom Cama*. New Delhi: Publications Division, Ministry of Information and Broadcasting, Government of India.

Singh, (Lt Cdr.) K.V. *The Indian Tricolour*, New Delhi: Rupa & Co in association with Flag Foundation of India, 2005.

Sircar, D.C. *Aśokan Studies*. Calcutta: Indian Museum, 1979.

Sircar, D.C. *Inscriptions of Aśoka*. Revised edition. New Delhi: Publications Division, Ministry of Information & Broadcasting, Government of India, 1967. (First published in 1957.)

Smith, Vincent Arthur. *Asoka: The Buddhist Emperor of India*. Oxford: Clarendon Press, 1901.

Sri Prakasa Papers, Nehru Memorial Museum and Library (NMML).

Stein, M.A. *Kalhana's Rajatarangini: A Chronicle of the Kings of Kaśmīr*. Reprint edition. Delhi: Motilal Banarasidas Publishers, 1989. (First published by Archibald Constable & Company in 1900.)

Stroud, Scott R. *An Intellectual Biography of B.R. Ambedkar: The Evolution of Pragmatism in India*, Gurugram: HarperCollins Publishers, 2023.

Subramanian, Lakshmi, *Singing Gandhi's India, Music and Sonic Nationalism*. New Delhi: Roli Books Pvt. Ltd, 2020.

Thaakur, Rabindranath. *Jābhā Jātrir Patra*. Reprint edition. Kolkata: Visva-Bharati, 1970. (First published in 1956.)

Thaakur, Rabindranath. *Geet Panchoshikaa*. Edited by Dinendranath Thaakur. Kolkata: Visva-Bharati, 1919–36.

Thapar, Romila. *Asoka and the Decline of the Mauryas*, Third Edition, twenty-first reprint. New Delhi: Oxford University Press, 2021.

The All-India Theistic Conference: Calcutta Session, 1911. Calcutta: Brahmo Mission Press; printed and published by A.C. Sarkar, 1911.

The Imperial Gazetteer of India: The Indian Empire, Vol. 4, Administrative. New Edition. Oxford: Clarendon Press, 1909.

Tirmizi, S.A.I. (ed.). *Paradoxes of Partition (1937–47): Vol. 1, 1937–1939*. New Delhi: Hamdard University, 1998.

Tirunavukarasu, K. *DMK Varalaru: Vol. 3—1949–1969*. Third edition. Chennai: Nakkheeran Pathippagam, 2015.

U Nu. *Saturday's Son*. Translated by U Law Yone. Edited by U Kyaw Win. New Haven and London: Yale University Press, 1975.

Vajpeyi, Ananya. *Righteous Republic: The Political Foundations of Modern India*. Cambridge, MA: Harvard University Press, 2012.

Vatsyayan, Kapila (ed.). *Culture of Indigo in Asia: Plant, Product, Power*. New Delhi: Niyogi Books, 2014.

Venkatachalapathy, A.R. *Swadeshi Steam: V.O. Chidambaram Pillai and the Battle Against the British Maritime Empire*. Gurugram: Penguin Random House India, 2023.

Venkayya, P.A. *National Flag for India*. Masulipatam: Self-published, 1916.

Virmani, Arundhati. *A National Flag for India: Rituals, Nationalism, and the Politics of Sentiment*. Ranikhet: Permanent Black, 2016.

Viswanathan, C. *Kaala Varisayil Bharati Padalgal*. Chennai: C Viswanathan, 2012.

Watters, Thomas. *On Yuan Chwang's Travels in India*. Oriental Translation Fund, New Series, Vol. 2. Edited by T.W. Rhys Davids and S.W. Bushell. London: Royal Asiatic Society, 1905.

Yengde, Suraj and Anand Teltumbde (eds). *The Radical in Ambedkar: Critical Reflections*. Gurugram: Penguin Random House, 2018.

ARTICLES/CHAPTERS/REPORTS

Ahmed, Shabbir. 'RSS Stage-Managed Anna Hazare Movement, Says Ex-India Against Corruption Team Member'. *The News Minute*, 30 July 2023.

Ali, Asim. 'Citizen Activism That Is Missing from the Wrestling Ring'. *The Hindu*, 5 June 2023.

Allen, Nick. 'Varnas, Colours, and Functions: Expanding Dumézil's Schema'. *Zeitschrift für Religionswissenschaft*, 6, no. 2 (1998).

Barnard, Alan. '!Ke e: /xarra //ke—Multiple Origins and Multiple Meanings of the Motto'. *African Studies*, 62, no. 2 (December 2003).

Barnard, Alan. 'Coat of Arms and the Body Politic: Khoisan Imagery and South African National Identity'. *Ethnos*, 69, no. 1 (February 2004).

Bevir, Mark. 'The Formation of the All-India Home Rule League'. *The Indian Journal of Political Science*, 52, no. 3 (July–September 1991).

Bharati, Subramania. *Writings in* The Hindu. Edited and an Introduction and Notes by A.R. Venkatachalapathy, THG Publishing Private Limited, 2022.

Bhattacharya, Subhas. 'The Indigo Revolt of Bengal'. *Social Scientist*, 5, no. 12 (July 1977): 13–23.

Bilgrami, Akeel. 'Gandhi and Liberal Modernity: The Vexed Question of Caste'. The India Forum, 2 August 2023.

Biswas, Sujay. 'Gandhi's Approach to Caste and Untouchability'. *Social Scientist*, Vol. 46 (September–October 2018).

Chandar, B. Tilak. 'Sattankulam Custodial Deaths | Police Tortured Jayaraj and Benicks Knowing It Will Result in Death, Says CBI Charge Sheet'. *The Hindu*, 28 October 2020.

Chattopadhyaya, V. 'India and the Second International'. *The Pan-Pacific Monthly*, 11 (1930).

Chopra, P.N. (ed.). *Towards Freedom, Vol. 1: Experiment with Provincial Autonomy, 1 January–31 December 1937*. New Delhi: Indian Council of Historical Research, 1937.

Curtis, John, Nigel Walker and Timothy Robinson. Persecution of Christians and Religious Minorities in India. Commons Library Debate Pack CDP-2022-0042. UK Parliament, 22 February 2022.

Death Penalty India Report. National Law University, Delhi, 2016.

Dhawan, Himanshi. 'President Pratibha Patil Goes on Mercy Overdrive'. *The Times of India*, 22 June 2012.

Dhillon, Amrit. '"Free Pass for Mobs": India Urged to Stem Vigilante Violence Against Minorities'. *The Guardian*, 19 February 2019.

Dunn, Geoffrey. 'Photographic License'. *New Times: San Luis Obispo*, 17 January 2002.

Gandhi, Gopalkrishna. 'A Moth-Eaten Nation?' *Hindustan Times,* 15 August 2010.

Gandhi, Gopalkrishna. 'Chitto Jaetha Bhoy Shunno'. *The Telegraph*, 1 June 2017.

Gandhi, Gopalkrishna. 'Nehru and Bose: Parallel Lives'. *Hindustan Times*, 23 November 2014.

Gandhi, Gopalkrishna. 'Our Anthem'. *Hindustan Times*, 3 December 2016.

Gandhi, Gopalkrishna. 'Two Nations'. *Hindustan Times*, 15 August 2017.

Gandhi, Gopalkrishna. 'Uphold the Lofty Ideals Symbolised by the Tricolour'. *The Hindu*, 22 July 2023.

Geetha, V. 'Can Powerful Words and Unfettered Love Help Shape the Future of Politics These Dark Times?' *Scroll.in*, 8 March 2023.

Geetha, V. 'Of Whales and Wheels: Buddhist Lessons in Democracy'. *Economic & Political Weekly*, 55, no. 32 (8 August 2020).

Guha, Ramachandra. 'Truths About the Tricolour'. *The Hindu* (Chennai), 26 September 2004.

Imlay, Talbot. 'Socialist Internationalism After 1914.' In *Internationalisms: A Twentieth-Century History*, edited by Glenda Sluga and Patricia Clavin, pp. 213–243. Cambridge: Cambridge University Press, 2017.

Indian National Congress. *Indian National Congress, 1920–1923: Being a Collection of the Resolutions of the Congress and of the All-India Congress Committee and of the Working Committee of the Congress from September 1920 to December 1923*. Allahabad: Allahabad Law Journal Press, 1924.

Indian National Congress. *Report of the National Flag Committee.* Ahmedabad: All India Congress Committee, 1931.

Indian National Congress. *The Indian National Congress, 1930–34: Being the Resolutions Passed by the Congress, the All India Congress Committee, and the Working Committee Between January 1930 and September 1934.* Allahabad: All India Congress Committee, n.d.

Indian National Congress. *The Indian National Congress, 1934–36: Being the Resolutions Passed by the Congress, the All India Congress Committee and the Working Committee During the Period Between May 1934 and April 1936.* Allahabad: Allahabad Law Journal Press, 1936.

Indian National Congress. *Indian National Congress 1936–37: Being the Resolutions Passed by the Congress, the All India Congress Committee and the Working Committee During the Period Between April 1936 and January 1938.* Allahabad: Allahabad Law Journal Press, n.d.

Indian National Congress. *Indian National Congress, Feb. 1938 to Jan. 1939: Being the Resolutions Passed by the Congress, the All India Congress Committee and the Working Committee During the Period Between Feb. 1938 to Jan. 1939.* Allahabad: All India Congress Committee, n.d.

Institute on Religion and Public Policy. *Religious Freedom in France: Report Submitted to the United Nations Universal Periodic Review.* Washington, DC: Institute on Religion and Public Policy, 2008.

James, Jacqui. 'Dark and Light, Light and Dark'. Unitarian Universalist Association Reading.

Jeyaraj, D.B.S. '"Sri Lanka Thaayae": How the National Anthem Written by Ananda Samarakoon Was Translated into Tamil by "Pundit" M. Nallathamby with Government Approval'. D.B.S. Jeyaraj.com, 13 February 2025.

Jha, Sadan. 'A History of Bharat Mata and Why We Need to Draw a Parallel with the National Anthem'. *The Indian Express*, 18 March 2016.

Jha, Sadan. 'The Life and Times of Bharat Mata: Nationalism as Invented Religion'. *Manushi*, no. 142 (2004).

Jha, Sanjay K. 'Centre Accused of Tying Food for Poor to Flag Purchase'. *The Telegraph*, 11 August 2022.

Jin, Hang. 'Buddhism and Political Rule: Rethinking on Ashoka's Attempt to Reshape India'. *Advances in Social Science, Education and Humanities Research*, 232 (2018).

Kamar. 'Die Kolonialfrage', In *Internationaler Sozialisten-Kongreß, Stuttgart 18. bis 24. August 1907*. Berlin: 1907.

Keerthi, Naresh. 'Spring Blossoms and Forgotten Poetry'. *The Hindu*, 15 April 2017.

Kelly, Michael. 'France's laïcité: Why the Rest of the World Struggles to Understand It'. *The Conversation*, 20 November 2020.

Krishna, T.M. 'Periyar Urged Change at Personal Level, Nanguneri Shows It Hasn't Happened'. *Deccan Herald*, 27 August 2023.

Library of Congress. 'Dorothea Lange's "Migrant Mother" Photographs in the Farm Security Administration Collection'. Library of Congress Guides, 12 June 2025.

Mehendale, M.A. 'Satyam Eva Jayate Nānṛtam. *Journal of the American Oriental Society*, 81, no. 4 (1961).

Mukherjee, Rudrangshu. 'Dharma and Caste in the Mahabharata'. The India Forum, 1 February 2021.

Nair, Janaki. 'Battles for Bangalore: Reterritorialising the City'. SEPHIS Paper No. 3. Amsterdam: SEPHIS (South–South Exchange Programme for Research on the History of Development), 1999.

Nauriya, Anil. 'Gandhi's Little-Known Critique of Varna'. *Economic & Political Weekly*, Vol. 41, No. 19 (2006).

Observatoire de la Laïcité. Freedoms and Prohibitions in the Context of 'Laïcité' (Constitutional Secularism). Paris: Observatoire de la Laïcité, Government of France, 2017.

Pandey, Rajesh Kumar. 'Judge Backing UCC at VHP Event Wanted Cow as "National Animal"'. *The Times of India*, 10 December 2024.

Parekh, Bhikhu. 'Defining India's Identity'. *India International Centre Quarterly*, 33, no. 1 (Summer 2006).

Parthasarathy, Sambavi, et al. 'Custodial Deaths: Police Convictions Remain Zero in Tamil Nadu and Beyond'. *The Hindu*, 3 July 2025.

Patel, Sardar Vallabhbhai. Proceedings of the Constituent Assembly (Legislative), 26 February 1948.

Prasad, K.V. 'Is Learning Hindi as a Third Language Necessary?' *The Hindu*, 14 March 2025.

Pratibha Devi and Indira Devi (eds). *Ananda Sangeet Patrika*. Kolkata: Ananda Sangeet Patrika Office.

Rajagopal, Krishnadas. 'Perarivalan, Rajiv Gandhi Case Convict, Released by Supreme Court Citing Extraordinary Powers'. *The Hindu*, 18 May 2022.

Rana, S.R. 'Hyndman and India'. *The Modern Review* (Calcutta), 87, no. 1 (January 1950).

Report of the Proceedings of the Indian National Congress 1885 to 1939.

Saha, Poulomi. 'President Signs Off on Farm Laws Repeal Bill'. *India Today*, 1 December 2021.

Scroll Staff. 'Less Than 3% Arrests Under UAPA Led to Conviction Between 2015 and 2020, Shows PUCL Draft Report'. *Scroll.in*, 16 September 2022.

Sebastian, John and Faiza Rahman. 'Improving Preventive Detention Laws'. The India Forum, 15 May 2023.

Sen, Probodh Chandra. 'India's National Anthem'. *The Visva-Bharati Quarterly*, 15, no. 1 (May–July 1949).

Singh, Ratna and Areeb Uddin Ahmed. 'Demolitions as Collective, Illegal Punishment, with Mainly Muslim Properties Destroyed After Riots'. *Article 14*, 25 April 2022.

Sridevan, Prabha. 'Take These Men off Death Row'. *The Hindu*, 6 July 2012.

Sugandhi, Namita. 'Context, Content, and Composition: Questions of Intended Meaning and the Aśokan Edicts'. *Asian Perspectives*, 48, no. 2 (2009).

Sujato, Bhikkhu (trans.). 'SN 56.11: Rolling Forth the Wheel of Dhamma'. SuttaCentral.

Sundar, S. 'Assistant Superintendent of Police in Ambasamudram Accused of Breaking the Teeth of Suspects; Tirunelveli District SP Recommends Inquiry'. *The Hindu*, 11 April 2023.

Swami Paramārthananda. Lectures on the Muṇḍaka Upaniṣad. Transcribed by disciples. Unpublished lecture transcripts, 2014–2015.

The Hindu Bureau. 'After Peace Talks, Scheduled Caste Devotees Enter Temple in Gummidipoondi'. *The Hindu*, 17 September 2024.

The Hindu Bureau. 'Caste Hindus Object to Dalits Using Main Road for Funeral Procession in Tiruvannamalai'. *The Hindu*, 2 October 2024.

The Hindu Bureau. 'Separate Cemeteries for Dalits'. *The Hindu*, 4 June 2011.

The Hindu Bureau. 'Tirunelveli "Honour" Killing Case: Victim Kavin's Mother, Teachers Express Shock'. *The Hindu*, 29 July 2025.

The Indian Express. '"Golden Time to Remove Socialism, Secularism from Constitution": Himanta Joins Debate on Preamble'. *The Indian Express*, 29 June 2025.

Theodorou, Angelina E. '64 Countries Have Religious Symbols on Their National Flags'. Pew Research Center, 25 November 2014.

Tripathi, Rahul. 'Outgoing President Ram Nath Kovind Turned Down Six Mercy Petitions. *The Economic Times*, 7 July 2022.

Tripathi, Shishir. 'A Lawyer for Lord Ayyappa: Advocate Sai Deepak Turns Heads in SC Arguing for Sabarimala Deity's Right to Celibacy'. *Firstpost*, 31 July 2018.

Tyabji, Laila. 'How the Tricolour and Lion Emblem Really Came to Be'. *The Wire*, 14 August 2018.

United States Commission on International Religious Freedom. The Religion-State Relationship and the Right to Freedom of Religion or Belief: A Comparative Textual Analysis of the Constitutions of Majority Muslim Countries and Other OIC Members. Washington, DC: United States Commission on International Religious Freedom, 2012.

Venkatachalapathy, A.R. 'A British Journalist & the Tamil Poet'. *The Hindu*, 4 December 2021.

Virmani, Arundhati. 'National Symbols Under Colonial Domination'. *Past & Present*, 164 (August 1999).

Visva-Bharati Quarterly. November 1942–January 1943. (Translated by Amiya Chakravarty.)

Widdess, Richard. 'Raga'. In *The Garland Encyclopedia of World Music, Vol. 5: South Asia*, pp. 54–64. Edited by Alison Arnold. New York and London: Routledge, 2000.

World Coalition Against the Death Penalty. 'Ending the Death Penalty in Africa'. Last modified 10 June 2022.

Yengde, Suraj. 'State Attacks Dalits via Anti-Left Rhetoric, as Directly Attacking Them Would Cost It Heavily'. *The Indian Express*, 3 May 2020.

'Addition of "Socialism", "Secularism" to Preamble of Constitution Is Sacrilege to Spirit of "Sanatana": Vice President Dhankhar'. *The Hindu*, 28 June 2025.

'Court Accepts Closure Report to Cancel Sexual Harassment Case Against Brij Bhushan'. *The Hindu*, 26 May 2025.

'Disabled Man Abused for Not Standing Up During National Anthem'. *The Times of India*, 2 October 2017.

'For Stan Swamy, UAPA Became His "Death Warrant": The Judicial Murder of Stan Swamy'. *The Quint*, 5 July 2021.

'Government Clarifies Motto Usage'. *The Hindu*, 2 June 1949.

'Periyar Warned Against Installing Ganesha Idols, Says K. Veeramani'. *The Hindu* (Chennai), 11 January 2024.

'Writer and Disability Campaigner Thrashed in Goa Theatre for Not

Standing Up During National Anthem'. *The Indian Express*, 20 October 2016.

'"Socialist", "Secular" Don't Reflect India's Core Cultural Values: Chouhan'. *Hindustan Times*, 28 June 2025.

ONLINE SOURCES

'100 Years Since "Jana Gana Mana" Was Born'. *The Hindu*, 4 January 2012. https://www.thehindu.com/features/friday-review/history-and-culture/100-years-since-jana-gana-mana-was-born/article2752111.ece.

'A Revolutionary and a Singer'. *The Hindu*, 20 July 2012. https://www.thehindu.com/features/metroplus/a-revolutionary-and-a-singer/article3682419.ece.

'A Short Recorded History of the Contentious National Song "Vande Mataram"'. *Scroll.in*, 24 March 2015. https://scroll.in/article/675445/a-short-recorded-history-of-the-contentious-national-song-vande-mataram.

'A Slice of South India in Balochistan'. *Mint* (Sunday Magazine), 12 February 2017. https://www.livemint.com/Sundayapp/lWCoIZ2K5dPycrhS1gk6nJ/A-slice-of-south-india-in-Balochistan.html.

'A Song of Unity'. *Sunday Observer* (Sri Lanka), 14 May 2006. https://archives.sundayobserver.lk/2006/05/14/jun02.asp.

'Abolitionist and Retentionist Countries'. Death Penalty Information Center. https://deathpenaltyinfo.org/policy-issues/policy/international/abolitionist-and-retentionist-countries, accessed 1 December 2025.

'Amid Massive Tiranga Drive, Naga Flag Hoisted in Parts of Nagaland, Manipur'. NDTV, 14 August 2022. https://www.ndtv.com/india-news/amid-massive-tiranga-drive-naga-flag-hoisted-in-parts-of-nagaland-manipur-3254491.

Arora, Ramesh. 'Why the Lions in the Emblem for the New Parliament Are Disturbing'. *The Indian Express*, 28 July 2022. https://indianexpress.com/article/opinion/columns/why-the-lions-in-the-emblem-for-the-new-parliament-are-disturbing-8027139/.

Banerjee, Shoumojit. 'How a British War Memorial Became a Symbol of Dalit Pride'. *The Hindu*, 2 January 2018. https://www.thehindu.com/news/national/other-states/the-legend-of-the-1818-battle-of-bhima-koregaon/article22352514.ece.

Baubérot, Jean. 'France's La Cité: Why the Rest of the World Struggles to Understand It'. *The Conversation*, 10 December 2020. https://theconversation.com/frances-la-cite-why-the-rest-of-the-world-struggles-to-understand-it-149943.

'BBMP Receives 50,000 Faulty Flags in Last Three Days'. *The New Indian Express*, 6 August 2022. https://www.newindianexpress.com/states/karnataka/2022/Aug/06/bbmp-receives-50000-faulty-flags-in-last-3-days-24849092.ece.

'Bhama Vijayam (1934)'. *The Hindu*, archived 28 May 2017. https://archive.ph/20170528112751/http://www.thehindu.com/todays-paper/tp-features/tp-cinemaplus/bhama-vijayam-1934/article3022445.ece.

Bhattacharya, Sanjukta. 'Gandhi's Little-Known Critique of Varna'. *Economic & Political Weekly,* 41, no. 19 (13 May 2006). https://www.epw.in/journal/2006/19/commentary/gandhis-little-known-critique-varna.html.

Bhattacharya, Sudeep Chandra. 'Ambedkar: A Biography of Caste and Conversion'. *Himal Southasian*, 15 December 2021. https://www.himalmag.com/politics/ambedkar-biography-caste-dalit-bahujan-savita-hindutva-gandhi-phule-buddha.

'Bombay HC Dismisses PIL against Satyamev Jayate'. *The Indian Express*, 22 June 2016. https://indianexpress.com/article/india/india-news-india/bombay-hc-dismisses-pil-against-satyamev-jayate-2868092/.

Brown, Neil. 'Reform, Revolution and Opportunism: Debates in the Second International (1900–1910)'. *Counterfire*, 15 May 2021. https://www.counterfire.org/article/reform-revolution-and-opportunism-debates-in-the-second-international-1900-1910-book-review/.

'Cakkavatti Sutta: The Wheel-turning Emperor'. *Access to Insight*. https://www.accesstoinsight.org/tipitaka/dn/dn.26.0.than.html, accessed 1 December 2025.

'Can Powerful Words and Unfettered Love Help Shape the Future of Politics in These Dark Times?' *Scroll.in*, 12 March 2023. https://scroll.in/article/1045530/can-powerful-words-and-unfettered-love-help-shape-the-future-of-politics-these-dark-times.

Chandrachud, Chintan. 'How a Case on Minerva Mills Challenged and Undid Indira Gandhi's Damage to the Constitution'. *The Print*, 12 January 2020. https://theprint.in/pageturner/excerpt/how-minerva-mills-case-challenged-indira-gandhi-damage-to-constitution/348426/.

'China's Global Ambitions Expand'. *Xinhua News*, 12 November 2023. https://english.news.cn/20231112/7320d385bd1c4590882e4e01decaca31/c.html.

'Condemning the Condemned: How India's Death Penalty Targets the Vulnerable'. *Article 14*, 8 December 2022. https://www.article-14.com/post/condemning-the-condemned-how-india-s-death-penalty-targets-the-vulnerable-6393ef5cd2e01.

Constitution of the Republic of South Africa (1996). Pretoria: Department of Justice, Republic of South Africa, 1996. https://www.justice.gov.za/legislation/constitution/saconstitution-web-eng.pdf.

'Coup and Counter-Coup in Niger: How the World Is Reacting'. BBC News, 28 July 2023. https://www.bbc.com/news/world-africa-66308724.

'Court Declares Cow the National Animal'. *The Indian Express*, 20 August 2021. https://indianexpress.com/article/india/cow-national-animal-india-court-7482909/.

Death Penalty Information Center. 'Botched Executions'. https://deathpenaltyinfo.org/executions/botched-executions, accessed 1 December 2025.

'Declare Cow the National Animal, Says Allahabad HC'. *The Hindu*, 1 September 2021. https://www.thehindu.com/news/national/declare-cow-the-national-animal-says-allahabad-hc/article36239391.ece.

Dhammika. The Edicts of King Asoka. *Access to Insight*. https://www.accesstoinsight.org/lib/authors/dhammika/wheel386.html#fn-39, accessed 1 December 2025.

'Dissecting Melodies: Placing the Nation's Songs in Context'. *The Telegraph* (India), 28 January 2023. https://www.telegraphindia.com/opinion/dissecting-melodies-placing-the-nations-songs-in-context/cid/1912378.

'DN 3 (Sujato translation).' SuttaCentral. https://suttacentral.net/dn3/en/sujato?lang=en&layout=plain&reference=none&notes=asterisk&highlight=false&script= latin, accessed 1 December 2025.

'DN 26 (Sujato translation).' SuttaCentral. https://suttacentral.net/dn26/en/sujato?lang=en&layout=plain&reference=none&notes=asterisk&highlight=false&s cript=latin, accessed 1 December 2025.

'86 Killed in Cow-Related Violence Since 2010 Are Muslims'. *Hindustan Times*, 29 June 2017. https://www.hindustantimes.com/india-news/86-killed-in-cow-related-violence-since-2010-are-muslims-97-attacks-after-modi-govt-came-to-power/story-w9CYOksvgk9joGSSaXgpLO.html.

'Eminent Personalities'. A.J. Vidyā Pariṣad. https://www.ajvidyaparishad.org/eminentpersonalities#, accessed 1 December 2025.

'Eshwarappa Stops Tamil Nadu State Song at Campaign Meet in Shivamogga, Insists on Playing Karnataka State Song'. *The Hindu*, 28 May 2023. https://www.thehindu.com/news/national/karnataka/eshwarappa-stops-tamil-nadu-state-song-at-campaign-meet-in-shivamogga-insists-on-playing-karnataka-state-song/article66784351.ece.

Estrin, James. 'The Roadside Encounter That Led to Dorothea Lange's "Migrant Mother"'. *The New York Times*, 28 November 2018. https://www.nytimes.com/2018/11/28/lens/dorothea-lange-migrant-mother.html.

Express News Service. 'Bombay HC Dismisses PIL against Satyamev Jayate'. *The Indian Express*, 22 June 2016. https://indianexpress.com/article/india/india-news-india/bombay-hc-dismisses-pil-against-satyamev-jayate-2868092/.

'The Fateful Roadside Encounter That Led to Dorothea Lange's Migrant Mother'. *Artsy*, 18 January 2019. https://www.artsy.

net/article/artsy-editorial-fateful-roadside-led-dorothea-langes-migrant-mother.

'Flag Code Amendment Explained'. *The Indian Express*, 22 July 2022. https://indianexpress.com/article/explained/india-flag-code-amendment-explained-8028772/.

'For Perarivalan, Turning Point Was Commuting of Death Sentence by Supreme Court in 2014'. *The Hindu*, 19 May 2022. https://www.thehindu.com/news/national/for-perarivalan-turning-point-was-commuting-of-death-sentence-by-supreme-court-in-2014/article65426826.ece.

'Former Supreme Court Judges Raise Concerns over Misuse of UAPA'. *The Hindu*, 12 July 2021. https://www.thehindu.com/news/national/former-supreme-court-judges-raise-concerns-over-misuse-of-uapa/article35516005.ece.

'Four Versions of "Vande Mataram" by Hindustani Maestros Mark National Week'. *Scroll.in*, 24 January 2015. https://scroll.in/article/718188/four-versions-of-vande-mataram-by-hindustani-maestros-mark-national-week.

'France'. In 2022 *Report on International Religious Freedom*. U.S. Department of State, 2023. https://www.state.gov/reports/2022-report-on-international-religious-freedom/france/.

'Fraternity: The Missing Link of India's Democracy'. The India Forum. https://www.theindiaforum.in/article/fraternity-missing-link-india-s-democracy, accessed 1 December 2025.

Gandhi, Rajmohan. 'Inclusion of the Word "Fraternity" in Preamble Is of Historic Importance and Contemporary Relevance'. *The Indian Express*, 22 October 2020. https://indianexpress.com/article/opinion/columns/india-constitution-preamble-fraternity-fundamental-rights-6824790/.

Ghosh, Devarsi. 'The Madras High Court Judge Who Banned Gay Conversion Therapy Spoke of Fighting His Own Biases'. *Scroll.in*, 10 June 2021. https://scroll.in/article/997159/the-madras-high-court-judge-who-banned-gay-conversion-therapy-spoke-of-fighting-his-own-biases.

Guha, Ramachandra. 'Gandhi and Liberal Modernity: The Vexed Question of Caste'. The India Forum, April 2023. https://www.

theindiaforum.in/essay/gandhi-and-liberal-modernity-vexed-question-caste.

'How and When the Anthems Can Be Used'. New Zealand Ministry for Culture and Heritage. https://www.mch.govt.nz/our-work/flags-anthems-and-emblems/national-anthems#how-and-when-the-anthems-can-be-used, accessed 1 December 2025.

'How "Vande Mataram" Came to Be Chosen as India's National Song'. *Scroll.in*, 27 March 2015. https://scroll.in/article/680336/how-vande-mataram-came-to-be-chosen-as-indias-national-song.

'How "Vande Mataram" Came to Be Performed in a Variety of Classical Ragas'. *Scroll.in*, 25 March 2015. https://scroll.in/article/677562/how-vande-mataram-came-to-be-performed-in-a-variety-of-classical-ragas.

'How the Tricolour and Lion Emblem Really Came to Be'. *The Wire*, 13 August 2018. https://thewire.in/history/india-national-flag-emblem-suraiya-badruddin-tyabji.

'Huge Blow: Why Karnataka Khadi Unit Fears the Worst Post Flag-Code Amendment, Rahul Gandhi Assures Help'. *The Financial Express*, 3 August 2022. https://www.financialexpress.com/india-news/huge-blow-why-karnataka-khadi-unit-fears-the-worst-post-flag-code-amendment-rahul-gandhi-assures-help/2618057/.

Human Rights Watch. *Violent Cow Protection in India: Vigilante Groups Attack Minorities*. 19 February 2019.

Hyndman, Henry M. 'The Colonies and Dependencies'. *Justice*, August 1904. https://www.marxists.org/archive/hyndman/1904/08/colonies-dependencies.htm.

'I Am Trying to Break My Own Preconceived Notions on Same-Sex Relationships, Says Judge'. *The Hindu*, 8 April 2021. https://www.thehindu.com/news/national/tamil-nadu/i-am-trying-to-break-my-own-preconceived-notions-on-same-sex-relationship-says-judge/article34202202.ece.

Improvateur, Asalha Puja. In The Dhammacakkappavattana Sutta. Thai Forest Wisdom. https://thaiforestwisdom.org/asalha-puja/, accessed 1 December 2025.

'Indian Courts Sentence Record 165 Death Penalties in 2022: Report'. WION News, 28 December 2022. https://www.wionews.com/

india-news/indian-courts-sentence-record-165-death-penalties-in-2022-report-557643.

'Indian Durbar Celebration'. *The Argus* (Melbourne), 1 January 1901. https://trove.nla.gov.au/newspaper/article/5135515.

'Indian Student in London Unfurls Karnataka Flag at Graduation Ceremony'. *Hindustan Times*, 10 January 2023. https://www.hindustantimes.com/cities/bengaluru-news/indian-student-in-london-unfurls-karnataka-flag-at-graduation-ceremony-watch-101674386080752.html.

'Indians Should Stop Reading Too Much into the Artwork on the Constitution and Instead Heed Its Words'. *Scroll.in*, 7 February 2021. https://scroll.in/article/984978/indians-should-stop-reading-too-much-into-the-artwork-on-the-constitution-and-instead-heed-its-words.

'India's Only BIS-Certified Flag-Making Unit Trumped by Polyester Flags'. *The Hindu*, 3 August 2022. https://www.thehindu.com/news/national/karnataka/indias-only-bis-certified-flag-making-unit-trumped-by-polyester-flags/article65673892.ece.

'India's Death Penalty System Under Scrutiny'. BBC News, 21 April 2023. https://www.bbc.com/news/world-asia-india-65347773.

'Inheritance in Uttarakhand UCC: Hindus, Muslims and Christians'. *The Indian Express*, 12 February 2024. https://indianexpress.com/article/explained/explained-law/inheritance-in-uttarakhand-ucc-hindus-muslims-and-christians-9149092/.

'International Socialist Congress of Amsterdam, 1904'. Marxists Internet Archive, 1904. https://www.marxists.org/history/international/social-democracy/1904/international-socialist-congress.htm.

'Islam Was the World's Fastest-Growing Religion from 2010 to 2020'. Pew Research Center, 10 June 2025. https://www.pewresearch.org/short-reads/2025/06/10/islam-was-the-worlds-fastest-growing-religion-from-2010-to-2020/.

'It's Time for the Government to Redeem Itself and Repeal the UAPA'. *The Wire*, 10 July 2021. https://thewire.in/law/its-time-for-the-government-to-redeem-itself-and-repeal-uapa.

'Jammu and Kashmir State Flag Removed from Civil Secretariat in

Srinagar'. *The Hindu*, 6 August 2019. https://www.thehindu.com/news/national/jammu-and-kashmir-state-flag-removed-from-civil-secretariat-in-srinagar/article61580201.ece.

Jeyaraj, D.B.S. 'History of Sri Lanka's National Anthem Mired in Controversy'. *Daily Mirror* (Sri Lanka), 5 June 2015. https://www.dailymirror.lk/print/dbs-jeyaraj-column/history-of-sri-lanka-s-national-anthem-mired-in-controversy/192-67545.

Jeyaraj, D.B.S. 'History of the National Anthem of Sri Lanka Has Been Mired in Controversy' DBS Jeyaraj, 31 March 2015. https://dbsjeyaraj.com/dbsj/?p=39972.

'Judge Wants to Learn About Same-Sex Relationships Before Penning Judgment'. *The Hindu*, 2 May 2021. https://www.thehindu.com/news/national/tamil-nadu/judge-wants-to-learn-about-same-sex-relationships-before-penning-judgment/article61818725.ece.

Kandasamy, Surya. 'A British Journalist & the Tamil Poet'. *The Hindu*, 13 October 2002. https://www.thehindu.com/opinion/lead/A-British-journalist-amp-the-Tamil-poet/article12447901.ece.

'Karnataka BJP Office Sells Poorly Stitched Tricolour'. *Deccan Herald*, 13 August 2022. https://www.deccanherald.com/india/karnataka/karnataka-bjp-office-sells-poorly-stitched-tricolour-1132884.html.

'Karnataka Government Unveils the State Flag, Awaits Centre's Approval'. *Hindustan Times*, 9 March 2018. https://www.hindustantimes.com/india-news/karnataka-government-unveils-the-state-flag-awaits-centre-s-approval/story-i4aMgmK3uaIyd8mhNwf94K.html.

'Karnataka Govt to Drop State Flag Issue'. *Times of India*, 29 August 2019. https://timesofindia.indiatimes.com/city/bengaluru/karnataka-govt-to-drop-state-flag-issue/articleshow/70908984.cms.

'Kenya Reinstates the Death Penalty after Decade-long Abolition'. BBC News, 12 October 2018. https://www.bbc.com/news/world-45835584.

Krishnan, Murali. 'In the Process of Evolving: How a Madras HC Judge Is Making Tamil Nadu LGBTQIA+ Friendly'. *The Print*, 4 September 2022. https://theprint.in/judiciary/in-the-process-of-evolving-how-a-madras-hc-judge-is-making-tamil-nadu-lgbtqia-friendly/1124442/.

Kumar, Sandeep. 'Revisiting the First Amendment to the Indian Constitution'. *NewsClick*, 10 June 2021. https://www.newsclick.in/revisiting-first-amendment-indian-constitution.

Kuru, Ahmet T. 'Veiled Meaning: The French Law Banning Religious Symbols in Public Schools'. Brookings Institution, 2004. https://www.brookings.edu/articles/veiled-meaning-the-french-law-banning-religious-symbols-in-public-schools/.

'The Last Word on the State and Temples'. *The Hindu*, 29 April 2021. https://www.hindu.com/opinion/lead/the-last-word-on-the-state-and-temples/article34379441.ece.

'Last Day of Sabarimala: Rights of the Deity as a Juristic Entity Are for Suing and Being Sued — Indira Jaising's Additional Rejoinder', *The Leaflet*. https://theleaflet.in/supreme-court/last-day-of-sabarimala-rights-of-deity-as-a-juristic-entity-are-for-suing-and-being-sued-read-indira-jaisings-additional-rejoinder-submissions, accessed 1 December 2025.

'Lawyers March to Protest against CAA–NRC–NPR and Police Repression'. *Bar and Bench*, December 2019. https://www.barandbench.com/news/lawyers-march-to-protest-against-caa-nrc-npr-and-police-repression.

'Lawyers Stage Protest against CAA.' *The Hindu*, 22 December 2023. https://www.hindu.com/news/cities/puducherry/lawyers-stage-protest-against-caa/article67965001.ece.

Lenin, Vladimir Ilyich. 'Notes for a Report on the Stuttgart Congress'. Marxists Internet Archive, October 1907. https://www.marxists.org/archive/lenin/works/1907/oct/00.htm.

Lenin, Vladimir Ilyich. 'Report on the International Socialist Congress in Stuttgart'. Marxists Internet Archive, 20 October 1907. https://www.marxists.org/archive/lenin/works/1907/oct/20.htm.

'Madras HC Judge Fought His Own Prejudices in Landmark LGBTQIA+ Order'. *The News Minute*, 9 June 2021. https://www.thenewsminute.com/tamil-nadu/madras-hc-judge-fought-his-own-prejudices-landmark-lgbtqia-order-150313.

Mahmood, Saif. 'Mirza Ghalib and the Law: A Curious Romance'. *The*

Wire, 4 July 2021. https://thewire.in/culture/mirza-ghalib-and-the-law-a-curious-romance.

Mehta, Pratap Bhanu. 'Liberty and the Republic'. *Seminar*, no. 615 (March 2010). https://www.india-seminar.com/2010/615/615_pratap_bhanu_mehta.htm.

'Migrant Mother—New Deal & the Great Depression'. *History.com*. https://www.history.com/articles/migrant-mother-new-deal-great-depression. Accessed 1 December 2025.

'Migrant Mother: Guide to Sources'. Library of Congress. https://guides.loc.gov/migrant-mother. Accessed 1 December 2025.

Modi, Narendra. '#HarGharTiranga Movement Tweet'. X (formerly Twitter), 2 August 2022. https://x.com/narendramodi/status/1554296310425358337.

'Moratorium Stays in Place in Sri Lanka'. World Coalition Against the Death Penalty, 28 March 2023. https://worldcoalition.org/2023/03/28/moratorium-stays-in-place-in-sri-lanka/.

'Naga Flag Not Negotiable, Says NSCN-IM Calendar as Peace Talks Remain in Limbo'. *ThePrint*, 1 January 2023. https://theprint.in/india/naga-flag-constitution-not-negotiable-nscn-im-calendar-asserts-as-peace-talks-in-limbo/1369366/.

'The Naga Flag and Constitution Invoke Pride and Hope of the Naga People: LPO'. *Eastern Mirror Nagaland*, 13 August 2022. https://easternmirrornagaland.com/the-naga-flag-and-constitution-invokes-pride-and-hope-of-the-naga-people-lpo.

'Nagaland Polls: Parties Promise Settlement on Naga Issue, Voters Unconvinced'. *Hindustan Times*, 17 February 2023. https://www.hindustantimes.com/cities/others/nagaland-polls-parties-promise-settlement-on-naga-issue-voters-unconvinced-101677331589064.html.

'National Anthem Must Be Played Before Screening of Films: Supreme Court'. *The Hindu*, 30 November 2016. https://www.thehindu.com/news/national/National-anthem-must-be-played-before-screening-of-films-Supreme-Court/article16729264.ece.

'National Anthem Sung in Sinhala and Tamil'. *Sunday Observer* (Sri Lanka), 5 February 2023. https://archives1.sundayobserver.lk/2023/02/05/news/national-anthem-sung-sinhala-and-tamil.

'National Anthem'. Government of South Africa. https://www.gov.za/about-sa/national-anthem-0. Accessed 1 December 2025.

'National Coat of Arms'. Government of South Africa. https://www.gov.za/about-sa/national-coat-arms#:~:text=The%20motto%20is%3A%20!,unity%20between%20thought%20and%20action. Accessed 1 December 2025.

'National Flag Can Now Be Machine-Made in Polyester'. *The Hindu*, 1 August 2022. https://www.thehindu.com/news/national/national-flag-can-now-be-machine-made-in-polyester/article65480414.ece.

'National Monument Status Sought for Jatheeya Kalasala'. *The Hindu*, 26 February 2015. https://www.thehindu.com/news/national/andhra-pradesh/national-monument-status-sought-for-jateeya-kalasala/article6931666.ece.

'New Times (San Luis Obispo)—Photographic License (Archive)'. NewTimesSLO, 3 December 2003. https://www.newtimesslo.com/archive/2003-12-03/archives/cov_stories_2002/cov_01172002.html.

'New Times SLO Investigative Feature (Archived)'. New Times SLO, archived 2 June 2002. https://web.archive.org/web/20020602103656/https://www.newtimes-slo.com/archives/cov_stories_2002/cov_01172002.html.

'No Concept of National Song in Constitution, Says SC'. *Hindustan Times*, 18 January 2017. https://www.hindustantimes.com/india-news/no-concept-of-national-song-in-constitution-says-sc/story-UYFUDprZTPnLUorcQIJ6dJ.html.

'No Negotiation over Naga National Flag: NSCN-IM'. *The Hindu*, November 22, 2022. https://www.thehindu.com/news/national/other-states/no-negotiation-over-naga-national-flag-nscn-i-m/article66174324.ece.

'No Jammu and Kashmir Flag on Srinagar's Civil Secretariat.' *Hindustan Times*, 6 August 2019. https://www.hindustantimes.com/india-news/no-jammu-and-kashmir-flag-on-srinagar-s-civil-secretariat/story-lizUKGtSsyChmW8p3HfY1N.html.

Orwell, George. 'A Hanging'. The Orwell Foundation, 1931. https://

www.orwellfoundation.com/the-orwell-foundation/orwell/essays-and-other-works/a-hanging/.

'The Other Indian at The Hague: When Britain and France Sought International Arbitration Over Savarkar'. *Scroll.in*, 17 June 2017. https://scroll.in/article/838809/the-other-indian-at-the-hague-when-britain-france-sought-international-arbitration-over-savarkar.

'Pañcavaggi Sutta: Five Brethren'. *Access to Insight*. https://www.accesstoinsight.org/tipitaka/sn/sn22/sn22.059.than.html, accessed 1 December 2025.

'Pakistan's Pandemic of Insecurity'. *Dawn*, 31 July 2020. https://www.dawn.com/news/1571797.

'Perarivalan Pardon: Rajiv Gandhi Assassination Case'. *The Wire*, 19 May 2022. https://thewire.in/government/perarivalan-pardon-rajiv-gandhi-assassination-case-tm-krishna.

'Polyester Flags: Gandhi Would Have Protested This Desecration of His Beloved Khadi'. *The Hindu*, 26 September 2022. https://www.thehindu.com/society/polyester-flags-gandhi-would-have-protested-this-desecration-of-his-beloved-khadi/article65923206.ece.

Preambles of Constitutions: A Comparative Study of 194 Current Constitutions. Constitutional-Change.com, 2018. https://www.constitutional-change.com/preambles-of-constitutions-a-comparative-study-of-194-current-constitutions/.

'Public Renditions of the National Anthem Have Long Been Rife with Code Violations'. *Scroll.in*, 17 December 2015. https://scroll.in/article/773143/public-renditions-of-the-national-anthem-have-long-been-rife-with-code-violations.

Rajagopal, Krishnadas. 'Bharat Mata: From Freedom Struggle Metaphor to Patriotism's Litmus Test'. *The Indian Express*, 21 August 2020. https://indianexpress.com/article/explained/in-fact-bharat-mata-from-freedom-struggle-metaphor-to-patriotisms-litmus-test/.

Rajangam, Stalin. 'Iyodhee Thass Pandithar: A Pioneer in Dalit History and Literature'. *The Wire*, 20 May 2019. https://thewire.

in/history/iyodhee-thass-pandithar-a-pioneer-in-dalit-history-and-literature.

'Ram Nath Kovind Rejects Mercy Pleas of Death-row Convicts'. *The Indian Express*, 26 May 2018. https://indianexpress.com/article/explained/ram-nath-kovind-mercy-plea-death-row-convicts-5204074/.

'Record Discs That Helped Defeat the British Empire: Tagore Sings "Bande Mataram"'. *Scroll.in*, 22 March 2015. https://scroll.in/article/674383/record-discs-that-helped-defeat-the-british-empire-tagore-sings-bande-mataram.

'Re-searching Ashoka in Thailand'. *The Hindu*. https://www.thehindu.com/opinion/op-ed/Re-searching-Ashoka-in-Thailand/article14401691.ece, accessed 1 December 2025.

'Salayatana Sutta: The All'. *Access to Insight*. https://www.accesstoinsight.org/tipitaka/sn/sn35/sn35.028.nymo.html, accessed 1 December 2025.

Samuel, Sigal. 'France's Hijab Ban and Its Controversies'. *Time*, 7 May 2021, https://time.com/6049226/france-hijab-ban/.

'Sale of Khadi Flags from Hubballi Unit Affected for the Second Year in Succession', *The Hindu*, 19 August 2023, https://www.thehindu.com/news/national/karnataka/sale-of-khadi-flags-from-hubballi-unit-affected-for-the-second-year-in-succession/article67194474.ece.

Sastri, S. Sitarama, *Mundaka Upanishad with Śaṅkara's Commentary*, 1905, Wisdom Library, https://www.wisdomlib.org/hinduism/book/mundaka-upanishad-shankara-bhashya.

'SC Modifies Order, Says National Anthem Not Mandatory', *The Hindu*, 10 January 2018, https://www.thehindu.com/news/national/sc-modifies-order-says-national-anthem-not-mandatory/article22403095.ece.

Senaratne, Kalani Kumarasinghe, 'The Fate of Sri Lanka's Tamil National Anthem', *The Diplomat*, 18 November 2019, https://thediplomat.com/2019/11/the-fate-of-sri-lankas-tamil-national-anthem/.

Shankar, Aishwarya, 'Gandhi in the Age of Post-Truth', *The Hindu*, 29

September 2022, https://www.thehindu.com/society/gandhi-in-the-age-of-post-truth/article65944957.ece.

Shankar, Anusha, 'Tilak and Jinnah: Why Their Pact Is Still Relevant for India–Pakistan Peace', *The Quint*, 31 July 2020, https://www.thequint.com/voices/blogs/tilak-why-his-pact-with-jinnah-is-relevant-for-india-pakistan-peace.

'Sri Lanka Scraps Tamil National Anthem at Independence Day', *Al Jazeera*, 4 February 2020, https://www.aljazeera.com/news/2020/2/4/sri-lanka-scraps-tamil-national-anthem-at-independence-day.

'Sri Lanka Scraps Tamil Version of Its National Anthem', *Economic Times*, 23 July 2010, https://economictimes.indiatimes.com/news/politics-and-nation/sri-lanka-scraps-tamil-version-of-its-national-anthem/article7088138.cms.

'Sri Lankan Independence Day Celebrations 2016', BBC News, 4 February 2016, https://www.bbc.com/news/world-asia-35495567.

'Spring Blossoms and Forgotten Poetry', *The Hindu*, 20 April 2017, https://www.thehindu.com/books/spring-blossoms-and-forgotten-poetry/article18059973.ece.

'StNp 1.7', Dhamma Talks, https://www.dhammatalks.org/suttas/KN/StNp/StNp1_7.html, accessed 1 December 2025.

'Sun Yat-sen: Biography and Influence', Zhongshan Government Portal, http://www.zs.gov.cn/ywb/aboutzhongshan/celebrities/content/post_1637856.html, accessed 1 December 2025.

'Symbols of the State', The India Forum, July 2022, https://www.theindiaforum.in/amp/article/symbols-state.

'Tamil Anthem and Reconciliation', *Sunday Times* (Sri Lanka), 4 February 2001, https://sundaytimes.lk/010204/plus5.html.

Tharoor, Shashi, 'The Secular Condition', *The Hindu*, 30 December 2017, https://www.thehindu.com/opinion/lead/the-secular-condition/article22347527.ece.

'The Artist Who Designed the State Emblem', *Madras M.*

'The Common Thread Between a Chinese Collaborator and the Chinese Communist Party', *The Diplomat*, 10 April 2023, https://

thediplomat.com/2023/04/the-common-thread-between-a-chinese-collaborator-and-the-chinese-communist-party/.

'The Dark Chronology of India's Cow Slaughter Laws', *Article-14*, 3 April 2023, https://article-14.com/post/the-dark-chronology-of-india-s-cow-slaughter-laws.

'The Delhi Durbar and the Proclamation of Queen Victoria'. Library of Congress Blogs, 14 November 2017. https://blogs.loc.gov/international-collections/2017/11/the-delhi-durbar-and-the-proclamation-of-queen-victoria/.

'The Democratic Imagination of a Poem'. *Bangalore Mirror*, 23 September 2016. https://bangaloremirror.indiatimes.com/opinion/views/the-democratic-imagination-of-a-poem/articleshow/ 54486261.cms.

'The Last Word on the State and Temples', *The Hindu*, 29 April 2021, https://www.hindu.com/opinion/lead/the-last-word-on-the-state-and-temples/article34379441.ece.

'The Other Indian at The Hague: When Britain and France Sought International Arbitration Over Savarkar', *Scroll.in*, 17 June 2017, https://scroll.in/article/838809/the-other-indian-at-the-hague-when-britain-france-sought-international-arbitration-over-savarkar.

'The Secular Condition', *The Hindu*, 30 December 2017, https://www.hindu.com/opinion/lead/the-secular-condition/article22347527.ece.

'The State Flag Issue', *The Times of India*, 29 August 2019, https://timesofindia.indiatimes.com/city/bengaluru/karnataka-govt-to-drop-state-flag-issue/articleshow/70908984.cms.

'Thoothukudi Anti-Sterlite Protest and Vedanta: Autopsy Report', *The Wire*, 15 June 2018, https://thewire.in/law/thoothukudi-anti-sterlite-protest-vedanta-autopsy-report.

'Those Foiling Reconciliation Are Anti-national, Says Sirisena', *The Hindu*, 6 February 2017, https://www.thehindu.com/news/international/Those-foiling-reconciliation-are-anti-national-says-Sirisena/article17195536.ece.

'Three Freedom-Movement-Era Versions of "Vande Mataram" in March Time', *Scroll.in*, 26 March 2015, https://scroll.in/

article/679051/three-freedom-movement-era-versions-of-vande-mataram-in-march-time.

'The Tilak-Jinnah Pact Embodied Communal Harmony That Is Much Needed in Modern-Day India', *Scroll.in*, 31 July 2020, https://scroll.in/article/968926/the-tilak-jinnah-pact-embodied-communal-harmony-that-is-much-needed-in-modern-day-india.

'Two Years After Official Flag of Karnataka Was Mooted, Here's Where the Proposal Stands', *The News Minute*, 25 November 2020, https://www.thenewsminute.com/karnataka/two-years-after-official-flag-karnataka-was-mooted-heres-where-proposal-stands-136633.

Tyabji, Laila, 'How the Tricolour and Lion Emblem Really Came to Be', *The Wire*, 13 August 2018, https://thewire.in/history/india-national-flag-emblem-suraiya-badruddin-tyabji.

'UN "Disturbed" by Death of Indian Activist Stan Swamy in Jail', *Al Jazeera*, 6 July 2021, https://www.aljazeera.com/news/2021/7/6/un-disturbed-by-death-of-indian-activist-stan-swamy-in-jail.

UNESCO, *Philosophy: A School of Freedom*, Paris: UNESCO, 2007, https://unesdoc.unesco.org/ark:/48223/pf0000064300.

'Uniform Cut-and-Paste? Quick Appraisal of Uttarakhand's Uniform Civil Code Bill', *Bar and Bench*, 8 February 2024, https://www.barandbench.com/columns/uniform-cut-and-paste-quick-appraisal-uttarakhand-uniform-civil-code-bill.

'Violent Clashes Over Cow Protection by Vigilantes', *The Guardian*, 20 July 2016, https://www.theguardian.com/world/2016/jul/20/violent-clashes-cow-protection-vigilantes-low-caste-india.

'What Is the 13th Amendment to the Sri Lankan Constitution, and Why Is It Contentious?' *The Hindu*, 30 September 2020, https://www.thehindu.com/news/international/the-hindu-explains-what-is-the-13th-amendment-to-the-sri-lankan-constitution-and-why-is-it-contentious/article32531844.ece.

'Why the Death Penalty Is Not a Solution to India's Rape Problem', *Article-14*, 17 July 2020, https://article-14.com/post/why-the-death-penalty-is-not-a-solution-to-india-s-rape-problem.

Index

Acknowledgements

When I embarked on writing this book, I thought of it as a pocket-sized collection of brief essays. But, as I began following the many threads and rabbit-holes I encountered during my research, the book grew to become a deeper investigation into these symbols, their histories, impressions and metaphors, and how we have come to embrace, revere and critique them. In particular, I wanted to understand their relevance through the lens of social and political shifts. This required the exploration of diverse fields of intellectual activity. I would have been quickly overwhelmed, had it not been for the generosity shown by innumerable scholars, writers, musicians, researchers and friends. To receive so much warmth and sharing from them—many of whom I had no acquaintance with when I first wrote to them—was overwhelming to say the least.

I must begin, undoubtedly, with Amlan Dasgupta. Over the past four years, I have sent him hundreds of queries, asked for translations from scores of Bengali texts, requested him to check or cross-check sections of my writings and constantly probed deeper on every bit of information he sent my way. Not once did he say he had no time or show any sign of fatigue or irritation. All he sought was time. After a while, I would receive a message or email with a clarification, often with the excitement of having uncovered something new. Thank you so much, Amlan-da, for being you. Jairam Ramesh explored the emblem and motto alongside me, and most graciously shared with me anything new, documents and insights, that he stumbled upon. Patrick Olivelle and Naresh Keerthi were patient with my questions on Hindu mythology, philosophy and language, often untangling complex constructions and directing me towards further reading. Sugata Bose and Sukanta Chaudhuri provided me insights into the mind and actions of Subhas Chandra Bose and Rabindranath Tagore respectively. Understanding the imports in religious texts was essential for this book. Shravasti Dhammaka and Amarasiri Bikkhu were there for any clarification on Buddhism and the Buddha. Faizur Mahmood eloquently brought to life the relationship between the colour green and Islam. Abhi Janamanchi described the scriptural significance of the colour white in Christianity. Sree Narayana Guru has been a part of my musical life for about five years now, and whenever I have wondered about events in his life or the layered meanings in his texts, I have reached out to S. Gopalakrishnan. Sadan Jha and Ole Lausen helped me understand various events surrounding the emergence of the Indian National Flag. Uma Dasgupta was my go-to person to find rare Bengali books and articles. Rudrangshu Mukherjee was always available for questions regarding the National Anthem. Reconstructing music from old notations is never easy. Monali Balasubramanian and Srijan Deshpande were magnificent in bringing them to life for me. I am also indebted to Srijan for his succinct analyses of the music, and for sharing any piece of information he came across in Marathi writings. Monali translated notations from Bengali to Hindi, which helped me compare the various versions of *Jana Gana Mana* and *Vande Mataram*.

When I began exploring this book, I was introduced to Raghunandan Sriram, then a young law student, by my friend Suhrith Parthasarathy. As my research assistant, Raghu went out of his way to gather and organise information, file RTI applications and offer clarifications. Without him, I would have not known how to proceed. My writing has to first pass the test at home. My sister-in-law Krithika Rajagopalan (associate editor,

The Hindu) is my first stop. Only after she vets my text a couple of times do I send it to my editor. Similarly, my mother and educationist, Prema Rangachary, has to have a look and give me the go-ahead.

At the very early stages of research, when Covid was raging, I had four video conferencing conversations that shaped the trajectory of the book. They were with the scholar and diplomat Gopalkrishna Gandhi, historian Nayanjot Lahiri, lawyer Suhrith Parthasarathy, Kandyan dancer and choreographer Ravibandu Vidyapathy, journalist Meera Srinivasan, and researcher and activist Mirak Raheem.

Right from the beginning, my young friend Varisha Narayanan has been there to help with research. My students were also of immensely helpful. Vignesh Ishwar was my information cataloguer, fact- and footnote-checker and bibliographer. S. Adityanarayanan used his knowledge of Western classical music to reconstruct *Shubh Sukh Chain* from what is probably the earliest available notation. Similarly, he reconstructed the music of the first published military band notation of *Jana Gana Mana*, and did a comparative study with other renditions. G. Ravikiran went through the history of the Karnataka anthem with me, gathering information from the scholar Ra Nam Chandrasekar on my behalf. On the same subject, Sailaja Venu of Mysore offered me great clarity. Anup Surendranath and the entire team from the Square Circle Clinic at NALSAR University of Law, Hyderabad, provided me with all the history, information and data I needed on the death penalty in India.

Without Kendra Leigh, none of my books may have come to fruition. When I am looking for a book, article, newspaper or image that no one has been able to find, I email her. She has come to my rescue on innumerable occasions over the past five years. Similarly, Arthanari Hari is another person I have relied upon to find material that is hard to come by. I have to thank my daughter Arya Krishna, who sacrificed a few days at college to find documents for me at the British Library. Not only did she access the material that I was looking for, but also discovered additional files that had not been referred to in earlier publications. I also thank Pinaki Talukdar, Srutokirti Basak and Samprita Sengupta for translating crucial pages from Bengali texts and Seralathan Paneerselvam of Goethe-Institut Max Mueller Bhavan Chennai for translating German texts for me. As always Rajesh Garga was there to check all translations from Tamil. The highly knowledgeable Kinnari Bhatt at the Sabarmati Ashram Archives, Jaishree Kannan at the Surendra Narayan Archives at the Theosophical Society, Chennai, and Sabahat Nausheen at Rabindra Bhavana Library, Santiniketan, were of immense help.

In April 2025, I spent a couple of weeks at the Watson Institute for Public and International Affairs, Saxena Center for Contemporary South Asia at Brown University as an 'Artist in Residence'. The academic environment was just perfect for me to fine-tune my chapters.

The one person to whom I owe a lot is my editor Ajitha G.S. We have worked together now for over a decade, and without her hard questions and tough pushbacks, none of my books would be what they are. V.K. Karthika and Sonia Madan did the final edits, tightening the text and making my arguments sharper. I would also like to thank Amrita Talwar and the marketing team for putting in place a comprehensive plan well in advance.

There are many more academicians, scholars, musicians and friends with whom I had informal discussions, some who emailed me their thoughts, passed on nuggets of information or pointed to another scholar's work. I would like to thank them all for their gifts.

In alphabetical order: A.R. Venkatachalapathy, Akshaya Mukul, Ammad Ali, Beena Sarwar, Carl Malamud, Devajit Bandyopadhyay, G. Sundar, Indira Jaising, Manoj Mitta, Namit Arora, Perumal Murugan, Priya Purushothaman, R.K. Shriramkumar, Rajmohan Gandhi, Ramachandra Guha,

Ranjani Ramachandran, Rohit De, Saif Mahmood, Sanjoy Ghose, Shahid Amin, Shwetha Prachande, Sunil Khilnani, Surasika Parthasarathy, Tapati Guha-Thakurta, Tony Joseph, Uddalak Mukherjee and Vikram Raghavan.

I am able to be a musician and writer without administrative burden consuming my time because my manager Ramya Rajaraman and the Artspire team take care of all these requirements.

Sangeetha Sivakumar, my partner, watched from a distance as I rummaged through archival documents and wrote in obsessive spurts, all the while wondering what this book was all about. She is about to find out! I promised my daughters, Arya and Anantha, that I will take a break from plunging into another book project because the last two have taken up nine years of my life. I will keep that promise. In the meantime, I send to my fellow citizens love and the hope that we will still find our way back to the optimism and foresightedness of our founding years.